Essential Articles for the Study of

Henry Vaughan

The Essential Articles Series

Essential Articles for the Study of

Henry Vaughan

Edited with an Introduction by
ALAN RUDRUM

Archon Books
1987

Printed in the United States of America

The paper used in this publication meets the
minimum requirements of American National Standard
for Information Sciences—Permanence of Paper for
Printed Library Materials, ANSI Z39.48-1984. ∞

Essential articles for the study of Henry Vaughan.

  (The Essential articles series)
  Includes bibliographies.
    1. Vaughan, Henry, 1622–1695—Criticism and
Interpretation.   2. Christian poetry, English—History and
criticism.   I. Rudrum, Alan.   II. Series.
PR3744.E87   1987   821'.4   87–11377
ISBN 0–208–02045–4 (alk. paper)

Acknowledgments

I am grateful to the authors of the pieces collected here, for permission to reprint without fee; and to editors and publishers for their cooperation.

Contents

CONTENTS

CONTENTS

Foreword

The resources available for the study of literature are so vast as to be almost overwhelming, particularly in the case of major authors. Few libraries have copies of all the important articles a serious student might wish to read, and fewer still can keep them easily accessible. The aim of the Essential Articles series is to bring together from learned journals and scholarly studies those essays on a standard writer or area of English literature which are genuinely essential—which will continue to appear on syllabus and reading list.

Introduction

Like many of his contemporaries, Vaughan has been more widely read and appreciated in our time than in his own. While he was not without admirers, there was no contemporary commendation to match Carew's splendid "Elegie upon the death of Dr. *John Donne*," and as L. C. Martin pointed out, none of his works reached a genuine second edition during his lifetime, and none was reprinted during the eighteenth century. During the first half of the nineteenth century a few of his poems found their way into the anthologies in which that time abounded, and one compiler conceded that "he has some few scattered thoughts that meet our eye."[1]

Vaughan's modern publishing history begins close to the mid-point of the nineteenth century, with the Reverend H. F. Lyte's edition of *Silex Scintillans* (1847) which was followed by the Reverend A. B. Grosart's edition of the *Complete Works* (1871). The fact that these two early editors were both clergymen may speak of the learned leisure enjoyed by some clerics in those days; and it may serve to remind us that Vaughan's growing popularity was in part a by-product of the Oxford Movement; as a Royalist and member of the Laudian wing of the Church of England Vaughan might well be thought more acceptable in Victorian England than in his own time.

Victorian criticism of the metaphysicals may not be generally well regarded nowadays; but it was astute of H. C. Beeching to sense the force of an observation first made of Wordsworth and to say of Vaughan too that "he makes us feel that Nature is not a mere collection of phenomena, but infuses into her least approach some sense of her mysterious whole."[2] As I have suggested elsewhere,[3] if we put this beside James Smith's celebrated *Scrutiny* essay on metaphysical poetry, in which he argues for the validity of the label on the ground that Donne's central preoccupation is the metaphysical one of the relationship between the One and the Many, there is an implication that Vaughan's major work may be within the metaphysical tradition in a more important sense than is indicated by the obvious stylistic borrowings of the early verse.

Similarly, A. N. Whitehead was later to say of Wordsworth, that "he always grasps the whole of nature as involved in the tonality of the particular instance."[4] The theory of Vaughan's direct influence upon Wordsworth is now pretty well demolished,[5] but that so non-trivial a description may plausibly be applied to both may suggest affinities which go beyond the usually cited case of the poets' attitudes to childhood. Nor need this be surprising, since Wordsworth, through his association with Coleridge, was in contact with a system of thought fundamentally akin to hermeticism, which may indeed be characterized as a later phase of hermeticism.

Modern Vaughan scholarship and criticism was launched by the publication in 1914 of L. C. Martin's edition of the *Works*. Martin cleared up most of the textual muddle bequeathed by careless seventeenth century compositors and uncritical nineteenth century editors; and his notes, while comparatively sparse, were accurate, useful, and suggestive enough to spur other scholars on. Martin's pupil Elizabeth Holmes gave impetus to one of the main lines of Vaughan criticism with the publication in 1932 of *Henry Vaughan and the Hermetic Philosophy*, a mere trifle as to size, making no pretence of being definitive, yet so resonant of grace and sympathetic feeling that we realize the author's immersion in a mode of thought that has brought her nearer to Vaughan. In addition to Elizabeth Holmes's work, many articles on Vaughan and hermeticism appeared in the twenties and thirties, most of them documenting verbal parallels; more recently, much of my own work has attempted to take the discussion further by showing that the influence goes beyond verbal borrowing, and that hermeticism was important in shaping Vaughan's *quidditas*, that special quality which cannot be expressed merely in terms of his indebtedness to Herbert or the Bible.

Given the nature of the poems in *Silex Scintillans*, and the tone and substance of Vaughan's own 1654 preface, it is not surprising that he should have attracted critics of a theological bent, or that the question of the relationship between his "conversion" and the poems of *Silex* should come to seem important. The tendency for writing along these lines to become an "industry" was halted by Frank Kermode, with an iconoclastic article in which he asserted that "something happened, something to do with poetry, and not with prayer."[6] Of course poetry and prayer are not mutually exclusive, as critics soon pointed out; but it was possible to disagree with Kermode's thesis while finding his argument intelligent and salutary. Perhaps the effect within Vaughan studies was comparable with that of Christopher Ricks's *Milton's Grand Style* among Miltonists, that is to remind us of the need within literary criticism of close reading and careful argument. While most Vaughan critics concentrated on the religious poems, the American scholar E. L. Marilla went his own way and produced a heavily annotated edition of the secular poems (1958). While there are several errors of detail in Marilla's work, he deserves gratitude for an act of sustained attention which made it easier for subsequent scholars to read Vaughan in his entirety, an important matter given the points of contact between the secular poems and those of *Silex*. Marilla has been deservedly influential, especially upon Vaughan scholarship in the United States.

If we are to speak of influence, then Louis Martz's 1963 article "Henry Vaughan: The Man Within" has perhaps had a potency within Vaughan studies like that of *The Poetry of Meditation* within seventeenth century studies generally. One of the tendencies of Vaughan criticism has been to read and interpret his poems as "timeless" religious lyrics. In contrasting Herbert's "The Church Porch" and Vaughan's "Rules and Lessons," Martz drew our attention vividly to the importance of what had happened historically between Herbert's time and Vaughan's: "Vaughan's advice bears no relation to any ecclesiastical symbolism ... It is as though the earthly church had vanished, and man were left to work alone with God." It may be largely due to Martz that we are now asking in what ways Vaughan's characteristic expressions and themes relate to his immediate historical context. Claude J. Summers and Ted-Larry Pebworth, in the essay reprinted here and in "Herbert, Vaughan, and Public Concerns in Private Modes,"[7] have found Vaughan's symbolism and allusions relating to the stresses of his time even in apparent acts of disengagement. I have come to feel that more of Vaughan's poems than previously suspected are implicitly contentious, and that this is true even of those major poems which have been read as "timeless" Christian lyric. One might take issue with Barbara Lewalski's sense of Vaughan as standing "upon the firm common ground of the English Protestant tradition in theology and poetics."[8] Surely that phrase "firm common ground" suggests a monolithic quality about the English Protestant tradition which was not there in Vaughan's immediate and relevant experience of it. One might cite, for example, the fissure between Calvinism and Arminianism within the English church during Vaughan's formative years. We need to consider possible connections between Vaughan's "philosophical" and "political" concerns; to ask, say, how his hermetic and alchemical interests might relate to Laudian Arminianism: are there connections between hermeticism and freewill, between alchemy and the universal sacramental grace of the Arminian position?[9]

In annotating Henry Vaughan's poems and his brother Thomas's works I naturally became keenly aware of the *influences* upon their thinking; we are now asking what Vaughan made of his complex intellectual inheritance in defining his own position within his stressful age. My own sense, and hope, is that Vaughan criticism is alive and well; in recent years two journals have devoted special numbers to consideration of his work,[10] and it is obvious that younger critics are making significant advances. I am especially glad in this selection to print a recent intelligent attack on Vaughan, together with an appreciation of his work from a viewpoint that many readers will find novel.

Notes

1. Campbell's *Specimens* (1819), cited by L. C. Martin (ed.), *The Works of Henry Vaughan*, 2nd ed., 1957, xx.

2. *The Poems of Henry Vaughan, Silurist*, edited by E. K. Chambers, with an introduction by H. C. Beeching, London and New York, 1896, xliv.

3. "Vaughan's 'Each'," a review of Imilda Tuttle, *A Concordance to Vaughan's "Silex Scintillans,"* in *Essays in Criticism*, Vol. 21, No. 1 (1971), 86–91. However, I there ascribed the remark to Grosart, following an error in my dissertation, and am glad of this opportunity to make a correction.

4. *Science and the Modern World*, Cambridge, 1929, 103.

5. June Sturrock, "Wordsworth and Vaughan," *Notes & Queries*, New Series 24, No. 4 (1977), 322–323.

6. "The Private Imagery of Henry Vaughan," *The Review of English Studies*, New Series, I (1950), 206–25. I am sorry that Professor Kermode did not wish to reprint this article.

7. *The George Herbert Journal*, Vol. 3 (1979–80), 1–21.

8. *Protestant Poetics and the Seventeenth Century Religious Lyric*, Princeton, 1979, 332.

9. I read a paper, "Alchemical Philosophy and Religio-Political Implication in the Poems of Henry Vaughan" at the 1985 conference of the Renaissance Society of America.

10. *Poetry Wales*, Vol. 11, No. 2 (1975) and *The George Herbert Journal*, Vol. 7, No. 1 (Fall 1983) and No. 2 (Spring 1984). Both will be found of great interest by students of Vaughan.

M. M. MAHOOD

Vaughan: The Symphony of Nature

A single lyric by Henry Vaughan rescued him from the obscurity which
engulfed the Metaphysical poets between their age and our own. *The
Retreate*, in its apparent foreshadowing of Wordsworth's belief that childhood retains contact with a former country of the soul, led to a revival
of interest in the Silurist as a Romantic born out of due season. In the
century and a half which have passed since the Immortality Ode was
written, we have, perhaps, travelled far enough from both poets to view
Vaughan's writings in what we feel to be a truer perspective—not as a
foothill to Romantic heights, but as a peak of a distinct previous range.
The axioms of Vaughan's thought are presuppositions about life which
were common to the seventeenth century; and the weariness and fret
that he experiences are quite different, in their cause and cure, from
nineteenth-century melancholia. Yet the distinctions which Victorian
critics made between Vaughan's poetry and that of other Metaphysical
writers is a very real one, even if our enlarged sympathy for the wittiness
of Donne and Herbert prevents us from drawing the same conclusions
as the Victorians. To turn to the study of *Silex Scintillans* with the poetry
of Herbert and his lesser imitators fresh in our memory is a bewildering
experience. We feel ourselves beginners in a foreign language. We have
acquired its basic vocabulary and grammar, but we cannot as yet relish
its *nuances*, the cultural incrustations of each epithet and phrase in its
finer writings. The surface-meaning of Vaughan's lyrics is always
plain—often much plainer than that of his contemporaries among re-

Reprinted, by permission of the author, from *Poetry and Humanism*, London (1950),
252–95.

ligious poets; but beneath lie complex undercurrents of meaning, each springing from some now unfamiliar source.

All poetry, and Metaphysical poetry in especial, loads words with multiple charges of meaning, but Vaughan's way of doing this is rather different from the method of Donne or Herbert. When Herbert (for example) uses the word 'Temper' as title to two of his lyrics, he fuses together its various meanings in order to express the ill-temper with which he suffers the fluctuations of hope and despair whereby God tempers the soul to perfection of pitch (as a musical instrument) and to a serviceable firmness (as steel is tempered) and to suggest his desire that God will moderate these extremes of high and low and of hot and cold—in fact, temper the wind to the shorn lamb. All these meanings of the word are matter-of-fact: the poem's impression of depth derives from their fusion in a white-hot intensity of feeling. With this we may compare the poetic process which underlies Vaughan's use of equally everyday words. Here we find the ambiguity which characterises all Metaphysical poetry, but whereas Herbert's ambiguities arise from different verbal meanings, those of Vaughan are due to different symbolic values in the object itself—the method used by the modern Symbolist poets.[1] The word 'stone', in Vaughan's poetry, is charged with the Druidic significance that his childhood imagination infused into an old cromlech near his home,[2] with the mystical value attached to Egyptian hieroglyphic tablets by the Hermetist writers, and with the symbolic import of Joshua's stone that cried aloud in witness of the Covenant, Zechariah's stone with seven eyes, and the white stone of the Apocalypse. In consequence of this symbolism, Johnson's stricture on the Metaphysicals remains true of Vaughan: more than any other poet of his age, he draws his images from recesses of learning not much frequented by readers of poetry.

Few English readers have been able to explore what may well be the most important of these recesses: the vernacular literature of Vaughan's native Wales. His compatriot, Miss Gwenllian Morgan, was convinced that the Silurist habitually thought in Welsh[3]; and the feeling of beginning a new language, which we experience in reading Vaughan, may in part be due to the fact that English was not his mother-tongue. It is perhaps possible to attain in another language than one's own to the perfection of the *mot juste*, according to the principle, 'so many things, almost in an equal number of words'[4]; but it is reserved for the native writer to choose a word which is right for half a dozen different reasons.

6

Yet Vaughan gains more than he loses from the fact that he writes a Welshman's English. His independence of the traditional sense of many words results in some brilliant and audacious usages, and enables him to revitalise many words of Latin origin. Thus he uses 'conspire' in the sense of 'sympathise' and 'resentment' with the meaning of 'responsive feeling'.[5] Herbert's verbs are made strikingly effective by his fusion of different shades of meaning derived from the context. Vaughan's verbs are often equally effective because he neglects all but a single, unfamiliar connotation of each word. 'To blood' would, to an Englishman, mean 'to let blood; to bleed'. But Vaughan's usage is quite independent of this customary meaning:

> O how it *Blouds,*
> And *Spirits* all my Earth!
> *The Morning-watch*

To dust is to remove dust rather than to raise it; but this does not detract from the energy of the line

> Let folly dust it on, or lag behind.
> *Rules and Lessons*[6]

I question whether Vaughan, if English had been his mother-tongue, could have hit upon a verb so logically inexact, and yet so perfectly right in its context, as that in

> I see them walking in an Air of glory,
> Whose light doth trample on my days.

Such examples as these, which are all that can be offered by a reader with no knowledge of Welsh, suggest that only Vaughan's compatriots can savour the full richness of the Silurist's English. There must be many instances of his diction gaining force from the Welsh equivalent of an English word—his use of 'white' to mean, like the Welsh *gwyn,* both snow-coloured and innocent is a well-known example—and many others where his imagery reflects that of Celtic poetry. But our inquiry is perforce limited to its English and Continental sources.

By far the largest of Vaughan's English debts is to the Authorised Version. Probably there is no poet of the period whose work reveals a more intimate knowledge of the Bible. This is a sweeping claim to make for any writer in a century when men got the whole of the Scriptures by heart; but Vaughan, I feel, had a deeper and finer knowledge of them than even Bunyan attained. In an age when religious controversy

7

often degenerated into a mere bandying of texts, all factions tended to look on the Bible as the chief ammunition-dump of the book-war. Although Vaughan was by no means indifferent to the doctrinal issues of the day, he never searched the Scriptures for the wherewithal to confute his opponents. Others might expound the letter; Vaughan lived the text. He surrendered his sensibility as a poet to the Authorised Version with a wholehearted abandonment which would have been impossible to such poet-priests as Donne and Herbert. The Welsh and English countryside appeared to him as they did to a later mystic, Samuel Palmer, 'apparell'd in celestial light', like the symbolic landscapes of Hebrew poetry or the visions of St. John. When he rode into an English town 'that cities shining spires' became a foresight of the New Jerusalem; and the Brecknock Beacons which bounded the horizon at Newton-by-Usk were for Vaughan the holy hill whence the Psalmist looked for help, or Solomon's mountains of myrrh and hills of frankincense.

After the translators of the 1611 Bible, Vaughan's chief literary creditor is Herbert. He freely acknowledges the debt in the Preface to *Silex Scintillans* and there is scarcely a poem in that volume which does not owe its title or thought, its phrasing, metre or imagery—and sometimes all of these together—to *The Temple*. 'There is no example in English literature of one poet borrowing so extensively from another', writes F. E. Hutchinson.[7] Besides this indebtedness to Herbert, Vaughan's poetry is full of echoes from other contemporary devotional poets and prose-writers. The extreme receptivity of mind which is a source of his greatness as a nature poet leads him to absorb, and unwittingly to reproduce, whole phrases from those imitators of Herbert whom he affected to despise. Just as his early verse is often a *cento* of lines and images taken from Donne and the Sons of Ben Jonson, so *Silex Scintillans* echoes many religious poets of the preceding decade from Crashaw to Milton.[8]

If Vaughan, about the year 1649, was reading thus widely in the devotional writings which had appeared since *The Temple* was published in 1633, he can scarcely have failed to feel the influence of the Emblem Book, a literary form which had become highly popular during the intervening years.[9] It is probable that once Vaughan's interest in the form was aroused he would investigate the Jesuit originals from which the English emblematists took their plates. Thus to the Celtic and English sources of his imagery we may perhaps add the European Catholic tradition of the emblematists. The reading of Jesuit devotional literature was by no means limited to recusants in seventeenth-century England; that

Vaughan shared the prevalent interest is shown by his translations of odes by the Polish Jesuit, Casimir, and by his use of Jesuit sources for the prose volume, *Flores Solitudinis*. He also borrowed phrases and images from another Jesuit writer, Drexelius, who was well known to English readers of the time. Several of his devotional treatises were translated into English during the seventeenth century, and Ralph Winterton's translation of his *De Aeternitate Considerationes* ran through eight editions between 1636 and 1716. Although Drexelius's fierce gloom and taste for grotesque illustrations can have had small appeal for Vaughan, there were other qualities in the Jesuit's work to which he readily responded: his impatience at the limitations imposed upon thought and feeling by man's earthly state, his half-mystical apprehension of the relations between time and eternity,[10] his longing for a perfect conformity of the human and divine wills.

Such a conformity is symbolised by Drexelius in the traditional image of the sunflower and the sun, upon which he bases his *Heliotropium*. Both the idea and the image would make a strong appeal to Vaughan, who repeatedly compares humanity's indifference to its Creator with Nature's readier response. Like most of Drexelius's books, the *Heliotropium* is illustrated by emblems, in which the vicissitudes of the human will in its attempt to conform with the Divine Will are given visual form by means of flourishing or drooping sunflowers, flying and falling hearts. This sunflower *motif*, which is used by Vaughan ('Man is such a Mary-gold')[11] is a favourite with the emblematists. It is found in Quarles (who derives his plates from Jesuit emblem-books) and forms the most beautiful of a famous series of engravings, Vaenius's *Amoris Divini Emblemata*.[12] Another strikingly emblematic image in *Silex Scintillans* is the 'paire of scales' which forms part of Vaughan's allegorical vision in *Regeneration*, a poem which has the air of being a string of emblems.[13] Even so individual and visionary a poem as *The World* may partly owe its 'great Ring of pure and endless light' to the Jesuits' repeated use of a ring (often made by a serpent biting its own tail) as the symbol of eternity.[14]

Many other images in *Silex Scintillans* have their counterpart in the Jesuit emblemata. But there are yet others which cannot be explained by reference either to earlier English writers or to the Continental tradition. Neither will, for example, elucidate the opening stanzas of *Cock-crowing*:

> Father of lights! what Sunnie seed,
> What glance of day hast thou confin'd

Into this bird? To all the breed
This busie Ray thou hast assign'd;
  Their magnetism works all night,
  And dreams of Paradise and light.

Their eyes watch for the morning hue,
Their little grain expelling night
So shines and sings, as if it knew
The path unto the house of light.
  It seems their candle, howe'r done,
  Was tinn'd and lighted at the sunne.

If such a tincture, such a touch,
So firm a longing can impowre
Shall thy own image think it much
To watch for thy appearing hour?
  If a meer blast so fill the sail,
  Shall not the breath of God prevail?

Here Vaughan develops, in great detail, an image based upon a philosophical theory which is usually quite unfamiliar to his modern reader;
words such as 'glance', 'ray', 'tincture', are laden with esoteric meaning.
Nearly all Vaughan's lyrics bear some such oblique reference to a little-
known system of thought, but the particular interest of these stanzas is
that they have an exact parallel in a prose passage which will guide us
to one principal source of his symbolism:

> The Soul ... is guided in her operations by a spiritual, me-
> taphysical grain, a seed or glance of light, simple and without
> any mixture, descending from the first Father of Lights. For
> though His full-eyed love shines on nothing but man, yet
> everything in the world is in some measure directed for his
> preservation by a spice or touch of the First Intellect.... [15]

If the prose passage is not actually the source of *Cock-crowing*, it suggests
a complete affinity of mind between the two writers; and in fact it is to
be found in the *Anima Magica Abscondita* of Henry Vaughan's twin
brother, Thomas. A perfect harmony of thought and interest united the
twins. One complimentary poem prefixed to Henry's *Olor Iscanus* asks:

> What *Planet* rul'd your *birth*? what *wittie star*?
> That you so like in *Souls* as *Bodies* are!

During the most critical years of Henry Vaughan's inner life, he and
his brother were physician and priest respectively at Newton-by-Usk

and the periods of their most characteristic writings exactly coincide. Thomas was the leading Hermetic philosopher of his day; and nearly all the many scholars who have investigated the writings of both twins in their interrelations are agreed that, through Thomas's influence, Henry Vaughan studied the Hermetic philosophy which, after sinking to the level of alchemy and magic during the Middle Ages, had been restored as a metaphysical system by Renaissance thinkers.[16] Although Samuel Butler and Swift both poured scorn upon the writings of 'Eugenius Philalethes', as Thomas Vaughan chose to call himself,[17] it is not really to Henry Vaughan's discredit that he allowed himself to be so deeply influenced by his brother's Hermetic thought. Thomas's determination to establish correspondences between everything in Heaven and earth leads him to some fantastic statements; he loves to shroud platitude in an air of mystification, and all too often the mountainous travail of his learning results in the merest mouse. But there is in him a touch of his own 'star-fire', and its intermittent light reveals him as a genuine mystic. Henry Vaughan's thought gained a great deal in depth and subtlety from the Hermetic philosophy which he learnt directly from his brother or studied with his guidance; while his own strong sense of 'conversion' enabled him to assimilate the unfamiliar system of ideas into his Christian world-view. It is this power to synthesise, much in the manner of an earlier Hermetist, Pico della Mirandola, which safeguards the Silurist from the madder excesses of Thomas Vaughan's thought. 'He has passed the Hermetic ideas and terms so integrally into the common language of Christian tradition that they do not disconcert the reader; they are not resented as the technical terms of an unfamiliar philosophy, but are accepted as the poet's way of expressing his conviction of the "commerce" between earth and heaven.'[18]

Through his brother's guidance, Henry Vaughan studied the writings of 'Thrice-great Hermes' and probably also those of Dionysius the Areopagite, for whom Thomas had a special veneration, and whose central paradox is restated in *The Night*:

> There is in God (some say)
> A deep, but dazling darkness.

Besides drawing upon such neo-Platonists as Dionysius for certain images, Vaughan sometimes seems to have Plato's own work in mind. In *The World* the apostrophe to the 'fools' who would rather 'live in grots and caves' than in the light of Heaven recalls, in the context of the

11

poem's Platonic symbolism, the cave allegory in *The Republic*. So does part of the elegy on the twins' younger brother, which begins 'Silence, and stealth of dayes!'

> As he that in some Caves thick damp
> Lockt from the light,
> Fixeth a solitary lamp,
> To brave the night
> And walking from his Sun, when past
> That glim'ring Ray
> Cuts through the heavy mists in haste
> Back to his day....

'Eugenes Philalethes' seems also to have encouraged his brother to study the Hermetists of modern times. Henry Vaughan interpolates a reference to Paracelsus into one of the translations in *Flores Solitudinis*[19]; and besides the allusion to Thomas's chief hero, Cornelius Agrippa, in *The Mount of Olives*, it has been shown that one of the lyrics in *Silex Scintillans*, *The Ass* is based upon a chapter of that writer's *The Vanity of Arts and Sciences*.[20] Lastly, it is probable that Henry Vaughan knew the mystical writings of a contemporary Hermetist, Jakob Boehme. In the poem *Repentance* he speaks of 'All that have *signature* or life', recalling Boehme's stress upon the Hermetic theory of the *signatura rerum*; and in translating Nollius's *Hermetical Physick* he interpolates an explanation of the word.[21]

There is a real danger that, in tracking some of Vaughan's images to these rather recondite origins, we may miss their more obvious source in the mountains and woods, lake and waterfalls which were continually before his eyes. Both twins believed Nature to be a second word of God, and thus far more rewarding of study than any volume of pagan philosophy. 'Now for thy study', writes Thomas Vaughan: 'in the summer translate thyself to the fields, where all are green with the breath of God and fresh with the power of heaven'.[22] Of the many winds which played upon the Aeolian harp of Henry Vaughan's sensibility, his native mountain air awakened the clearest and purest tones. He is alone among the poets of the time in repeatedly suggesting the hour and place of his lyrics' composition. In *The Lampe*, "Tis dead night round about'; 'They are all gone into the world of light' is written in the afterglow of

> those faint beams in which this hill is drest,
> After the Sun's remove,

and *The Dawning* is an urgently impressionistic sketch of quickly-changing effects of light:

> The whole Creation shakes off night,
> And for thy shadow looks the light,
> Stars now vanish without number,
> Sleepie Planets set, and slumber,
> The pursie Clouds disband, and scatter,
> All expect some sudden matter,
> Not one beam triumphs, but from far
> That morning star.

So Vaughan's immediate delight in a beautiful countryside blends, in his poetry, with his recollections of native and English verse, of the Bible, of Jesuit emblemata and of both ancient and modern Hermetists. These sources of his imagery are often themselves complex, since the Jesuits' learning extended to the Hermetic philosophy, a Hermetist such as Thomas Vaughan made use of emblemata,[23] and the emblematists drew many of their symbols from the Bible. Such complications often make it impossible to decide the exact source of an image; notwithstanding, I think an inquiry in the provenance of some dominant *motifs* in Vaughan's poetry is worth attempting.

Vaughan, like all mystics, was dejected at his own powerlessness to experience union, or even illumination, except at the rarest intervals. It was as if God had interposed a veil between Himself and the human mind which the poet could penetrate only in those visionary moments when

> some strange thoughts transcend our wonted theams,
> And into glory peep.

This image of the veil occurs frequently in Vaughan's writings. Besides using it some score of times in his original verse and prose, he introduced it into his translations where there is nothing in the source to suggest it.[24] Of the word's lyrical occurrences, none is more effective than that in *L'Envoy* with which *Silex Scintillans* ends:

> Arise, arise!
> And like old cloaths fold up these skies,
> This long worn veyl....

There is rich Metaphysical complexity here; at least four symbolic meanings of 'veil' coalesce in the intensity of Vaughan's feeling. The cry of 'Arise!' and the allusion to folded clothes bring the Resurrection to mind, and thus suggest the idea of the body as a veil covering the soul. This

13

is the dominant thought behind several occurrences of the image in *Silex Scintillans*. In *The Night*, it is Christ's mortal body:

> That sacred vail drawn o'r thy glorious noon.

In *Cock-crowing* it represents all human flesh:

> Onely this Veyle which thou hast broke,
> And must be broken yet in me,
> This veyle, I say, is all the cloke
> And cloud which shadows thee from me.
> This veyle thy full-ey'd love denies,
> And onely gleams and fractions spies.

Closely joined with the idea of the Resurrection as the rending of a veil is the memory of the veil before the Sanctuary, which was rent at the eleventh hour in token of the Old Law's supersession. Some of Vaughan's uses of the image refer especially to this symbolic event:

> Veiles became useles, Altars fel,
> Fires smoking die;
> And all that sacred pomp, and shel
> Of things did flie.
>
> *Faith*

Not the veil of the flesh alone, but the whole fabric of the physical world impedes the 'love-sick souls exalted flight',[25] and the image in *L'Envoy* contains a third symbolic meaning of 'veil' as the boundary between the natural and supernatural worlds. Edmund Blunden has pointed out how Vaughan is exceptional among poets in his indifference to the moon's beauty.[26] The reason for this seems to be that the moon's sphere, as the supposed bound and limit of the elemented world, bars Vaughan's access to those 'brave, translunary things' towards which he aspires. Thus in *The Mount of Olives* he speaks of the moon as the planet 'whose *sphere* is the *veil* or *partition* drawn betwixt *us* and *Immortality*', and in the Elegy on Walbeoffe there is a slighting allusion to the '*Moon's* ruder veil'.[27] Lastly, the limits set by time are no less irksome to the aspiration of Vaughan's spirit than are those imposed by space; and the *L'Envoy* image, by its reminiscence of the Apocalyptic, 'And the heavens were removed as a scroll when it is rolled up', suggests yet a fourth symbolic meaning of 'veil' as time's shadow eclipsing the light of eternity. This meaning preponderates in *The day of Judgement*:

All other days, compar'd to thee,
Are but lights weak minority,
They are but veils, and Cypers drawn
Like Clouds, before thy glorious dawn.

Thus in this one passage of *L'Envoy*, the word 'veil' stands for the Old Law, time, the body, and the limits of the physical world: four barriers between the soul and God which were penetrated in the first Resurrection and which are to be destroyed at the last.

To take the image to pieces in this way is not, of course, to show how it works—that remains the poet's secret—but it can suggest the richness of the harmonics which reverberate over Vaughan's clearest notes. This complexity, as I have tried to demonstrate, is symbolistic rather than semantic; in consequence, Vaughan's subtle use of 'veil' owes much to the veil symbolism to be found in Hermetic and neo-Platonic writers. These include Cornelius Agrippa, whose plea 'Cast off the veil that is before your faces' is quoted by Thomas Vaughan.[28] The German mystics have a particular liking for the image.[29] It is also found among the seventeenth-century emblematists. Quarles's verses to a plate showing a curtain drawn between Divine Love and Anima are very similar in tone to Vaughan's *Cock-crowing*:

Thou are my Sun, Great God! O when shall I
View the full beams of thy meridian eye?
Draw, draw this fleshly curtain, that denies
The gracious presence of thy glorious eyes.
                    Book V, Emblem xii

But the main source of Vaughan's symbol is the Bible, where St. Paul had already achieved a fusion between different symbolistic uses of the word 'veil'. For the Apostle, Isaiah's prophecy, 'And he wil destroy in this mountaine the face of the couering cast ouer all people, and the vaile that is spread ouer all nations',[30] was fulfilled when the rent veil of the Temple disclosed 'a new and liuing way which hee hath consecrated for vs, through the vaile, that is to say, His flesh'[31] Vaughan made these last words the epigraph to his poem, *Resurrection and Immortality*; and his symbolistic use of 'veil' often echoes another passage, in which St. Paul writes of the veil which covered the face of Moses on his descent from Mount Sinai:

which vaile is done away with in Christ. But even vnto this
day, when Moses is read, the vaile is vpon their heart.
Neuerthelesse, when it shall turne to the Lord, the vaile shall
be taken away.

2 Cor. iii.14–16

The complex origins of this image are simple in comparison with
the possible sources of another image much favoured by Vaughan—a
stone as symbol of the unregenerate heart. Sometimes the metaphor is
of a *silex scintillans*—the flint which must be struck before it can emit
fire:

> Lord! thou didst put a soul here; If I must
> Be broke again, for flints will give no fire
> Without a steel, O let thy power cleer
> Thy gift once more, and grind this flint to dust!
>
> *The Tempest*

At other times, Vaughan compares the obdurate heart to the rock in
the wilderness which flowed with water when struck by Moses. In *The
Mount of Olives* he pleads, 'Take away, O my God! this heart of stone
and give me a heart of flesh. . . . O thou that didst cause the waters to
flow out of the stonie rock . . . give to me true remorse'.[32] Both metaphors
mingle in the Latin verses accompanying the emblem of a flinty heart
struck by the thunderbolt of divine fire which appears on the title-page
of *Silex Scintillans*. I give Edmund Blunden's translation, which is beau-
tifully in keeping with Vaughan's English verse manner:

> *The Flashing Flint*
> O I confess, without a wound
> Thou oft hast tried me,
> And oft Thy Voice without a sound
> Hath longed to guide me;
> Thy zephyr circled me from heaven
> On a calm wing,
> And murmuring sought t'allure me, given
> To no such thing.
>
> A Flint I was, both deaf and dumb,
> But Thou, unceasing,
> (So lov'st Thou all Thy tribe) didst come
> To my releasing;

16

Thou hast tried all Thy powers, until
  Thou show'st Thy love,
With whose vast Will my stubborn will
  Thou dost remove.

Thy siege comes sharper; by Thy shock
  My wall's o'erthrown;
Thou shatter'st even my breast of rock,
  And what was stone
Is flesh and blood: O see, I bleed:
  At last these Heaps
Burn with Thy heaven, and, changed indeed!
  The Marble weeps.

Thus in the world's first age Thy hand
  Made fountains ripple
From Rocks, and Cliffs at Thy command
  Refreshed Thy people;
Thy secret busy care, my Lord,
  Hath here been plain:
My dying is my life restored;
  My loss, my gain.[33]

Vaughan's printer probably had the block for the engraving which
accompanies these verses cut in imitation of a design in some continental
emblem book; the sentient Petrarchan heart is the dominant *motif* with
many emblematists of the period.[34] With or without an emblem, the
image is frequent in Jesuit books of devotion. In that part of Nieremberg's *De Arte Voluntatis* which Vaughan translated, there occurs the
simile, 'Certaine Divine Raies breake out of the Soul in adversity, like
sparkes of fire out of the afflicted *flint*'.[35] It would be most familiar to
such writers in its liturgical use, although its ultimate source is, of course,
the Old Testament: in the promise made to Ezekiel, 'and I will take
away the stonie heart out of your flesh, and I will giue you an heart of
flesh', in Jeremiah's 'Is not my word like a fire, saith the Lord? and like
a hammer that breaketh the rocke in pieces', and in the Psalmist's
recollection that it was the presence of God 'Which turned the rocke
into a standing water: and the flint into a fountaine of waters'.[36] These
texts were combined with Petrarchan heart-imagery by many religious
poets of Vaughan's day. For example, Martin Lluelyn builds a lyric
upon the sonneteering conceit that only the heat of Divine Love can
melt the frozen heart; it concludes with this stanza:

After thy *Love* if I continue hard,
If Vices *knit* and more *confirm'd* are grown,
If guilt *rebell*, and stand upon his Guard,
And what was *Ice* before freeze into *Stone*,
    Reprove, Reprove,
And let thy *Pow'r* assist thee to revenge thy *Love*,
For thou hast still thy *threats* and *Thunder* left;
'*The Rock that can't be melted, may be cleft*'.[37]

An even closer parallel with Vaughan's emblematic verses is to be found
in the writings of his brother Thomas, who inserts into his *Anthroposophia
Theomagica* a lyric which may have been written for the same emblem
of the flashing flint, perhaps by way of a rhyming contest with his twin:

    Lord God, this was a stone
    As hard as any one
    Thy laws in Nature framed.
    'Tis now a springing well
    And many drops can tell,
    Since it by Art was framed.

    My God, my heart is so;
    'Tis all of flint and no
    Extract of tears will yield.
    Dissolve it with Thy fire,
    That something may aspire
    And grow up in my field.

    Bare tears I'll not entreat,
    But let Thy Spirit's seat
    Upon those waters be;
    The I—new form'd with light—
    Shall move without all night
    Or eccentricity.[38]

Thomas Vaughan absorbs the image into his alchemical lore in his
endeavour to give a philosophical and religious meaning to the search
for the Philosopher's Stone. 'In a word', he claims in *Lumen de Lumine*,
'salvation itself is nothing else but transmutation.... God of His great
mercy prepare us for it, that from hard, stubborn flints of this world we
may prove chrysoliths and jaspers in the new, eternal foundations'.[39]
The power whereby the Divine Fire revitalises a cold and rocky heart

is for Thomas Vaughan the primal secret of creation which alchemists have long sought in vain:

> This, Reader, is the Christian Philosopher's Stone—a Stone so often inculcated in Scripture. This is the Rock in the wilderness—in the wilderness because in great obscurity and few there are that know the right way unto it. This is the Stone of Fire in Ezekiel; this is the Stone with Seven Eyes upon it in Zachary; and this is the White Stone with the New Name in the Revelation.
>
> *The Works of T. Vaughan*, ed. Waite, p. 113

So the transcendental alchemy of the Hermetists can be added to the Bible, the emblem-books and contemporary religious poetry as among the possible sources of the stone and flint imagery in the title and contents of *Silex Scintillans*.

A further recurrent image in Vaughan's poetry, 'the Candle of the Lord', again shows a mixed ancestry. Although the Silurist writes with scorn of the Puritan illuminists who used the metaphor for the Inner Light, his own lyrics abound in allusions to

> the earnest thy love sheds,
> The *Candle* shining on some heads.
>
> Dedication to *Silex Scintillans*

Vaughan, like the Cambridge Platonists and Milton, means by the symbol the small light of natural reason which remained with man even in the obscurity of his Fall and might be rekindled by grace. There are several Biblical sources of the image: 'O that I were as in moneths past, as in the dayes when God preserued me. When his candle shined vpon my head, and when by his light I walked through darkenesse'; 'For thou wilt light my candle: the LORD my God will enlighten my darkenesse'; 'The spirit of man is the candle of the LORD'.[40] Vaughan's choice of the image may have been encouraged by its widespread adaptation as an emblem. Thus the first engraving in Drexelius's *Zodiacus Christianus* shows 'Cereus ardens, quo designatur *Lux interna*, quæ beneficia Dei, vanitatem mundi, vitæ brevitatem, peccatorum cœnum, voluptatum omnium vanescentes vmbras sic ostendit'.[41] It was not, however, necessary for Vaughan to go to the continental emblem book for visual instances of the image. In England in 1638 there appeared two books which between them fairly exhausted the emblematic uses of the *Lux interna*—Quarles's *Hieroglyphics of the Life of Man* and Robert Farley's *Lychnocausia*. Every one of Vaughan's light images could be matched either in the engravings or in the text of these two works.[42] A third source is suggested by the candle which appears in the emblematic frontispiece to Thomas Vaughan's *Lumen de Lumine*; the symbol was traditional with the Hermetists. Thus Thomas describes the Fire-Soul which is the central concept of his philosophical system as 'the Secret Candle of God, which he hath tinned in the elements: it burns and is not seen, for it shines in a dark place. Every natural body is a kind of black lantern; it carries this Candle within it, but the light appears not: it is eclipsed with the grossness of the matter'.[43] Once again, three different symbolistic traditions, those of the Old Testament writers, the Hermetists and the Renaissance allegorists who evolved the emblem, contribute to the richness of associations in Vaughan's use of an image.

This glance at the complex origins of a few images is not intended to detract from Vaughan's poetic individuality, but rather to enhance it. A poet of more superficial feelings might cull each image from a different source and offer us an indifferent pot-pourri of other men's flowers. Vaughan, however, did not seek in books the substitute for devotional experience; he found in them its confirmation, and the repeated discovery gives us the multiple overtones of his imagery. He was vividly, almost physically, aware of his own hardness of heart; in consequence he seizes upon every symbolistic use of stone or flint to typify such hardness. He is oppressed by a feeling of God's inaccessibility; accordingly each veil-symbol in the writings of St. Paul, the emblematists and the Hermetic philosophers stamps itself deeply upon his imagination.

That Vaughan controls, and is not controlled by, his borrowings is evident if we consider what he did not take from his sources. Donne's legal and martial metaphors, Herbert's musical terms, the homely, scientific or classical images of the Jesuits, have no place in the Silurist's poetry except as awkward intruders. For a physican, he makes surprisingly little use of medical terms, and *The Temple* probably has more of these than *Silex Scintillans*. Vaughan's originality can be seen if we compare his *Son-dayes* with its model, Herbert's *Prayer* (I). Both poems are an attempt to define their theme by a string of symbols. But when Vaughan tries to imitate Herbert's tactile, manipulative type of image— 'The Christian plummet sounding heav'n and earth' (a favourite emblem of the period)—he can only produce the insipid 'Pulleys unto headlong man', while his attempt at a monetary image, of the kind Herbert uses to convey his strongest feelings, falls equally flat:

> ... Times Prerogative,
> And Interest
> Deducted from the whole.

But when he is able to transfuse his own experience of Nature's part in the devotional life into Herbert's images, he handles the earlier poem with a Midas touch, and what was merely fanciful becomes imaginative. Herbert's 'The milkie way' is too pallid for Vaughan, who transforms the phrase with one of his audacious verbs—

> The milky way Chalkt out with Suns

and into Herbert's 'six-daies world transposing in an houre' he infuses the memory of a time when outer and inner experience harmonised as 'A Gleam of glory, after six-days-showres'.

Thus Vaughan, for all his seeming eclecticism, is a selective borrower. He takes his good where he can find it, but he takes only *his* good. For this reason, the imagery of Vaughan's poems offers the surest and swiftest guide to his philosophy and to the devotional experience which is that philosophy's source.

Vaughan's images group themselves in a few well-defined clusters. One of the largest and most recurrent of these groups has, for common factor, the idea of magnetism. The phenomenon interested Vaughan before he came to see it as a universal principle of Nature. Already in the 1646 *Poems* there are signs that Vaughan is beginning to explore the 'secret commerce', kept between all parts of the cosmos, of which the lodestone is only one manifestation:

> Thus to the North the Loadstones move,
> And thus to them th'enamour'd steel aspires:
> Thus, *Amoret*,
> I doe affect;
> And thus by winged beames, and mutuall fire,
> Spirits and Stars conspire,
> And this is LOVE.
> (*To* Amoret, *of ... what true Love is*)

This 'conspiration' of spirit (that is, of the star-fire in all created forms) with star is a dominant theme of *Silex Scintillans*, and represents one form of the belief in a correspondence between diverse planes of being which is found in all Baroque poetry. Thomas Vaughan gives striking expression to the idea in words which (he claims) originally formed a Hermetic inscription:

> Heaven above, heaven beneath,
> Stars above, stars beneath,
> All that is above is also beneath:
> Understand this, and be happy.
>
> Waite, p. 183

Vaughan, more than other poets, sees this correspondence as a circulation of sympathy between the various planes of existence. Terms such as 'busy ray', 'influence', 'sympathy' are used by him to convey this feeling of an active commerce. The heavenly bodies emit beams to seek out in the terrestrial forms below some inner light which burns with responsive desire towards its influential star. Thus the cock's 'little grain' of star-fire compels him to herald the sun's rising. Plants feel the same attraction:

> Some kinde herbs here, though low & far,
> Watch for, and know their loving star.
>
> *The Favour*

In one of his night-watches, Vaughan checks the impulse of his imagination to 'outstep' the stars, in order that he may reflect upon the 'conspiration' of each star with its earthly counterpart as a symbol of God's call and the soul's response. If the terrestrial form is to attract the star's radiance it must itself have

> a restless, pure desire
> And longing for thy bright and vitall fire,
> Desire that never will be quench'd,
> Nor can be writh'd, nor wrench'd.

> These are the Magnets which so strongly move
> And work all night upon thy light and love,
> As beauteous shapes, we know not why,
> Command and guide the eye.

> For where desire, celestiall, pure desire,
> Hath taken root, and grows, and doth not tire,

> There God a Commerce states, and sheds
> His Secret on their heads.

The Starre

Even stones experience this magnetism, for they too have their share of the 'star-fire'. In most jewels this fire is clearly to be seen—'We have astronomy here under our feet' writes Thomas Vaughan[44]—but the pearl's opacity clouds its brilliance. This gives pearls a special significance in Vaughan's imagery, where they symbolise the semi-obscurity of the immortal soul in the mortal body:

> So *Souls* shine at the *Eyes*, and *Pearls* display
> Through the *loose-Chrystal-streams* a glaunce of day.

This conception of the spirit or soul as an imprisoned star recurs in *The Bird*

> For each inclosed Spirit is a star
> Inlightning his own little sphære,

and again in 'They are all gone into the world of light':

> If a star were confin'd into a Tomb
> Her captive flames must needs burn there;
> But when the hand that lockt her up, gives room,
> She'l shine through all the sphære.

In this poem, Vaughan once more employs the magnetism, which he believes to exist in Nature, as an analogy with the relationship between God and the soul; and once again he speaks of it as the response of light to light and fire to fire. For the star-fire hidden within the forms of birds and plants and stones corresponds to the divine spark in man, the Candle of the Lord which is kindled at the 'new world's new, quickning Sun'.[45] In instances far too numerous to list here, Vaughan apostrophises God as the Light of Lights. One passage from *The Mount of Olives* must serve to recall the luminous effect given to all Vaughan's writings by this light symbolism; it is the poet's Meditation at the setting of the Sun:

> This Sun of the firmament hath his Course; it riseth, setteth, comes up again, and again goes down: But thou Lord, knowest no vicissitudes, thou art the *Ancient of dayes*, thou art the *Rock of ages from Everlasting to Everlasting.* O thou, *the same to day and yesterday, and for evermore! Thou bright and morning Starre springing from on high,* illuminate me, who am now sitting in darknesse

23

and in the shadow of death. *O light of light, the brightnesse of thy Fathers glory,* inlighten all inward obscurities in me, that after this life I may never be cast into the outward darknesse. *O most blessed, most merciful, and Almighty Jesu!* abide I beseech thee with me, *for it is towards Evening, and the day is far spent.* As long as thou art present with me, I am in the light, but when thou art gone, I am in the shadows of death, and amongst the stones of emptinesse. When thou art present, all is brightnesse, all is sweetnesse, I am in my Gods bosome, I discourse with him, watch with him, walk with him, live with him, and lie down with him. All these most dear and unmeasurable blessings I have with thee, and want them without thee. Abide then with me, O thou whom my soul loveth! Thou Sun of righteousnesse with healing under thy wings arise in my heart; refine, quicken, and cherish it; make thy light there to shine in darknesse, and a perfect day in the dead of night.

The chiaroscuro of this passage reminds us that by comparison with such heavenly radiance as Vaughan envisages even the sun and stars are dark. Beside the images which suggest influence and illumination are as many others which convey the ideas of deprivation and darkness. Life in the world is dark by comparison with Heaven's 'pure and endless light'. Vaughan borrows from Paracelsus the metaphor of the soul as a candle obscured in the dark-lantern of the body, and interpolates it into his translation of Nieremberg.[46] At other times he sees life as a dark cavern or as a long night's journey.[47] At best, it is no more than the reflected glow of sunset, since the bright morning of Eden and of childhood have long since passed. Because the Second Coming will be the daybreak to this long darkness, all dawns have the beauty of symbolic meaning for Vaughan:

> *Mornings* are *Mysteries*; the first worlds *Youth*,
> Mans *Resurrection*, and the futures *Bud*
> Shrowd in their births.
> *Rules and Lessons*

Christ is repeatedly called the day-spring and the morning star in *Silex Scintillans*; and Vaughan adds a characteristic paradox to hundreds of others in which the Baroque poets struggled to express the mystery of the Resurrection:

24

> To put on Clouds instead of light,
> And cloath the morning-starre with dust,
> Was a translation of such height
> As, but in thee, was ne'r exprest.
>
> *The Incarnation and Passion*

The cloud-image contained in these lines is, on a quantitative reckoning, Vaughan's favourite symbol for the human soul's separation from the Divine Light. Like the veil-image with which they are often associated, Vaughan's clouds and mists stand for all the limitations that mortal life imposes on the soul: the body, space and time. All are suggested by the last stanza of *Resurrection and Immortality* in which the Soul speaks thus to the Body:

> Then I that here saw darkly in a glasse
>   But mists, and shadows passe,
> And, by their owne weake *Shine*, did search the springs
>   And Course of things
>   Shall with Inlightned Rayes
>   Pierce all their wayes;
> And as thou saw'st, I in a thought could goe
>   To heav'n, or Earth below
> To reade some *Starre*, or *Min'rall*, and in State
>   There often sate,
>   So shalt thou then with me
>   (Both wing'd, and free,)
> Rove in that mighty, and eternall light
>   Where no rude shade, or night
> Shall dare approach us; we shall there no more
>   Watch stars, or pore
> Through melancholly clouds, and say
>   *Would it were Day!*
> One everlasting *Saboth* there shall runne
> Without *Succession*, and without a *Sunne*.

Sometimes Vaughan seeks to express the impenetrable nature of this barrier between God and Nature by the image of a hard, translucent shell—the 'mundane shell' of Blake's emblems. In *Resurrection and Immortality* this image is fused with a traditional Christian symbol of eternal life, the silk-moth's liberation from her cocoon.[48] The same symbolism is implicit in *The Search*:

25

> The skinne, and shell of things
> Though faire,
> are not
> Thy wish, nor pray'r
> but got
> By meer Despair
> of wings.

With the growth of its wings, the enclosed spirit knows itself to be an exile from its true home, and this unrest is another dominant theme of Vaughan's poetry and prose. Man is a traveller, who 'only is a stranger here, where all things else are at home'.[49] Vaughan repeats the idea in *Man*, where he laments human waywardness—

> He hath no root, nor to one place is ty'd,
> But ever restless and Irregular
> About this Earth doth run and ride,
> He knows he hath a home, but scarce knows where,
> He sayes it is so far
> That he hath quite forgot how to go there

and contrasts it with the unerring instinct of homing birds and bees. Man's loss of Eden is the cause of his homesickness: in *Man's Fall, and Recovery* Vaughan represents him as a 'sully'd flowre' transplanted from the hills of Paradise.

This metaphor brings us to a second large group of images, as numerous as those which cluster around the idea of magnetism, which we may call images of fructification. Scarcely a poem in *Silex Scintillans* is without some image of the human soul as a plant watered by the dew of grace, hardened by the frosts and storms of affliction, and yielding sound fruit or ripe grain when 'the white winged Reapers come'. In such a lyric as *The Sap*, the idea is worked out in a series of fanciful metaphors; but in his finer poetic moments Vaughan overleaps the distinctions implicit in such analogies and enters imaginatively into the life of growth:

> O Joyes! Infinite sweetnes! with what flowres,
> And shoots of glory, my soul breakes, and buds!
> All the long houres
> Of night, and Rest
> Through the still shrouds

26

> Of sleep, and Clouds,
> This Dew fell on my Breast.
>
> *The Morning-watch*

God's grace is spoken of as a quickening and nourishing dew in many
parts of Vaughan's work, and in *The Night* this concept is fused with an
echo from the Song of Songs to create one of the richest images in *Silex
Scintillans*: night is

> Gods silent, searching flight:
> When my Lords head is fill'd with dew, and all
> His locks are wet with the clear drops of night. . . .

Another verse from the same book of the Bible—'Awake, O North winde,
and come thou South, blow vpon my garden, that the spices thereof
may flow out'[50]—finds an echo whenever Vaughan uses images of soft
winds and spicy airs, which nourish the leaves of his symbolic plant as
vitally as the dew and rain sustain its roots. Sometimes these mild airs
are turned to a storm, or frost chills the growing plant; yet Vaughan is
able to say 'Blest be thy Dew and blest thy Frost' in the certain hope
that both ensure a good harvest:

> For as thy hand the weather steers,
> So thrive I best, 'twixt joyes, and tears,
> And all the year have some grean Ears.
>
> *Love, and Discipline*

Another Biblical echo is heard in the poem from which these lines are
taken: the parable of the Sower whose seed is the Word of God. Many
of Vaughan's fructification images, especially in *The Mount of Olives*,
derive from this source; the stony ground of the parable corresponds to
Vaughan's favourite image of the flinty heart in which no seed of conformity to the Divine Will can grow. But God can make the most barren
soil fruitful; and we have already seen how Vaughan symbolises this
power when he associates the image of the flinty heart with the 'springing
Rock' struck by Moses in the wilderness.

Vaughan's allusions to this miracle introduce a further group of
fructification images, those connected with springing or running water.
In the music, purity and beneficence of mountain streams, and in their
impetuous movement towards the sea, the poet found a perfect symbol
of the Christian life, which he uses in *The Waterfall* and *The Dawning*.
Wells bore a similar significance; the desert wells which watered the

27

flocks of Abraham and his tribe were to the first Chosen People such springs of living water as the Sacraments were to the Church. The weather's circulation of water between earth and sky was also rich in meaning for Vaughan, who saw in it a symbol of the 'busy commerce' between God and man: the descent of grace as dew or rain, the ascent of prayer as an exhalation.

If we attempt to define the intellectual bias which impels Vaughan's choice of these two imagic clusters—the magnetism group and the fructification group—we shall, I believe, discover a single philosophical concept underlying them both. Since no book of lyrics supplies an orderly account of the poet's philosophy, all such inferences remain in the nature of guesses; but in Vaughan's case these guesses come a little nearer to certainties when they are found to correspond almost exactly with the philosophical system of his twin brother, Thomas.

Both the Vaughans retained in maturity that sense of the momentous with which children imbue the most trivial-seeming events. The 'shootes of everlastingnesse' that pierced Henry Vaughan's imagination as he gazed at a cloud or flower were felt by Thomas while the brothers watched their schoolmaster dabble in chemistry—or, more properly, alchemy:

> There is scarce anything in it [i.e. the world] but hath given me an occasion of some thoughts; but that which took me up much and soon was the continual action of fire upon water. This speculation—I know not how—surprised my first youth, long before I saw the university; and certainly Nature, whose pupil I was, had even then awakened many notions in me which I met with afterwards in the Platonic philosophy.
>
> Waite, pp. 395–6

This union of elemental extremes—the hot and dry fire operating upon the cold and fluid water—became the basis of Thomas Vaughan's theories of the physical world. The Creation, as he describes it in his first book, *Anthroposophia Theomagica*, was itself such a union of a divine light and fire with the cold, dark mass of chaos. Through this 'incubation', as Thomas Vaughan terms it, chaos was resolved into its elements. First, fire was removed to an outer sphere—the 'fire-liquid light' of Henry Vaughan's poem *Midnight*. Next, air was extracted from the chaos, leaving the elements of earth and water from which the Spirit, working through the refined elements of air and fire, wrought all forms of life. This concept of the upper light and lower darkness is given visual form in Henry Vaughan's ring of light above a sphere of darkness; and a paragraph from *Lumen de Lumine* will serve to stress this resemblance between the world-pictures of the brothers:

> When I seriously consider the system or fabric of this world I find it to be a certain series, a link or chain which is extended *a non gradu ad non gradum*,[51] from that which is beneath all apprehension to that which is above all apprehension. That which is beneath all degrees of sense is a certain horrible, inexpressible darkness. The magicians call it active darkness, and the effect of it in Nature is cold, etc. For darkness is the visage of cold—the complexion, body and matrix of cold—as light is the face, principle and fountain of heat. That which is above all degree of intelligence is a certain infinite, inaccessible fire or light. Dionysius calls it Divine Darkness, because it is invisible and incomprehensible.... The middle substance or chain between these two is that which we commonly call Nature. This is the *Scala* of the great Chaldee which doth reach from the subternatural darkness to the supernatural fire.
>
> Waite, p. 269

This action of the upper light upon the lower darkness did not cease with the Creation; it is repeated in the procreation of every living form, by a process described in Thomas Vaughan's last work, *Euphrates*. There remain in every part of the cosmos fragments, or seeds, of the First Matter from which all things were originally made. This First Matter, the Mercury of the alchemists, is not an elemented substance, but an earth-water, the feminine principle which must receive the embrace of its contrary, fire, before a new life can be engendered. This fire is similarly not one of the elements, but is a star-fire which remains in nature as the counterpart of the heavenly bodies. 'There is not an herb here below but he hath a star in heaven above; and the star strikes him with her beam, and says to him: Grow.'[52] Here is our union of the two ideas of magnetism and fructification; the star-fire which is rayed into every living creature by its corresponding luminary unites with the seed of the First Matter to produce generation and growth.

Sometimes Thomas Vaughan writes of this generative process as if he believed it to be delegated to Nature in the rôle of God's viceregent;

but more often he depicts Nature as the means of God's continual activity in the cosmos:

> For Nature is the Voice of God, not a mere sound or command but a substantial, active breath, proceeding from the Creator and penetrating all things.
>
> Waite, p. 84

Thus the sun and stars which infuse the star-fire into matter themselves derive this creative heat from a celestial source:

> This Fire is at the root and about the root—I mean, about the centre—of all things, both visible and invisible. It is in water, earth and air; it is in minerals, herbs and beasts; it is in men, stars and angels. But originally it is in God Himself, for He is the Fountain of heat and fire, and from Him it is derived to the rest of the creatures in a certain stream or sunshine.... It is an influence of the Almighty God, and it comes from the Land of the Living Ones.
>
> Waite, pp. 279–80, 294–5

One further quotation must represent the many passages in Thomas Vaughan's work where he affirms this belief in God's continued intervention in Nature:

> Truly the great world itself lives not altogether by that heat which God hath enclosed in the parts thereof, but it is preserved by the circumfused, influent heat of the Deity. For above the heavens God is manifested like an infinite burning world of light and fire, so that He overlooks all that He hath made and the whole fabric stands in His heat and light, as a man stands here on earth in the sunshine. I say then that the God of Nature employs Himself in a perpetual coction, and this not only to generate but to preserve that which hath been generated; for His spirit and heat coagulate that which is thin, rarefy that which is too gross, quicken the dead parts and cherish the cold.
>
> Waite, pp. 218–9

Critically considered, Thomas Vaughan's natural philosophy is a lunatic farrago of alchemy, astrology, neo-Platonic cosmology and sexual symbolism. But fantastic and wayward as his theories must appear to the post-Newtonian reader, they are identical with those held by his brother, Henry, and revealed in his images of magnetism and fructification. And the reader who is exasperated by Thomas Vaughan's alchemical jargon will not be departing from the author's intention if he reads his cosmology as the allegory of spiritual experiences. Like all Hermetists, Thomas Vaughan believes in the closest correspondences between microcosm and macrocosm: 'For between man and the world there is no small accord, and he that knows not the one cannot know the other'.[53] For this reason God's perpetual operation in Nature is matched by His perpetual communion with the human mind. Indeed, the whole of Thomas Vaughan's fantastic natural philosophy is based on a determination to find physical analogies for the central belief of his metaphysic: God's penetration of the material world.

As a result of this correspondence, the relationship between the divine and human natures is the exact counterpart of that between terrestial and celestial forms. *The Starre* and *Cock-crowing* in *Silex Scintillans* are built upon the theory that there is in every soul a glance of the Divine Light, a Candle of the Lord, of which Thomas Vaughan writes: 'The influx from Him is the true, proper efficient of our regeneration, that *sperma* of St. John, the seed of God which remains in us.'[54] Sin has nearly extinguished this original light; but just as the star-fire in plants and stones draws down the magnetic ray from their guiding stars, so the faint light of natural reason attracts the illumination of grace.[55] In its turn, the soul's candle aspires to the sun of its origin; that is, the mind 'is satisfied with nothing but God, from Whom at first she descended'.[56] We have already seen that when Thomas Vaughan writes about the Philosopher's Stone he means a transmutation of the soul; the highest alchemy is such a revelation of the First Matter as consists in freeing the heart from all material impurities, and thus preparing it for that 'secret incubation of the Spirit of God' whereby the spiritual elements of the mind are reunited with their heavenly counterparts— the will conspiring (in Henry Vaughan's sense of the word) with the wind that blows whither it lists, and the light of natural reason coalescing with the Pentecostal fire.

In the same way that God's work of generation through natural processes repeats His initial act of Creation, this regeneration of the heart by grace is the renewal of His descent into Nature as God Incarnate. This last concept does not hold the central place we might expect it to occupy in Thomas Vaughan's thought. The reason for this may be that while he shared his intellectual system with his brother he never underwent those profound experiences which we are forced to call, conventionally, the 'conversion' of Henry Vaughan. He may have been unsuited for them by a temperamental difference which has been well defined by George Macdonald. In his view, the Silurist—

> develops his mysticism upwards, with relation to his higher nature alone: it blossoms into poetry. His twin-brother Thomas developed his mysticism downwards in the direction of the material sciences—a true effort still, but one in which the danger of ceasing to be true increases with increasing ratio the further it is carried.
>
> *England's Antiphon*, p. 251

Yet there are passages in Thomas Vaughan's writing which suggest that the difference in devotional experience between the brothers was not extreme. Among his crucibles, Thomas reached an understanding of the Incarnation which, to judge by these words from *Anima Magica Abscondita*, was scarcely less sure and certain than that experienced by Henry Vaughan in his nightly vigils:

> I am certain the world will wonder I should make use of Scripture to establish physiology; but I would have them know that all secrets—physical and spiritual, all the close connections and that mysterious kiss of God and Nature—are clearly and punctually discovered there. Consider that merciful mystery of the Incarnation, wherein the fulness of the Godhead was incorporated and the Divine Light united to the Matter in a far greater measure than at the first creation. Consider it—I say—and thou shalt find that no philosophy hath perfectly united God to His creature but the Christian, wherefore also it is the only true philosophy and the only true religion; for without this union there can be neither a natural temporal nor a spiritual eternal life.
>
> Waite, p. 93

'*A quickness, which my God hath kist*': Henry Vaughan's definition of life is almost identical with his brother's 'mysterious kiss of God and Nature'. For the poet, as well as the alchemist, this union of Creator with creature, enacted in innumerable ways at each instant, is the fundamental truth underlying all branches of learning. For him too, 'the universal magnet which binds this great frame and moves all the members of it to a mutual compassion'[57] unites God with the microcosm, man, no less than with the great world of physical Nature. As generation in that 'great world' is effected through the supra-terrestrial elements of air and fire working upon the earth-water of the First Matter, so the Pentecostal breath and flame of the Spirit re-animate the lifeless heart. Vaughan's delight in the transformations wrought upon land and water by changes in atmosphere and light owes a good deal to this 'elemental' theory of renewal. It can be said with almost literal truth that his poetry is 'all air and fire'. He envies birds their power to outsoar the grosser elements with a freedom that the human imagination struggles to obtain; and the beauty of starlight draws from him the plea that the Divine Light may irradiate his dark spirit as stars illuminate and quicken the dark world:

> Thy heav'ns (some say,)
> Are a firie-liquid light,
> Which mingling aye
> Streames, and flames thus to the sight.
> Come then, my god!
> Shine on this bloud,
> And water in one beame,
> And thou shalt see
> Kindled by thee
> Both liquors burne, and streame.
> O what bright quicknes,
> Active brightnes,
> And celestial flowes
> Will follow after
> On that water,
> Which thy spirit blowes!
>
> *Midnight*

This 'elemental' concept of generation and growth directs Vaughan's choice of images of magnetism and fructification to symbolise God's descent into Nature and man's responsive longing to ascend to God. The association of ideas is made clear by these lines from *Disorder and Frailty*, in which I have italicised the words which suggest the four elements:

> I threaten heaven, and from my Cell
> Of *Clay*, and frailty break, and bud

> Touch'd by thy *fire, and breath*; Thy bloud
> Too, is my *Dew*, and springing *wel.*

But this analogy between the divine descent into the macrocosm and God's union with the microcosm of man is by no means perfect. Nature, although she is supposed to share in the corruption of man's Fall, makes a far readier response than he to the heavenly influences. 'Each Bush and Oak doth know I AM'; beasts, birds and plants seem to live in the expectation of their Creator's second descent.[58] Only man, who should as a High Priest offer the sacrifices of all other creatures, fails in his calling.[59] His response, in Vaughan's experience, comes only at moments when that of the other creatures is so joyous that man is compelled to share it. *The Morning-watch* is the record of such a time:

> In what Rings
> And *Hymning Circulations* the quick world
> Awakes, and sings;
> The rising winds,
> And falling springs,
> Birds, beasts, all things
> Adore him in their kinds.
> Thus all is hurl'd
> In sacred *Hymnes*, and *Order*, The great *Chime*
> And *Symphony* of nature.

Vaughan's clearest expression of his belief that Nature can teach man by the example of her greater loyalty to her Maker is to be found in *The Tempest*:

> O that man could do so! that he would hear
> The world read to him! all the vast expence
> In the Creation shed, and slav'd to sence
> Makes up but lectures for his eie, and ear.

> Sure, mighty love foreseeing the discent
> Of this poor Creature, by a gracious art
> Hid in these low things snares to gain his heart,
> And layd surprizes in each Element.

> All things here shew him heaven; *Waters* that fall
> Chide, and fly up; *Mists* of corruptest fome
> Quit their first beds & mount; trees, herbs, flowres all
> Strive upwards stil, and point him the way home.

How do they cast off grossness? only *Earth*,
　　And *Man* (like *Issachar*) in lodes delight,
　　Water's refin'd to *Motion*, Aire to *Light*,
Fire to all three, but man hath no such mirth.

Plants in the *root* with Earth do most Comply,
　　Their *Leafs* with water, and humiditie,
　　The *Flowres* to air draw neer, and subtiltie,
And *seeds* a kindred fire have with the sky.

All have their *keyes*, and set *ascents*; but man
　　Though he knows these, and hath more of his own,
　　Sleeps at the ladders foot; alas! what can
These new discoveries do, except they drown?

The allusion in the last stanza is to Jacob's Ladder, which Thomas
Vaughan declared the greatest Cabbalistic mystery; for both the brothers it was a symbol of the Great Scale of Nature which is a recurrent
concept of seventeenth-century humanism. Milton, with his strong faith
in the power of natural reason, sees this ladder as man's means of ascent
to the Intelligible World; to the mystic Vaughan it represents the descent
of the Spirit into the mind's wise passivity, the process which his brother
termed 'that most secret and silent Lapse of the Spirit *per Formarum
naturalium Seniem*'.[60] The difference is only the mark of differing temper-
aments, and does not affect the strength of either poet's belief, as the
central tenet of his faith, in the interpenetration of two worlds, whereby
'the influences of the spirit animate and quicken the matter, and in the
material extreme the seed of the spirit is to be found'.[61]

　　This union of divine and human natures is the intellectual core of
both brothers' philosophy; for Henry Vaughan it was a living experience
besides. In the poetry of Vaughan's master, George Herbert, this experience is always related to the historical accomplishment of this reconciliation in the life and death of Christ. The theme is less frequent in
Silex Scintillans; but the reason for this lies rather in the altered character
of devotional life in Vaughan's day than in any difference of belief. His
two poems on the Holy Communion show that for Vaughan it represented, in the superlative degree, God's penetration through the veil of
Nature. But whereas Herbert's own celebrations of the Eucharist kept
this historical union constantly in his thoughts, the Parliamentary victory deprived Vaughan of a sacrament which was ministered, if at all,
with very little of the Laudian 'beauty of holiness'. As long as the

35

Puritans were in power, Vaughan could seek only the grace without the sign:

> Give to thy wretched one
> Thy mysticall *Communion*,
> That, absent, he may see,
> Live, die, and rise with thee.
>
> *Dressing*

Fortunately for Vaughan's spiritual well-being, he had a nature particularly fitted for such solitary experience. Every aspect of Nature was for him so instinct with the Divine Presence that he was well content to seek his 'mysticall *Communion*' by night and alone, as Nicodemus had done when

> No mercy-seat of gold,
> No dead and dusty *Cherub*, nor carv'd stone,
> But his own living works did my Lord hold
> And lodge alone.
>
> *The Night*

The danger in such a search was that it might lead the seeker into a mere pantheism. But the Silurist's sense of 'something far more deeply in terfused' in Nature does not obscure his belief in the ultimate 'otherness' of that Spirit's source. His certainty that Nature is only a shadow of a greater world saves him from the excesses of many illuminist sects and seers of the seventeenth and eighteenth centuries, for whom the Inner Light seemed to comprise the whole of divinity; and it distinguishes his thought from the pantheism of some Romantic nature poets. That a sense of the Divine Immanence was, for Vaughan, only the first step towards a transcendental faith is made clear by the closing stanzas of one of his elegies for his younger brother:

> O thou! whose spirit did at first inflame
> And warm the dead,
> And by a sacred Incubation fed
> With life this frame
> Which once had neither being, forme, nor name,
> Grant I may so
> Thy steps track here below,
>
> That in these Masques and shadows I may see
> Thy sacred way,

And by those hid ascents climb to that day
Which breaks from thee
Who art in all things, though invisibly;
Show me thy peace,
Thy mercy, love, and ease,

And from this Care, where dreams and sorrows raign
Lead me above
Where Light, Joy, Leisure, and true Comforts move
Without all pain,
There, his in thee, shew me his life again
At whose dumbe urn
Thus all the year I mourn.

'I walkt the other day...'

Pantheism was one extreme result of the Renaissance humanism which produced as its opposite distortion the Cartesian dualism inherent in much seventeenth-century thought. Vaughan's vivid awareness of the physical world's intersection with the spiritual world makes nonsense of this dualism; and Thomas Vaughan also seeks to refute it. In this, as in other matters, Thomas Vaughan speaks from speculation, Henry Vaughan from experience. To the poet's way of thinking, the book of Nature affords better proof of the Creator's presence in His world than any volume of metaphysics; and in the migrations of birds, the flickering of marsh-fire, and the resentient cry of cut timber at an approaching storm, Henry Vaughan found the symbols of a greater union between God and His image wherewith to support his brother's contention that—

> the mystery of salvation can never be fully understood without (natural) philosophy—not in its just latitude—as it is an application of God to Nature and a conversion of Nature to God, in which two motions and their means all spiritual and natural knowledge is comprehended. To speak then of God without Nature is more than we can do, for we have not known Him so; and to speak of Nature without God is more than we may do, for we should rob God of His glory and attribute those effects to Nature which belong properly to God and to the Spirit of God, Which works in Nature.
>
> Waite, pp. 394–5

Vaughan's unfailing power to recognise in all natural objects the signature of their Creator, and to experience within himself that perpetual union symbolised by that signature, give him his place here as a humanist of the seventeenth century. In many ways, however, his outlook differs from that of other humanist poets of the period. He lacks the sanctified worldliness that balances the transcendent faith of many Metaphysicals, and which creates that tension between being and becoming which is at the root of their paradoxical wit. Unlike Donne and the continental Jesuits, he does not retain an imagery based upon the secular arts and sciences when he leaves Helicon for Jordan. The same lack of a mundane stress shows itself in his assent to the Platonic doctrine that the body impedes and corrupts the soul; he shares none of the Baroque delight in the body and its senses, that delight which inspires the Christian Epicureanism of Thomas Traherne and prompts the triumphant claim of a cantata of the period that 'Every man who eats and drinks, and is of good cheer in all his doings, is a gift from God'.[62] At times the melancholy of Vaughan's otherworldliness deepens to the anti-humanist tone of Goodman and other Jacobean pessimists:

> We could not have lived in an age of more instruction, had we been left to our own choice. We have seen such vicissitudes and examples of humane frailty, as the former world (had they happened in those ages) would have judged prodigies. We have seen Princes brought to their graves by a new way, and the highest order of humane honours trampled upon by the lowest. We have seene Judgement beginning at Gods Church, and (what hath beene never heard of, since it was redeem'd and established by his blessed Son,) we have seen his Ministers cast out of the Sanctuary, & barbarous persons without *light* or *perfection*, usurping holy offices.
>
> *Man in Darkness* in *The Mount of Olives*

In itself, this passage explains the cause of Vaughan's melancholy. The Parliamentary victory, which filled Milton with a buoyant trust in the new theocracy, meant death or destitution for many of Vaughan's relations and friends; and *Silex Scintillans* was composed mainly between 1647 and 1649, a time which was the nadir of Royalist hopes. Society, in the sense of a traditional order corresponding to the hierarchic plan of the natural and spiritual worlds, seemed to Vaughan shattered beyond hope of repair; and the loss robs his poetry of the practical, mundane imagery by which *The Temple* is distinguished.

Yet there is in Vaughan's writings an earthward stress which balances his transcendent impulses and which justifies Miss Guiney's claim that 'Henry Vaughan is a true humanist'.[63] Its nature is suggested in a verse letter, in the form of an invitation, which Vaughan wrote during the Civil Wars:

> Let us meet then! and while this world
> In wild *Excentricks* now is hurld,
> Keep wee, like nature, the same *Key*.
> *To ... Master T. Lewes*

Man might do his worst to spoil the divinely-ordained pattern of being, but Nature remained in harmony with Heaven. In *The Constellation* Vaughan contrasts the social chaos of his times with the ordered motions of the stars:

> Yet O for his sake who sits now by thee
> All crown'd with victory,
> So guide us through this Darknes, that we may
> Be more and more in love with day;
>
> Settle, and fix our hearts, that we may move
> In order, peace and love,
> And taught obedience by thy whole Creation,
> Become an humble, holy nation.
>
> Give to thy spouse her perfect, and pure dress,
> *Beauty* and *holiness*,
> And so repair these Rents, that men may see
> And say, *Where God is, all agree.*

Thus even in the most ephemeral forms of natural life, Vaughan finds that stability which society has lost. 'Turn my eyes from all transitory objects', he prays in *The Mount of Olives*, 'to the things which are eternal, and from the *Cares* and *Pride* of this world to the *fowles of the air* and the *Lillies of the field*;[64] the implication is that Nature has for Vaughan an immortality denied to whatever moth and rust can corrupt. Milton transposed his social pleasures to Heaven; Vaughan exhibits the same Baroque impulse when he translates his solitary pleasures thither, in conceiving a new heaven and a new earth that will not be too unlike the old. In *The Jews* he imagines the Resurrection of Nature, when long-dead trees will spring into green life; and he returns to the same theme in *The Book*. Other poets of the time liked to expatiate on the ultimate reunion of the body's dispersed dust; Vaughan gives an individual turn to the idea when he reflects that the flax which furnished the book's pages, the tree from which its boards were made, and the animal with whose skin they are covered, will all be restored in eternity to their original form:

> O knowing, glorious spirit! when
> Thou shalt restore trees, beasts and men,
> When thou shalt make all new again,
> Destroying onely death and pain,
> Give him amongst thy works a place,
> Who in them lov'd and sought thy face!

This earthward stress was very strong whenever Vaughan found himself in the presence of a Nature undisturbed by human waywardness. But it never outweighs the transcendent urge—the 'I want! I want!' of another of Blake's emblems—which is the compelling force of all seventeenth-century devotional verse. Indeed the sensitivity of Vaughan's response to the beauty of light and weather was in itself a source of his belief in an unseen world; such fleeting splendours could only be the 'gleams and fractions' of a real and enduring beauty veiled from mortal sight. Nearly all his lyrics record his struggle to—

> outrun these skies,
> These narrow skies (narrow to me) that barre,
> So barre me in, that I am still at warre,
> At constant warre with them.
>
> *Love-sick*

This feeling of being debarred from a beauty which has been revealed to him in brief moments of illumination makes exile and estrangement dominant themes in Vaughan's poetry. Exile is the subject of the Ovidian elegies which he translated for *Olor Iscanus*, as well as of many lyrics in *Silex Scintillans*. In *The Pilgrimage*, for example, man in Nature is symbolised as a bird driven from its native wood and as a traveller whose uneasy sleep is interspersed with dreams of home.

This sense of estrangement causes Vaughan to set special store by childhood as a time when the veil between the material and the spiritual worlds is kept transparent by innocence, and to look back regretfully to the 'white time' of the Chosen Race, before their subjugation to the Mosaic Law. Sometimes Vaughan's mystical apprehension of time, his belief that what has happened once happens always, brings about a fusion of the two states of innocence. In *Corruption* the man who

> saw Heav'n o'r his head, and knew from whence
> He came (condemned,) hither,
> And, as first Love draws strongest, so from hence
> His mind sure progress'd thither,

represents the childhood phase of each individual life, but at the same time he stands for Abraham and his descendants who, in the days before Jacob's ladder was withdrawn into Heaven, enjoyed the company of angelic guests:

> Angels lay *Leiger* here; Each Bush, and Cel,
> Each Oke, and high-way knew them,
> Walk but the fields, or sit down at some *wel*,
> And he was sure to view them.

The Romantic poets, for their part, have much to say about the age of innocence; but Vaughan's handling of the theme is totally different from theirs. *The Retreate* expresses more than the idea that children, being closer to eternity than their elders, are able to view the things of time by its light. It also affirms the belief that the grown man can re-enter this state of felicity, because 'this life to Vaughan is like a great circle; birth and death begin at the same point'.[65] One line in particular brings out this idea of a circular progress which is a journey both from and towards home, and not the separation of irrevocable exile. Vaughan speaks of his starting-place in life as

> that plaine,
> Where first I left my glorious traine,
> From whence th'Inlightned spirit sees
> That shady City of Palme trees.

This last line is a highly emotive echo from the biblical account of the death of Moses, who was granted one sight of the Promised Land and 'Iericho, the citie of palme trees'.[66] In its context in Vaughan's poem, it points to the vital difference between the Baroque and the Romantic poets' treatment of the theme of estrangement. For Vaughan, life is not the exile by the waters of Babylon that it seemed to Christina Rossetti; it is a pilgrimage to a known shrine, the journey into the Promised Land. The way lies through the wilderness, but even there God sends manna from the sky and water from the rock, and guides His people as a pillar of cloud by day and a pillar of fire by night. Poem after poem in *Silex Scintillans* alludes to this guidance of the Chosen Race as a symbol of the Providence which shelters all strangers and pilgrims here. Life may be a dark labyrinth, but Vaughan cannot lose his way, since he holds the end of a golden string—

> My *love-twist* held thee up, my *unseen link.*
> *Retirement*

Vaughan's melancholy is undeniable, but it never becomes the weary despondency of later poets, because his faith is sufficiently theocentric for him to see in this sense of exile God's way of directing human nature towards its real home. To man alone among creatures 'God order'd motion, but ordain'd no rest'[67] because

> Hadst thou given to this active dust
> A state untir'd,
> The lost Sonne had not left the huske
> Nor home desir'd.
> *The Pursuite*

This assurance, which he shares with other Metaphysical poets, underlies even his profoundest melancholy and is the ultimate source of his greatness as a devotional poet. I have stressed the esoteric complexity of Vaughan's imagery; but his great moments occur whenever this assurance imparts a rich simplicity and he abandons his emblematic and hermetic symbols for the tone and imagery of the medieval lyric:

> If thou canst get but thither,
> There growes the flowre of peace,
> The Rose that cannot wither,
> Thy fortresse, and thy ease.
> Leave then thy foolish ranges;
> For none can thee secure,
> But one, who never changes,
> Thy God, thy life, thy Cure.

Notes

1. T. S. Eliot's double inheritance of the Metaphysical and the Symbolist traditions is one cause of his work's imagic richness. In his latest poetry, the blend of semantic and symbolist overtones is particularly exciting.

2. F. E. Hutchinson, *Henry Vaughan*, p. 24.

3. *Ibid.*, p. 156.

4. From a famous passage in Thomas Sprat's *History of the Royal Society*, which records the birth of scientific prose, but which implies also a despoiling of language to a 'close, naked, natural way of speaking' which threatened the life of poetry.

5. The former in 'Sure, there's a tye of Bodyes!' and the latter in *The Timber*; there are other examples.

6. All quotations from Vaughan in this chapter are from L. C. Martin's edition of his *Works*. It is rather interesting to find that, according to the *New English Dictionary*, this use of the verb 'to dust', and also that of the verb 'to line', in the sense of 'to make a bee-line for' (see *Rules and Lessons*, 53–4), are common to Vaughan and to modern colloquial American. Have the seventeenth-century meanings been preserved in America? Or are they there the consequence of liberties similar to Vaughan's taken by U.S. citizens for whom English was not the mother-tongue?

7. *Op. cit.*, pp. 102–3.

8. Martin, p. 696, has shown Vaughan's debt to Felltham's *Resolves*, from the ore of which Vaughan extracted his 'shootes of everlastingnesse', to give them a golden setting in *The Retreate.*

9. Rosemary Freeman, *op. cit.*, pp. 229–40, lists eight English religious emblem-books published between 1633 and 1648. There are also the emblematic *Kalendarium humanæ vitæ* of Robert Farley (1638) and Mildmay Fane's *Otia Sacra* (1648).

10. Thus in his *Considerations upon Eternitie*, Drexelius enlarges upon the Hermetic notion that 'The Soul is the Horizon between time and eternity', and in the *Heliotropium* occurs a mechanistic image, of the kind much favoured by Jesuit preachers, which is, I think, echoed in *Silex Scintillans*: 'As it is usual to regulate all clocks by one chief clock; so it is most fitting that we should regulate our little timepieces or, in other words, each his own will, according to that Supreme and Heavenly Horologe of infinite magnitude, that is to say, according to the Divine Will' (trans. by Shutte, pp. 96–7). Vaughan may be remembering this when he puns upon the title of *The Morning-watch*:

> Heav'n
> Is a plain watch, and without figures winds
> All ages up.

But the source of Vaughan's image may equally well lie in Herbert's *Temple*, e.g. in *Evensong*.

11. Martin, p. 429.

12. *Emblem 15*. It is reproduced by Mario Praz, *Seventeenth-century Imagery*, p. 124. Quarles's plate is the fourth in his fifth book.

13. Scales figure in Quarles's *Emblems* as the balance in which the world is weighed and found no heavier than a bubble (I, iv). In the emblems which Christopher Harvey adapted from van Haeften, the heart is weighed against the Law and proves too light (No. 20), but in the religious emblems of another Jesuit, Cramer, it outweighs the Law once the symbols of Christianity are added to its side of the balance. The *motif* reappears in Bolswert's emblems to Sucquet's *Via vitae aeternae*, and even when there are no accompanying emblems it is a common image in the writings of Drexelius and other Jesuits.

14. Vaenius and Bolswert are especially addicted to it, and it occurs in every emblem to Drexelius's *De Aeternitate Considerationes.*

15. *The Works of Thomas Vaughan*, ed. A. E. Waite, p. 81.

16. See A. C. Judson, 'Cornelius Agrippa and Henry Vaughan', *M.L.N.*, XLI, 1926; 'Henry Vaughan as a Nature Poet', *P.M.L.A.*, XLII, 1927; "The Source of

Henry Vaughan's Ideas concerning God in Nature', *S.P.*, XXIV, 1927; Elizabeth Holmes, *Henry Vaughan and the Hermetic Philosophy*; William O. Clough, 'Henry Vaughan and the Hermetic Philosophy', *P.M.L.A.*, XLVIII, 1933; Ralph M. Wardle, 'Thomas Vaughan's Influence upon the Poetry of Henry Vaughan', *P.M.L.A.*, LI, 1936; L. C. Martin, 'Henry Vaughan and *Hermes Trismegistus'*, *R.E.S.*, XVIII, 1942; Richard Walters, 'Henry Vaughan and the Alchemists', *R.E.S.*, XXIII, 1947.

17. Hutchinson, *op. cit.*, p. 151.
18. *Ibid.*, p. 155.
19. Martin, p. 305.
20. See A. C. Judson, 'Cornelius Agrippa and Henry Vaughan'.
21. Martin, p. 583. According to the *Stationers' Register*, the Vaughans' publisher, Humphrey Blunden, who seems to have devoted himself to the propagation of astrological and hermetical writings, was the first to issue translations of Boehme's works in England.
22. Waite, pp. 115–16.
23. Thus Drexelius wrote a *Trismegistus Christianus*; and the emblematic frontispiece to Thomas Vaughan's *Lumen de Lumine* contains three of Henry's favourite images: the ring of eternity (here a dragon biting its tail), pearls as a symbol of the Kingdom of Heaven, and the Candle of the Lord.
24. Martin, p. 272, 11.22–4; p. 289, 1.39.
25. *Cock-crowing*.
26. *On the Poetry of Henry Vaughan*, p. 41.
27. Martin, p. 176 and p. 610.
28. Waite, pp. 134–5.
29. See Helen White, *The Metaphysical Poets*, p. 297.
30. Isa. xxv. 7.
31. Heb. x. 20.
32. Martin, p. 159.
33. Blunden, *op. cit.*, p. 62.
34. I cannot, however, find the *Silex Scintillans* plate among the Jesuit emblem books. The nearest to it are the emblems of a German Jesuit, Daniel Cramer, whose *Decades Quatuor Emblematum Sacrorum* (1617) abound in plates showing the hand of God emerging from a cloud, exactly as it does in Vaughan's emblem, to strike or shield a large human heart. The only reason why Cramer might have attracted the notice of the brothers Vaughan is that he describes himself as of the '*Societas Iesu et Roseae crucis vera*'. This would have interested Thomas Vaughan, whose writings contain many admiring references to the Rosicrucians. Among other heart emblems, Vaughan is likely to have seen the plate depicting 'The Hardness of the Heart' in Harvey's *Schola Cordis*.
35. Martin, p. 249.
36. Ezek. xxxvi. 26; Jer. xxiii. 29; Ps. cxiv. 8.
37. *Man-Miracles*, p. 152. The same image is used by Thomas Washbourne. See *The Rock*, p. 76 of Grosart's edition of Washbourne's *Works*.
38. Waite, p. 32.
39. *Ibid.*, p. 302.
40. Job xxix. 2–3; Ps. xviii; Prov. xx. 27.
41. Drexelius, *Opera Omnia*, 1643, I, p. 267.
42. Some examples: Farley's title-page represents the saints as stars shedding their light upon the candles of human life below; compare Vaughan's *Joy of my life*: 'Stars are of mighty use ... God's Saints are shining lights.' Vaughan's poem *The Lampe* might have been compiled out of Farley's emblems. In particular, Farley's lines—

> But if I love to shine with glorious ray
> Then by my flames in teares I melt away,
>
> *Emblem* 12

approximate to Vaughan's—

> And thy aspiring, active fires reveal
> Devotion still on wing; Then thou dost weepe
> Still as thou burn'st . . .

Farley's emblem of a guttering candle aspiring towards the morning star, a symbol of the soul's impatience to be released from the dying flesh, would have appealed to Vaughan. Both Quarles and Farley use the spent candle as an image of death; compare Vaughan's description of how he tried to recall the features of his younger brother:

> I search, and rack my soul to see
> Those beams again,
> But nothing but the snuff to me
> Appeareth plain.

Quarles and Farley both favour the uncommon verb, 'tin', meaning to kindle, which is used by both the Vaughans.

43. Waite, pp. 266–7.
44. *Ibid.*, p. 23.
45. Martin, p. 541—*L'Envoy.*
46. *Ibid.*, p. 305.
47. In *Silence and Stealth of dayes* . . . and *Joy of my life. . . .*
48. It is possible that Vaughan encountered the image in the writings of St. Teresa.
49. Martin, p. 352.
50. Song of Solomon iv. 16.
51. I keep the Latin. Waite renders it: 'from conditioned to unconditioned'.
52. Waite, p. 299.
53. *Ibid.*, p. 395.
54. *Ibid.*, p. 49.
55. *Ibid.*, pp. 46–7.
56. *Ibid.*, p. 47.
57. *Ibid.*, p. 193.
58. Martin, p. 436—*Rules and Lessons.*
59. *Ibid.*, p. 442—*Christ's Nativity.*
60. Quoted by E. Holmes, *op. cit.*, pp. 34–5, in her discussion of the *scala naturæ* in Hermetic thought. The fullest treatment of the subject is A. O. Lovejoy's *The Great Chain of Being*. The matter was also discussed by 'Eirionnach' in a series of articles entitled '*Aurea Catena Homeri*', *Notes and Queries*, Second Series, III, pp. 63–5, 81–5, 104–6; XII, pp. 161–3 and 181–3.
61. Waite, p. 199.
62. From Schütz's *Symphoniae Sacrae.*
63. *The Mount of Olives* (1902), Introduction.
64. Martin, p. 145.
65. From Helen McMaster's essay on Vaughan and Wordsworth, *R.E.S.*, XI, 1935.
66. Deut. xxxiv. 3.
67. Martin, p. 477—*Man.*

L. C. MARTIN

Henry Vaughan
and the Theme of Infancy

As the poetry of Henry Vaughan gained standing in the nineteenth century its correspondences with that of Wordsworth were frequently pointed out. Both, it was noticed, were poets of nature in the sense that they not only admired its phenomena but recommended a communing with it which would have beneficial effects of a moral or spiritual order; and both were poets of childhood, which they represent as a time when the soul, fresh from its Source and unspotted by the world, has at least some clearer spiritual perceptions than the grown man can compass or comprehend. There is the important difference that whereas Vaughan longs

> to travell back
> And tread again that ancient track,

Wordsworth would make the most of the capacities and appreciations proper to the years which bring the philosophic mind; but they agree that with the passing of childhood a paradise is lost that can never be wholly found again.

When, therefore, it was alleged that Wordsworth owned a copy of *Silex Scintillans* it could easily seem to follow that he had been influenced by its writer and even that the existence of the *Immortality Ode* had depended upon the example of *The Retreate*. The evidence was supplied

Reprinted, by permission of Oxford University Press, from *Seventeenth Century Studies presented to Sir Herbert Grierson*, Oxford (1938), 243–55.

by Archbishop Trench in a note in *A Household Book of English Poetry*[1]:
'A correspondent, with date July 13, 1869, has written to me, "I have
a copy of the first edition of the *Silex*, incomplete and very much damp-
stained, which I bought in a lot with several other books at the poet
Wordsworth's sale" '; to which Grosart[2] added a statement, not founded
on fact, that *Silex Scintillans* is entered in the sale-catalogue of Wordsworth's books. The volume may, of course, have been one of a group
listed without titles or other description.

It has recently been observed[3] that the grounds for associating the
two poets in this way are not very satisfactory, that there is no mention
of Vaughan in the whole body of Wordsworth's writings, and that even
if the volume in question was in Wordsworth's library it has yet to be
proved that he took any influence from it. So far as the *Immortality Ode*
is concerned there were other channels through which its main doctrine
could have reached him, if indeed any definite 'sources' are to be alleged.
Wordsworth himself remarked that 'a pre-existent state has entered into
the popular creeds of many nations; and, among all persons acquainted
with classic literature, is known as an ingredient in Platonic philosophy'.
And although it is quite possible that *The Retreate* and other poems by
Vaughan may have consciously or unconsciously affected Wordsworth's
imagination, the question of origins still deserves further investigation
with a view to showing in what conditions of thought and sentiment
Vaughan himself may have been moved towards the speculative attitude
which *The Retreate* implies. It is indeed a question of conditions rather
than of 'influences', although these are categories which cannot always
be kept distinct. The theories of pre-existence which had often been
held since the time of Plato are part of these conditions. We have,
however, to consider, not a simple expression of the Platonic theory or
myth, but a fusion of it with the widespread sentiment which attributes
a special innocency and insight to children. The occurrence in literature
of this fusion is relatively rare, and when it occurs it is not to be accounted
for merely by showing that it has occurred before, but by considering
also what factors in the writer's nature and experience might cause any
antecedent or contemporary thought of a similar kind to appeal to him.

A study of Henry Vaughan's works reveals him as one who, for
reasons which a modern psychologist might try to discover, was particularly interested in images of freshness, purity, and primal vigour,
and his attitude to infancy may be seen as one more instance of the
tendency which attracted him to the primrose and the lily, to whiteness

among the colours, and to spring and the dawn among times and seasons. Or it may be regarded as the transference to the individual plane of thoughts concerning the childhood of the race and the degeneration of 'civilized' man from a Golden Age typified otherwise in Vaughan's poetry by the original sinlessness of Adam, by the artless fidelities of the Jewish patriarchs, or by the uncorrupted condition of the early Christian community.

In what degree his numerous reflections of this kind were brought about or intensified in him by the political events of the mid-century and by personal troubles partly connected with those events it would be hard to estimate; but from his references it is clear that the Civil War and especially the harsh measures adopted by the Puritan revolutionaries did much to induce in him a state of depression favourable, as Wordsworth was to show in circumstances partly analogous, to nostalgic exaltations of nature and childhood. 'We could not', Vaughan writes in *The Mount of Olives* (1652),

> have lived in an age of more instruction, had we been left to
> our own choice. We have seen such vicissitudes and examples
> of humane frailty, as the former world (had they happened in
> those ages) would have judged prodigies. We have seen
> Princes brought to their graves by a new way, and the highest
> order of humane honours trampled upon by the lowest. We
> have seene Judgement beginning at Gods Church, and (what
> hath beene never heard of, since it was redeem'd and estab-
> lished by his blessed Son,) we have seen his Ministers cast
> out of the Sanctuary[4], & barbarous persons without *light* or
> *perfection*, usurping holy offices.... Suddenly do the high things
> of this world come to an end, and their delectable things passe
> away.... And surely the ruine of the most goodly peeces seems
> to tell, that the dissolution of the whole is not far off.

A quarter of a century had passed since George Hakewill had in 1627 first published his *Apologie or Declaration of the Power and Providence of God in the Government of the World*, maintaining that the world had still as many potentialities for good as at any time in the past and attacking 'the weake grounds which the contrary opinion of the Worlds decay is founded vpon'. Henry Vaughan, however, was evidently still of those who in spite of Hakewill accepted the doctrine of world or universal degeneration. This doctrine and the melancholy attending it[5] had gained force from recent astronomical discoveries in the light of which the most ancient heavens could no longer seem so fresh and strong, so pure and incorruptible, as the traditions would have them seem to be. The stellar system was now, it appeared, demonstrably unexempt from processes of change and decay. Vaughan apparently never accepted this subversive astronomy; he needed the stars as an image of orderliness and willing obedience to law contrasting with the instability and frowardness of man. With his deep sense of human decadence he needed also, for his imaginative solace, the concept of human nature in earlier unspoilt phases; and could easily pass from this to the idealization of childhood. It is not a far cry from the beginning of Boethius's *Metrum 5* as translated by Vaughan in *Olor Iscanus:*

> Happy that first white age! when wee
> Lived by the Earths meere Charities,

to the beginning of *The Retreate*:

> Happy those early dayes! when I
> Shin'd in my Angell-infancy.

'Those early days' had been spent in the impressive mountainous regions of South Wales; and after studying at Oxford and having some experience of London and the Civil War Vaughan went to live again, and to practise as a doctor, in his native place. This he did at about the age at which after the French Revolution Wordsworth went to settle in the Lake District, and with a mind similarly disillusioned regarding the ways of sophisticated man. In each case the poet's 'retreàt' to childhood appears to be bound up with his return, in fact and in imagination, to the nature by which his childhood had been surrounded.

These are circumstances which may well have affected the poet's attitude towards the theme of infancy, but they do not explain his development of it, the terms and images which he employs; in particular they do not explain the doctrine hinted in *The Retreate*, of a sinless pre-existent state, which the child in some sort remembers and in some degree inherits. It may be said that it was an easy step for the poet thus to rationalize his sentiment, but the answer to this might be that Wordsworth has made it easy for us to think so. In point of fact it was a step that apparently had not been taken before by an English poet. Correspondences, however, may be found for the doctrine, not only in the literature of past ages but in that of Vaughan's own time; and since they appear in works of which some at least were readily accessible and

likely to be attractive to him on general grounds, it is of some moment
to take account of them as aids to the recognition of the background,
the intellectual atmosphere, in which his poetry took its shape.
The inquiry leads into the by-ways rather than the main tracks of
speculative literature. Vaughan's attitude in *The Retreate* may seem to
be related to the Platonic ἀνάμνησις and so in some degree it is, but
the relationship is not very close; indeed Vaughan, who respects the
child's emotional and quasi-sensuous intuitions, who had *felt*

> through all this fleshly dress
> Bright shootes of everlastingnesse,

contradicts the Platonic teaching that ἀνάμνησις is the hard-won result
of processes, ratiocinative in essence, whose higher functions are possible
only to an adult intelligence; and Vaughan's conception of the grown
man's descent from a childhood more closely in touch with divine things
does not merely repeat the notion of the soul's descent into its fleshly
tenement. What it adds to that notion is something which Hellenic
thought, untouched by alien speculation, was perhaps not very likely
to add or to encourage.

There is, however, one striking anticipation in the Neo-Platonic
writings attributed to 'Hermes Trismegistus', still in seventeenth-
century England a name for some to conjure by; it occurs in Libellus
X of the *Hermetica*, where the sage adjures his disciple thus:

> Look at the soul of a child, my son, a soul that has not
> yet come to accept its separation from its source; for its body
> is still small, and has not yet grown to its full bulk. How
> beautiful throughout is such a soul as that! It is not yet fouled
> by the bodily passions; it is still hardly detached from the soul
> of the Kosmos. But when the body has increased in bulk, and
> has drawn the soul down into its material mass, it generates
> oblivion; and so the soul separates itself from the Beautiful
> and Good, and no longer partakes of that; and through this
> oblivion the soul becomes evil.[6]

Mr. Walter Scott, the recent editor of *Hermetica*, whose translation
is here adopted, holds that Libellus X is entirely Hellenistic in origin;
in a note on this passage, however, he quotes from Abelson's *The Immanence of God in Rabbinical Literature* the remark that 'The Rabbins emphasize untiringly the spotless purity of the new-born babe'.[7] Here again

it seems necessary to qualify, for Rabbinical teaching is not consistent in this respect. According to Schechter, *Some Aspects of Rabbinic Theology*, 'the general notion seems to be the one accepted by R. Judah, which is that the Evil Yezer accompanies man from his earliest childhood to his old age, by reason of which he enjoys a priority of not less than thirteen years over the Good Yezer, who only makes his appearance at the age of puberty'.[8] It nevertheless appears to be true that the innocence of earliest childhood was a Jewish doctrine enjoying no little respect; and this is a point of some significance in view of the greatly increased vogue of Hebrew studies in England during the sixteenth and seventeenth centuries. In the Talmud, Joma, 22*b*, reference is made to 'a child aged one year who has not tasted sin'; Berachoth P., 4*d*, on Eccles. iii. 2, has 'Happy the man whose hour of death is like the hour of his birth; as at his birth he is free of sin, so at his death may he be free of sin'; and Shabbath, 152*b*, comments on Eccles. xii. 7 ('the spirit shall return unto God who gave it'): 'Give it back to Him as He gave it to you, in a condition of purity.[9]

There are, moreover, other places in which the childish state is connected with a still more excellent pre-natal condition. Schechter[10] refers to legends based upon the Talmud tending to the view of the newly born child 'as a higher being, which, but a few seconds before, had been conversing with angels and saints, and had now condescended into our profane world to make two ordinary mortals happy'. Thus according to Niddah, 30*b*,[11] 'it is said that before the birth of man he is shown and taught all the things which he will experience in life; but, as soon as he enters the world, all is forgotten by him'. The Midrash Tanchuma gives an expanded account of the same myth:

> While the child is still in its mother's womb ... a light illumines round about its head, whereby it looks and sees from one end of the world to the other. ... During this interval, too, it gains an insight into all the knowledge that is available, all the rules of life whereby, if a man observe them, he will live,— the veritable secrets of Almighty Wisdom. Once, however, arrived in the world of phenomena, an angel comes forward, and closes its mouth; the knowledge it has acquired is all but forgotten. ... Yet, on the strength of these dim recollections, the new-born is adjured thus: 'Be thou righteous, be not wicked.' ... Understand that the Almighty is pure, His mes-

51

sengers are pure; and the soul which He has placed within thee is pure. If thou preservest thy soul in purity, well and good; but if not, I will take it from thee.[12]

It may appear strange that the concept of a Golden Age in the life of the individual, before or after birth, should not have attracted the poets who preceded Vaughan more often than it appears to have done. It represents certainly a somewhat precarious idealization of the childish state, but it is neither unintelligible nor baseless, in spite of the rude refutations which children themselves can so readily seem to supply. There are traces of it in Roman culture and literature,[13] and Christian poets in particular might have been expected to make much of the symbolism in which the child becomes a type of the Kingdom of Heaven, and of which Luther makes some interesting applications.[14] It may be supposed that what chiefly stood in the way was the doctrine of original sin. Christians who harboured ideas resembling the Jewish notions alluded to above would risk the charge that they were straying from the paths of orthodox belief in the direction of the Pelagian heresy. But Pelagianism was one of the many heretical tendencies, new and old, which enliven the history of religious thought in the seventeenth century. It was an essential part of 'Anabaptist' teaching that children who die unbaptized would nevertheless be saved, and a similar heterodoxy was recommended by Jeremy Taylor in his *Unum Necessarium* (1655), where the doctrine of original sin loses some of its harshness and is interpreted in its bearings upon childhood in a way that Henry Vaughan was likely to find agreeable:

> But it is hard upon such mean accounts to reckon all children to be born enemies of God ... full of sin and vile corruption, when the Holy Scriptures propound children as imitable for their pretty innocence and sweetness, and declare them rather heirs of heaven than hell. 'In malice be children': and, 'unless we become like to children, we shall not enter the kingdom of heaven'; and 'their angels behold the face of their Father which is in heaven'.... These are better words than are usually given them; and signify, that they are beloved of God, not hated, designed for heaven, and born to it, though brought thither by Christ, and by the Spirit of Christ, not born for hell: that was 'prepared for the devil and his angels', not for innocent babes. This does not call them naturally

wicked, but rather naturally innocent, and is a better account than is commonly given them by imputation of Adam's sin.[15]

It is indeed a better account than was commonly given them. Milton is nearer to orthodoxy when he writes in *Areopagitica*:

> Assuredly we bring not innocence into the world, we bring impurity much rather: that which purifies us is triall, and triall is by what is contrary. That vertue therefore which is but a youngling in the contemplation of evill, and knows not the utmost that vice promises to her followers, and rejects it, is but a blank vertue, not a pure.

There are, however, other signs that the 'climate of thought' in the seventeenth century was becoming favourable to the inspiration of *The Retreate* and the poems of similar drift in *Silex Scintillans* and *Thalia Rediviva*. Probably Henry Vaughan was not himself aware of all the precedents which the literature of his time had furnished; but the sort of imaginative fuel which lay to his hand and which in those poems he kindled into life is represented in any allusions and adherences to the Platonic theory of pre-existence, any contrastings of childish innocence with adult depravity, and, above all, any suggestions that the youthful superiority is connected with a pre-existent state.

Henry More's poem, *The Prae-existency of the Soul* (1647), no doubt extended the currency of the Plotinian doctrine which it develops but is not of first importance in the present connexion. The soul descends to its embodiment and is

> A spark or ray of the Divinity
> Clouded in earthly fogs, yclad in clay,
> A precious drop sunk from Aeternitie,

but for aught that More says the fogs are as dense in childhood as at any later stage of life.

Nearly twenty years before this John Earle in his 'character' of a child in *Microcosmographie* (1628) had made much of the contrast between the child and the grown man, without, however, committing himself to a theory of pre-existency:

> A *Child* is a Man in a small letter, yet the best Copie of *Adam* before he tasted of *Eue*, or the Apple; and hee is happy whose small practice in the World can only write his Char-acter. Hee is natures fresh picture newly drawne in Oyle,

which time and much handling dimmes and defaces. . . . His father hath writ him as his owne little story, wherein he reades those dayes of his life that he cannot remember; and sighes to see what innocence he has out-liu'd. The elder he growes, he is a stayre lower from God; and like his first father, much worse in his breeches. He is the Christians example, and the old man's relapse: The one imitates his purenesse, and the other falls into his simplicitie. . . .

Earlier still Bacon, in his essay *Of Youth and Age*, had quoted Jewish authority for the view that youth has stronger powers of spiritual insight depending upon a closer walk with God:

> A certain rabbin, upon the text, *Your young men shall see visions, and your old men shall dream dreams*, inferreth that young men are admitted nearer to God than old, because vision is a clearer revelation than a dream; and certainly, the more a man drinketh of the world the more it intoxicateth.

Owen Felltham's *Resolves* (c. 1623) have the special importance that they were well known to Henry Vaughan, who often quoted from them although never with acknowledgement. Vaughan derived from Felltham one of the most striking phrases in *The Retreate*, 'Bright shootes of everlastingnesse', Felltham having written of the soul that 'The *Conscience*, the *Caracter* of a *God* stampt in it, and the apprehension of *Eternitie*, doe all proue it a shoot of everlastingnesse'.[16] Vaughan may well also have dwelt upon the following passages, the first of which testifies to the prevalence of Neo-Platonic theory:

> 'Tis the *bodies contagion*, which makes the *Soule* leprous. In the opinion that we all hold, at the first infusing 'tis *spotlesse* and *immaculate*.[17]

And

> How blacke a *heart* is that, which can giue a *stabbe*, for the *innocent smiles* of an *Infant*? Surely *Innocence* is of that purity, that it hath more of the *God* in it, than any other *qualitie*; it intimates a freedom from *Generall Vice*.[18]

The intellectual relations between Henry Vaughan and his twin brother Thomas,[19] minister and 'chymist', were closer still. Their writings show that they explored some of the same imaginative fields, although Thomas was less controlled in his thought and more obscure in

54

his utterance. In the turbid stream of his speculations many currents met, themselves already of diverse origins, Neo-Platonic and Jewish, Hermetic and Kabalistic, western theosophy and oriental magic. But he clearly belonged to the class of mystical investigator represented before him by Paracelsus and Cornelius Agrippa, the type which is drawn to the study of 'Nature', *naturans* and *naturata*, its essence and its processes, with a view to the mastery of its physical secrets but ultimately to establishing contact with a super-sensible Reality and acquiring some of its spiritual power, to an alchemy of the soul rather than of metals. 'Nature', moreover, is to be studied at first hand, without the contaminating influence of bookish theory, and in this respect Thomas Vaughan shares the attitude of those mystics who favour the negative way, suspecting calculation and relying more exclusively upon perceptions and intimations of a more intuitive order. How in this frame of mind bookish ignorance and learned insensibility can be contrasted with the instinctive wisdom or insight not only of humble men but of untutored children may be illustrated from a passage in Valentine Weigel's treatise *Of the Life of Christ* (translated 1648):

> Hence the way to Faith is close shut up to wicked proud men, although they read the Bible in many Tongues. And on the contrary, the way to Faith and Christ, stands open for all hungry and humble hearts, which cannot so much as reade one letter, as all your Infants which hear and learne only of God; for he that hath within him the inward School-master, looseth nothing of his Salvation, although all Preachers should be dead, and all Bookes burned.[20]

And Thomas Vaughan, observing in his *Euphrates, or the Waters of the East* (1655) how even in his early youth he had been Nature's pupil, proceeds in a still more Wordsworthian vein:

> This *Consideration* of my self, when I was a Child, hath made me since examine Children, namely, what thoughts they had of these *Elements*, we see about us, and I found thus much by them, that *Nature* in her simplicity, is much more wise, than some men are with their acquired parts, and *Sophistrie*; ...A Child I suppose, *in puris Naturalibus*, Before education alters, and ferments him, is a Subject hath not been much consider'd, for men respect him not, till he is companie for them, and then indeed they spoile him. Notwithstanding I should think, by what I have read, that the naturall disposition

of Children, before it is *Corrupted* with *Customes* and *Manners*, is one of those things, about which the *Ancient Philosophers* have busied themselves even to some *curiosity*.[21]

Thomas Vaughan refers in one place[22] to 'Jacob Behmen *his most excellent and profound* Discourse of the Three Principles', and it is very likely that his indebtedness to the mystic of Görlitz went farther than this single reference would suggest. Boehme, whose works were much translated into English during the fifth and sixth decades of the seventeenth century, is another who recommends seekers after divine truth to cultivate the childlike spirit:

> Our whole Religion is but a child-like worke; namely, that we wholly forsake and disclaime our owne knowing, willing, running, disputing . . . and persevere in the way which bringeth us againe to our owne native Countrey.[23]
>
> Loving Sir, it is a simple *childlike way* that leadeth to the highest wisedome, the World knowes it *not*.[24]

Moreover, Boehme in his *XL Questions* (translated 1647) introduces a doctrine of reminiscency in connexion with the theme of childish innocence:

> Little Children are our Schoolmasters[25] till evill stirre in them, and so they embrace the *Turba Magna*, but they bring their sport from the Mothers wombe, which [sc. the sport] is a Remnant of Paradise: but all the rest is gone till we receive it againe.[26]

When we receive it again 'we shall lead a life like children, who rejoyce and are very merry in their Sports'.[27] And if Henry Vaughan had needed any authority for the phrase 'Angell-infancy' he could have found it in Boehme's *Aurora* (translated 1656), where the question 'To whom now shall I liken the Angels?' is answered:

> I will liken them to *little* children, which walk in the fields in *May*, among the *flowers*, and pluck them, and make curious Garlands, and Poseys, carrying them in their hands rejoycing.
> . . .[28]

During the century which separates Vaughan and Traherne from William Blake English poets showed little interest in the theories concerning childhood which attracted these predecessors. Even Blake, who recognized the visionary powers of children, attaches to those powers no definite lore of preexistency and reminiscence. Mr. Garrod has argued that although 'the ultimate source of the doctrine of reminiscence is, of course, Plato and the Neo-Platonists', the immediate source upon which Wordsworth drew in the *Immortality Ode* was 'not Plato, but Coleridge'. It then becomes tempting to ask what near or remote authority, if any, Coleridge himself may have found for a doctrine which, in Wordsworth's presentation of it, is not very much like Plato's.

> Oft o'er my brain does that strong fancy roll
> Which makes the present (while the flash doth last)
> Seem a mere semblance of some unknown past,
> Mixed with such feelings, as perplex the soul
> Self-questioned in her sleep; and some have said
> We lived, ere yet this robe of flesh we wore.

Thus Coleridge began the sonnet written in 1796 on hearing of the birth of his son, Hartley; and in connexion with it he referred to Plato and to Fénelon. 'Almost all the followers of Fénelon', he wrote to Poole, 'believe that men are degraded intelligences, who had all once lived together in a paradisiacal or perhaps heavenly state.' It will be noticed that although there may be significance in the fact that the occasion for this sonnet was the birth of a child, Coleridge does not here or elsewhere claim that the reminiscent faculty is stronger in childhood than in later life. Coleridge was, however, widely versed in mystical literature. In the *Biographia* (ch. ix), besides acknowledging a great debt to Plato and his followers, he alludes with special reverence to Boehme and other Christian illuminati; and whether Wordsworth knew Vaughan's poetry or not it seems possible that the *Immortality Ode* derives in part, and chiefly through Coleridge, from the same traditions of thought and sentiment which lay behind the conception of *The Retreate*.[29]

Notes

1. Second edition, 1870.
2. *Vaughan's Complete Works*, 1871, ii, p. lxiv.
3. By Miss Helen N. McMaster in an article on 'Vaughan and Wordsworth', *Review of English Studies*, July 1935.
4. As was Thomas Vaughan, Henry's twin brother.
5. See George Williamson, 'Mutability, Decay, and Seventeenth-Century Melancholy,' *Journal of English Literary History*, Sept. 1935.
6. Cited by Q. Iredale, *Thomas Traherne*, 1935, p. 48.

7. *Op. cit.*, p. 281.

8. *Op. cit.*, p. 254.

9. These passages are cited by A. Cohen, *Everyman's Talmud*, p. 102.

10. *Studies in Judaism*, First Series, p. 347.

11. See Gollancz, *Paedagogics of the Talmud*, p. 38.

12. See Gollancz, *Paedagogics of the Talmud*, pp. 93–4.

13. See W. Warde Fowler, 'On the toga praetexta of Roman children', *Classical Review*, Oct. 1896, p. 317. I am indebted to Professor J. F. Mountford for this reference.

14. Mr. John Purves kindly refers me also to Dante, *Paradiso*, xxvii, ll. 127–9.

15. Ch. IV, sect. 51.

16. Edition of 1631, p. 197.

17. Ed. cit., p. 65. This perhaps suggested some of the imagery in Vaughan's *St. Mary Magdalen*, ll. 68 ff. The address is to the 'self-boasting Pharisee':

> Go Leper, go; wash till thy flesh
> Comes like a childes, spotless and fresh;
> He is still leprous, that still paints:
> Who Saint themselves, they are no *Saints*.

18. Ed. cit., p. 206.

19. What is said here on this subject was substantially written before I had seen the article in *Publications of the Modern Language Association of America*, Dec. 1936, by Mr. Ralph M. Wardle: 'Thomas Vaughan's influence upon the Poetry of Henry Vaughan.'

20. *Op. cit.*, pp. 111–12.

21. *Op. cit.*, pp. 20–1.

22. *Coelum Terrae*, p. 110.

23. *Epistles*, translated 1649, p. 12.

24. *Ibid.*, p. 200.

25. Cf. *The Threefold Life of Man* (translated 1650), p. 191: 'Children are our Schoolmasters (in all our witt and cunning wee are but fooles to them)'. Quoted by R. M. Wardle, op. cit. Cf. also Thomas Vaughan, *Coelum Terrae*, pp. 91–2.

26. *Op. cit.*, p. 130.

27. *Op. cit.*, p. 129.

28. *Op. cit.*, p. 239. Cited by Elizabeth Holmes, *Henry Vaughan and the Hermetic Philosophy*, p. 55.

29. See also *Biographia Literaria*, ed. Shawcross, vol. ii, pp. 242–3.

L. C. MARTIN

Henry Vaughan and
"Hermes Trismegistus"

In 1614, seven or eight years before the birth of Henry and Thomas
Vaughan, the origin and date of the Hermetic books had been determined with considerable accuracy by Isaac Casaubon. Before the publication in that year of his *Exercitationes XVI* it had been generally believed
that the Libelli represented the deliverances of the Egyptian god Thoth,
named Hermes by the Greeks, that they were written at about the time
of Moses, and that they were the foundation on which Pythagoras and
later teachers had built the fabric of Greek philosophy. Casaubon ascribed the Hermetic writings to the first century of the Christian era,
thus antedating them, but by no more than one or two hundred years,
and justly pronounced them to be 'in part' of Platonist derivation. He
might have said 'almost wholly', for his further association of them with
Christian doctrine has not been substantiated and it can now be taken
as established that their authors were pagan Greeks resident in Egypt
under the Roman Empire, or Egyptians who had come under the influence of Greek culture.[1]

But the old suppositions were not immediately and universally
dispelled and it was still possible for Thomas Vaughan to imply, in one
of his fairly numerous references to the *Hermetica*, that they faithfully
reflected the theology of ancient Egypt;[2] and they could thus be made
to lend the support of pristine and almost sacred authority to the very

Reprinted, by permission of Oxford University Press, from *Review of English Studies*,
18 (1942), 301–07.

questionable compound of theosophy, alchemy, astrology and natural magic which Thomas Vaughan offered a heedless world in a jargon of professional terminology. Henry Vaughan, on the other hand, who mentions the Hermetic writings but once, and then in a translation, had studied them apparently with care and certainly with imaginative profit; and may well seem to have been better employed than his brother in giving new poetic life to some of the Hermetic notions without as a rule unduly perplexing, by his terms or his contexts, the mind of the common reader. It is not intended here to estimate the varying merit of these poetic transmutations but merely to point out certain loci in which the Hermetic influence is either manifest or probable and also to show that the Hermetic writings occasionally throw some light upon the poet's meaning.

Perhaps the clearest instance of his indebtedness is supplied by a a passage in '*The importunate Fortune, written to Doctor* Powell *of* Cantre' (*Thalia Rediviva*, 1678, pp. 614–17).[3] The argument is to the effect that Vaughan's speculative and visionary gifts enable him to despise worldly affluence and to soar into a heaven of spiritual wellbeing. As he rises he casts off the impedimenta of human frailty and leaves them in the spheres to which they belong:

> First my dull Clay I give unto the *Earth*,
> Our common Mother, which gives all their birth.
> My growing Faculties I send as soon
> Whence first I took them, to the humid *Moon*.
> All Subtilties and every cunning Art
> To witty *Mercury* I do impart.
> Those fond affections which made me a slave
> To handsome Faces, *Venus* thou shalt have.
> And saucy Pride (If there was ought in me)
> *Sol*, I return it to thy Royalty.
> My daring Rashness and Presumptions be
> To *Mars* himself an equal Legacy.
> My ill-placed Avarice (sure 'tis but small;)
> *Jove*, to thy Flames I do bequeath it all.
> And my false *Magic*, which I did believe,
> And mystic Lyes to *Saturn* I do give.
> My dark Imaginations rest you there,
> This is your grave and Superstitious Sphære.

Apart from the first two lines quoted here this is clearly based upon the following passage from Libellus I ('The Poimandres') describing the processes which succeed the dissolution of the material body:

60

And thereupon the man mounts upward through the structure of the heavens. And to the first zone of heaven he gives up the force which works increase and that which works decrease; to the second zone, the machinations of evil cunning; to the third zone, the lust whereby men are deceived; to the fourth zone, domineering arrogance; to the fifth zone, unholy daring and rash audacity; to the sixth zone, evil strivings after wealth; and to the seventh zone, the falsehood which lies in wait to work harm (p. 129).[4]

The several association of these various human tendencies with the Moon, Venus, Mars and the rest is of course not peculiar, but it would probably be difficult to find a closer parallel to this elaboration of the doctrine than Vaughan has supplied.

In the lines which follow in Vaughan's poem he is no doubt indebted to the corresponding Hermetic passage, but apparently had other passages also in mind.

Get up my disentangled Soul, thy fire
Is now refin'd & nothing left to tire,
Or clog thy wings. Now my auspicious flight
Hath brought me to the *Empyrean* light.
I am a sep'rate *Essence*, and can see
The *Emanations* of the Deitie,
And how they pass the Seraphims, and run
Through ev're *Throne* and *Domination*.
So rushing through the Guard, the Sacred streams
Flow to the neighbour Stars, and in their beams
(A glorious Cataract!) descend to Earth
And give Impressions unto ev'ry birth.
With Angels now and Spirits I do dwell.
And here it is my Nature to do well,
Thus, though my Body you confined see,
My boundless thoughts have their *Ubiquitie*.

The Hermetic writer continues thus:

And thereupon, having been stripped of all that was wrought upon him by the structure of the heavens, he ascends to the substance of the eighth sphere, being now possessed of his own proper power, and he sings, together with those that dwell there, hymning the Father; and they that are there rejoice with him at his coming. And being made like to those with whom he dwells, he hears the Powers, who are a substance

of the eighth sphere, singing praise to God with a voice that
is theirs alone.

The two passages are similar in outline and in one or two details but
some further citations will suggest that other Hermetic conceptions were
at this juncture fused in the processes of Vaughan's imagination:
(a) Libellus XI (ii), p. 221, on the soul's powers to transcend in thought
the limits of space:

> Bid it fly up to heaven, and it will have no need of wings;
> nothing can bar its way, neither the fiery heat of the sun, nor
> the swirl of the planet-spheres; cleaving its way through all,
> it will fly up till it reaches the outermost of all corporeal things.
> And should you wish to break forth from the universe itself,
> and gaze on the things outside the Kosmos (if indeed there is
> anything outside the Kosmos), even that is permitted to you.

(b) Libellus V, p. 161, where the drift is much the same:

> Would that it were possible for you to grow wings and
> soar into the air! Poised between earth and heaven, you might
> see the solid earth, the fluid sea and the streaming rivers, the
> wandering air, the penetrating fire, the courses of the stars,
> and the swiftness of the movement with which heaven encom-
> passes all.

(c) Libellus X, p. 203, the apparent source of Vaughan's thoughts about
'*Emanations*' and their effects upon 'ev'ry birth':

> The divine forces operate by means of the Kosmos, and their
> operation reaches man by means of the cosmic radiations to
> which birth and growth are due.

It cannot be maintained with confidence that wherever Vaughan's
notions correspond to those of the Hermetic writers there is a necessary
sequence of cause and effect, but once the association has been made
in an instance permitting of little doubt it is legitimate to suppose that
where other resemblances occur the same factor may possibly be at
work. Several such resemblances are to be noted in connexion with the
poem 'Resurrection and Immortality' (*Silex Scintillans*, 1650, pp. 400–
402). This is in the form of a dialogue between Soul and Body, and the
Body, speaking first, tries to argue that the emergence of a butterfly
from the 'dead' chrysalis justifies the hope that 'death' is not the end
of all. The argument is not unlike that of St. Paul (I Cor. xvi. 35 *sqq.*);

but the Soul, which is better instructed in Hermetic lore, chides the Body for its limited outlook, affirming that there is no such thing as death, and observing

> how of death we make
> A meere mistake.
> For no thing can to Nothing fall, but still
> Incorporates by skill,
> And then returns, and from the wombe of things
> Such treasure brings
> As *Phenix*-like renew'th
> Both life, and youth. . . .

Several passages in the *Hermetica* are relevant to these lines, but the following may suffice:

(a) in Libellus VIII, p. 175:

> The word 'death' is a mere name, without any corresponding fact. For death means destruction; and nothing is destroyed.

(b) in Libellus XI (ii), p. 217:

> . . . But men call the change 'death', because, when it takes place, the body is decomposed, and the life departs and is no more seen.

(c) in Libellus XII (ii), p. 233:

> Dissolution is not death; it is only the separation of things which were combined; and they undergo dissolution, not to perish, but to be made new.

Vaughan continues with a doctrine of general conservation in the material universe which he combines later with another, more in accord with Christian belief, that when the body dissolves the separation from it of the soul is merely temporary:

> For a preserving spirit doth still passe
> Untainted through this Masse,
> Which doth resolve, produce, and ripen all
> That to it fall;
> Nor are those births which we
> Thus suffering see
> Destroy'd at all;

in which there are perhaps reminiscences of Libellus XII (ii), p. 235:

Considered as one whole, my son, the Kosmos is exempt from change; but all its parts are subject to change. But there is nothing in it that suffers corruption or destruction; if men think otherwise, their thoughts are confused by the terms in use.

and of Libellus XVI, p. 267:

he puts life into the things in this region of the Kosmos, and stirs them up to birth, and by successive changes remakes the living creatures and transforms them.

In the rest of the poem, which is of a more orthodox Christian tendency, inspection will show that nevertheless some of the imaginative material is paralleled by sentences in the *Hermetica* already cited.

In other poems or passages by Vaughan it seems at least arguable that the Hermetic influence can be perceived although it may not always be direct or unmixed with that of notions more peculiar to later thought.

1. It has already been suggested[5] that the theory of childhood set forth in 'The Retreate' may owe something to Libellus X, p. 197:

Look at the soul of a child, my son, a soul that has not yet come to accept its separation from its source; for its body is still small, and has not yet grown to its full bulk. How beautiful is such a soul as that! It is not yet fouled by the bodily passions; it is still hardly detached from the Kosmos. But when the body has increased in bulk, and has drawn the soul down into its material mass, it generates oblivion. . . .

Compare also Libellus XII (ii), p. 235: 'Birth is not a beginning of life, but only a beginning of consciousness'.

2. In several places Vaughan gives an animistic turn to the words of St. Paul in Romans viii. 19 and 22, about the earnest expectation of the creature, and might have quoted Libellus XII (ii), p. 233, as his sanction:

Now this whole Kosmos . . . is one mass of life. . . . There is not, and never has been, and never will be in the Kosmos anything that is dead.

And when Vaughan wrote in stanza 3 of 'Rules and Lessons', p. 436:

Walk with thy fellow-creatures: note the *hush*
And *whispers* amongst them. There's not a *Spring*,

> Or *Leafe* but hath his *Morning-hymn*; Each *Bush*
> And *Oak* doth know *I AM*; canst thou not sing?

he may have remembered the following passage in the same Libellus, p. 235:

> God foretells the future to him in manifold ways, by the flight
> of birds, by the inward parts of beasts, by inspiration, or by
> the whispering of an oak-tree.

3. Whatever earlier or later instances may be adduced, there is Hermetic authority also for Vaughan's admiration of the orderly and obedient behaviour of the stars in their courses, which he contrasts with the frowardness of man. In 'The Constellation,' p. 469, he writes:

> Fair, order'd lights (whose motion without noise
> Resembles those true Joys
> Whose spring is on that hil where you do grow
> And we here tast sometimes below,)
>
> With what exact obedience do you move
> Now beneath, and now above,
> And in your vast progressions overlook
> The darkest night, and closest nook!
>
> Some nights I see you in the gladsome East,
> Some others neer the West,
> And when I cannot see, yet do you shine
> And beat about your endles line.

and in *The Mount of Olives*, p. 144:

> Contemplate the *Order* of the Stars, and how they all in their
> several stations praise their Creator.

thus echoing Libellus VIII, p. 177:

> But it is only the living creatures upon earth that are involved
> in this disorder. The bodies of the celestial gods [sc. the heav-
> enly bodies] keep without change that order which has been
> assigned to them by the Father in the beginning; and that
> order is preserved unbroken by the reinstatement of each of
> them in its former place.

and Libellus V, p. 159:

If you wish to see Him, think on the course of the Moon, think
on the order of the stars. Who is it that maintains that order?.
. . . Each of these stars too is confined by measured limits, and
has an appointed space to range in.

4. It is just possible that the well-known opening of 'The World',
p. 466:

> I saw Eternity the other night
> Like a great *Ring* of pure and endless light,
>   All calm, as it was bright,
> And round beneath it, Time in hours, days, years
>   Driv'n by the spheres
> Like a vast shadow mov'd, In which the world
> And all her train were hurl'd.

owes something to Hermetic doctrine, although Vaughan is more certainly influenced by a passage in Felltham's *Resolves* ('*Of Time's continuall
speede*', 4th ed., 1631, p. 25), where there is a vision of '*Eternities* Ring'
cast round the attractions of Virtue and Vice.[6] The relevant Hermetic
passage is in Asclepius III, p. 353:

> Eternity then is not limited by the conditions of time; and
> time, which admits of numerical limitations, is eternal in virtue
> of its cyclic recurrence. Thus time as well as eternity is infinite,
> and is thought to be eternal. But eternity is rightly held to
> rank above time, in virtue of its fixity; for it is firmly fixed, so
> as to be able, by its rigid immobility, to sustain those things
> which are in motion. . . . For the Kosmos, changeless in virtue
> of the unalterable law by which its motion is determined,
> revolves with an everlasting movement.

It must be emphasized that in these remarks no account has been
taken of any annotations or modifications of the original Hermetic doctrines which may have been made between the third century and the
time when Henry Vaughan wrote his poetry. There is room and need
for a full listing of the analogies which the intervening period might
provide. Nor is any claim made that the similarities pointed out above
are exhaustive even of the limited field here entered. But such as they
are they may serve to illustrate a relationship which appears not to have
been duly appreciated, and they show that several of Vaughan's characteristic ideas have their correspondences and partly originated in the
writings attributed to 'thrice-great Hermes'.

Notes

1. See Mr. Walter Scott's discussion in his edition of the *Hermetica* (1924), vol. I, pp. i-iii.

2. In *Magia Adamica* (1650), *Works*, ed. A. E. Waite (1919), p. 179.

3. The page-numbers refer to my edition of Vaughan's *Works* (1914).

4. The translations are those of Mr. Walter Scott, *op. cit.*, vol. I, to which the page-numbers given refer. I follow also his numbering and arrangement of the Libelli.

5. In *Seventeenth Century Studies presented to Sir Herbert Grierson* (1938), p. 247.

6. This correspondence was pointed out to me a few years ago by one of my students, Mr. Matthew Murphy. Vaughan knew the *Resolves* very well.

E. L. MARILLA

The Religious Conversion
of Henry Vaughan

The religious conversion of Henry Vaughan has long been a subject of
critical interest, but no one has yet carefully examined this biographical
problem. Inquiry on the subject usually begins and ends with incautious
inference from confusing bibliographical details. These may be briefly
reviewed.

On 17 December 1647 Vaughan wrote a dedication from some
work (described in the dedication merely as 'these *papers*') which he did
not at once publish. In 1651 his *Olor Iscanus* (composed of twenty-two
original secular poems and twenty-five translations) appeared, the title-
page bearing the imprint 'Published by a Friend'. The volume contains
the ambiguous dedication of 1647, but 'The Publisher to the Reader'
informs us (not altogether accurately): '*The* Author *had long agoe condemn'd
these* Poems *to* Obscuritie... *I present thee then not onely with a* Book, *but
with a* Prey... *I have not the Author's* Approbation *to the* Fact...'. In the
meantime, Vaughan himself had published *Silex Scintillans* (1650), con-
sisting entirely of religious verse; and five years later he published an
augmented re-issue of this volume, including a preface (30 September
1654) in which he denounces those who continue 'after years of discre-
tion' to write '*vitious verse*' and '*idle books*', and repents that he has not
always been an influence against this evil.

These facts are the basis of the theory that at some time between

Reprinted, by permission of Oxford University Press, from *Review of English Studies*,
21 (1945), 15–22.

1647 and 1650 Vaughan experienced a religious conversion, renounced his secular poems, and resolved to devote his poetic talents thereafter exclusively to spiritual themes.[1]

The purpose of the present study is two-fold: first, to show that accessible evidence disproves the theory of a complete conversion before 1650 and reveals that Vaughan's spiritual experience represents a gradual deepening of religious sentiment which continued after 1650, reaching fulfilment probably about 1654; second, to consider a later significant change in Vaughan's attitude that has been neglected in criticism.

The fact that *Olor Iscanus* contains poems obviously written throughout 1647–50,[2] when the first *Silex Scintillans* was also being composed, makes untenable a previous assumption that Vaughan's turning from secular to exclusively religious themes was a result of a complete conversion before 1650. The inclusion of these later poems in *Olor Iscanus* also discredits the further inference that the notice, 'The Publisher to the Reader', records a consequent and immediate decision of the poet to suppress the secular work of his 'unregenerate' years. Recognition of these errors in the theory being discussed leads us to consider the related assumption that Vaughan's attitude in *Silex Scintillans* of 1650 is fundamentally different from that of the secular verse of former years. Examination of the writings does not support this notion. The preface of the *Poems* (1646) is certainly no expression of lightheartedness; and the dominant tone throughout the original verse (as well as that of the work which the poet chose to translate and include) is one of reflection and contemplation. *Olor Iscanus* manifests maturing interests and philosophic habits of mind. Throughout this work are passages revealing strong moral convictions and deep concern about the current political and ecclesiastical turmoil. The attentive reader of the whimsical verses inspired by the war will distinguish between the truly facetious and those that echo Democritean mirth. In most instances, the poet's reflections on contemporary conditions bear a tone of dejection and disclose a tendency to escape disheartening reality through meditation. Contempt for the Puritans is quite recognizable in *Olor Iscanus*, and it is no less relevant that in poems excluded from this volume and published much later in *Thalia Rediviva* (1678)[3] Vaughan even more clearly identifies himself as a Royalist and Anglican and reveals that he viewed with real apprehension the progress of the Parliamentarians. Actually, the mood of the 1650 *Silex Scintillans*, far from representing a distinct departure from the poet's previous manner of thinking, appears as a logical sequence of his increasing seriousness as revealed in the secular verse.

It now becomes apparent that 'The Authors Preface' of 1654 in the second *Silex Scintillans* is not to be interpreted as an expression of Vaughan's views in 1650. The Preface is both a denunciation of current abuse of literary ambition and artistic talent and a pronouncement that obedience to 'Gods *sacred exhortations*' requires that able writers devote themselves wholly 'to pious *Themes* and *Contemplations*'. Vaughan has much to say here about degenerate authors whose 'willingly-studied and wilfully-published vanities' are mere manifestations of 'sensual volutation or wallowing in *impure thoughts* and *scurrilous conceits*' for public notice. But his arraignment of these only sharpens his censure of capable writers who inadvertently encourage the evil by their preoccupation with 'lean *conceptions*, which in the most inclinable *Reader* will scarce give any nourishment or help to *devotion*. 'The true remedy', we are told, 'lies wholly in their bosoms, who are the gifted persons, by a wise exchange of *vain* and *vitious subjects*, for *divine Themes* and *Celestial praise*'. Plainly, in Vaughan's opinion in 1654 those who did not devote their poetic powers exclusively to spiritual themes were wilfully encouraging the 'evil disease' which he here assails. It is relevant that in the same document he contritely acknowledges that he himself was once one of these offenders:

> And here, because I would prevent a just *censure* by my free *confession*, I must remember, that I my self have for many years together, languished of this very *sickness*; and it is no long time since I have recovered. But (blessed be God for it!) I have by his saving assistance supprest my *greatest follies*,[4] and those which escaped from me, are (I think) as innoxious, as most of that *vein* use to be; besides, they are interlined with many virtuous, and some pious mixtures. What I speak of them, is truth; but let no man mistake it for an *extenuation* of faults, as if I intended an *Apology* for *them*, or my *self*, who am conscious of so much *guilt* in *both*, as can never be expiated without *special sorrows*, and that cleansing and pretious *effusion* of my Almighty Redeemer. . . .[5]

Since Vaughan is known to have continued throughout 1647–50 the 'wrong-doing' for which he here repents, we are forced to conclude that the Preface of 1654 represents an advance in his spiritual development definitely beyond that which produced the *Silex Scintillans* of 1650.

Criticism has too much neglected *The Mount of Olives* and *Flores*

Solitudinis (registered on 16 December 1651 and 15 September 1653, respectively) as sources of commentary on Vaughan's thinking during 1650–4. The works in these volumes evince engrossing interest of the author in 'divine themes'[6] but even more explicit evidence of increasing religious sentiment is found in the prefaces. Whereas the *Silex* of 1650 contains no prefatory remarks, in the dedication (1 October 1651) of *The Mount of Olives* Vaughan appeals 'To the Truly Noble and Religious S'. Charles Egerton' for support in this attempt to exalt the Christian life in the current '*bad times*' when 'It must be counted for a great *blessing*, that there is yet any left which dares *look* upon, and *commiserate* distressed Religion'. An additional preface in this work points again to the ungodliness of the times and urges the '*Christian Reader*' to pursue his way with patience, and for comfort and courage to '*Look not upon transitorie, visible things, but upon him that is eternal, and invisible*'. The note 'To the Reader' (17 April 1652) of *Flores*, reflecting increasing intensity, declares that through great suffering the poet has attained the revelation that in his previous concern about the trials of life (a prominent theme in *Olor Iscanus*) he was '*Quarrelling with* [God's] light' and exhibiting '*the foolish testinesse of man arising out of his* misconstruction *and* ignorance *of the wise method of* Providence'. It is proof of that 'wise method', we are informed, that his error brought '*those sad* Conflicts' which impelled him to seek retirement where he found the peace that comes of spiritual illumination. In true evangelistic fashion he exhorts the Reader to seek like peace in similar channels, and commends, with significant discrimination and persuasion, his '*little booke*' of precepts (whose title '*was found in the* woods *and the* wildernesse'):

> It may be thy spirit is such a popular, phantastick flye, as loves to gad in the shine of this world; if so, this light I live by in the shade, is too great for thee. I send it abroad to bee a companion of those wise Hermits, who have withdrawne from the present generation, to confirme them in their solitude, and to make that rigid necessity their pleasant Choyse. To leave the world, when it leaves us, is both sordid and sorrowfull; and to quitt our station upon discontents, is nothing else, but to be the Apes of those Melancholy Schismaticks ... They are Spirits of a very poore, inferiour order, that have so much Sympathy with worldlie things, as to weepe at Parting.[7]

In a further dedicatory note 'To the Truely Noble And Religious Sir *Charles Egerton*' (1653), a year later, Vaughan writes with even more fervour, and the vehemence of his judgment upon the vanity of worldly interests represents a close approach to the militant attitude in the Preface of the following year. In this dedication he declares:

> *Nothing can give that, which it hath not, this transitory changeable and corrupt world cannot afford permanent treasures. All it gives, and all it shewes us, is but* trash & illusion. *The true incorruptible riches dwell above the reach of rust and theeves.* . . .
>
> *All the gay appearances in this life seeme to me but a swift succession of rising* Clouds, *which neither abide in any certaine* forme, *nor continue for any* long time; *And this is that, which makes the* sore travell of the sonnes of men *to be nothing else but a meere chasing of shadowes.* All is vanity (*said the Royall Philosopher,*) and there is no new thing under the Sun.
>
> *I present you therefore with a discourse perswading to a* contempt & *a* desertion *of these* old things which (*our Saviour tells us*) shall passe away.[8]

From these records it is clear that Vaughan's attitude in 1654 was the result of a steady intensification of his religious experience after 1650.

Under close examination, then, the theory of a complete conversion before 1650 becomes a misinterpretation of the evidence. *Silex Scintillans* (1650) represents, not a fundamental change in Vaughan's attitude toward life, but rather a logical stage in a development begun in the earlier secular verse. Furthermore, bibliographical evidence forbids interpretation of 'The Publisher to the Reader' of *Olor Iscanus* as testimony that Vaughan had decided *out of piety* to suppress his secular poems. And, finally, that *Olor Iscanus* contains poems written after 1647 and as late as 1650 invalidates previous acceptance of the Preface of 1654 as a statement of the poet's views during the late 1640's. Careful consideration of the facts reviewed here reveals that Vaughan's conversion was a gradual development beginning as early as the middle 1640's and continuing as late as 1654, and discloses also that it was after 1650, not before, that his experience became most dynamic.

When we recognize the true nature of Vaughan's religious experience, we can see more clearly its relationship to biographical facts which have been used to account for its origin.[9] It may be that the loss of friends and relatives was a factor in the poet's spiritual growth, but it is unnecessary to regard losses of this kind after 1650 as less relevant than those during the 1640's.[10] If we consider Vaughan's interest in the

Hermetica also a force in his conversion, it remains relevant that Hermetic influence is present not only in *Silex Scintillans* of 1650 but also in *Olor Iscanus* and is prominent in the *Silex* of 1655, in which year, let us observe, Vaughan published his translation of Henry Nollius's *Hermetical Physick*. My interpretation admits Vaughan's acknowledgment in the 1650 *Silex Scintillans* of Herbert's influence and also his reference to himself as Herbert's convert in the Preface of 1654. Moreover, it is consistent with my thesis that whereas none of Vaughan's expressions prior to 1652 (including the note to the Reader of *The Mount of Olives* and its dedication of 1 October 1651) contains mention of ill-health, the prefatory addresses (as well as the title-page) of *Flores Solitudinis* and the Preface of the 1655 *Silex* record an increasingly severe illness during 1653–4 and clearly testify to its influence on the poet's thinking during these years.

It is evident, however, that the Civil War and its political consequences, hitherto regarded only as an influence in Vaughan's attitude before 1650, represent the principal force in his spiritual development during the period of 1647–54. Scholars who have acknowledged that Vaughan, an ardent Royalist, was deeply concerned about the national turmoil of the 1640's have failed to make the logical inference that his anxiety would increase as he witnessed the last stages of the war. The conclusion is supported by evidence of Vaughan's persistent allegiance to the Royalist cause. It is practically confirmed by the Latin poem '*Ad Posteros*', prefixed to *Olor Iscanus*, which records in studied enigma the poet's distress about the recent Parliamentarian victory and the execution of King Charles I in 1649.[11] No less reasonable is the inference that his anxiety would settle into despair as he realized the full significance of the Parliamentarian triumph. It is only by ignoring the relevance of historic fact or by denying Vaughan's sensibility, which his expressions during the 1650's attest, that we can deny that for him the early years of the republican regime were a period of crisis. In logic we must recognize that the cumulative effect of the Royalist catastrophe in 1649 helped to intensify Vaughan's religious feeling, which culminated in complete renunciation of secular interests and found austere expression in the Preface of 1654—written, let us note, exactly ten days after Parliament made Cromwell 'Protector for life'.

That Vaughan's devout mood of the 1650's later underwent a permanent modification has not been sufficiently recognized. His letters to John Aubrey during the 1670's,[12] his first direct expressions after

1655 of which we have record, reveal that he had long before broken his retirement and taken a new view on life. In the initial letter of 15 June 1673 Vaughan states that 'My profession allso is physic, wch I have practised now for many years with good successe (I thank god!) & a repute big enough for a person of greater parts than my selfe'. This statement clearly shows an interest in life, as does his correspondence with Aubrey about the inclusion of himself and his brother Thomas in Anthony à Wood's *Historia et Antiquitates Universitatis Oxoniensis* (1674). And apparently Henry felt no restraint in acknowledging (9 December 1675) his pleasure in the fact 'That my dear brothers name (& mine) are revived, & shine in the Historie of the Universitie. . . . ' Obviously, he had regained respect for values which he had repudiated during the 1650's. Among the biographical details that he considered worth publishing in Wood's *Historia* was his residence in London as a young law student, an experience reflected in some early verses which, though quite inoffensive, Vaughan would not have regarded in 1654 as his most 'innoxious'. Even more revealing is his bibliography included in the letter of 15 June 1673. Although for some reason the *Poems* are omitted, Vaughan lists, not only *Silex Scintillans*, but also *Olor Iscanus*, and he adds *Thalia Rediviva* (then unpublished), which contains secular poems written as early as 1647,[13] including love verses neither more nor less reprehensible than those in the *Poems* of 1646. Vaughan's attitude in 1673 is distinctly less ascetic than his attitude of 1654. And that his renewed interest in life continued throughout his remaining twenty-two years is attested by his correspondence with Aubrey and Wood, which records not only vigorous professional activity but also lively interest in current affairs and in various literary pursuits up to some six months before his death in 1695.

The chief explanation for the change in Vaughan's views between 1654 and 1673 almost certainly resides, as in the case of his earlier conversion, in the political developments of the time. The Commonwealth, let us recall, came to an end five years after the publication of the second *Silex Scintillans*. The Restoration was a happy event for Royalists. And when we consider that Vaughan was then less than forty years old, it becomes almost inconceivable that he should fail to respond to new conditions affording, among other benefits, a liberation of spirit that challenged retirement. His medical career, which in 1673 had extended for 'many years', shows his adjustment to these better times, which was as natural as his previous reaction to political ostracism.

The account of Vaughan's religious conversion becomes, then, a simple and understandable story. During and immediately after his residence in London, the young law student indulged his poetic impulses in imitative experiments with various literary forms and themes. Results of these first attempts he later saw fit to publish, along with a Latin translation, as the *Poems* in 1646. In the meantime, the frustration of his study of law proving an incentive to literary effort, he continued to write with growing earnestness. Although his interest in conventional themes continued, as the true import of the war became manifest Vaughan, disturbed by the social and political confusion, was impelled to turn his poetic attention also to themes relating to the conflict and frequently to infuse into other expressions his concern about the moral issues of the strife. In 1647 such writings—probably along with some translations—had accumulated considerably, and on 17 December he wrote a dedication with a view to publishing the work when sufficiently augmented. Having been attracted to the sacred writing of George Herbert, however, Vaughan was already experimenting with religious themes, and he now began to find relief for his increasing perturbation not only in secular compositions which more overtly attacked the prospering Parliamentarians (and were therefore unpublishable) but also in pious verses reflecting the manner and mood of *The Temple*. His dejection deepening as the signs of a Royalist defeat increased, he turned more and more to Herbert as a source of inspiration and guidance and eventually came to devote his literary talent chiefly to pious compositions. The final overthrow of the monarchy and the execution of the King supplied the impulse in 1650 to bring forth the sacred verse as appropriate testimony to the efficacy of Christian faith during the current triumph of evil.

Although Vaughan could publish *Silex Scintillans* with impunity, his unpublished secular writing remained a problem. It contained war poems which he could no longer consider publishing and also love verse that might perturb sympathetic readers of his later religious poetry. He decided that he could do no better than to place the secular compositions in the competent editorial hands of his friend Thomas Powell and let him determine the solution of the problem. This 'understanding editor' performed his task well, carefully selecting for *Olor Iscanus* that part of the work which would be most acceptable to the public and reasonably safe for the author and adding, for his special protection against potential enemies among Parliamentarian sympathizers, an ingenious preface which deceived no less his commentators for nearly a century.

Vaughan's religious fervour was accentuated by ill-health and other trying circumstances after 1650. He found comfort in the lives and writings of saintly characters of the past and was inspired to make these sources of reassurance available for others who shared his anxiety and his need of spiritual consolation. For his method of escape from recognition of defeat as outlined in *The Mount of Olives, Flores Solitudinis,* and *Silex Scintillans* of 1655 Vaughan had many precedents.

Subsequent recovery from illness and earnest pursuit of his medical interests (originally a part of his piety and recorded in his translation of the *Hermetical Physick*) signalized adjustment to existing conditions and the passing of the poetic mood. A little later the Restoration brought new opportunities, and continuous professional success and prosperity thereafter dispelled the attitude induced by a long series of frustrations, and engendered in the poet the equanimity reflected in his letters to Aubrey and Wood during his last twenty-two years.

Notes

1. This theory begins with Vaughan's first modern editor, the Rev. H. F. Lyte (*Silex Scintillans*, 1847, pp. xxx–xxxii), and has gained wide acceptance in subsequent criticism. See, for instance, J. C. Sharp, 'Henry Vaughan, Silurist,' *The North American Review*, CXXXVIII (1884), 125; Anonymous, 'Henry Vaughan,' *Littell's Living Age*, CLXXXVIII (1891), 237; H. C. Beeching, *Poems of Henry Vaughan*, ed. E. K. Chambers (London, 1896), I, pp. xxiv–xxvi; J. Vaughan, 'Henry Vaughan, Silurist,' *The Nineteenth Century*, LXVII (1910), 495–6; Anonymous, 'Henry Vaughan', *The Spectator*, CXV (1915), 543; Percy H. Osmond, *The Mystical Poets of the English Church* (London, 1919), p. 142; P. E. More, *The Demon of the Absolute* (Princeton, 1928), pp. 151–5; Elizabeth Holmes, *Henry Vaughan and the Hermetic Philosophy* (Oxford, 1932), pp. 12–18; Gwenllian E. F. Morgan, 'Henry Vaughan, Silurist', *The Times Literary Supplement*, 3 November 1932, p. 815; Anonymous, 'Henry Vaughan', *The Times Literary Supplement*, 13 October 1932, p. 724; F. E. Hutchinson (a review), *The Review of English Studies*, X (1934), 232; J. B. Leishman, *The Metaphysical Poets* (Oxford, 1934), pp. 148–51; Ralph M. Wardle, 'Thomas Vaughan's Influence upon the Poetry of Henry Vaughan', *P.M.L.A.*, LI (1936), 938; Helen C. White, *The Metaphysical Poets* (New York, 1936), pp. 264–73. Apparently no one has recognized that this interpretation of the problem has a counterpart in the investigations of one of Vaughan's most important editors, the Rev. A. B. Grosart (*Works of Vaughan*, The Fuller Worthies' Library, 1871, II, pp. xxv–xxviii, xlvi–xlix), whose conclusion is that the conversion was a development of the 1650's.

2. See William R. Parker, 'Henry Vaughan and his Publishers', *The Library*, Fourth Series, XX (1940), 408, and Harold R. Walley, 'The Strange Case of *Olor Iscanus*', *The Review of English Studies*, XVIII (1942), 30–1.

3. See Parker, *Library*, pp. 407–10.

4. See Parker, *Library*. p. 411.

5. *Works of Vaughan*, ed. L. C. Martin (Oxford, 1914), ii, 390.

6. *The Mount of Olives* consists of a treatise on 'Man in Darkness, Or, A Discourse of *Death*", twenty-four devotional exercises suitable *'for most times and occasions'* in the life of the *'Christian Reader'*, and a translation of 'Man in Glory: Or, A Discourse of the blessed state of the Saints in the New Jerusalem' ('Written . . . by the most Reverend and holy Father *Anselmus* Archbishop of *Canterbury*'). *Flores Solitudinis* is composed of 'Primitive Holiness, Set forth in the Life of blessed Paulinus, The most Reverend . . . Bishop of *Nola*' and translations of 'Of Temperance and Patience', 'Of Life and Death' (both 'Written . . . by *Johan: Euseb: Nierembergius*'), and 'The World Contemned (' . . . written by the Reverend Father *Eucherius*, Bishop of *Lyons'*).

7. *Works*, ed. Martin, i, 216.

8. *Works*, ed. Martin, i, 214–15.

9. Previous interpretation (see p. 15, n., above) assigns the following as principal influences: loss of friends in the Civil War; the untimely death both of a younger brother and of his first wife; the general confusion of the war; the inspiration of *The Temple* of George Herbert; association with his brother Thomas and their common interest in the Hermetic philosophy; a severe and protracted illness.

10. No poem in *Olor Iscanus* lamenting the death of acquaintances is more expressive of grief than are the verses in *Thalia Rediviva* occasioned by Charles Walbeoffe's death in 1653. Nor are the poems in *Silex Scintillans* (1650) that are said to have been written on the loss of his brother William more burdened with bereavement than are those in the *Silex* of 1655 that were no less certainly inspired by the recent death of his wife.

11. See the translation and interpretation of the poem in my 'Henry Vaughan and the Civil War', *Journal of English and Germanic Philology*, XLI (1942), 514–26.

12. *Works*, ed. Martin, ii 667, ff.

13. See Parker, *Library*, pp. 408–10.

DON CAMERON ALLEN

Vaughan's "Cock-Crowing" and the Tradition

Vaughan lived in the narrow space between two worlds: one was a world of crystal translucency and one was of blind darkness. The black world he knew sadly enough and well; the world of light he saw indistinctly because the veil of mortality thwarted his vision: "And onely see through a long night/Thy edges and they bordering light."[1] The veil, which Christ alone had penetrated[2] and which Vaughan knew would cover his eyes until Doomsday,[3] becomes a constant symbol of the poet's spiritual frustration. He lives "under veyls here";[4] he hopes to have "his Curtaines off";[5] or he awaits the time when his "callous veyl"[6] will be purged away by fire. His realization of spiritual insufficiency has, on occasion, a conscious edge of violence:

> Since in these veyls my Ecclips'd Eye
> May not approach thee, (for at night
> Who can have commerce with the light?)
> I'le disapparell, and to buy
> But one half glance, most gladly dye.[7]

It is not enough for him that at times he sees the great Light in dreams or in visions that are almost ecstatic; but, fortunately, the failure of spiritual sight is not a prompter of mortal despair. Vaughan remembers his "glimpses" and he is cheered by the knowledge that a candle shines on "some heads,"[8] that in him is the seed, the tiny inner warmth. "That

Reprinted, by permission of The Johns Hopkins University Press, from *Journal of English Literary History*, 21:2 (1954), 94–106.

Sacred Ray/Thy Spirit plant."[9] Sometimes his deeds mist within him "and put out that lamp";[10] sometimes this ray, a star captive in a tomb, cannot blaze with the full ardor of the stars;[11] yet he is blessed when he finds that all creatures, even those lesser than he, possess a glimmering of the secret light.

All creatures, he tells us in "Palm Sunday," have an interior flickering that permits them to recognize their incarnate Creator.[12] Vaughan wishes to share in this gift, to interpret with the birds the splendid doctrine of Providence.[13] He yearns to be a star or a bird; then he "should be/Shining, or singing still to Thee."[14] The doctrine of the world of light is partially expressed in "The Eagle,"[15] but from time to time he recalls the old contention between light and darkness and knows that he is on the edge of a terrible forest.

> But as these Birds of light make a land glad,
> Chirping their solemn Matins on each tree:
> so in the shades of night some dark fowls be,
> Whose heavy notes make all that hear them, sad.[16]

The rent between the two worlds is here made plain, but Vaughan, while doubtful of satisfaction in the veiled life, seeks constantly to see light in darkness, even though this light is filtered and is not God's "Center and mid-day." In "Cock-Crowing" he selects the bird of light as a commanding symbol. Here he can gloss darkness by light and know his own soul in terms of a lesser creature. Before we trace the history of this symbol, we should read the poem.

> Father of lights! what Sunnie seed,
> What glance of day has thou confin'd
> Into this bird? To all the breed
> This busie Ray thou hast assign'd;
> Their magnetisme works all night,
> And dreams of Paradise and light.
>
> Their eyes watch for the morning hue,
> Their little grain expelling night
> So shines and sings, as if it knew
> The path unto the house of light.
> It seems their candle, howe'r done,
> Was tinn'd and lighted at the sunne.
>
> If such a tincture, such a touch,
> So firm a longing can impowre

Shall they own image think it much
To watch for thy appearing hour?
If a meer blast so fill the sail,
Shall not the breath of God prevail?

O thou immortall light and heat!
Whose hand so shines through all this frame,
That by the beauty of the seat,
We plainly see, who made the same,
Seeing thy seed abides in me,
Dwell thou in it, and I in thee.

To sleep without thee, is to die;
Yea, 'tis a death partakes of hell:
For where thou dost not close the eye
It never opens, I can tell.
In such a dark, Ægyptian border,
The shades of death dwell and disorder.

If joyes, and hopes, and earnest throws,
And hearts, whose Pulse beats still for light
Are given to birds; who, but thee, knows
A love-sick souls exalted flight?
Can souls be track'd by any eye
But his, who gave them wings to flie?

Onely this Veyle which thou hast broke,
And must be broken yet in me,
This veyle, I say, is all the cloke
And cloud which shadows thee from me.
This veyle thy full-ey'd love denies,
And onely gleams and fractions spies.

O take it off! make no delay,
But brush me with thy light, that I
May shine unto a perfect day,
And warme me at thy glorious Eye!
O take it off! or till it flee,
Though with no Lilie, stay with me!

This poem is plainly a minor metaphor in the three larger images
that are the major centers of Vaughan's poetic theology. There is, first,
the seed planted by God in the flinty soil of the human heart, watered
by the showers and streams of his Grace and warmed to growth by the

essential light. As the seed grows, it is whipped by the winds of the world, strangled by weeds, blighted by the frost of sin. In time it will be a lily, blossoming to its maker's hand. The growth of the plant from its green root is likened in a second sense to a great journey back to the noble, yet "shady City of Palme trees." The traveler often goes, like Nicodemus, by night to find his Lord; and the way lies through a blasted land, over treacherous rocks and past dangerous woods. The voyage is sometimes starlighted, but often light is shut out by cloud and darkness. Finally, there is the metaphor of union, when God receives the flower, and the saved poet returns to the soul-land from whence he came. "Cock-Crowing" does not overlook any of these capital topics, but it belongs to the first metaphoric center, fixing our attention on the seed of light that God, according to Vaughan, has planted in all his creatures. Here the creature celebrated is the cock, and behind Vaughan's choice of this bird to expound his doctrine lies the usual tradition, both pagan and Christian.

In the history of symbols, the mysteries of the cosmos are frequently suggested by birds that live between heaven and earth, for wings are necessary to the exploration of celestial pastures and man must listen to birdsong, as Marvell did, in order to learn something about celestial harmony. The gods of the ancients, when not winged themselves, were attended by significant birds of their own choosing. The eagle accompanies Jove as the hawk had once journeyed with Horus; the peacock is holy to Juno; the dove, to Venus. Though Hades is a land where no birds sing, the Elysian Fields could not have been endured or enjoyed without them. Tibullus imagines the great goddess walking with lovers in the Hearafter and listening to the viols and flutes of choral birds.

> Sed me, quod facilis tenero sum semper Amori,
> Ipsa Venus compos ducet in Elysios.
> Hic choreae cantusque vigent, passimque vagantes
> Dulce sonant tenui gutture carmen aves.[17]

The cock, master of the raucous song praised in Vaughan's poem, was to antiquity the most familiar of birds, the *dux et rex* of the yard and doorway; yet, though he was common, he was also a holy bird, sacred to Athena, to Hermes, to Latona, to Demeter, and to the half-gods, Hercules and Aesculapius. It was natural that he was the symbol of the sun; and it was for this reason that Idomeneus, the fighting flame of the *Iliad*, who was descended from Helios, bore an effigy of the bird on his shield.[18] For the Greek and Latin world, the rooster was the "bird of light," and as such he not only expelled the dark but the evils that walked by night.

> Nocte Deae Nocti cristatus caeditur ales,
> Quod tepidum vigili provocat ore diem.[19]

The sunless hours, as these lines from Ovid imply, are filled with uncertain dread that the cock with his "instinct of light" (so Heliodorus[20] calls it) banishes. The dread that the pagans define with uncertainty is made clear for us when Basil states that the call of the sun-bird puts demons to flight.[21] The fact that the early Church used the rooster as a funereal ornament and that the bird is mentioned in epitaphic verse is, consequently, not surprising; he is not only the bird of light, but a symbol of the eternal light that guides and protects the souls of the dead. The cock's conversion to Christianity was easy, and it was facilitated not only by his pagan repute but also by the special qualities that Christian writers gave to all birds.[22]

When Vaughan wrote the first two stanzas of this poem, he was rephrasing in Christian terms what any classical poet might have said. The same classical knowledge helps us read stanzas five, seven, and eight, but we must go to the Scriptures and the tradition of the Church for full comprehension. The cock of St. Peter's denial is supported by an impressive passage in Job (38:36) where the admonishing Jehovah states: "Who placed wisdom in the heart of man, or who gave understanding to the cock?" With this text, men and the bird of dawn are brought together in the benefits of God though their shares are qualitatively different. It is the memory of this fecundating verse and the history of the human symbolism of the cock in the Christian world that effect the transition between the first and last stanzas of Vaughan's poem. The Christian cock is the Christian man; so a poem is produced that is, in all it says, an invocation. What comes from God is thus returned to him.

To bring this about, the pagan symbolism of the cock combines with Biblical expressions to make the Christian symbol. It is St. Ambrose who provided poets with the text on the cock that filled their imaginations with crowing metaphors.

> When this bird sings, the highwayman leaves his ambush, for the morning star, called forth, rises and lights the heaven. With this singing, the anxious sailor puts aside sorrow, for the tempests and storms stirred up by the strong night

winds are quieted. The devout man, moved by this singing, rises to pray and to read the offices. Finally, with this song, the cornerstone of the Church himself washes away his sin contracted by denying when once before the cock crowed. With this song hope returns to all. The tedium of sickness is lightened; the pain of wounds lessens; the heat of fevers lowers; faith returns to the fallen; Jesus regards the hesitant and corrects the wanderers.[23]

With these praises, the cock becomes a Christian bird, for the references in both Testaments have made him the angel at the door, or, as Cassiodorus calls him, "spiritualis gallus."[24] But he is more commonly recognized in the beginning as one of those minor saints, "qui in nocte saeculi per fidem clamant in Dominum,"[25] and this is a figuration that would have pleased Vaughan. Once Gregory had written his *Moralia in Job*, the cock became the personal analogue of the priest,[26] a man divinely moved, who has a special understanding of God's ways and whose duty, like that of the cock, is not only to bring light to men but to warn those who sleep in darkness of the imminent coming of God. The responsibilities of these instructed men on the eve of Doomsday are described by Rupertus with the metaphor of the cock: "And just as the rooster by crowing shakes off with his notes the sleep of sloth, announcing the coming light, the priest. . . . " In Vaughan's final four stanzas, the Christian cock becomes, as tradition will have it, the sign of the Last Judgment.

All of these texts are nonpoetical, and we must turn to the Latin poetry of the Middle Ages to find the literary way to Vaughan. In his great hymn, "Aeterne rerum conditor," Ambrose brought the cock into the liturgy.

> Surgemus ergo strenue,
>   Gallus jactantes excitat,
> Et somnolentes increpat,
>   Gallus negantes arguit.
> Gallo canente, spes redit,
>   Ægris salus refunditur,
> Mucro latronis conditur
>   Lapsis fides revertitur.[27]

Prudentius, the successor of Ambrose, made the bird's place sure when he put him at the entrance of the *Liber Cathemerinon*; here in the "Hymnus ad Galli Cantum," the singing cock awakens men from spiritual slumber, warning them of the coming splendour. "Nostri figura est iudicis," says the poet and then solemnly expands the idea.

> Hic somnus ad tempus datus
> Est forma mortis perpetis:
> Peccata, ceu nox horrida,
> Cogunt iacere ac stertere.

> Sed vox ab alto culmine
> Christi docentis praemonet
> Adesse iam lucem prope,
> Ne mens sopori serviat.

> Ne somnus usque ad terminos
> Vitae socordis opprimat
> Pectus sepultum crimine
> Et lucis oblitum suae.

Vaughan almost says this in English: "To sleep without thee, is to die;/Yea, 'tis a death partakes of hell."[28] Prudentius, who strives for the fullest interpretation, continues, reminding his readers that Peter's denial came as Christ conquered Hell and Death. His bird, too, has further lessons for those who sleep in darkness and dream vainly of gold, glory, and pleasure. "Fit mane, nil sunt omnia." For the cock, we are then assured, is not only the herald of God's light, the resonant shout of Doomsday, but also the grave Judge.

> Tu, Christe, somnium dissice,
> Tu rumpe noctis vincula,
> Tu solve peccatum vetus
> Novumque lumen ingere.[29]

The hymns of Ambrose and Prudentius made the cock a divine analogue, and thereafter he finds a sure place in the ritual. The Mozarabic hymns included one song for matins, "Gallo canente venimus"[30] and in two other hymns—"Gallus diei nuntius"[31] and "Gallus auroram resonis/Salutans cantibus"[32]—the bird has a symbolic rôle. The poets of the age of Charlemagne naturally celebrated the priestly rooster who called men to worship[33] and who predicted the day of God's Coming.[34] The latter theme is handsomely embroidered in the *Carmina Centulensis*, where the poet presents the cock and the thrush singing a doomsong together after the morning choir; a relatively somber hymn it is, in which they urge the righteous to prepare immediately for the new age of gold.[35] But all of these poems are minor compared to the fourteenth-century, "Multi sunt presbyteri qui ignorant, quare/Super domum domini gallus solet stare."

By the time this poem was written the cock had obviously taken a firm perch on spires, and this poem attempts to tell us why he is so honored. Throughout this poem, the mutual duties of priest and layman are carefully annotated in terms of the symbolic legend of the cock; for though the cock is a priest in analogy—"si bonus presbyter eius fit figura"—the secular can also take instruction from the bird. Actually, the poem is a series of contrasts. The care of the bird for his flock is balanced against the fact that the hellish basilisk is hatched from his eggs. "Sic crescit diabolus ex presbyterorum/Magna negligentia." Once more we hear of the cock as a mighty ward against evil, of his strict warnings in God's service, of his premonitions of the Day of Judgment.

> Sic et bonus presbyter, respuens terrena,
> Ducat suos subditos ex inferni poena,
> Praebens iter caelicum caeli per amoena
> Ut cum Christus venerit, turba sit serena.[36]

Without this tradition, Vaughan's poem might not have come into being in the text we have; with the tradition, it is richer and fuller in all its implications. For centuries before Vaughan saw visions by the Usk, the cock had been famed for his instinctive knowledge of light, not only that of the lesser light of the sun but also of the divine light. For this reason he was associated with the priest as an expeller of spiritual darkness and of evil. In the natural world he made lions afraid; in the higher world, he was victor over the lions of Hell. While he reminded men of their duties to God and roused them from their worldly slumber, he also warned them of Christ's Second Coming and urged them to prepare for the Day of Judgment. These traditions make the fabric of the early and late stanzas of "Cock-Crowing," but there is another connection that must be established because Vaughan says that the bird has within him a "busie Ray," "a little grain expelling night," whereas man, "thy own image," has a soul that is far broader in its comprehension of the divine. Hence, if the rooster can dream "of Paradise and light,"

> Shall thy own image think it much
> To watch for thy appearing hour?

The difference between man and the cock implies the difference between "sapientia" and "intelligentia." For Vaughan this difference is expressed by the breeze that fills a sail and that which fills the soul of the poet, the very breath of God. But as the poem proceeds, the soul becomes like a bird.

> If joyes, and hopes, and earnest throws
> And hearts, whose Pulse beats still for light
> Are given to birds; who, but thee, knows
> A love-sick souls exalted flight?
> Can souls be track'd by any eye
> But his, who gave them wings to flie?

The translation of soul into bird is also part of a long poetic process.

Drawing on the bank of pagan symbolism, the early Christians associated the soul with flying things. The Greeks had represented the soul as a winged replica of the person who was dead, and Psyche, the soul-butterfly, set the pattern for the iconographical description of the Christian soul with her colored wings.[37] The relationship between the soul or mind of man, and birds, was strongly perceived by the Greeks, and it is not surprising to find that Plato compares the mind to an aviary,[38] or that Plotinus discovers three kinds of souls among men and compares them to three classes of birds.[39] This decorous symbol was appropriated by the Fathers of Christian belief because it was also authorized by the Scriptures.

As we stand at the deathbeds of the saints of antiquity, we see, if we believe their chroniclers, their souls ascending to heaven as birds. St. Benedict saw the soul of his sister, leaving her body in the form of a dove;[40] and St. Gregory in his record of the death of Abbot Spes says that the soul of that devout man was seen "in columbae specie."[42]In the *Peristephanon*, Prudentius turns his experience into poetry.

> Emicat inde columba repens
> Martyris os nive candidior
> Visa relinquere et astra sequi;
> Spiritus hic erat Eulaliae
> Lacteolus, celer, innocuus.

Colla fluunt abeunte anima
Et rogus igneus emoritur,
Pax datur artubus exanimis,
Flatus in aethere plaudit ovans
Templaque celsa petit volucer.

Vidit et ipse satelles avem
Feminae ab ore meare palam,
Obstupefactus et attonitus
Prosilit et sua gesta fugit,
Lictor et ipse fugit pavidus.[42]

Though for most early Christian poets the soul assumes the form of a dove or a nameless bird,[43] the Renaissance was also able to associate the soul with the cock. The translation is due not to Christian tradition, but once again, to Plato.

"I owe, Crito," says the dying Socrates, "a cock to Aesculapius; do not forget to pay it." The interpretation of this final request of the great philosopher has caused men of all times to whip their minds. The irreverent Lucian observes that the remark shows what little regard Socrates had for Zeus.[44] The testimony of this scoffer was hardly acceptable to early Christians; yet, in this case, Tertullian agrees with the pagan and observes that Socrates, the atheist, ordered the sacrifice out of filial consideration for his father.[45] Origen thinks the demand shows that Socrates, in spite of his wisdom, abandoned eminent principles for the trivial and unimportant.[46] Chrysostom[47] and Theodoret[48] smell idolatry. Lactantius is more brutal: Socrates feared the judge of the dead, stern Rhadamanthus.[49]

The humanists, to whom Plato was the master that Aristotle was to the scholastics, rose to the defence of their philosopher. Ficino saw in the dying request of Socrates a statement of Christian intent. Socrates, he insists, sought among the gods for a physician who could cure the diseases of the soul; and when at last he had resolved his own diseases (doubts and fears), he was eager to thank God.[50] Pico della Mirandola fully agrees with his friend and extends the allegory. The cock, he states, is the soul of man; this is the reason that Socrates said he owed a cock to Aesculapius. By this ultimate statement he meant that he owed his own soul to the doctor of souls.[51] So for the Florentine Platonists the cock of the *Phaedo* was the soul of the philosopher, but their concept was strengthened by another citation in the books of the past.

As every educated man of the seventeenth century knew, there is among the cryptic and almost mystical sayings of Pythagoras the strict advice: "Feed the cock." The baffling command was explained by the sixteenth-century editor, Lilius Gyraldus—a great explainer of enigmas—as golden doctrine. Pythagoras, he tells us, was encouraging his disciples to feed the divine part of the soul (the cock) with celestial knowledge just as they fed their bodies with more mundane food.[52] So the cock of Erasmus' St. Socrates and the cock of Milton's St. Pythagoras become in the sixteenth century the immortal soul of man. The symbol of solar light arrives with pagan help at a greater definition, for it changes into the "seed," the created light that dwells in all humankind.

With this alteration we can better understand how Vaughan could move from the allegory of the cock to the Christian desires of his inner self. Behind much of the transformation may rest his philosophical belief in the mysterious doctrines of the universe that he shared with his brother,[53] but enforcing these and making them real is the poetical result of the long struggle of men to express in terms of the lower world what their hearts tell them about the unknowable. In the darkness, the heart of flint sparks, and from its little lights the poet gains courage to await the rending of the veil. The seed has grown into a plant though the plant may not yet have brought forth a bright flower.

> O take it off! make no delay,
> But brush me with thy light, that I
> May shine unto a perfect day,
> And warme me at thy glorious Eye!
> O take it off! or till it flee,
> Though with no Lilie, stay with me!

In this last stanza, reminded by the cock, Vaughan writes his own "Venite rerum Conditor"; but as he writes it, he also realizes that the time may be far away, that he may have to visit with the night before he sees the eternal brightness of God. He draws his comfort and he frames his prayer according to the text of the creature instinct with light. This symbol remains with us, for Vaughan's cock crows again for Masefield.

> But in the darkest hour of night
> When even the foxes peer for light
> The byre-cock crows; he feels the light.

VAUGHAN'S "COCK-CROWING"

So, in this water mixed with dust
The byre-cock spirit crows from trust
That death will change because it must.

Notes

1. *Works*, ed. L. C. Martin (Oxford, 1914), p. 521.
2. P. 485.
3. P. 542.
4. P. 535.
5. P. 399.
6. P. 396.
7. P. 419.
8. P. 395.
9. P. 448.
10. P. 433.
11. P. 421.
12. P. 501.
13. P. 506.
14. P. 422.
15. P. 606.
16. P. 497.
17. I.3.57–60.
18. Pausanias *Itinerary* V.25.9.
19. Ovid *Fasti* I.455–56; see *Met.* XI. 597–98 and Lucretius *De. Rer. Nat.* IV.
710–14.
20. *Aethiopicus* I.18.3.
21. J.-F. Boissonade, *Anecdota Graeca* (Paris, 1829–1833), III, 445. The traditional fear of the lion for the cock is recorded by Pliny (X.48), and this account,
repeated in the Middle Ages and Renaissance, is read on the basis of Ps. 21:22 and
I Pet. 5:8 as an allegory in which the lion is Satan.
22. Classical poets sometimes gave birds human characteristics. Propertius
makes the cock an author: "Tum queror, in toto non sidere pallia lecto,/ Lucis et
auctores non dare carmen aves" (IV.3.31–32), and Ovid makes the crow "auctor
aquae" (*Amores* II.6.34). Late Latin and mediaeval poets often turn birds into musical
instruments or human musicians. Sedulius makes them little organs: "Tempora veris
celebrant crespante sussurro,/ Produnt organulis tempora veris aves" (*Poetae Latini
Aevi Carolini*, ed. Traube [Berlin, 1896], III, 227). John of Garland has them playing
cithers while the organ plays a requiem (G. Mari, "Poetris magistri Johannis Anglici
de arte prosayca metrica et rithmica," *Rom. Forsch.*, XIII [1902], 894). St. Jerome
in a prose account of spring describes them as singing psalms (*Epistulae*, ed. Hilberg
[Vienna, 1910], XLIII, 3). In the *Carmina Burana*, there is a poem describing the
nightingale as a cither-player: "Citharizat cantico dulcis philomena" (eds. Hilka and
Schumann [Heidelberg, 1951], poem 138, st. 4, 1.1); elsewhere in the same collection,
birds are said to sing to the drum, the psalter, the lyre, and the viol (92.60–64), or
"melodia sonant garrule" (151.2). Alanus de Insulis relates them to sirens and gives
them many musical duties: "Syrenes nemorum, cytharistae veris, in illum/ Convenere
locum, mellitaque carmina sparsim/ Commentantur aves, dum gutturis organa pul-

89

sant./ Pingunt ore lyram, dum cantus imbibit istos/ Auditus, dulces effert sonus auribus escas" (*Anticlaudianus, The Minor Anglo-Latin Satirists*, ed. Wright [London, 1872], II, 276). The idea that birds are poets as well as authors is suggested in early Italian literature: "E gli augelleti riprendon lor lena/ E fanno dolci versi in loro usanza" (*Early Italian Literature*, ed. Grillo [London, 1920], I, 213).

23. *Hexameron* (*PL*, XIV, 255).

24. *Expositio in Psalterium* (*PL*, CXX, 817).

25. Pseudo-Jerome, *Expositio* (*PL*, XXIII, 1529).

26. *PL*, LXXVI, 527–28. This account is followed with expansions by Hugo of St. Victor in *De Bestis Aliis et Rebus* (*PL*, CLXXVII, 33–35); see also St. Eucherius, *Formulae spiritalis* (*PL*, L, 750); Rupertus, *Commentarius in Job* (*PL*, CLXVIII, 1163); and *Le Bestiare*, ed. Walberg (Paris, 1900), 11.230–313.

27. *PL*, XVI, 1473.

28. Vaughan's "dark Ægyptian border," which also appears in "The Relapse" as "a thick, Egyptian damp" (p. 433) has a symbolism of sin and sinners; see Tertullian, *De Spectaculis* (*PL*, I, 635); and St. Prosper, *Psalmorum . . . Expositio* (*PL*, LI, 326).

29. *Carmina*, ed. Dressel (Leipzig, 1860), pp. 4–9.

30. *PL*, LXXXVI, 935.

31. J.-F. Gergier, *Lyricus Sacer* (Bensaçon, 1889), R, poem 21.

32. J. Santolius, *Hymni Sacri et Novi* (Paris, 1698), p. 192.

33. Paulus Albarus, *Carmina*, ed. Traube, *PLAC* (Berlin, 1896), III, 128.

34. Milo, *Carmina, PLAC*, III, 582–84, 661.

35. III.332. There is an enigma on the cock by Tatwin (Wright, II, 543) in which the bird is associated with adventual prophecies.

36. *The Oxford Book of Medieval Latin Verse*, ed. Gaslee (Oxford, 1925), pp. 178–80.

37. See Chapter Two.

38. *Theaetetus* 197C.

39. *Enneads* V.9.1, 6–21.

40. *Prolegomena* (*PL*, LXVI, 196).

41. *Dialogi* (*PL*, LXXVII, 336).

42. *Op. cit.*, p. 338.

43. See Rabanus Maurus (*PL*, CXII, 871); Rupertus (*PL*, CLXVIII, 294); Garnerus de St. Victor, (*PL*, CXCIII, 65).

44. *Bis. Accus.* 5.

45. *Ad Nationes* (*PL*, I, 589).

46. *Contra Celsum* (*PG*, XI, 1294).

47. *Commentarius in Epistolam ad Romanos* (*PG*, LX, 414).

48. *Graecorum Affectionum Curatio* (*PG*, LXXXIII, 1006).

49. *Institutiones Divinae* (*PL*, VI, 417).

50. Plato, *Opera* (Lyons, 1548), p. 333.

51. *Commentationes* (Bologna, 1496), p. 134r.

52. *Pythagorae Symbolorum Interpretatio*, in *Opera* (Leyden, 1696), II, 659–60.

53. See *The Works of Thomas Vaughan*, ed. Waite (London, 1919), pp. 81–82, 266–67.

FREDSON BOWERS

Henry Vaughan's
Multiple Time Scheme

Henry Vaughan built up his poems by a series of interpenetrating al-
legories, each one of which is likely to have more than a single level of
significance. We do violence to the texture of this closely knit thought,
then, if we attempt to analyze any one part of it independently. We also
do an injustice, for no one allegorical theme or subject in Vaughan is
self-sufficient. If we start to unravel any thread in the texture of his
thought, we logically end only when the last knot of the whole has
slipped free.

So much for a warning, since this note is concerned with a single
thread: with Vaughan's use of a multiple time scheme as one of the
layers of his allegory. Central to the whole question is the equation of
time with space in his major allegory of the pilgrimage. This pilgrimage
opens up different layers of time, since it may represent one day in the
life of a man; this one day may stand for the man's whole lifetime; the
life of a man may represent one day in the history of the race of mankind;
and man's whole history itself on earth to date may typify only one day
in his great pilgrimage from the Day of Creation to the Day of Judgment.

Vaughan's special interpretation of the pilgrimage seems to depend
upon the verse from Hebrews that he affixed to his poem "The Pilgrimage": *"And they Confessed, that they were strangers, and Pilgrims on the earth."*
Man is a stranger because his proper home is Heaven, and he is a

Reprinted, by permission of the publisher, from *Modern Language Quarterly*, 23 (1962),
291–96.

traveler on the earth in order to return to his home: "So strengthen me, Lord, all the way,/ That I may travel to thy Mount" ("The Pilgrimage," 465).[1] His heavenly home is a place of light, for light is the basic attribute of divinity. Thus in "The Pilgrimage," as in other poems, the world is like night in comparison to the heavenly day. Man's eye (the traditional window of the soul) is darkened by the sins of the flesh after the Fall:

> in these veyls my Ecclips'd Eye
> May not approach thee, (for at night
> Who can have commerce with the light?)
> ("Vanity of Spirit," 419)

Since the Fall, the earth is a "land of darkness and blinde eyes" ("The Night," 522):

> A neast of nights, a gloomie sphere,
> Where shadowes thicken, and the Cloud
> Sits on the Suns brow all the yeare,
> And nothing moves without a shrowd.
> ("Death," 399)

Through the ancient union of Sin with Death, this night in which the sinful world lingers is "the shadow of death" (Job x.21). But there is a sun to restore the light. Christ the Son is, conventionally, typified by the sun. Hence the dawn of every day prefigures the salvation that Christ offers to His faithful, and their restoration to their true home in Heaven where the cycle of night and day, sin and cleansing, has no part, but all is bathed in the light of one everlasting day.

At the lowest level of Vaughan's allegorical time scheme, then, the twenty-four hour revolution of the sun represents one day in the devout man's life. During the hours of light, like the plant or the tree he should put forth the leaves of his good deeds, for these deeds represent the labors of the day. When night comes, the pious man will watch and pray. He will take Christ for his bedfellow and will awake with Him. If, on waking, one's first thoughts are of Christ, "so shall thou keep / Him company all day, and in him sleep" ("Rules and Lessons," 436). The succession of busy days and pious nights builds up to a life of Christian effort; and when the great night of death overtakes the soul, the dawn of heavenly light will immediately follow.

In this manner the working hours of light in a single day come to stand for the individual man's good deeds throughout his lifetime, and the pious prayers and religious sleep of the ensuing night typify the painless coming-on of the night of death and the easy transition to the eternal dawn that follows. This is one part of what Vaughan means in "Rules *and* Lessons":

> *Mornings* are *Mysteries*; the first worlds *Youth*,
> Mans *Resurrection*, and the futures *Bud*
> Shrowd in their births.   (436)

In the world two paths or tracks meet. "The *One* of goodness, peace and life, / The *other* of death, sin and strife" ("The Ass," 518). Man has the free-will to choose either path, and if through Love he unlocks the "little gate" ("Repentance," 448), he enters upon Christ's "Sacred way" (479) which is "the path unto the house of light" ("Cock-crowing," 488). In the end, after all the foul roads, "dark hills, swift streames, and steep ways / As smooth as glasse" (423), the path leads from the earth "Above the stars, a track unknown, and high" ("*Isaacs Marriage*," 409), until the pilgrim at last reaches "that plaine... From whence th' Inlightned spirit sees / That shady City of Palme trees" ("The Retreate," 419).

Vaughan imagines this pilgrimage in a simultaneous double time sense. He had called mornings "the first worlds *Youth*" by analogy with the dawn of the first day during the Creation when the sun was placed in the heavens and itself became a pilgrim. The childhood of mankind followed on the creation, or "birth," of Adam and Eve; and their life in Eden coincided with the youth of the world when, figuratively, all were sunshine days and there was no night of sin. After the Fall sin drew the clouds of night across the sky, and the unobstructed sun threw its rays on Eden no more. Thus a post-lapsarian man in the dawn of his own birth is, paradoxically, exiled from heaven to a land of darkness and night through which he travels on pilgrimage, and it is only when his own night, or death, comes to him that he can be born again in the dawn of heaven. (For this reason children who died young, corresponding in their innocence to mankind still in Eden, found the path of their pilgrimage smooth and even, and could "by meer playing go to Heaven" ["Childe-hood," 520].)

The pilgrimage of the race of mankind also begins in the darkness of sin that followed on Adam's expulsion from Eden and his sunshine days there. As in the Hebrews quotation, Adam himself was a stranger in the world to which he had been thrust. The pilgrimage of his descendants, that is of mankind, required them to travel the ages through the world to recover their lost Paradise. The stages of this pilgrimage are delineated in "Mans fall, and Recovery."

> Farewell you Everlasting hills! I'm Cast
> Here under Clouds, where stormes, and tempests blast
> This sully'd flowre
> Rob'd of your Calme.   (411)

Continuing the Eden-Heaven parallel, Vaughan's pre-Mosaic man laments:

> I've lost
> A traine of lights, which in those Sun-shine dayes
> Were my sure guides, and only with me stayes
> (Unto my cost,)
> One sullen beame, whose charge is to dispense
> More punishment, than knowledge to my sense.
>   (411–12)

This state of darkness endured for two thousand years until the institution of the Old Law under Moses. It is true that the Old Law was not a law of salvation but one of punishment, and it is true that as a consequence "sinne tooke strength, and vigour from the Law" (412). Nevertheless, inherent in the Old Law was the Promise of ultimate reconciliation for the chosen seed, and for this reason even though Vaughan compares the history of mankind under the Old Law to a night, the darkness is not absolute as before. True, the veil of clouds that ushers in the night has been drawn across the heavens to intervene between God's light and the earth, and this veil is to be associated with the Old Law. Yet there is a "weake *Shine*" ("Resurrection and Immortality," 402) through the veil; and, indeed, in "Faith" Vaughan describes the reign of the Old Law as

> A glorious night,
> Where Stars, and Clouds, both light, and shade
> Had equal right.   (451)

It is this light of the Promise that leads Vaughan to link the early wanderings of the Jews with man's pilgrimage and to call them

> those first and blessed swains [who]
> Were pilgrims on the those plains
> When they receiv'd the promise.
> ("The Shepheards," 471)

Christ's crucifixion was "Under that stately and mysterious cloud / Which his death scatter'd" ("Jacobs Pillow, and Pillar," 527). His resurrection thereupon becomes the dawning sun of a new day:

> Then did he shine forth, whose sad fall,
> And bitter fights
> Were figur'd in those mystical,
> And Cloudie Rites.
> ("Faith," 451)

Under this New Covenant of salvation, Christ's blood broke the stone tablets of the Mosaic covenant:

> This makes me span
> My fathers journeys, and in one faire step
> O're all their pilgrimage, and labours leap,
> For God (made man,)
> Reduc'd th'Extent of works of faith; so made
> Of their *Red Sea*, a *Spring*; I wash, they wade.
> ("Mans fall, and Recovery," 412)

Although the application is partly to the individual, I take it that the "me" here is really mankind. The long painful years of the pilgrimage under the Old Law are over, and with a vast new spring forward, man has grasped at offered salvation.

We are now in a position to recapitulate for a moment before pressing on to the final layer of the allegorical time sequence. Vaughan's direct association of day and the divine sun makes the rotation of day and night a perpetual allegory in which the light of saving grace is welcomed at every dawn. With each day's labor and pious sleep, man enacts in little his lifetime of good works and the quiet sleep of death that will usher him through the clouds to eternal light. In its progress from dawn to dark, the day itself prefigures the year with its seasons of warmth and cold, of growth and decay, life and death, all of which Vaughan allegorizes in some of his most moving Nature poetry. The growth of a man from childhood to old age is also typified by the passage of the hours from dawn to dark, and thence of the days to weeks, and to the twelve months.

This history of mankind on earth after his innocent childhood in the sunshine light of Eden, followed by his cold aging in the dark and winter-stormy world of sin under a law of punishment, is also a pilgrimage exactly like the pilgrimage through life of the individual man. This constant equation of the individual's life with the history of the race of mankind is an important key to Vaughan's thought. Without it, the double nature of childhood cannot be grasped. Vaughan knows himself for a child of the New Law, whereas his fathers lived under the Old. When he writes so delightfully of childhood, then, his nostalgia for lost innocence is not concentrated alone on any single, mortal child, but it refers simultaneously, as well, to the bright childhood of mankind in Eden before the dark Old Law was imposed after the Fall. In truth, Vaughan can strive back toward the innocence of his own childhood and, in one of his pilgrimage phrases, "love a backward motion," only because under the New Law his own childhood typifies Eden before the mistakes of free-will of his maturity duplicated the Fall of Adam.

In "Rules *and* Lessons" Vaughan had written,

> *Mornings* are *Mysteries*; the first worlds *Youth*,
> Mans *Resurrection*, and the futures *Bud*
> Shrowd in their births.   (436)

We have seen the equation of the first world's youth with man's resurrection under the multiple allegory of the sun's diurnal passage. We come, finally, to "mornings are the bud of the future." Vaughan had written, in "The Search,"

> I see a Rose
> Bud in the bright East, and disclose
> The Pilgrim-Sunne.   (405)

This is a heavily symbolic passage, in which Christ the Sun is the Rose, and it would seem that the buds, as conventionally, are his wounds from which come salvation. Christ the Sun, in one time scheme, not only brought the dawn of the New Law to mankind to speed its pilgrimage through time; as the Sun, Christ also will usher in the dawn of the last day of that historic pilgrimage, the Day of Judgment. This Day of Judgment—and its consequences—are the future's bud that should be allegorized from the dawn of any day on earth; and in this last day Vaughan extends the time scheme to its farthest limits—the end of the world. On Judgment Day, Christ is no longer prefigured by the natural sun. It is not the natural sun that rises on this great Day, but Christ Himself:

> So when that day, and hour shal come
> In which thy self wil be the Sun,
> Thou'lt find me drest and on my way,
> Watching the Break of thy great day.
>
> ("The Dawning," 452)

To Vaughan, the Day of Judgment was not a day of horror, but instead one of utmost joy, for it meant the final defeat of sin and the end of man's long pilgrimage to his heavenly home, not as an individual but as a race.

This concept brings to a close his mystical time scheme, for in the long day of eternity after Judgment the allegory of the diurnal round of the sun and its seasonal progress can have no place. Thus at one time Vaughan writes that this ultimate Sun in eternity "shall never set" ("Death," 400). But even a sun that never sets proved inadequate for Vaughan's greatest moment of insight. The denial of setting still contains the idea of setting, a concept that cannot for a moment be admitted for the great light of God now freely shining forth to all. (It is like defining good as the absence of evil.)

Hence even the divine Sun that "tramples on" ("The Recovery," 645) the natural sun is too dim a comparison, and indeed its very name brings in connotations of a setting that cannot be in eternity. So Vaughan gathers all his powers, and in "Resurrection and Immortality," awaiting the Judgment, he cries in the night of the world and his sin:

> *Would it were Day!*
> One everlasting *Saboth* there shall runne
> Without *Succession*, and . . .
> [in the last moment of mystical ecstasy]
> without a Sunne.   (402)

Notes

1. All references are to pages in Volume II of the *Works of Henry Vaughan*, ed. L. C. Martin (Oxford, 1914).

LOUIS L. MARTZ

Henry Vaughan: The Man Within

The earlier poets in the English meditative tradition, Southwell, Alabaster, Donne, Herbert, and Crashaw, were all poets of Catholic or Anglo-Catholic tendency, where the Continental art of meditation found a fertile ground in which to develop an English counterpart.[1] It is significant that all five of these earlier poets became priests: Southwell, bred and executed as a Catholic; Alabaster, shifting from Anglican to Catholic to Anglican; Donne, born and bred a Catholic, but turning finally to the English Church; Crashaw, born and bred a Protestant, but turning finally to the Roman Church; and Herbert, happy all his life within the English communion. They had their doctrinal differences, and I do not wish to minimize those differences; but they had something more in common: a devotion to the central mysteries of the Passion, a devotion to the symbols and a liturgy that served to celebrate those mysteries. All would have agreed with George Herbert's vision of "The Agonie":

> Who knows not Love, let him assay
> And taste that juice, which on the crosse a pike
> Did set again abroach; then let him say
> If ever he did taste the like.
> Love is that liquour sweet and most divine,
> Which my God feels as bloud; but I, as wine.

But with Crashaw's death in 1649 this kind of eucharistic vision died away in English poetry of the seventeenth century: 1649, a highly significant date, being also the year that saw the execution of King

Reprinted, by permission of the publisher, from *Publications of the Modern Language Association of America*, 78 (1963), 40–49.

Charles. In 1650 appeared Henry Vaughan's *Silex Scintillans*, marking in its central symbols and central inspiration one of those sudden and drastic mutations that occur in human affairs from time to time. I should like here to consider the poetry of Henry Vaughan as a symbol of this vital transformation.

It is important to begin by looking closely at *Silex Scintillans*, 1650. For Vaughan's enlarged volume of 1655, with its second part and its greatly expanded opening matter, presents us with a modified outlook, a less consistent fabric, and a weaker body of poetry— despite the fact that some half-dozen of Vaughan's finest poems did not appear until 1655. The common charges against Vaughan's poetry—that his poems often begin with a flash of power, but then dwindle off into flat and tedious rumination, that he works by fits and starts, and lacks sustained powers of construction—such charges find their chief support in Book II of *Silex*, which reveals many signs of a failing inspiration. But the volume of 1650 is a whole, like Herbert's *Temple*; and indeed there are many signs that the volume was deliberately designed as a sequel, a counterpart, and a tribute to Herbert's book.

Vaughan's subtitle is exactly the same as Herbert's: "Sacred Poems and Private Ejaculations"; but the main title represents a vast difference, enforced, in the 1650 volume alone, by the engraved title-page presenting the emblem of the Flashing Flint—the stony heart weeping, bleeding, and flaming from the hand of God that strikes direct from the clouds, steel against flint. Furthermore, if we look closely at this flinty heart, we may see something that I never noticed until my friend Professor Evelyn Hutchinson, examining this title-page with his scientific eye, asked, "Do you see a human face peering forth from within the heart?" It is certainly so: a man within can be clearly seen through an opening in the heart's wall. And facing this we have, again in the 1650 volume only, an intimate confession in the form of a Latin poem, explaining the emblem. Perhaps a literal version of this cryptic Latin will show how essential this poem and this emblem are for an understanding of the 1650 volume as a whole:

> The Author's Emblem (concerning himself)
> You have often touched me, I confess, without a wound,
> and your *Voice*, without a voice, has often sought to counsel
> me; your diviner breath has encompassed me with its calm
> motion, and in vain has cautioned me with its sacred murmur.
> I was deaf and dumb: a *Flint*: You (how great care you take

99

of your own!) try to revive another way, you change the Remedy; and now angered you say that *Love* has no power, and you prepare to conquer force with *Force*, you come closer, you break through the *Rocky* barrier of my heart, and it is made *Flesh* that was before a *Stone*. Behold me torn asunder! and at last the *Fragments* burning toward your skies, and the cheeks streaming with tears out of the *Adamant*. Thus once upon a time you made the *Rocks* flow and the *Crags* gush, oh ever provident of your people! How marvellous toward me is your hand! In *Dying*, I have been born again; and in the midst of my *shattered means* I am now *richer*.[2]

At once, after this story of a sudden, violent illumination, comes the short and simple poem headed, like the opening poem of Herbert's *Temple*, "The Dedication";[3] it contains a number of verbal echoes of Herbert and the whole tone and manner of the poem represents a perfect distillation of Herbert's intimate mode of colloquy:

> Some drops of thy all-quickening bloud
> Fell on my heart, these made it bud
> And put forth thus, though, Lord, before
> The ground was curs'd, and void of store.

These three elements, then: engraved title-page, Latin confession, and Herbertian Dedication form the utterly adequate preface to *Silex Scintillans*, 1650; they prepare us for a volume that will have two dominating themes. First, we will have the record and results of the experience of sudden illumination; and second, we will have a tribute to the poetry of George Herbert, which, it seems, played an important part in preparing the way for, or cultivating, Vaughan's peculiar experience. Thus, toward the middle of Vaughan's volume, after hundreds of unmistakable echoes of Herbert in title, phrasing, theme, and stanza- form,[4] Vaughan at last openly acknowledges his debt by accepting the invitation of Herbert's poem "Obedience," where Herbert offers his poetry as a written deed conveying himself to God, with this conclusion:

> He that will passe his land,
> As I have mine, may set his hand
> And heart unto this Deed, when he hath read;
> And make the purchase spread
> To both our goods, if he to it will stand.

> How happie were my part,
>   If some kinde man would thrust his heart
> Into these lines; till in heav'ns Court of Rolls
>   They were by winged souls
>   Entred for both, farre above their desert!

Vaughan, in "The Match," answers in Herbert's own mode of familiar address:

> Dear friend! whose holy, ever-living lines
>   Have done much good
>   To many, and have checkt my blood,
> My fierce, wild blood that still heaves, and inclines,
>   But is still tam'd
>   By those bright fires which thee inflam'd;
> Here I joyn hands, and thrust my stubborn heart
>   Into thy *Deed*...

As we look back, this joining of hands and hearts between Vaughan and Herbert is almost equally evident in the opening poem of the volume proper: "Regeneration." Here the allegorical mode of the painful quest, the imagery of struggling upward toward a "pinacle" where disappointment lies, the sudden cry mysteriously heard upon this hill, and even some aspects of the stanza-form—all these things show a poem that begins by playing skilful variations on Herbert's poem "The Pilgrimage," which leads the speaker through "the wilde of Passion" toward the hill suggesting Calvary:

> When I had gain'd the brow and top,
> A lake of brackish waters on the ground
>   Was all I found.
>
> With that abash'd and struck with many a sting
>   Of swarming fears,
>   I fell, and cry'd, Alas my King!
>   Can both the way and end be tears?
> Yet taking heart I rose, and then perceiv'd
>   I was deceiv'd:
>
> My hill was further: so I flung away,
>   Yet heard a crie
> Just as I went, *None goes that way*
> *And lives*: If that be all, said I,

> After so foul a journey death is fair,
> And but a chair.

But Vaughan's pilgrimage has quite a different theme: in the fourth stanza the Herbertian echoes fade out, as Vaughan's pilgrim is called away into an interior region of the soul, here imaged with the combination of natural and Biblical landscape that often marks Vaughan at his best:

> With that, some cryed, *Away*; straight I
> Obey'd, and led
> Full East, a faire, fresh field could spy
> Some call'd it, *Jacobs Bed*;
> A Virgin-soile, which no
> Rude feet ere trod,
> Where (since he stept there,) only go
> Prophets, and friends of God.

The allusion to Jacob's vision and journey toward the East (Genesis xxviii.10–22; xxix.1) is only the first of many such allusions by Vaughan to the "early days" of the Old Testament; here the scene begins an allegorical account of the mysterious workings of grace; the pilgrim enters into a state of interior illumination, where he is prepared to apprehend the presence of God and to hear the voice of the Lord. In the remaining six stanzas the setting mysteriously changes to another landscape, a springtime scene, where a grove contains a garden with a fountain; the state of grace is imaged by combining the natural imagery of spring with subtle echoes of the most famous of all spring-songs: the Song of Solomon. The key to these stanzas is given by Vaughan himself in a verse from the Canticle appended to the poem: "Arise O North, and come thou South-wind, and blow upon my garden, that the spices thereof may flow out." It is the Garden of the Soul: one of the great central symbols in the Christian literature of meditation and contemplation. For Vaughan's poem here we need to recall especially the four verses of the Canticle (iv. 12–15) that immediately precede Vaughan's citation:

> A garden inclosed is my sister, my spouse; a spring shut up, a fountain sealed.
> Thy plants are an orchard of pomegranates, with pleasant fruits; camphire, with spikenard,

Spikenard and saffron; calamus and cinnamon, with all
trees of frankincense; myrrh and aloes, with all the chief spices:
A fountain of gardens, a well of living waters, and streams
from Lebanon.

So in Vaughan's spiritual landscape "The aire was all in spice," while

Only a little Fountain lent
Some use for Eares,
And on the dumbe shades language spent
The Musick of her teares;
I drew her neere, and found
The Cisterne full
Of divers stones, some bright, and round
Others ill-shap'd, and dull.

The first (pray marke,) as quick as light
Danc'd through the floud,
But, th'last more heavy then the night
Nail'd to the Center stood;

Vaughan is developing his favorite image-cluster of light and darkness
through symbols that suggest one of his favorite Biblical passages: the
third chapter of St. John's gospel, where Nicodemus hears the words of
Jesus by night:

Except a man be born of water and of the Spirit, he cannot
enter into the kingdom of God.
That which is born of the flesh is flesh; and that which
is born of the Spirit is spirit.

So in Vaughan's allegory, the spiritual part of man is here reborn, made
bright and "quick" as light; while the fleshly part remains dull and
heavy, nailed to the earth. Much the same significance is found in the
following scene, where in a bank of flowers, representing his own interior
state, the speaker finds

Some fast asleepe, others broad-eyed
And taking in the Ray...

And finally, all the images and themes of this poem coalesce with a
three-fold allusion to the "winds" of grace: the "rushing mighty wind"
of Pentecost (Acts ii.2), the winds that are prayed for in Vaughan's
quotation from the Canticle, and the wind described in the words of

Jesus to Nicodemus: "The wind bloweth where it listeth, and thou hearest the sound thereof, but canst not tell whence it cometh, and whither it goeth: so is every one that is born of the Spirit." And so the poem concludes:

> Here musing long, I heard
> A rushing wind
> Which still increas'd, but whence it stirr'd
> No where I could not find;
>
> I turn'd me round, and to each shade
> Dispatch'd an Eye,
> To see, if any leafe had made
> Least motion, or Reply,
> But while I listning sought
> My mind to ease
> By knowing, where 'twas, or where not,
> It whisper'd; *Where I please.*
>
> Lord, then said I, *On me one breath,*
> *And let me dye before my death!*

So the poem,[5] like dozens of others by Vaughan, begins with echoes of George Herbert, whose simplicity of language and intimacy of tone pervade the whole poem and the whole volume of 1650; but, like all of Vaughan's better poems, "Regeneration" moves away from Herbert to convey its own unique experience through its own rich combination of materials, in which we may discern three dominant fields of reference: the Bible; external Nature; and the interior motions of the Self. There is in "Regeneration" not a single reference that could be called eucharistic. Yet Herbert opened the central body of his poems with an emblematic Altar, typographically displayed upon the page, and he followed this with the long eucharistic meditation entitled "The Sacrifice," where he develops the meaning of the Passion through a variation on the ancient Reproaches of Christ, spoken from the Cross as part of the Good Friday service. Nothing could speak more eloquently of the vast difference between these two poets.

At the outset of his *Temple* Herbert gave seventy-seven stanzas of epigrammatic advice on how to lead a good life, under the title, "The Church-porch"; these stanzas form a preparation for the mental communion that constitutes the heart of Herbert's central body of poetry, "The Church," as he makes plain by these lines on the threshold:

Thou, whom the former precepts have
Sprinkled and taught, how to behave
Thy self in church; approach, and taste
The churches mysticall repast.

Now Henry Vaughan also has a group of stanzas in this epigrammatic form, under the title "Rules and Lessons"; they come exactly in the center of the 1650 volume, as though the advice there given formed the center of the volume's devotional life. But Vaughan's advice bears no relation to any ecclesiastical symbolism; there is no reference to the Passion. It is as though the earthly church had vanished, and man were left to work alone with God. I think it is worth remembering that by 1650 Vaughan's earthly Church of England had in fact vanished: Vaughan's twin-brother Thomas, the parish priest of Vaughan's own church, was evicted from his post in 1650; and the post remained vacant for nearly eight years. At any rate, Vaughan's rules and lessons for the devout life lay down, in twenty-four stanzas, certain ways of individual communion with God in every hour of the day, from early morning, through the worldly work of midday, and on through night, until the next day's awakening: one couplet gives the essence of the rules:

A sweet *self-privacy* in a right soul
Out-runs the Earth, and lines the utmost pole.

Man's duty is to cultivate the inner self, using as aids the two "books" that we have seen in "Regeneration": the Book of Nature, and the Book of Scripture, as Vaughan suggests in his advice for morning devotions:

Walk with thy fellow-creatures: note the *hush*
And *whispers* amongst them. There's not a *Spring*,
Or *Leafe* but hath his *Morning-hymn*; Each *Bush*
And *Oak* doth know *I AM*; canst thou not sing?
O leave thy Cares, and follies! go this way
And thou art sure to prosper all the day.

Serve God before the world; let him not go
Until thou hast a blessing, then resigne
The whole unto him; and remember who
Prevail'd by *wrestling* ere the *Sun* did *shine*.
Poure *Oyle* upon the *stones*, weep for thy sin,
Then journey on, and have an eie to heav'n.

Note the rich and curious complex of the Biblical and the natural: the allusion to the bush from which Moses heard the voice of God; the extended reference to the occasion when Jacob wrestled with the mysterious stranger "until the breaking of the day," when he won the stranger's blessing, and knew at last that he had "seen God face to face" (Genesis xxxii.24–30); and the shorter allusion to the familiar scene of Jacob's vision, after which "Jacob rose up early in the morning, and took the stone that he had put for his pillows, and set it up for a pillar, and poured oil upon the top of it" (Genesis xxviii.18).

The Bible, Nature, and the Self thus come together in a living harmony, as we see in Vaughan's poem "Religion," a poem that, typically, seems to take its rise from Herbert's poem "Decay":

> My God, when I walke in those groves,
> And leaves thy spirit doth still fan,
> I see in each shade that there growes
> An angell talking with a man.
>
> Under a *Juniper*, some house,
> Or the coole *Mirtles* canopie,
> Others beneath an *Oakes* greene boughs,
> Or at some *fountaines* bubling Eye;
>
> Here *Jacob* dreames, and wrestles; there
> *Elias* by a Raven is fed,
> Another time by th' Angell, where
> He brings him water with his bread;
>
> In *Abr'hams* Tent the winged guests
> (O how familiar then was heaven!)
> Eate, drinke, discourse, sit downe, and rest
> Untill the Coole, and shady *Even*...

We must read several stanzas before it becomes clear that the "leaves" here are essentially the leaves of the Bible,[6] where the self can learn to live intimately with God; but at the same time the vivid apprehension of natural life here may suggest that nature itself is still inspired by the divine presence.

The fact that Vaughan so often, in his best poems, seeks out these individual ways of communion with God does not mean that he chooses to neglect or ignore traditional devotions to the Eucharist. On the contrary, Vaughan is acutely aware of the importance of the eucharistic allusions in Herbert's *Temple*, for he makes frequent efforts to follow

Herbert's central mode of mental communion. But he does not often succeed, as we may see in four sizeable poems in the 1650 volume that are devoted to eucharistic celebration. His poem "The Passion" is an extended effort to meditate upon the traditional themes, but the poem is wooden, labored, and forced in its effect. One may perhaps trace one cause of this failure to the fact that Vaughan does not visualize the Passion "as if he were present," in the ancient tradition of such meditations; instead, he puts the whole occasion in the past. He does not memorialize the Passion as a present reality. In another poem, "Dressing," he performs a preparation for "Thy mysticall *Communion*," but the poem is so worried by contemporary doctrinal quarrels that it ends with a bitter attack on Puritan views, and not with any devotional presence. Another poem, entitled "The Holy Communion," begins by echoing the first two lines of George Herbert's eucharistic poem, "The Banquet": "Welcome sweet, and sacred feast; welcome life!" but Vaughan's poem immediately veers away from the feast to ponder the action of grace within the self, and the operation of God's creative power over the entire universe.

Vaughan's one and only success in this kind of poetic celebration comes significantly in his poem "The Sap," where he approaches the Eucharist indirectly, through a tale told to himself by his inmost self:

> Come sapless Blossom, creep not stil on Earth
>   Forgetting thy first birth;
> 'Tis not from dust, or if so, why dost thou
>   Thus cal and thirst for dew?
> It tends not thither, if it doth, why then
>   This growth and stretch for heav'n? . . .
> Who plac'd thee here, did something then Infuse
>   Which now can tel thee news.
> There is beyond the Stars an hil of myrrh
>   From which some drops fal here,
> On it the Prince of *Salem* sits, who deals
>   To thee thy secret meals . . .
> Yet liv'd he here sometimes, and bore for thee
>   A world of miserie . . .
> But going hence, and knowing wel what woes
>   Might his friends discompose,
> To shew what strange love he had to our good
>   He gave his sacred bloud
> By wil our sap, and Cordial; now in this

> Lies such a heav'n of bliss,
> That, who but truly tasts it, no decay
> Can touch him any way . . .

The whole poem, as several readers have pointed out, bears some resemblance to Herbert's poem "Peace," but the contrasts are more significant. In Herbert's poem the seeker after peace comes upon a "rev'rend good old man" who tells him the story of "a Prince of old" who "At Salem dwelt"—alluding to Christ under the figure of Melchizedek, who "Brought forth bread and wine" (Genesis xiv.18; Hebrews vii). Herbert's poem presents an allegory of the apostolic succession: the "good old man" offers the bread of life derived from the "twelve stalks of wheat" that sprang out of Christ's grave:

> Take of this grain, which in my garden grows,
> And grows for you;
> Make bread of it: and that repose
> And peace, which ev'ry where
> With so much earnestnesse you do pursue,
> Is onely there.

But Vaughan does not end his poem with such an echo of the ecclesiastical ritual; instead he closes with what appears to be yet another tribute to the poems of George Herbert, as he seems to echo here at least four of Herbert's eucharistic poems:[7]

> Then humbly take
> This balm for souls that ake,
> And one who drank it thus, assures that you
> Shal find a Joy so true,
> Such perfect Ease, and such a lively sense
> Of grace against all sins,
> That you'l Confess the Comfort such, as even
> Brings to, and comes from Heaven.

But this comfort remains, in Vaughan's poetry, a promise and a hope: his central channels of communion lie elsewhere, channels with a long and venerable history.

Perhaps my discussion of Vaughan's favorite triad, Bible, Nature, and Self, has already suggested the three "books" cultivated by the medieval Augustinians, and especially by St. Bonaventure: The Book of Scripture, The Book of Nature, and the Book of the Soul.[8] The three books are, essentially, one: the revelation given us in the Bible shows man how to read, first nature, and then his own soul. That is to say, in Augustinian terms, man, enlightened by Biblical revelation, can grasp the Vestiges, the "traces," of God in external nature; and from this knowledge he can then turn inward to find the Image of God within himself.[9] It is an Image defaced by sin, but with its essential powers restored by the sacrifice of Christ. Man is not simply fallen: he is fallen and redeemed. It is man's responsibility, with the omnipresent help of Grace, to clear and renew this Image, until it may become a true Similitude. But the journey of renewal can never be wholly accomplished in this life: thus, as in "Regeneration," the poems that relate Vaughan's journey of the mind toward God end with a cry for help, a prayer for some momentary glimpse of perfection, as in his "Vanity of Spirit," where he performs a journey very much akin to Bonaventure's *Itinerarium*, first searching through all Nature, and then finding at last within himself

> A peece of much antiquity,
> With Hyerogliphicks quite dismembred,
> And broken letters scarce remembred.
> I tooke them up, and (much Joy'd,) went about
> T' unite those peeces, hoping to find out
> The mystery; but this neer done,
> That little light I had was gone:
> It griev'd me much. At last, said I,
> *Since in these veyls my Ecclips'd Eye*
> *May not approach thee, (for at night*
> *Who can have commerce with the light?)*
> *I'le disapparell, and to buy*
> *But one half glaunce, most gladly dye.*

In this effort to piece together broken letters scarce remembered, by the aid of an interior light, we have the essential action of that kind of meditation which may be termed Augustinian. Its finest explanation is still the one most easily available, and one certainly well known to Vaughan: it lies in the great climactic section of St. Augustine's *Confessions*, the chapters of the tenth book (vi–xxvii) where he marvels at and meditates upon the power of Memory. If we read and reread these chapters, we may come to feel them acting more and more as a commentary upon the poems of *Silex Scintillans*, 1650; and we may come to understand more clearly the ways in which Vaughan's finest poetry draws its strength from the great central tradition of Platonic Christianity.

The Augustinian meditation begins, as Vaughan's volume of 1650 begins, with an effort to apprehend the meaning of an experience of sudden illumination: "percussisti cor meum verbo tuo, et amavi te"— "Thou hast strucken my heart with thy word, and therupon I loved thee.... What now do I love, whenas I love thee?"

> not the beauty of any *corporall thing*, not the order of times; not the brightnesse of the *light*, which to behold, is so gladsome to our eyes: not the pleasant *melodies* of songs of all kinds; not the fragrant smell of flowers, and oyntments, and spices: not *Manna* and honey, nor any *fayre limbs* that are so acceptable to fleshly embracements.
>
> I love none of these things, whenas I love my God: and yet I love a certaine kinde of *light*, and a kind of *voyce*, and a kinde of *fragrancy*, and a kinde of *meat*, and a kind of *embracement*. Whenas I love my God; who is both the *light*, and the voyce, and the sweet *smell*, and the *meate*, and the *embracement* of my inner man: where that *light* shineth unto my soule, which no place can receive; that *voyce* soundeth, which time deprives me not of; and that fragrancy *smelleth*, which no wind scatters ...
> This is it which I love, when as I love my God.[10]

Here is the spiritual landscape of the redeemed soul, described by Vaughan in his "Regeneration," glimpsed throughout his volume in the many fresh images from nature that he uses to relate the experience, and summed up once again for us near the close of the volume, in the poem "Mount of Olives." This title represents a traditional symbol of the soul's retirement to prayer and meditation, here to recall, like Augustine, the moment which gave his life its meaning:

> When first I saw true beauty, and thy Joys
> Active as light, and calm without all noise
> Shin'd on my soul, I felt through all my powr's
> Such a rich air of sweets, as Evening showrs
> Fand by a gentle gale Convey and breath
> On some parch'd bank, crown'd with a flowrie wreath;
> Odors, and Myrrh, and balm in one rich floud
> O'r-ran my heart, and spirited my bloud ...
> I am so warm'd now by this glance on me,
> That, midst all storms I feel a Ray of thee;

> So have I known some beauteous *Paisage* rise
> In suddain flowres and arbours to my Eies,
> And in the depth and dead of winter bring
> To my Cold thoughts a lively sense of spring.

With the memory of such an experience within him, the Augustinian seeker turns to question external nature:

> I askt the *Earth*, and that answered me, *I am not it*; and whatsoever are in it, made the same confession. I asked the *Sea* and the *deepes*, and the *creeping things*, and they answered me, *We are not thy God, seeke above us.* . . . I asked the heavens, the Sunne and Moone, and Starres, Nor (say they) are wee the *God* whom thou seekest.

All creatures give the same answer: "they cryed out with a loud voyce, *He made us*" (Ch. vi). It is the questioning of nature that we find throughout Vaughan's poetry, where "Each *tree, herb, flowre/* Are shadows of his *wisedome*, and his Pow'r" ("Rules and Lessons"), where Vaughan prays that man "would hear/The world read to him!"

> all the vast expence
> In the Creation shed, and slav'd to sence
> Makes up but lectures for his eie, and ear.

—Lectures in the old medieval sense: readings of the book, with commentary and elucidation:

> All things here shew him heaven; *Waters* that fall
> Chide, and fly up; *Mists* of corruptest fome
> Quit their first beds & mount; trees, herbs,
> flowres, all
> Strive upwards still, and point him the way home.
> ("The Tempest")

And the way home lies through an interior ascent, climbing upward and inward through the deepest regions of the human soul:

> I beg'd here long, and gron'd to know
> Who gave the Clouds so brave a bow,
> Who bent the spheres, and circled in
> Corruption with this glorious Ring,
> What is his name, and how I might
> Descry some part of his great light.
> I summon'd nature: peirc'd through all her store,

> Broke up some seales, which none had touch'd before,
> Her wombe, her bosome, and her head
> Where all her secrets lay a bed
> I rifled quite, and having past
> Through all the Creatures, came at last
> To search my selfe, where I did find
> Traces, and sounds of a strange kind.
>
> ("Vanity of Spirit")

So Augustine turns to search within himself and comes "into these fields and spacious palaces of my *Memory*, where the treasures of innumerable *formes* brought into it from these things that have beene perceived by the *sences*, be hoarded up."

> And yet doe not the things themselves enter the *Memory*; onely the *Images* of things perceived by the *Sences*, are ready there at hand, when ever the *Thoughts* will recall them. . . .
> For there have I in a readinesse, the heaven, the earth, the sea, and what-ever I can thinke upon in them. . . . There also meete I with my *selfe*, I recall my *selfe*, what, where, or when I have done a thing; and how I was affected when I did it. There be all what ever I remember, eyther upon mine owne experience, or others credit. Out of the same store doe I my selfe compare these and these likelyhoods of things: eyther of such as I have made experience of, or of such as I have barely beleeved upon experience of some things that bee passed: and by these do I compare actions to *come*, their *events* and *hopes*: and upon all these againe doe I meditate, as if they were now present. . . .
> Great is this force of *memory*, excessive great, O my *God*: a large and an infinite roomthynes [*penetrale*: inner room], who can plummet the bottome of it? yet is this a *faculty* of mine, and belongs unto my nature: nor can I my self comprehend all that I am. (Ch. viii)

Yet things even more wonderful lie beyond, as he probes ever and ever more deeply into the recesses of the memory. "Here also bee all these precepts of those *liberall Sciences* as yet unforgotten; couch as it were further off in a more inward place" (Ch. ix). These things could not have been conveyed within the senses; how was it then that he came to accept these precepts as true?

unlesse because they were already in my memory; though so
farre off yet, and crowded so farre backeward as it were into
certaine secret caves, that had they not beene drawne out by
the advice of some other person, I had never perchance beene
able so much as to have thought of them? (Ch. x)

Here the hint of the presence of something like innate ideas in the deep
caves of the soul leads directly to a long account of what might be called
the dramatic action of Augustinian meditation. It is an action significantly different from the method of meditation later set forth by Ignatius
Loyola and his followers; for that later method shows the effects of
medieval scholasticism, with its powerful emphasis upon the analytic
understanding, and upon the process of "picturing out" the conceptions
of the mind.[11] Ignatian meditation is thus a precise, tightly articulated
method, moving from the images that comprise the composition of place
into the threefold sequence of the powers of the soul, memory, understanding and will, and from there into the affections and resolutions of
the aroused will. But in Augustinian meditation, there is no such precise
method; there is, rather, an intuitive groping back into regions of the
soul that lie beyond sensory memories. The three faculties of the soul[12]
are all used, but with an effect of simultaneous action, for with Augustine
the aroused will is using the understanding to explore the memory, with
the aim of apprehending more clearly and loving more fervently the
ultimate source of the will's arousal.

Wherfore we find, that to learne these things whose *Images*
we *sucke* not *in* by our Sences, but perceive *within* by themselves,
without Images, as they are; is nothing else, but by *meditating*
to *gather together*, and by diligent *marking*, to take notice of those
same *notions* which the *memory* did before contayne more scat-
teringly and confusedly... (Ch. xi)

But these things are evasive and elusive; unless we engage in a continual
act of re-collection, "they become so drowned againe, and so give us
the slip, as it were, backe into such remote and privy lodgings, that I
must be put againe unto new paines of meditation, for recovery of them
to their former perfection... they must be *rallied* and drawne together
againe, that they may bee knowne; that is to say, they must as it were
be *collected* and *gathered together* from their dispersions: whence the word
cogitation is derived" (Ch. xi).
The seventeenth-century translator has been frequently rendering

the word *cogitare* by the word *meditate*: thus providing his own account of Augustinian meditation: to draw together these things scattered in the memory. It would seem that poetry composed under the impulse of this kind of meditation would differ considerably in its structure from any poetry written under the impulse of the Ignatian mode of meditation—such as Donne's Holy Sonnets. The poetry of Augustinian meditation would perhaps tend to display an order akin to that which Pascal saw in the writings of Augustine: "Cet ordre consiste principalement à la digression sur chaque point qu'on rapporte à la fin, pour la montrer toujours."[13] That *Pensée* may at least suggest the poetry of Vaughan, where the order often consists chiefly in what appear to be digressions, but are really exploratory sallies or *excursus* in the manner indicated by the following passage of the *Confessions*:

> Great is this power of Memory; a thing, O my God, to bee amazed at, a very profound and infinite multiplicity: and this thing is the minde, and this thing am I. . . . Behold, in those innumerable fields, and dennes, and caves of my memory, innumerably full of innumerable kinds of things, brought in, first, eyther by the *Images*, as all *bodies* are: secondly, or by the *presence* of the *things* themselves, as the *Arts* are: thirdly, or by certaine *notions* or *impressions*, as the *Affections* of the mind are . . . Thorow all these doe I runne and tumble [*discurro et volito*]; *myning* into them on this side, and on that side, so farre as ever I am able, but can finde no bottome. So great is the force of memory, so great is the force of this life of man, even whilest hee is mortall.   (Ch. xvii)

But deep within all this multiplicity lies that essential memory toward which Augustine's digressive and "tumbling" meditations have been subtly and inevitably leading us: the memory of a "happy life," a "blessed life," the "beata vita."

> Is not an happy life the thing which all desire; and is there any man that some way or other desires it not? But where gate they the knowledge of it, that they are so desirous of it? where did they ever see it, that they are now so enamored of it? Truely we have it, but which way, I know not . . .
> How they come to know it, I cannot tell: and therefore have they it by, I know not, what secret notice; concerning which, in much doubt I am, whether it bee in the memory or no: which if it bee, then should wee sometimes have beene

blessed heretofore. [quia, si ibi est, iam beati fuimus aliquando; utrum singillatim omnes, an in illo homine, qui primus peccavit...non quaero nunc; sed quaero, utrum in memoria sit beata vita.]
But whether every man should have beene so happy as severally considered in himself, or as in the loynes of that man who first sinned...I now inquire not: but this I demaund, whether this blessed life bee in the memory, or no?

(Ch. xx)

It must be so, he concludes, for it is known to people in different languages, under different names: "And this could not bee, unlesse the thing it selfe expressed by this name, were still reserved in their memory." But what, precisely, is this thing?

there is a ioy which is not granted unto the ungodly; but unto those onely which love thee for thine owne sake; whose ioy thy selfe art. And this is the blessed life, *to reioyce unto thee, concerning thee, and for thy sake:* this is the happy life, and there is no other. (Ch. xxii)

a happy life is a ioying in the truth: For this is a ioying in thee, who art the truth, O God my light, the health of my countenance, and my God. This is the blessed life that all desire ...Where therefore gaynd they the knowledge of this happy life, but even there, where they learned the truth also?... which yet they would not love, were there not some notice of it remayning in their memory.... For there is a dimme glimmering of light yet un-put-out, in men: let them walke, let them walke, that the darknesse overtake them not.

(Ch. xxiii)

It is the central image of *Silex Scintillans:* the flash, the spark, the glance, the beam, the ray, the glimmering of light that comes from the memory of an ancient birthright of blessedness—"utrum singillatim omnes, an in illo homine, qui primus peccavit": whether it be a memory of each man's individual life, or whether it be a memory of Adam's original happy life—that memory remains, yet un-put-out in men. We find the image notably in the poem "Silence, and stealth of dayes," where this Augustinian motif is used in recalling the memory of a loved one who has died (evidently Vaughan's brother):

As he that in some Caves thick damp
    Lockt from the light,
Fixeth a solitary lamp,
    To brave the night
And walking from his Sun, when past
    That glim'ring Ray
Cuts through the heavy mists in haste
    Back to his day,
So o'r fled minutes I retreat
    Unto that hour
Which shew'd thee last, but did defeat
    Thy light, and pow'r
I search, and rack my soul to see
    Those beams again...

The "Sun" here is the "solitary lamp" within the cave of the speaker's soul: the memory of his loved one is the light within that serves as an interior sun. Sometimes, carried toward the things of the outer world, the speaker tends to walk away from that "glim'ring Ray," but, remembering that he has forgotten, he walks, he walks, in Augustine's way, back toward the memory of light. The beams of this loved one's soul, he comes to realize, now shine in heaven, and he cannot track them there; yet something bright remains within, as he concludes:

Yet have I one *Pearle* by whose light
    All things I see,
And in the heart of Earth, and night
    Find Heaven, and thee.

It is the indestructible Image of God, apprehending the Presence of God in the memory: "Sure I am, that in it thou dwellest: even for this reason, that I have preserved the memory of thee, since the time that I first learnt thee: and for that I finde thee in my memory, whensoever I call thee to remembrance" (*Confessions* x.25).

So the memory of that inner Presence runs throughout Vaughan's volume of 1650, as Vaughan struggles backward on his ancient journey of return toward the memory of blessedness. Sometimes the journey backward takes the form of "The Retreate" toward the days of the individual's childhood:

Happy those early dayes! when I
Shin'd in my Angell-infancy.
Before I understood this place
Appointed for my second race,
Or taught my soul to fancy ought
But a white, Celestiall thought,
When yet I had not walkt above
A mile, or two, from my first love,
And looking back (at that short space,)
Could see a glimpse of his bright-face;
When on some *gilded Cloud*, or *flowre*
My gazing soul would dwell an houre,
And in those weaker glories spy
Some shadows of eternity...
 O how I long to travell back
And tread again that ancient track!
That I might once more reach that plaine,
Where first I left my glorious traine,
From whence th' Inlightned spirit sees
That shady City of Palme trees;
But (ah!) my soul with too much stay
Is drunk, and staggers in the way.
Some men a forward motion love,
But I by backward steps would move,
And when this dust falls to the urn
In that state I came return.

The poem presents the essence of the *Phaedo*, as qualified and developed
by Christian Platonism. Indeed, the *Phaedo* gives us the closing image
of the drunken man, in an important passage that suggests the kernel
of this poem:

> And were we not saying long ago [asks Socrates] that
> the soul when using the body as an instrument of perception,
> that is to say, when using the sense of sight or hearing or some
> other sense... were we not saying that the soul too is then
> dragged by the body into the region of the changeable, and
> wanders and is confused; the world spins round her, and she
> is like a drunkard, when she touches change?...
> But when returning into herself she reflects, then she
> passes into the other world, the region of purity, and eternity,

117

and immortality, and unchangeableness, which are her kindred...[14]

In Vaughan, as in Augustine's *Confessions*, there is of course only the most guarded and glancing use of the Platonic doctrine of reminiscence: any hint of the soul's pre-existence is used by Vaughan as a metaphor of innocence; and the whole poem is toward the close clearly transmuted into orthodox Christianity. The poet superimposes upon the Platonic suggestions the concept of the "Inlightned spirit" which catches a vision of the promised land, as did Moses when he "went up from the plains of Moab unto the mountain of Nebo... And the Lord shewed him all the land of Gilead... and all the land of Judah, unto the utmost sea, And the south, and the plain of the valley of Jericho, the city of palm trees..." (Deuteronomy xxxiv. 1–3).

So the "early days" of the individual's childhood become one with the "early days" of the human race, as related in the Old Testament; and both together form powerful symbols of the memory of a happy life that lives, however glimmeringly, within the soul that has, through regeneration, come into yet a third state of childhood: the state of the "children of God" (Romans viii. 16).

> Sure, It was so. Man in those early days
> Was not all stone, and Earth,
> He shin'd a little, and by those weak Rays
> Had some glimpse of his birth...
> He sigh'd for *Eden*, and would often say
> *Ah! what bright days were those?*
> Nor was Heav'n cold unto him; for each day
> The vally, or the Mountain
> Afforded visits, and still *Paradise* lay
> In some green shade, or fountain.
>
> ("Corruption")

Such is the paradise within, compounded of the Bible, of Nature, and of the Self, which lies at the heart of Vaughan's *Silex Scintillans*, 1650: a vision that results from the constant effort to remember the beauty of the sudden illumination described in his opening Latin confession. That Latin poem and its emblem of the Flashing Flint, with its image of the man within, now once more come to mind as we read the well-known passage that concludes Augustine's sequence of meditations on the force of memory:

Too late beganne I to love thee, O thou beauty both so ancient and so fresh, yea too too late came I to love thee. For behold, thou wert *within* mee, and I *out* of my selfe, where I made search for thee; deformed I, wooing these beautifull pieces of thy workmanship. . . . Thou calledst, and criedst unto mee, yea thou even brakest open my *deafenesse.* Thou discoveredst thy beames, and *shynedst* out unto mee, and didst chase away my blindnesse. Thou didst most *fragrantly blow* upon me, and I drew in my *breath* and panted after thee. I *tasted* thee, and now doe *hunger* and *thirst after thee.* Thou didst *touch* mee, and I even *burne* againe to enjoy thy peace. (Ch. xxvii)

Notes

1. The present essay represents essentially the first chapter of *The Paradise Within.* Yale University Press.

2. I am indebted to the Rev. Marcus Haworth for suggesting some of the phrases in this translation.

3. In 1655 this 14-line poem becomes the first part of a poem in 46 lines, with the elaborate dedicatory heading: "To my most merciful, my most loving, and dearly loved Redeemer, the ever blessed, the onely Holy and Just One, Jesus Christ, the Son of the living God, And the sacred Virgin Mary."

4. Many of these echoes have been listed in the notes to Vaughan's *Works,* ed. L. C. Martin, 2nd edn., Oxford: Clarendon Press, 1957; and the echoes have been perceptively discussed by E. C. Pettet, *Of Paradise and Light: A Study of Vaughan's* Silex Scintillans (Cambridge University Press, 1960), Chap. iii. See also the recent helpful article by Mary Ellen Rickey, "Vaughan, *The Temple,* and Poetic Form," *SP,* LIX (1962), 162-170.

5. This brief account of "Regeneration" deals only with those aspects important to the present study; for detailed interpretations, differing in some respects from my own, see the illuminating studies of this poem by R. A. Durr, *SP,* LIV (1957), 14-28; by Ross Garner, *Henry Vaughan: Experience and the Tradition* (University of Chicago Press, 1959), 47-62; and by Pettet, op. cit., pp. 104-117.

6. For the trees of stanza 2, see I Kings xix. 4-8 (Elijah under the juniper tree); Zechariah i.8-11 ("the men that stood among the myrtle trees"); Judges vi.11 ("And there came an angel of the Lord, and sat under an oak which was in Ophrah").

7. See Herbert, "The H. Communion," two poems under one title; the first deals with the action of "grace against all sins"; the second celebrates the "ease" with which the soul now communicates with heaven: "Thou hast restor'd us to this ease / By this thy heav'nly bloud." See also "The Invitation," esp. st. 4, dealing with "joy"; and "The Banquet," celebrating the "sweet and sacred cheer" of the Communion, and its power of raising the soul to "the skie."

8. See G. H. Tavard, *Transiency and Permanence: The Nature of Theology According to St. Bonaventure* (Franciscan Institute, St. Bonaventure, N.Y., 1954), chaps. ii-iv.

9. See Etienne Gilson, *The Christian Philosophy of Saint Augustine,* trans. L. E. M. Lynch (New York: Random House, 1960), pp. 210-224.

10. *Confessions*, Book X, Chap. vi. All subsequent references are to Book X. Quotations in English are taken from *Saint Augustines Confessions translated*, by William Watts, London, 1631. This version, with some corrections, is included in the Loeb Library edition of the *Confessions*, which I have used for the Latin quotations.

11. See Bede Frost, *The Art of Mental Prayer* (London: S.P.C.K., 1940), p. 69.

12. Memory, Understanding, and Will are not discussed as "faculties" in the *Confessions*, although something close to this triad is implied in one chapter of the final book (xiii.11), where Augustine discusses the triad: *esse, nosse, velle*. The full development of Augustine's exploration of the interior trinity of powers, the Image of the Trinity in man is found in his treatise, the *De Trinitate*, completed about twenty years after the *Confessions*. See esp. Book X of the *De Trinitate*, and the excellent Introduction to this treatise by John Burnaby, prefaced to his translation of selected books: *Augustine: Later Works*, Library of Christian Classics, Vol. VIII, Philadelphia: Westminster Press, 1955.

13. *Pensées*, ed. Brunschvicg, no. 283.

14. *The Dialogues of Plato*, trans. B. Jowett (3rd edn. 5 vols., Oxford University Press, 1892), II, 222.

JAMES D. SIMMONDS

Henry Vaughan's Amoret and Etesia

In his *Henry Vaughan: A Life and Interpretation* (Oxford, 1947), pp.
51–52, Dr. F. E. Hutchinson expresses his conviction that the Amoret
to whom Vaughan addresses six love-poems in *Poems* (1646), and the
Etesia to whom he addresses seven in *Thalia Rediviva* (1678), were in
fact the same person. By this view, both series would be addressed to
Catherine Wise, who became the poet's first wife, for Dr. Hutchinson
also argues (p. 54) that poems in the 1646 volume celebrate Vaughan's
first courtship and marriage.[1] The latter point seems well taken, but
the evidence advanced for the single identity of Amoret and Etesia
appears too slight to support the conclusion. Dr. Hutchinson describes
his argument as "an almost inevitable inference" from the fact that "the
tone in the Amoret and Etesia poems is the same, and often even the
circumstances are similar or identical, and the expression the same" (p.
52). However, he does little to substantiate these assertions, presenting
no evidence of a uniformity of tone in the two series, and only one
example of similar expression and one of identical circumstances. The
question of Etesia's identity has important consequences both for
Vaughan's life and for the date of composition of the poems addressed
to her. It therefore seems warrantable to examine the poems in some
detail, and attempt to establish a broader and firmer base for inference.

The two examples of parallelism which Dr. Hutchinson provides
are inconclusive. The comparison of the lady's face or eye to a star,
which comprises the verbal parallel,[2] is a commonplace of Renaissance

Reprinted, by permission of the publisher, from *Philological Quarterly*, 42:1 (1963),
137–42.

love poetry, and the attendant emphasis on the star's remoteness from the earth results from a conventional insistence on the lover's inferiority to the beloved. In the other example,[3] the circumstantial parallel consists in Vaughan's declaration that he "first" met his beloved among the "shades" of a wooded retreat. But woods and groves were traditionally the settings in poetry of lovers' encounters; the scene of Vaughan's first meeting with Etesia is identified in terms too conventional for us to equate it with the scene of his first meeting with Amoret.[4] Dr. Hutchinson's argument, moreover, defies the *prima facie* evidence, which suggests that Amoret was one woman and Etesia another; for, if a poet uses two different names, the logical inference is that he intends to distinguish between two different people.

This basic distinction between Amoret and Etesia is further emphasized by the publication of each series in a different book. Had the Etesia poems been addressed to Catherine Wise, we might logically expect Vaughan not only to use the name "Amoret," but also (provided they were written before 1646), to publish them likewise in the 1646 volume. Dr. Marilla has suggested, in explanation of their omission, that "the Etesia pieces were written after the publication of the *Poems*, and . . . the author changed the poetic name in these later poems in order to avoid implying incompleteness in the volume which he wished to stand as a composite memorial" (*Secular Poems*, p. 333). This view is tenable, and even rather tempting, for it explains the change in name as well as the omission of these poems in 1646. However, while they may readily have been written after that date, the evident waning of Vaughan's interest in secular poetry after 1648 establishes a strong probability that they were available for publication in *Olor Iscanus* (1651). Dr. Marilla's suggestion does not fully explain why these poems were not published in 1651,[5] and although it is conceivable that Vaughan may have withheld them (as he perhaps changed the poetic name), in order to avoid implying incompleteness in the 1646 volume, their omission somewhat strengthens the *prima facie* evidence; for, if we assume that they were addressed to his wife, we have no real knowledge of any motive for his not publishing them at that time. On the other hand, if we assume that they were addressed to some other woman, we have, in Vaughan's delicacy of feeling for his wife (granted that his possession of such delicacy is also assumed), a satisfactory explanation of their omission from *Poems* and *Olor Iscanus*, and also, in the fact that Catherine Vaughan was no longer living in 1678, of their eventual publication in

Thalia Rediviva. If this explanation is correct, we are virtually compelled to make the further inference that the Etesia poems were written prior to Vaughan's attachment to Catherine Wise, and consequently that they belong to an earlier period than the Amoret poems.[6]

A relevant factor remaining to be considered is the emotional tone of the poems themselves. As previously mentioned, Dr. Hutchinson declares the tone in both series to be the same (p. 52), but offers no substantiation of this claim; in fact, impartial examination reveals that there is, fairly consistently, a sharp contrast of tone. This contrast, implying different emotional reactions on Vaughan's part, tends to support the *prima facie* evidence that each series was addressed to a different woman. The essence of the contrast may be readily grasped by a comparative reading of "Etesia *absent*," lines 1–12 (Martin, p. 647), and "*To* Amoret, *of the difference 'twixt him, and other Lovers, and what true Love is*," lines 15–28 (Martin, pp. 12–13). To facilitate such a reading, the passages are given here in the order named:

1. Love, the Worlds Life! what a sad death
   Thy absence is? to lose our breath
   At once and dye, is but to live
   Inlarg'd, without the scant reprieve
   Of *Pulse* and *Air*: whose dull *returns*
   And narrow *Circles* the Soul mourns.
       But to be dead alive, and still
   To wish, but never have our will:
   To be possess'd, and yet to miss;
   To wed a true but absent bliss:
   Are lingring tortures, and their smart
   Dissects and racks and grinds the Heart!

2. Just so base, Sublunarie Lovers hearts
       Fed on loose prophane desires,
           May for an Eye,
           Or face comply:
   But those removed, they will as soone depart,
           And shew their Art,
           And painted fires.

  Whil'st I by pow'rfull Love, so much refin'd,
       That my absent soule the same is,
           Carelesse to misse,
           A glaunce, or kisse,

Can with those Elements of lust and sence,
Freely dispence,
And court the mind.

It is evident at a glance that the tone in the former passage is much
more fervent than in the latter, and reflection manifests that this accords
with a difference in the nature of the poet's attachment. In the Etesia
poem, his affirming that the frustration occasioned by the lady's absence
causes him intense physical torture, his likening that absence to "a sad
death" and his own state to that of one "dead alive," all disclose that
he is attracted to Etesia by passionate desire. This poem reveals him
as one of those "Sublunarie Lovers" whom he contemns in the Amoret
poem. Here, by direct contrast, his mood does not change whether the
lady be present or absent, for his love does not consist in "loose prophane
desires" for "an Eye,/Or face," but is "so much refin'd" that he can
dispense with "Elements of lust and sence" and so be "Carelesse to
misse,/A glaunce, or kisse." His affection for Amoret obviously is more
balanced, more assured, more disinterested, and depends more upon
companionship and mutual interests than his feeling for Etesia, which
depends chiefly upon physical attraction. Since the former qualities are
usually ascribed to maturity and the latter to adolescence, we have here
a further basis for suggesting that the Etesia poems quite likely belong
to an earlier period.

The contrasting qualities of the two poems just examined are found
also in the rest. "*To* Etesia *(for* Timander,) *the first Sight*" (Martin, pp.
643–44), celebrates the lady's beauty in hyperbolical terms and describes
the "fever" of the lover "blinded by a face." "*The Character, to* Etesia"
(pp. 644–45), bases on her physical beauty a celebration of her as a
mysterious embodiment of nature's glory. "*To* Etesia *looking from her
Casement at the full* Moon" (pp. 645–46), is an autobiographical sketch,
the only point of which is the concluding affirmation of the enslaved
lover's misfortune. "*To* Etesia *parted from him, and looking back*" (p. 646),
and "*To* Etesia *going beyond Sea*" (pp. 646–47), likewise concentrate on
the pains of the "famish'd" lover whose "dying" heart the aloof beauty
threatens to "destroy."

These attitudes, conventional elements of love-poetry in the tradition of Petrarch, are found also in "To Amoret. The Sigh" (pp. 5–6), and
in the first two stanzas of "To Amoret, Walking in a Starry Evening"
(pp. 7–8). However, the final stanzas of the latter, as well as the rest of

the Amoret poems, reveal close affinities with the love-poems of Donne, Carew, Suckling and others who, discarding the Petrarchan conventions, expressed simpler, more independent, and (especially Donne) more philosophical attitudes.[7] "To Amoret gone from him" (p. 8), and the final stanzas of "To Amoret, Walking in a Starry Evening," reflect upon the spiritual affinity, independent of physical agencies, expressed in love, and upon the relation of this "sympathie" to the influence of planets on earthly creatures. "A Song to *Amoret*" (pp. 8–9) is a simple affirmation of the poet's "divine affection" for the lady, while "To Amoret Weeping" (pp. 13–14) assures her of the power of their love to transcend earthly misfortune.

It is possible that the contrast in emotional tone between the two series may imply that the Etesia poems reflect an early stage of Vaughan's attachment to Catherine Wise. If they do, then they may have been omitted from *Poems* and *Olor Iscanus* because of a feeling on Vaughan's part that their emphasis on physical attraction made them a less worthy record of his alliance than the Amoret poems. However, a contrary suggestion resides in the last four Etesia poems. At least three of these, and possibly four, are concerned with the separation of the lovers,[8] and seem to record a progressive frustration of the poet's desire, climaxed by an apparent abandonment of all hope of reunion. Upon reflection, it seems reasonable that some significance should attach to the fact that three poems recording Vaughan's infatuation with Etesia are followed by as many recording his distress over her parting from him. The suggestiveness of this phenomenon is intensified by the fact that these unhappy poems conclude the series, and that the nadir of his misery is attained in the final poem. By my view of these pieces, they imply that the romance was ended abruptly by the lady's departure *"beyond Sea."*[9]

The argument for the single identity of Amoret and Etesia must, it seems, be regarded as insubstantial. The clearest indications which can be obtained from a careful analysis of the poems all suggest that the Etesia poems record an earlier relationship between Vaughan and an unidentified woman. Certainly, these indications are not strong enough to support a positive conclusion; but, unless more penetrating analysis can provide surer direction, they must deter us from perpetuating a mere conjecture by allowing it to outweigh the *prima facie* evidence (supported mainly by a sharp contrast in emotional tone), that the Etesia poems were addressed to a woman with whom Vaughan was associated prior to his courtship of Catherine Wise.

Notes

1. For a more detailed presentation of this thesis, see *The Secular Poems of Henry Vaughan*, ed. with Notes and Commentary by E. L. Marilla, University of Uppsala Essays and Studies on English Language and Literature, vol. XXI (Uppsala, 1958), p. 100. In opposition to Chambers, Marilla also argues plausibly for the autobiographical significance of the Etesia poems (pp. 325–26).

2. "To Amoret, Walking in a Starry Evening," lines 14–15, and "The Character, to Etesia," lines 19–20, *The Works of Henry Vaughan*, ed. L. C. Martin, 2nd ed. (Oxford, 1957), pp. 7, 644. This edition is cited throughout as "Martin."

3. "Upon the Priorie Grove, His usuall Retyrement," lines 1–4, and "To Etesia *going beyond the Sea*," lines 5–10, Martin pp. 15, 646–67. "Upon the Priorie Grove" does not mention Amoret, but the reasons for believing that it concerns her are persuasive: see Hutchinson, *Life*, pp. 52–53, and Marilla, *Secular Poems*, pp. 147–48.

4. The following is an account of the seven equally inconclusive other parallels which may be found: 1) "*To* Amoret *of the difference 'twixt him, and other Lovers, and what true Love is,*" lines 33–34, and "*To* Etesia *(for* Timander), *the first Sight,*" lines 49–50 (Martin, pp. 13, 644): incidental use of the same words in different contexts. 2) "A Song to *Amoret*," line 19, and "*To* Etesia *looking from her Casement at the full* Moon," line 8 (Martin, pp. 9, 645): again, incidental repetition. 3) "A Song to *Amoret*," line 24, and "*To* Etesia *parted from him, and looking back,*" line 6 (Martin, pp. 9, 646): conventional language in love-poetry. 4) "To Amoret, The Sigh," line 6, and "*To* Etesia *going beyond Sea,*" line 6 (Martin, pp. 5, 646): Dr. Hutchinson points to this without comment (*Life* p. 52, and note); again, the terms are conventional. 5) "To Amoret gone from him," lines 19–20, and "The Character, *to* Etesia," lines 31–32 (Martin, pp. 8, 645): the concept of stellar "influence," popular in contemporary love-poetry, and found also in Vaughan's religious verse. 6) "To Amoret gone from him" (title), and "Etesia *absent*" (title), Martin, pp. 8, 647: the verbal similarity is less significant than the marked divergence in mood and situation. 7) "To Amoret Weeping" (title), and "In Etesiam lachrymantem" (title), Martin, pp. 13, 646: again the verbal repetition is less significant than the thematic contrast of the two poems.

5. Their omission has been explained formerly by the theory that Vaughan suppressed them because of their incompatibility with newly infused moral scruples. In "The Identity of Henry Vaughan's Suppressed Poems," *MLQ*, XXII (1961), 390–98, I argue that this theory is unsatisfactory.

6. "Vaughan's first wife is thought to have died during the early 1650's, and it appears that her sister became his second wife. But neither the evidence of Vaughan's troubled expressions during the 1650's nor our confidence in his sense of propriety allows the assumption that the Etesia poems were inspired by the latter attachment" (Marilla, *Secular Poems*, p. 333). Some suggestion of different periods of composition may perhaps reside in the fact that all of the Etesia poems are written in rhyming couplets, and that although this is true also of "To Amoret gone from him" and "To Amoret Weeping," the rest of the Amoret poems are written in stanzas with more evolved rhyme patterns.

7. The influence of Donne's diction and imagery on the Amoret poems has long been recognized—see Martin's notes and the commentary by E. L. Marilla on "To Amoret, Walking in a Starry Evening," lines 19–24 (*Secular Poems*, p. 121); "To Amoret gone from him," lines 19–22 (*ibid.*, p. 123); "*To* Amoret, *of the difference 'twixt him, and other Lovers, and what true Love is,*" lines 15–28 (*ibid.*, pp. 137–38); "To Amoret Weeping," lines 9–12 (*ibid.*, p. 141).

8. The import of "In Etesiam lachrymantem" is dubious, since Vaughan does

not specify the cause of her grief; but it is likely that he relies here upon the suggestive implication of this poem's placement in the midst of others dealing with the dissolution of an apparently passionate relationship.

9. Dr. Hutchinson (*Life*, p. 54), sees "Etesia *absent*" as "addressed to a wife," and although he gives no reasons for this view, it might perhaps find a basis in lines 9–10 (Martin, p. 647): "To be possess'd, and yet to miss;/To wed a true but absent bliss." Vaughan's agonized mood here, however, seems inappropriate to a man temporarily parted from his wife, and contrasts strongly with the mood of "To Amoret gone from him," in which the poet expresses his feelings on a similar occasion. My view of this and the three preceding poems does not imply that Vaughan and Etesia parted following a rupture of their relationship, or that they knew their separation would be permanent; thus Vaughan might well consider himself still "possess'd" and (figuratively) "wed," although the intensity of his distress and the comparison of his state to that of the dead awaiting resurrection imply that he does not expect reunion within the foreseeable future.

S. SANDBANK

Henry Vaughan's
Apology for Darkness

Among several commendatory poems prefixed to Henry Vaughan's
Thalia Rediviva (1678), I. W.'s "To my worthy Friend, Mr.
Henry Vaughan the Silurist"[1] makes a critical point beyond mere commendation. Vaughan's muse is praised here for wisely demeaning herself to
express, not only the supreme bliss of "radiant Worlds," but also the
"hollow Joyes" of earthly life; not that the latter have any intrinsic
value: "hollow Joyes" here obviously means "the hollowness of joys."
If hollowness nevertheless deserves to be expressed, it is mainly because
it can serve to set off fullness. The king's majesty is "burnished" by his
own eclipse and suffering. His luster is best read in the shade, his
greatness best found in the shroud. Two analogues are then quoted—
from nature and from religion:

> So lightning dazzles from its night and cloud;
> So the first Light himself has for his Throne
> Blackness, and Darkness his Pavilion.

Lightning, King and God—the brightest manifestations of the physical,
the human, and the spiritual—owe much of their brightness to a background of night, suffering, or primeval Darkness, respectively. I. W.
here points to an image and an idea very central to Vaughan's poetry:
what may be called Vaughan's apology for darkness.

Reprinted, by permission of the publisher, from *Studies in English Literature*, 7 (1967),
141–52.

There is no need to show once again that terminology of light and darkness is prominent in Vaughan's vocabulary. Light, as often pointed out, is associated with God, Election, Heaven, life, happiness; darkness— with the Devil, Damnation, death, misery. The two images, or groups of images, thus serve to re-inforce a dramatic world-picture in which the opposition between heaven and earth, Grace and nature, is a very basic distinction. This more or less conventional use of light-darkness imagery in Vaughan's poetry has been traced back to numerous possible sources: Hermeticism, the Bible, Christian mysticism, the Christian Meditation, etc.

Essentially more important, however, though statistically less prevalent, is another, less conventional treatment of darkness, which critics often neglect. Darkness, to Vaughan, is not only the absence of light— and, figuratively, of all the values light stands for. It is also a necessary condition of light, the background which sets it off. As such, it cannot be branded as merely evil. Vaughan's popular epithet of "poet of light" needs some qualification. He is by no means a Boehme or a Blake, but the consciousness of darkness, indeed, the conviction that light cannot do without darkness, is essential to the understanding of what he says and of how he says it. This affirmation of darkness gives his work much of its unity, in that it is the embodiment in an image of several separate aspects of his thought. A visual experience here gives rise to a whole complex of analogous experiences: psychological, theological, mystical.

The visual experience itself has been noticed often, notably by E. C. Pettet, who speaks of the recurrence of the cloud-star image-cluster in Vaughan's poetry.[2] The phenomenon of starlight intensely shining forth from among dark clouds seems to have been particularly attractive to Vaughan. It produces parallel images, such as that of sun shining at midnight, or darkness at noon. A chamber in the Globe Tavern, "painted over head with a Cloudy Skie, and some few dispersed starres," gives rise to the playful paradox of "Darkness, & Stars i'th' mid day!", while outside, towards twilight, "the soft stirs/of bawdy, ruffled Silks, turne night to day" (pp. 10–11). Nicodemus speaks with the Sun at midnight (p. 522), and it is at midnight that Christ's "all-surprizing light" may break (p. 451).

Time and again Vaughan stresses the "value" light gains from night (p. 678). "Light," he says, "is never so beautifull as in the presence of darknes" (p. 217), and "stars never shine more glorious, then when they are neare black Clouds" (p. 370)[3]; "one beam i'th' dark outvies/

Two in the day" (p. 439). Darkness, here, is obviously more than the negation of light. One cannot discern light—one cannot, at any rate, do justice to its beauty—without a dark background to set it off. This visual experience—and the formula it can be reduced to—namely, the value of the negative as a foil for the positive—has several repercussions in Vaughan's thought. It is the object of this paper to consider some of these analogues.

A) The Cosmological Analogue.

Henry Vaughan's brother Thomas, practically obsessed by cosmogony and cosmogonical speculation, assigns a central place to darkness and night in his numerous accounts of creation.[4] Great as his influence on Henry be,[5] I cannot find any trace of such cosmogonical theories in Henry's work. Cosmologically, however, darkness plays an important part—and is vindicated—in Henry's work.

The cosmological vindication of darkness was an integral part of both the religious and the philosophical traditions Vaughan was working in. The God of the Bible is the creator of darkness as well as light, and darkness, originally a chaotic power, has been integrated, in creation, into the constitution of the universe. The alternation of day and night becomes essential to world-order, and darkness finds its legitimate place within this order.[6] Philosophically, the idea that universal harmony is based on reconciled opposites goes back to the Aristotelian definition of beauty as "discordia concors."

Both aspects appear in Vaughan. God is the creator of darkness as well as light: "Did not he, who ordain'd the day,/ Ordain night too?" (p. 459). "Light, and darknes," "days, nights" are all God's works (p. 436). But the religious aspect is inseparable from the philosophical. For not in vain did God "Ordain night too":

> Were all the year one constant Sun-shine, wee
>   Should have no flowres,[7]
> All would be drought, and leanness; not a tree
>   Would make us bowres;
> Beauty consists in colours; and that's best
>   Which is not fixt, but flies, and flowes;
> The settled Red is dull, and whites that rest
>   Something of sickness would disclose.

> Vicissitude plaies all the game,
>   Nothing that stirrs,
>   Or hath a name,
>   But waits upon this wheel,
> Kingdomes too have their Physick, and for steel,
>   Exchange their peace, and furrs. (p. 459)[8]

"Though temper'd diversly," elements are reconciled to each other in "sweet Concord," the cold assisting the hot etc. (p. 651). Night, far from taking away the use of light, "urgeth the Necessity of day" (p. 628). Darkness is not only inevitable. It is necessary for the success of its opposite.

B) The Psychological Analogue: Conversion.

The cosmological principle of harmony-based-on-contraries has for its counterpart, on the religio-psychological plane, the conviction that the bliss of the pious contains the consciousness of vanquished sinfulness. This experience of conversion, so central to Vaughan's world, is another version of the light-in-darkness image. A related theme is that of chastisement and affliction as essential to religious bliss. The main image to express this last theme is that of the "silex scintillans," or sparkling flint, again a variation on the light-out-of-darkness motif.

One source of Vaughan's conviction, that in the same way as light is brighter against darkness, holiness too is holier against the background of past sins and repentance, seems to be suggested in the poem "St. Mary Magdalen" (p. 507). Speaking of Mary's conversion, Vaughan refers to the story of Mary and Simon the Pharisee (Luke VII), rebuking the "Self-boasting Pharisee" for calling her a sinner. The relevant passage in Luke includes the following words, spoken by Christ: "Her sins, which are many, are forgiven; for she loved much: but to whom little is forgiven, the same loveth little."

Sin and forgiveness are thus closely associated with eventual Glory. The connection between the two is explained in a passage from Anselm's *Man in Glory*, translated by Vaughan, in which faith is said to grow out of a profound consciousness of one's own corruption and from the consequent gratitude to a redeeming God: "That therefore thou mayst for ever take delight in the singing of his prayses, thou wilt (I believe) have always in thy mind those great transgressions and eternal miseries from which he delivered thee" (p. 201). This theme is then developed in many of Vaughan's divine poems. The paradox of "Sighs make joy sure" (p. 491), "pious griefs Heavens joys awake" (p. 511), "through thick pangs, high agonies/ Faith into life breaks" (p. 512), finds its concrete embodiment in the image of light shining out of, and set off against, darkness. True joy, overcast with clouds and rain, is likened to "those clear heights which above tempests shine" (p. 491), while true grief is, paradoxically, bright enough to "outshine all joys" (p. 505). The simile is made explicit in "The Timber":

> But as shades set off light, so tears and grief
> (Though of themselves but a sad and blubber'd story)
> By shewing the sin great, shew the relief
> Far greater, and so speak my Saviors glory.   (p. 498)

A similar image used in this context of repentance is that of light-in-dew, where dew, like darkness, stands for grief and tears, out of which the light of glory shines, but also for the tears of merciful Grace.[9] "Dew" is then further associated with Christ's blood, on the one hand, and with blooming and budding, on the other hand.[10]

Finally, a motif related to that of the awareness of past sins as essential to true Glory is that of discipline and chastisement as breaking the armor of darkness, thus bringing forth the hidden light. The seeming darkness of affliction paradoxically leads to the light of happiness; man is rendered "most Musicall" through "Wholesome" sickness (p. 459), through "restorative" diseases (p. 662); truth, when afflicted, thrives like that light which "gains a value from the Night" (p. 678). There are many metaphoric variations on this theme: the bird that sings best when its nest is broken (p. 501), the tree which being bent grows best (p. 490), liberty in imprisonment (p. 472), or God's "easie yoke" (p. 516). Above all, the idea of bliss out of affliction is rendered through the famous "silex scintillans," or sparkling flint, image, in which sudden light breaks out of the dark stoniness of the sinful heart.

C) Night for Prayer and Vision.

Darkness also spells silence, rest, peace, refuge. Night is the antithesis of the fussiness and distraction of daylight, it is "this worlds defeat" (p. 522). Vaughan's favorite word here is "shade" rather than "darkness,"[11] and its use is often complex: for it stands not merely for shelter from the heat of earthly ill-guiding light, and as an epithet for "that shady City of Palme trees" (p. 419), but it also means "copy" or "image." When Sundays, therefore, are described as the "Bright shadows of true Rest" (p. 447), the oxymoron is justified because "shadows" stands for both refuge from the heat (shade) and "image" of the light of God's glory. More naturally, "shadow" stands for the image of death, in which its meaning as "copy" and its meaning as "darkness" combine. This use appears in a section from Nierembergius's *Of Life and Death*, translated by Vaughan. The section discusses sleep as a copy of death; the underlined words are Vaughan's additions:

> So life, by reason of the importunity, and the multitude of humane troubles, cannot endure or hold out till it reacheth the Inne, which is death; but is driven to rest *in the shade* upon the way-side; for sleep (*the shadow of death*) is nothing else but a reparation of weary and fainting life. . . . If death *in its shadow and projection* be the recreation of life, how delightful will it be at home, or in it self! (p. 285)

But night, beyond its being the antithesis of the heat of gaudy sunlight, is also the channel that leads to another light, the true Light of the spirit. Here, again, light shines out of darkness and needs the "shade" to be revealed. Night is the time of prayer and vision.

The dialectic of light-of-the-world→darkness→divine Light is particularly worked out in the two prefaces to *Flores Solitudinis*: the Epistle Dedicatory and the "To the Reader." The transition which the reader may expect from "the sun into the Shade," will lead him, not to the deadly "Occidentem & tenebras," but to "that happy starre, which will directly lead you to the King of light" (p. 213). Similarly, the "shine of this world" is contrasted to the other light that grows out of darkness— "this light I live by in the Shade" (p. 216). It was at midnight that Nicodemus spoke with the Sun of Christ (p. 522), and it was the other night that the poet himself saw the endless light of eternity (p. 466). The soul's ascent to God at night is likened to a star shining behind the "mistie shroud" of clouds (p. 425).

Night being the "day of Spirits" (p. 522), or the "working-time of Spirits" (p. 305),[12] no wonder that it is, in accordance with Luke XXI, 37,[13] Christ's "prayer time" (p. 522), and that it should be our own prayer-time as well (p. 143). For it is "the mother of thoughts" (p. 169), and of all other times "the most powerful to excite thee to devotion" (p. 187). But it is not only the concrete peace and quiet of night that makes it the most practical time for vision and prayer. Blocking the way to the ordinary senses, it frees man from the subjection to sense and makes possible purely spiritual meditation, thus becoming a metaphor similar to St. John of the Cross's Night of the senses and of the understanding. It is only when the eye of sense and reason closes that the mystical eye opens. Darkness is again vindicated as the gateway to the light, as that blindness which makes real sight possible:[14] one's eyes never open except when God closes them (p. 488). The man who walks in God is the man whose eyes are both put out (p. 525), and the poet is resolved to "seal my eyes up" (p. 520).

D) The Darkness of God.

St. John of the Cross adds a third Night to the Nights of the senses and of reason—the Night of God Himself; for God "is dark night to the soul in this life."[15] That is, the incomprehensibility of God to man's mind finds its embodiment in the image of light too dazzling to look at, that is, dark; as Milton puts it: "Dark with excessive bright thy Skirts appear."[16] The ultimate source of this much-discussed image is pseudo-Dionysius's "darkness above light,"[17] meant, as Thomas Vaughan understands it, not in an absolute sense, "but in a relative sense or, as the schoolmen express it, 'in respect of us,'" for He is "invisible and incomprehensible."[18] This "Dark Aleph" of the contracted pre-creative God later manifests itself in the "Bright Aleph" of Creation, or of Christ.[19]

Henry Vaughan's own much-discussed reference, in "The Night," to the "deep, but dazzling darkness" which is in God, may have been inspired by pseudo-Dionysius,[20] or by his own brother. Like Thomas, he makes it clear that the darkness derives from our own inability to see: "some say" there is darkness in God—in the same way as men say it is dusky, not because there is "objective" darkness in God, or because it is "objectively" dusky, but "because they/See not all clear." The final two lines, however, seem to "objectivize" God's darkness:

O for that night! where I in him
Might live invisible and dim.

But "dim," elsewhere used by Vaughan to describe the extinguishing effect of the greater on the smaller light,[21] could indirectly show these words to mean the very opposite: I wish I were united to God, so that His excessive *light* would dim my little candle.

E) The Darkness of Incarnation.

The darkness of Incarnation is a motif both opposed and complementary to the darkness of God. For if the inaccessibility of God's light makes Him dark, the darkness—or veil—of the Incarnate Christ makes God's light accessible. Man cannot see God's light and live; therefore—as well as for other reasons, of course—God puts on a dark veil of flesh that makes His sight possible.

The veil-image, elsewhere used by Vaughan to symbolize the limitations connected with existence in the flesh, here serves as a metaphor for the "epistemological" advantage of the incarnate phase of God, which makes possible the knowledge of God by dimming His dazzling light.[22] Vaughan speaks of Christ's "entrance through the veile," of His putting on "Clouds instead of light," of the breaking of the veil on Christ's death which gave man sight and led him to the knowledge of God.[23] Above all, the much discussed first stanza of "The Night" clearly states that Nicodemus could recognize God "through"—which undoubtedly means also "by means of"[24]—the "sacred vail" of flesh He had put on. We cannot see God unless He is shrouded, eclipsed, veiled; and the veil is Incarnation.[25] Glowworms can shine only when facing the semi-darkness of the moon, for daylight would extinguish them; man can live only when facing the semi-darkness of Incarnation, for the naked light of God would drown his light. But the wish to "live" by looking at the "sacred vail," instead of the "glorious noon" itself, later in the poem develops into a wish to "die before his death"—as he puts it in "Regeneration"—and "live invisible and dim" in the "night," or "dazzling darkness" of God, which actually is the very same "glorious noon" of the first stanza.

F) Light in Darkness and Life in Death.

The paradox of God in the flesh is superseded by the sharper paradox of divine death for the sake of human life. The saving Crucifixion is the core of Vaughan's light-in-darkness dialectic, and the climax of his apology for darkness.

Death, besides being traditionally associated with darkness, also leads to a world of light, and it is in this sense that "the jewel of the just (shines) nowhere, but in the dark" (p. 484), i.e., death is the dark corridor, the passage through which is indispensable for the vision of the Light. Above all, Christ died to give life to man; the paradox of this life-giving death is often inseparable in Vaughan's poetry from the act of Incarnation itself: "a God Enclos'd within [a] Cell" (p. 415) is both a God incarnated and a God buried. It finds its traditional type in the phoenix whose "custom 'tis/ To rise by ruin" (p. 657), but above all, in the light-in-darkness image. Christ's death, "dark and deep pangs" to Himself, "to me was life and light" (p. 394). Less directly, in "Disorder and frailty" (p. 444), the "grave and womb of darkness," from which Christ beckons to the poet's "brutish soul" at the beginning of the poem, is later replaced by "Thy stars, and spangled hall" at which the poet aims and stretches from his cell of clay; thus an implied picture emerges of a lowly dark grave containing a high heaven of stars. As the source of true light, the death of Christ is an eye-opener, His blood has cleared our eyes and given us sight (p. 458). Like the setting sun, the dead set in the west only to be reborn in the east (p. 59).

"As time one day" (p. 512), probably a lament over the death of his first wife, combines the paradox of light-in-darkness with that of green branches budding out of dry dust and of the "bleaching" blood of Christ. The latter is an image Vaughan is particularly fond of. From a more pedestrian use of the snow-blood cluster—for blood-stained truth as soiled snow (p. 673), or carnations washing their bloody heads in snow-white streams (p. 644),—he progresses (in thought, not in time) through Revelations VII, 4, prefixed to his translation of *Man in Glory* (p. 193), to the typically paradoxical "bleaching" blood.[26]

In Vaughan, as in the Bible, darkness, though integrated into the world-order, is naturally further from the divine plan and will than is light. It is light and day, not darkness and night, that represent Providence, Redemption, hope and life. None of the metaphorical uses that make darkness so significant in Vaughan's poetry implies a "Romantic" attraction to darkness as such. If Glory is set off against past sins and repentance, it is Glory, not repentance, that ultimately wins the day. If night, both literally and figuratively, is the mother of thoughts and of mystical vision, it is the final sudden ray of light that is the much-expected goal. If God is darkness, it is only to our imperfect mind that darkness must be His sole attribute. If death is the only way to true life, and Crucifixion the only way to salvation, it is true life and salvation, not death and Crucifixion, that Vaughan "groans" for. As in the Bible, in which the elimination of day-night alternation is an integral part of eschatological visions,[27] Vaughan, too, can occasionally visualize that state of Glory in which the earthly light-darkness dialectic is overcome and light alone reigns. If here on earth a "wreath of grief and praise" must be offered to Christ, "Praise soil'd with tears, and tears again/ Shining with joy, like dewy days," Christ's "quickning breath" ulti-mately bears

> Through saddest clouds to that glad place,
> Where cloudless Quires sing without tears,
> Sing thy just praise, and see thy face.
>
> (p. 539)

Silex Scintillans ends with a powerful description, in "L'envoy" (p. 541), of the disappearance of the veils of physical light, and the overflow into this world of the immaculate brightness of ultimate light, absolute, which is freed from the need to be set off against its opposite:

> Arise, arise!
> And like old cloaths fold up these skies,
> This long worn veyl: then shine and spread
> Thy own bright self over each head,
> And through thy creatures pierce and pass
> Till all becomes thy cloudless glass,
> Transparent as the purest day
> And without blemish or decay,
> Fixt by thy spirit to a state
> For evermore immaculate.
> A state fit for the sight of thy
> Immediate, pure and unveil'd eye.

Vaughan's muse here rises to the "radiant Worlds" of which I. W. speaks in his commendatory poem, for once leaving all "hollow Joyes" behind. But the dazzling force of rare lines such as these depends, for its effectiveness, on their general context, on the long passage through the semi-darkness which is Vaughan's more usual theme.

Notes

1. *The Works of Henry Vaughan*, ed. L. C. Martin (Oxford, 1957), 620. All references in my text are to this edition. For I. W.'s identity, see editor's note to p. 615.

2. *Of Paradise and Light: a Study of Vaughan's Silex Scintillans* (Cambridge, 1960), 24–26, 135–136.

3. These words are from *Primitive Holiness*, a work which is largely a translation of the *Vita diui Paulini Episc. Nolani ex scriptis eius & veterum de eo Elogiis concinnata* (Antwerp, 1621); the quoted words, however, seem to be Vaughan's own. See editor's note to p. 370.

4. Central to Thomas Vaughan's accounts of creation is the meeting between masculine fire and the feminine darkness of the Materia Prima. He identifies the biblical primeval darkness with the Kabbalist "Ensoph" and the Orphic "Night," and subscribes to "that position of all famous poets and philosophers—that 'all things were brought forth out of the night.'" (*The works of Thomas Vaughan: Eugenius Philalethes*, ed. A. E. Waite [London, 1919] p. 216.) His description of both sub-rational Materia Prima and super-rational God as "Darkness" (ibid., p. 269) seems to lead him astray in that it makes him mix up Materia Prima with the pseudo-Dionysian "nothingness" of God, and he says of the former that "It is that Transcendent Essence whose theology is negative" (ibid., p. 214). Darkness plays a central role in his thought as the mother of all things.

5. I find the long controversy about whether the twin-brothers had anything to do with one another after adolescence rather futile. The biographical fact that Henry was not sure whether his brother had an M.A. (see his letter to John Aubrey, p. 687), or what the name of the village was where he had been buried (p. 691), by no means disproves influence. After all, Henry did know his brother's work (pp. 687–688), and apparently sympathized with his brother in his ludicrously bad-tempered controversy with Henry More ("Daphnis," 11.35–38, p. 677). Thomas Powell's homage to the brothers—"Not only your faces, but your Wits are Twins" ("Upon the most Ingenious pair of Twins . . . ", p. 36) would have been absurdly tactless, had the brothers been completely estranged from each other. Above all, the many thoughts, terms and images they share in common clearly point to mutual knowledge and influence. A comparison such as Miss Elizabeth Holmes makes between Henry's "Cock-crowing" and a passage from Thomas' *Anima Magica Abscondita* (see editor's note to "Cock-crowing," p. 746) is an irrefutable proof of the latter's influence on the former.

6. See Sverra Aalen, *Die Begriffe 'Licht' und 'Finsternis' im Alten Testament, im Spätjudentum und im Rabbinismus*, Skrifter utgitt av Det Norske Videnskaps-Akademi i Oslo. II, Hist.-Filos. Klasse, 1951, no. 1 (Oslo, 1951) 9–19.

7. Cf. "Affliction" *(Thalia Rediviva)*, p. 662: "Flow'rs that in Sun-shines riot still,/Dye scorch'd and sapless"; cf. also Traherne, *Centuries* III, 21.

8. Cf. Sylvester's Du Bartas (1621 ed.) 12–13:

But yet, because all Pleasures wex unpleasant,
If without pause we still possesse them, present;
And none can right discerne the sweets of Peace,
That have not felt Wars irkesome bitterness;
And Swans seem whiter if swart crowes be by
(For, Contraries each other best discry)
Th'All's-Architect, alternately decreed
That Night the Day, the Day should Night succeed.

9. "Dew" in both its figurative senses is used in "The Sap" (p. 475) ll.3–4 and 39–41, "Jesus Weeping" (p. 503) ll.11,48–49, "Admission" (p. 453) ll.29–32, or "The Timber" (p. 497) in which there is a gradual progression from the tears of repentance to the spiritual waters of the celestial springs. The twofold sense of "dew" is discussed in Pettet's *Of Paradise and Light*, p. 133.

10. Pettet, pp. 30, 42–47. Vaughan's association of water with light is persistent: in "Midnight" (p. 421), God's Heaven is described as a "fierie-liquid light," both flaming and streaming, and the poet asks Heaven to make his own blood, or water, both "burne and streame." The star, in "The Starre" (p. 489), is said to "stream or flow," while God's emanations of light, in "The Importunate Fortune" (p. 634) are "Sacred streams," "A glorious Cataract," and they "flow." Also in "The Eagle" (p. 626), the beams of the sun rush upon the eagle "like so many Streams." The combination, in Heaven, of light, or fire, and water, may have something to do with the Jewish traditional interpretation of Shamayim (heaven) as derived from a combination of Esh (fire) and Mayim (water), an interpretation cited by Henry's brother Thomas *(The Works of Thomas Vaughan*, p. 278) and by two authors he admired: Pico della Mirandola, in *Heptaplus*, "Ad Lectorem Praefatio," and J. Reuchlin, in *De Arte Cabalistica* (in Johann Pistorius' *Artis Cabalisticae*, [Basel, 1587], p. 633).

11. In *The Mount of Olives* (p. 152) night as "shadow," as "rest and security," is even contrasted to night as "the hours and the powers of darknesse."

12. These are words Vaughan added to his translation of Nierembergius.

13. Quoted on the title-page of *The Mount of Olives*, p. 137; cf. Vaughan's marginal note to "The Night," 1.29.

14. This paradox is popular with the Metaphysicals: "To see God only, I goe out of sight" (Donne, "A Hymne to Christ, at the Authors last going into Germany"); "Shutt our eyes that we may see" (Crashaw, "In the Glorious Epiphanie of our Lord God, a Hymn . . . ").

15. *Ascent of Mount Carmel*, as quoted by Ross Garner, *Henry Vaughan: Experience and the Tradition* (Chicago, 1959), pp. 55–56.

16. *Paradise Lost*, III, 380.

17. ὑπέρρωτος γνόρος —*De Myst. Theol.* II.

18. *The Works of Thomas Vaughan*, p. 269.

19. *Works*, p. 15.

20. His reference to "Hierotheus" in the preface to the second edition of *Silex Scintillans* (p. 392) shows that he knew at least the *De divinis nominibus*, in which this fictitious writer of hymns is mentioned, though he could have picked up the name from a later writer.

21. E,g,, p. 472· "But to this later light they saw in him,/Their day was dark, and dim."

22. Cf. Hebrews X, 19–20. This motif is recurrent in 17th century poetry. Milton, in "Il Penseroso," ll.11–16, applies it to his admired Melancholy.

23. *Flores Solitudinis*, p. 288; "The Incarnation, and Passion," p. 415; "The Holy Communion," p. 457.

24. Cf. R. A. Durr, *Of the Mystical Poetry of Henry Vaughan* (Cambridge, Mass., 1962), p. 115.

25. The underlying assumption here seems to be that pure spirits must put on material "garments" when they descend to earth: "No spiritual thing descending below can operate without a garment," says Pico della Mirandola in the 35th of his "Conclusiones Cabalisticae," quoted as a "Kabalistic maxim" by Thomas Vaughan *(The Works of Thomas Vaughan*, p. 46) and paraphrased by Henry Vaughan (p. 366).

26. See "Ascension-Hymn," p. 482; "To my most merciful...Christ," p. 394; "As time one day," p. 512.

27. E.g., Zechariah XIV, 6–7; see Sverre Aalen, pp. 20–27.

ALAN RUDRUM

Vaughan's "The Night":
Some Hermetic Notes

In his excellent critical book on Vaughan, E. C. Pettet writes that 'his
best poems are among the ones that show a minimum of hermetic
influence'. In this he is supported by Ross Garner and R. A. Durr.[1] In
reviewing their books I have indicated disagreement with this view, and
in articles on 'The Book' and 'Regeneration' have argued for the subtlety
and centrality of Vaughan's hermeticism.[2] Here I want to focus on one
of the very best of Vaughan's poems, 'The Night'. Its quality being
generally acknowledged, I shall essay neither a general appreciation,
nor an exercise in practical criticism. These things have been well done
by Mr. Pettet, and I merely wish to supplement his account. My starting-
point is the phrase *'Virgin-shrine'* which occurs in the first line, and
which has never been satisfactorily explained. I believe that it must be
understood by reference to the concept, popular among Renaissance
hermetists, of the Cosmic Christ, and that this is a controlling concept
throughout the poem. Since my principal attention is required by a
phrase in the poem's first line, this account may well seem structurally
anti-climactic. Justification may be that this single phrase embodies the
entire universe of the poem. The unity of 'The Night' is generally felt,
but rarely correctly interpreted, indeed usually only dimly seen. My
supporting notes may serve to reveal some of the elements of thought,

Reprinted, by permission of the publisher, from *The Modern Language Review*, 64:1
(1969), 11–19.

tedious to relate and perhaps trivial in themselves, which coalesce into
that unity.

It will be best if the reader has the whole poem in front of him:

The Night

Through that pure *Virgin-shrine,*
That sacred vail drawn o'r thy glorious noon
That men might look and live as Glo-worms shine,
And face the Moon:
Wise *Nicodemus* saw such light
As made him know his God by night.

Most blest believer he!
Who in that land of darkness and blinde eyes
Thy long expected healing wings could see,
When thou didst rise,
And what can never more be done,
Did at mid-night speak with the Sun!

O who will tell me, where
He found thee at that dead and silent hour!
What hallow'd solitary ground did bear
So rare a flower,
Within whose sacred leafs did lie
The fulness of the Deity.

No mercy-seat of gold,
No dead and dusty *Cherub,* nor carv'd stone,
But his own living works did my Lord hold
And lodge alone;
Where *trees* and *herbs* did watch and peep
And wonder, while the *Jews* did sleep.

Dear night! this worlds defeat;
The stop to busie fools; cares check and curb;
The day of Spirits; my souls calm retreat
Which none disturb!
Christs progress, and his prayer time;
The hours to which high Heaven doth chime.

Gods silent, searching flight:
When my Lords head is fill'd with dew, and all
His locks are wet with the clear drops of night;
His still, soft call;

142

> His knocking time; The souls dumb watch,
> When Spirits their fair kinred catch.
>
> Were all my loud, evil days
> Calm and unhaunted as is thy dark Tent,
> Whose peace but by some *Angels* wing or voice
> Is seldom rent;
> Then I in Heaven all the long year
> Would keep, and never wander here.
>
> But living where the Sun
> Doth all things wake, and where all mix and tyre
> Themselves and others, I consent and run
> To ev'ry myre,
> And by this worlds ill-guiding light,
> Erre more then I can do by night.
>
> There is in God (some say)
> A deep, but dazling darkness; As men here
> Say it is late and dusky, because they
> See not all clear;
> O for that night! where I in him
> Might live invisible and dim.

I know of no parallels either in contemporary religious verse or in orthodox theology for the phrase *Virgin-shrine*, which refers to Christ's earthly body; and although it is no doubt a medieval and Catholic commonplace that Christ's flesh was virgin, both because he was a virgin and because he was born of one, nevertheless Vaughan's use of the phrase strikes many readers as odd, and attempts to explain it in orthodox terms are not entirely successful. Indeed R. A. Durr, in an article in 1960,[3] wrote that the phrase obviously refers to Mary, an error which is silently retracted in his book, though he does there suggest a reference to the Virgin Mary as the secondary meaning of the phrase (p. 115). E. C. Pettet understands the phrase as meaning that Christ's human form is both Virgin-born and immaculate (p. 142). This seems to me to do more justice to orthodoxy than to Vaughan's phrase, which surely means, whatever else it means, 'a shrine which contains a virgin'.

It is possible to argue that the phrase does not refer primarily to Christ's human person at all, that the 'pure *Virgin-shrine*' is the unclouded night-sky, showing forth in all her glory Diana, the moon, 'Queen, and huntress, chaste, and fair'. To the objection, 'What then becomes of the appositional phrase "That sacred veil", which is an obvious reference to the Pauline "the veil, that is to say, his flesh"?' one might reply that this is conceivably to mistake Vaughan's intention, since after all he twice at least uses the image of the veil in connexion with the moon.[4]

It seems to me likely that the argument is unnecessary. As Miss Mahood has pointed out[5] Vaughan's symbols are often complex. It is here possible that the images refer *both* to Christ and to the whole night-scene, indeed that the two are identical! One recalls that Vaughan believed both that Christ was incarnate as a human being on earth, and that He is in some sense the life of Nature. The Prologue to St John's Gospel seems to indicate that St John believed something of that sort, and, to judge from the first chapter of *Colossians*, so did St Paul. In our own time such ideas have been found suggestive by thinkers like Canon Charles Raven and Teilhard de Chardin; in Vaughan's time they were developed by the hermetists. Paracelsus thought of the universe as being God's incarnation, just as Christ was for orthodoxy, and Agrippa was not averse to visualising the created universe as a vast person, quoting 'a saying of Orpheus' which may well have been in Vaughan's mind when he wrote the sixth stanza.[6] It is in Jacob Behmen that one finds the concepts which explain Vaughan's images, which allow them to refer both to the whole night scene and to Christ's earthly body without contradiction. Behmen insists on the 'celestial and unlimited corporeity' of the Redeemer, pointing out that 'while God became man, His humanity was everywhere where His divinity existed', that is, Christ even during the Incarnation was immanent in the whole universe.[7] This reference to the Redeemer's 'unlimited corporeity' reconciles the ideas of the Cosmic Christ and of the Incarnate Lord, it is consonant with Agrippa's quotation referring to the universe as a vast person, and consonant too with the hermetic assimilation of Christ with the Adam Kadmon of the *Zohar*, the androgynous prototype of humanity who encompassed the whole of space.[8]

Behmen's further statement that Christ 'has the eternal celestial bride, the virgin of divine wisdom ... in His possession' seems to bring us closer to the sense of *'Virgin-shrine'* than does the recollection that Christ was born of a virgin, and suggests that it may be worthwhile to pause over Behmenite doctrine a little, especially as there are some grounds for believing that Vaughan may have been familiar with the particular work of Behmen's in which the quotations adduced so far occur.

An important element in Behmen's teaching is the concept of the Sophia, the Eternal Virgin. In his doctrine of the Divine Nothing, Behmen descries the shadows at the base of being, the 'deep, but dazzling darkness' of Vaughan's final stanza. The doctrine of the Sophia sets forth the light of the deity. The equation of Christ with the Sophia becomes a little more plausible when we recall that for Vaughan's twin brother Thomas 'the Second Person is the Light'[9] and that in the second line of the poem there is a reference to 'thy glorious noon'. One cannot separate the Sophia-concept from the concept of the Androgyne which has reference to the supposed initial wholeness of man. The androgynous state was the image of God in man, who had the Virgin, the Divine Wisdom, as his companion and the object of his contemplation.

The Fall, in Behmen's account, involved the loss of the Virgin, the loss of Adam's androgynity, and the appearance of Eve, the child of this world. Now the virginity of Adam in his original sophianic state was not meant by Behmen to signify that the masculine nature was isolated from the feminine, but rather that there was an essential union between the two natures; and this anthropological teaching of Behmen's is closely bound up with his teaching on the nature of Christ: Christ's nature, he thought, was androgynous. Traditional theology had never taken to its conclusion St Paul's teaching that Christ is the New Adam, but the hermetic philosophers did, probably because one of the sources of their system was a fountain from which St Paul also drew.[10] Paracelsus, for example, taught that Christ was the Adam Kadmon, to whom all creatures finally return, and Behmen wrote constantly of the old Adam and the new, to signify that in Christ God is humanized and man becomes divine: Christ, he claimed, lived in Adam and he in Christ. In the person of Christ, the original perfection, the androgynity and virginity of man was restored: Christ possesses the Virgin; his flesh might well be described as a *'Virgin-shrine'*:

> The regenerated soul receives Christ's flesh and blood . . . and
> the spirit of the new will becomes substantial and essential
> . . . and this essentiality is called Sophia, being the essential
> wisdom, and the body of Christ.[11]

If we accept that the phrase *'Virgin-shrine'* may have reference to Behmen's teaching then we can understand how Vaughan can think of Christ both as a human person and as the whole night-scene, since the Adam Kadmon, who had the Virgin of divine wisdom in his possession, and who is renewed in the incarnate Christ, did contain the whole cosmos within himself.[12] This part of cabalistic-hermetic teaching is revived in Behmen's insistence on the 'unlimited corporeity' of Christ while in the flesh.

The phrase 'That sacred vail drawn o'r thy glorious noon', in the second line of the poem, is in apposition to 'Virgin-shrine'. This image of the veil occurs frequently in Vaughan's work; he uses it some score of times in his original verse and prose, and introduces it in translation where there is nothing in the source to suggest it.[13] B. T. Stewart suggests a 'hermetic' reason for Vaughan's fondness for the image, arguing that as used in 'The Night' the word is coloured by the cabalistic doctrine of the *sephiroth*, the divine emanations which paradoxically hide and at the same time reveal the divine nature.[14] The doctrine is of course the cabalists' way of reconciling the doctrine of the unknowability of the deity with that of his manifestation in the universe. Stewart is correct in saying that Vaughan's use of the image of the veil here is in consonance with cabalism: the third and fourth lines make it clear that it is the veil thrown across the glory of God for the paradoxical purpose of revealing the divine nature. It seems reasonable to say that Vaughan's image fuses the Christian and the hermetic teachings about the manifestation of God. To the Christian, God manifests himself in the incarnate Christ, 'the image of the invisible God'. To the hermetist, He manifests himself in the universe, which is likewise His incarnation. My commentary on the phrase 'Virgin-shrine' and Stewart's on 'That sacred vail' support each other, since for the cabalists the whole of creation is a veil, as for the hermetic Christian Christ's corporeity is 'unlimited'. This is not to say that 'The Night' is really two poems operating through a set of images which contain irreconcileable ambiguities, one poem for the orthodox Christian, the other for the hermetic adept. It does mean that Vaughan found profound meaning in the concept of 'the Cosmic Christ'.

Vaughan's intentions, to a reader who knows the spirit of his work and is not mesmerized by the specific Biblical reference to Nicodemus, are made clear by the imagery: just as for the hermetists the emphasis was not on the historical aspects of the Incarnation so much as on its symbolical aspect and on Christ's cosmic function, so in the first stanza Christ is not mentioned by name, and when in the fifth stanza He is, the context is not that of his historical career. The imagery of the first stanza, down to the humble 'Glo-worms', is worked out in terms drawn from the world of nature rather than from human life, and an important function is assigned to generally cosmic imagery (noon, moon, light, night) which coalesces round the shadowy figure of Christ. Turning now to the second stanza, we find that again Christ's humanity and earthly career are not stressed. The 'Sun-Christ' parallel, implicit in the 'glorious noon' of the first stanza (a parallel which is Biblical but becomes vastly enriched in hermetic thought) is made explicit in the final couplet of the second stanza. Henry Vaughan's awareness of the hermetic equation *Anima-Mundi*:Christ:Sun informs 'Regeneration',[15] and elsewhere in his poetry he shows himself fond of using the image of the Sun in connexion with Christ; for example in 'Faith' where, as here, it is used in conjunction with the veil image, and in 'The Dawning', where we also find the image of Christ's 'locks' which occurs in the sixth stanza of 'The Night'. The image of the Sun shining at midnight finds a parallel in Thomas Vaughan's strangely beautiful work *Lumen de Lumine*, which throws light on 'Regeneration'. Moreover, in his notes to this passage in Thomas's work, Waite points out that the 'alchemical symbolism ... pictures a region of strange experience where the sun shines at midnight' (*Works*, p. 244). This would be enough to indicate that Vaughan's paradox has its background in the work of the hermetists, but more striking still is a parallel we find in Behmen:

> There is a wonderful time coming, but because it beginneth
> in the night, there are many that shall not see it, by reason
> of their sleep and drunkenness: yet the Sun will shine on the
> children at midnight.[16]

It is noteworthy that the thought of Vaughan's 'Who in that land of darkness and blind eyes' also finds its parallel in the immediate context of the 'Sun at Midnight' image. Moreover, our suggestion as to the link between Behmen's Sophia-concept and Vaughan's phrase *'Virgin-shrine'* is reinforced by Behmen's note on the word 'children' in the passage quoted. These are, he says, the children of 'Sophia, or the Divine Wisdom'. The reference to the Virgin of wisdom in Christ's possession comes from the same work of Behmen's, *The Three Principles of the Divine Essence*. The verbal parallels seem to make it likely that Vaughan had read this particular work, and they are supported by ordinary probability. Thomas Vaughan mentions it in his *Coelum Terrae*: 'Jacob Behmen in his most excellent and profound *Discourse* of the *Three Principles*' (*Works*, p. 213). It is worth adding that the first translations of Behmen's works in

England were issued by Humphrey Blunden, who seems to have devoted himself to the propagation of alchemical and hermetical writings. Humphrey Blunden was also publisher to both Thomas and Henry Vaughan. In the third and fourth stanzas of 'The Night' we have a beautiful rendering of the theme of the divine immanence. Vaughan has no disinclination to write in terms of humble natural objects; he moves quite naturally from the cosmic imagery of the Sun-Christ parallel to seeing divinity in a humble flower. In the first stanza, one notices, Christ as a historical personage is not invoked by the imagery; in these we have a positive expression of the concept of immanence divorced from any particular historical and personal manifestation. It is very much a piece with Vaughan's personality as a religious man that he could divine the 'fulness of the Deity' enfolded in the leaves of a flower. The theme of immanence is enlarged upon in the fourth stanza, where the whisper of devotion swells out into the organ note of affirmation. The Vaughans, while staunch Royalists, shared their mystical doctrines with the sectaries rather than with their political allies, and the mood expressed in the fourth stanza may seem to come oddly from an Anglican of rather strict tendencies; it is much more what we might expect from a George Fox, with his contempt for 'steeple-houses'. It is perhaps scarcely necessary to invoke the writings of the hermetists in order to explain the bias of Vaughan's mind, but we do find his mood paralleled very frequently in the works of Behmen, who would never admit that a building could be anything more than a building, and disliked the custom of calling 'stone houses' churches. Throughout his work Behmen insists on the necessity for individual salvation, for each man to be Nicodemus; he thought that the sacraments of the church were ineffectual unless considered as symbols of inward regeneration, and therefore dangerous, because likely to be misleading. This is a frequently recurring theme, particularly in his *Epistles*. For example we find him saying that it is not 'Temples or houses of stone (sc. 'which regenerate man') but the Divine Sun in... the Temple of Jesus Christ, in himself' (*Epistle* I, p. 12). We never find him directing his readers to the liturgy of the church, but he frequently exhorts them to seek God in Nature; the man who is 'born of God' may see 'in every spike of grass, his Creator in whom he liveth' (*Three Principles*, p. 57).

The thought of the final couplet of the fourth stanza, in which religious awareness and a desire for God is attributed to '*trees*' and '*herbs*' is by no means unique in Vaughan. Indeed it is very much part of him that he sees the world of nature as being essentially co- operative with God, while erring man goes astray. Perhaps the fullest expression of this attitude is found in his poem 'Man'. Now it may be that the image of the religious awareness of the plants, contrasted here with the sleeping Jews, is related to the hermetic philosophy, and related moreover in such a way as to link it with the phrase *'Virgin-shrine'* which I have attempted to elucidate by reference to Behmen's concepts of the Sophia and the Androgyne. The idea that man was originally androgynous, and that he originally lived in the Eternal Realm, is found in the hermetic books as well as in Behmen (*libellus* i). According to the hermetic author, Man fell from eternity into time because he fell in love with his own reflection in the world of becoming. Nature also fell in love, with 'the beauty of the form of God' in man. After Nature had 'wrapped man in her clasp' man and all the rest of the creatures were bisexual for a time, and consequently lived together in harmony, since the androgynous state, being the image of the bisexuality of the deity, was one in which matter was subordinated to mind. Then man lost his bisexuality and became afflicted with carnal desires. This helps us to see why it is that the *'trees'* and *'herbs'* 'watched' and 'wondered' while the Jews gave way to their bodily needs in sleep; and since it is only the vegetable world which has retained its primal integrity, it is not surprising that it should be a flower 'Within whose sacred leafs did lie / The fulness of the Deity'. Moreover, if our explanation of the phrase *'Virgin-shrine'* does carry the undertone that by retaining the divine bisexuality, Christ was able to mirror in human flesh the perfections of the eternal world, the word 'wise' as applied to Nicodemus becomes hermetically apt when we recall that it is 'the man who has mind in him' who recognises his immortality and can reascend to contemplation of the deity in the eternal realms.[17]

In the fifth and sixth stanzas Vaughan passes from the theme of the deity immanent in creation to a rhapsody on the theme of night. These stanzas form perhaps the most expressive, but by no means the only passage in which Vaughan deals with his religious love for the night. It seems that he could find God in Nature best by the light of dawn or the dimness of evening. It is at night that the earthly desires of the world are defeated, and even the 'busie fools' (contrasted with 'Wise *Nicodemus*') cease their activities. There is in these stanzas a wonderful fusion of Biblical with hermetic imagery. The phrase 'The day of Spirits' is an adaptation of Paracelsus's 'Night is the working-time of spirits', a sentence paralleled by Thomas Vaughan's assertion that the 'Night of the Body' (a phrase he says is cabalistic) is the rendezvous of all spirits.[18] The words 'Christ's progress' are referred by Vaughan in a footnote to the first chapter of St Mark's Gospel, in which Christ is said to have risen a great while before dawn to go out to pray, but we notice that the 'progress' of these stanzas is quite independent of any historical event, while in the following stanzas Christ is significantly referred to in the natural imagery of 'dew' and 'the clear drops of night'.

The lines in the sixth stanza, 'When my Lords head is fill'd with dew, and all / His locks are wet with the clear drops of night', are clearly Biblical in origin. In the second verse of the fifth chapter of the *Song of Solomon*, we read

> I sleep, but my heart waketh; it is the voice of my beloved that knocketh, saying, Open to me, my sister, my love, my dove, my undefiled: for my head is filled with dew, and my locks with the drops of the night.

As the *Song* was conventionally interpreted, these lines referred to Christ awakening the church with his calling; it is Christ who is here the beloved. In the words 'I sleep, but my heart waketh', we have the background of 'The souls dumb watch', and of course the phrase 'His knocking time' also refers to this passage. If the source of this wonderful passage is clearly Biblical, it may well be that its significance for Vaughan was deepened (along the lines of the orthodox reading of the allegory) by hermetic concepts or phrases. It is the more worthwhile to pause and notice these, since there has been controversy over the meaning of Vaughan's lines, and a hermetic interpretation, as in the case of *'Virgin-shrine'*, has the merit of reconciling the antagonists. Kermode writes, 'The conceit is daring; the sky is God's hair, and the stars are drops of night dew sprinkled upon it'.[19] Garner points out that 'the context of the echo from the *Song of Solomon*, in its traditional interpretation, concerns Christ and His church', and accuses Kermode of reading the echo from the *Song of Solomon* in terms that are imported from outside the religious context to prove that Vaughan's verse depends for its validity on literary associations entirely apart from his religious predilections. He argues (pp. 141–2) that 'the poet's primary intention is to give a picture of Christ as he appeared on this earth, and the physical wetness of the dew emphasizes His sacred humanity'. These two interpretations come closer together if we accept that Vaughan's imagination was moving

within the concept of the Cosmic Christ, reinforced probably by the cabalistic symbolism of the Vast Countenance adduced by Stewart.
In view of the fact that the poem is about the relationship between
man and God, and the fact that this theme is developed throughout in
terms of natural and very probably hermetic imagery, it is relevant that
the hermetists thought of the spirit of the world which lives on in man
as being a 'dew of light'. This is the same *Anima Mundi* which the
hermetists equated with Christ. This is another way they had of describing the *scintilla animae*, or the divine spark which lives on in man's
soul: that is, this 'divine spark' in the soul can be equated with Christ,
who for the hermetic Christian was immanent in each human soul as
a 'dew of light' to which Christ, when His head is 'fill'd with dew' makes
His 'still, soft call'. Vaughan's image encompasses both the shadowy
figure of Jesus, calling to His Church, as He was conventionally read
into the passage from Canticles, and the Cosmic Christ of the hermetists,
Fludd's 'spirit of God or Christ', which 'dwelleth not in artful Temples,
but maketh every natural thing his sanctuary'.[20]
In the seventh stanza the poem moves into Vaughan's personal
application of his meditation. This stanza, with its burden of dissatis-
faction with the level of his spiritual life, seems straightforward enough;
and indeed no-one has difficulty in understanding it. Yet Vaughan's
expression is still moving within distinctively hermetic bounds. The lines
should not be taken to mean that if the author could reach the 'calmness'
of the unmanifest deity—one recalls here the hermetic emphasis on the
imperturbability of God (*libellus* VI, I)—then he would be out of this
life altogether and consequently in the eternal realm. They mean that
he would be in a state of 'heaven-on-earth'. Now this is a possibility for
hermetic rather than for Christian mysticism. Even for the Christian
mystic who can ascend to the prayer of union, this final stage of contact
with God is only a fleeting thing, whereas Vaughan writes of being 'in
heaven all the long year'. Where hermetic is assimilated to Christian
thought that heresy arises which states that it is possible for good men
to be 'deified' in this life.[21] Of course Vaughan is not claiming that he
himself is deified—just the reverse in fact—but it is difficult to escape
the conclusion that the seventh stanza does depend on the idea that
deification is possible
The eighth stanza may also have reference to hermetic doctrines;
the Sun referred to is no longer Christ, but the natural celestial body
which measures time; the use of the image involves not a simple dropping

RUDRUM

of the Sun-Christ parallel, but a contrasting of eternity with time. The words 'where all mix and tyre I Themselves and others' may refer to the loss of harmony involved in the general loss of primal bisexuality; this state of discord can only be transcended by the man 'who has mind in him', while those who are led astray because they have set their affections on the body 'continue wandering in the darkness of the sense-world, suffering the loss of death' (*libellus* I, 19). In this passage it is perhaps legitimate to see in 'the darkness of the sense-world' a parallel with Vaughan's 'this world's ill-guiding light', in the words 'led astray' a parallel with his 'errs', while the hermetist's 'wandering in the sense-world' may be echoed in the final words of the seventh stanza. We are fairly certain that Vaughan had read this particular *libellus*.[22] However, while it is difficult to doubt that there is a reference in stanzas seven and eight to hermetic doctrines, the imagery can again be referred to the Bible, to such passages, for example, as 'I am the light of the world; he that followeth me shall not walk in darkness, but shall have the light of life'; and 'If therefore the light that is in thee be darkness, how great is that darkness'.

In the final stanza of the poem Vaughan's meditation moves from the contemplation of 'the image' to a prayer for union with 'the invisible God' himself. As in the first stanza, the two levels of reference tacitly assert the actuality both of a transcendental mystery and a human predicament: the poem may be seen as an attempt, through releasing the symbolistic ambiguities of language, to assert the potential continuity of experience from the mundane to the ecstatic. Underlying it is the hermetic preoccupation with the alchemy of experience: the winning of the Stone out of the barren earth, of the Elixir from the brackish waters of experience.

Notes

1. E. C. Pettet, *Of Paradise and Light* (Cambridge, 1960); Ross Garner, *Henry Vaughan: Experience and the Tradition* (Chicago, 1959); R. A. Durr, *On the Mystical Poetry of Henry Vaughan* (Cambridge, Mass., 1962).
2. Reviews: Garner, *AUMLA (Journal of the Australasian Universities Language and Literature Association)*, 14 (November 1960), 71–3; Pettet, *AUMLA*, 15 (May 1961), 90–3; Durr, *AUMLA*, 20 (November 1963), 369–71. Articles: 'Henry Vaughan's "The Book": A Hermetic Poem', *AUMLA*, 16 (November 1961), 161–6; 'Henry Vaughan and the Theme of Transfiguration', *Southern Review (An Australian Journal of Literary Studies)*, I (1963), 54–68.
3. 'Vaughan's "The Night"', *J.E.G.P.*, 59 (1960), 34–40.
4. '... that *planet* (whose *sphere* is the *veil* or *partition* drawn betwixt *us* and

152

"THE NIGHT": SOME HERMETIC NOTES

immortality)', *Works*, edited by L. C. Martin, second edition (Oxford, 1957), p. 176; 'the *Moon's* ruder veile', *Works*, p. 630.

5. *Poetry and Humanism* (1950), pp. 262–4.
6. A. Koyré, 'Paracelse', *Revue d'Histoire et de Philosophie Religieuses* (1933), pp. 67–8; H. C. Agrippa, *Three Books of Occult Philosophy*, translated by J.F. (1651), chapter 6.
7. See F. Hartmann, *Personal Christianity* (New York, 1957), p. 242.
8. *Jewish Encyclopedia*, new edition, (New York, 1925), I, 181–3.
9. *Works*, edited by A. E. Waite (1919), p. 14.
10. See the article 'Adam Kadmon' in the *Jewish Encyclopaedia*.
11. Epistle I, 9, *The Epistles of Jacob Behmen aliter, Teutonius Philosophus*, translated by Gyles Calvert (1649). For the basis of my account of Behmen's teaching on the Eternal Virgin, see N. Berdiaeff's introduction to the French translation of *Mysterium Magnum* (Paris, 1945); and H. L. Martensen, *Jacob Boehme*, translated by T. Rhys Evans, revised edition with notes and appendices by S. Hobhouse (1949), pp. 155 ff.
12. See Vol. III, pp. 135 ff., of *Hermetica*, edited by W. Scott, 4 vols (Oxford, 1924–36).
13. See M. M. Mahood, *Poetry and Humanism* (1950), p. 262.
14. 'Hermetic Symbolism in Henry Vaughan's "The Night"', *P.Q.*, 29 (1950), 417–22.
15. This aspect of the poem is discussed in my 'Henry Vaughan and the Theme of Transfiguration', cited above.
16. 'Preface to the Reader', *The Three Principles of the Divine Essence*, English translation (1648).
17. *Libellus* I, 18. For the hint developed here, I am indebted to M.-S. Røstvig's article 'Andrew Marvell's "The Garden": A Hermetic Poem', *English Studies*, 40 (1959), 65–76.
18. *Works*, p. 224.
19. F. Kermode, 'The Private Imagery of Henry Vaughan', *Review of English Studies*, New Series, I (1950), 206–25 (p. 222).
20. Robert Fludd, *Mosaicall Philosophy*, English version (1659), p. 12.
21. '... in the view of the Hermetists, every man is (potentially at least) what the Christians held Christ, but Christ alone, to be' (Scott, I, 12, note). The fact that some Renaissance hermetists allowed the possibility of a state of 'heaven-on-earth' is made clear by Behmen: 'the right man regenerate and born anew in Christ, is not in this world, but in the Paradise of God; and albeit he is in the liberty [i.e. in the world of revealed objects] yet he is in God' (*Epistle* 23, p. 178.)
22. See L. C. Martin's notes to 'The Importunate Fortune', *Works*, p. 758.

153

A. U. CHAPMAN

Henry Vaughan and Magnetic Philosophy[1]

> *Many other Magnetisms may be pretended, and the like*
> *attractions through all the creatures of Nature. Whether*
> *the same be verified in the action of the Sun upon inferior*
> *bodies, whether there be Æolian Magnets, whether the flux*
> *and reflux of the Sea be caused by any Magnetism from*
> *the Moon; whether the like be really made out, or rather*
> *Metaphorically verified in the sympathies of Plants and*
> *Animals, might afford a large dispute.* . . .
>
> *Pseudodoxia Epidemica*

I The Problem of Definition

In *Coelum Terrae*, Thomas Vaughan, the poet's Hermetist brother, rejects the idea that the concept of magnetism is to be confined to the attractive qualities of the lodestone and magnet. Iron and lodestone, he says, is but one of "a pack of small conspiracies," of "pitiful particulars" which some Platonists confuse with "the universall magnet which binds this great frame and moves all the members of it to a mutual compassion."[2] By this "universall" magnet, he tells us in *Anthroposophia Theomagica*, "all things may be attracted whether physical or metaphysical. . . . without this there is no ascent or descent, either influential or personal. . . . it is that which mediates between extremes, and makes inferiors and supe-

Reprinted, by permission of the publisher, from *Southern Review (Adelaide)*, 4:3 (1971), 215–26.

riors communicate."[3] Thomas's rival in Neoplatonic philosophy, Henry More, describes magnetism as "whatsoever doth immediately rule and actuate any body" and this encompasses the "spermatical" power of plants and the "plastical" power of animals, that is their formative and procreative virtues.[4] A quarter of a century earlier, the Flemish Paracelsian Jean Baptiste van Helmont refers to magnetism as "a *Celestial quality*, of near affinity to the *sidereal influences*"[5] and argues that "whoever denies the influential power of *Sublunaries* mutually transmitted and entertained each by other, to be performed by Magnetism; and requires an instance to be given him to the contrary: in sober truth he requires a flat absurdity, a Magnetism (forsooth) without Magnetism. . . ."[6] All of these are assertions of the existence of a magnetism of an altogether greater scope than, and of a nature different from, the lodestone/iron phenomenon. It is the purpose of this paper to examine Henry Vaughan's references to magnetism to discover whether his view of it coincides with that of his brother and these other authors or whether he merely sees magnetism "Metaphorically verified" in Nature at large.

Such an examination will, I hope, make a small contribution to the large dispute about the nature and extent of the Hermetic influence in Henry Vaughan's poetry. The works which, in the 1920's and 30's, pioneered the interpretative criticism of Vaughan stressed the nature mysticism and Hermetic philosophy in his poetry.[7] This view has been largely carried over into the notes and commentaries of L. C. Martin[8] and, more particularly, E. L. Marilla.[9] More recently published work has tended to relegate the influence of Hermeticism on Vaughan to the status of a source of metaphor.[10] None of these writers has critically examined Vaughan's references to magnetism, the earlier group being content to assume that he believed in a "universall magnetism," the later that he uses magnetic imagery in a figurative way.

The assumption that Henry Vaughan is a thoroughgoing adherent to Hermetic ideas would, of course, make this inquiry meaningless; for if the poet believes that magnetism *is* that which "makes inferiors and superiors communicate," *is* the medium of "the influential power of *Sublunaries*," then he is identifying it with those other manifestations of "influence," of "commerce"—most notably light—about which he also writes. Such an identification would preclude any discussion of the topic of magnetism by denying its discrete existence. We must, therefore, start with the hypothesis that Vaughan does indeed perceive that the *physical* difference between the iron/lodestone phenomenon and, say, light has, at the least, some *poetic* significance; that in those passages that refer explicitly to the effects of the lodestone and magnet or which include such words as "magnetic" and "magnetism" the choice of image or vocabulary is not accidental, that another image—for example light— would not have served as well. This analysis of the poetic uses to which Vaughan puts magnetism will allow us to proceed to an assessment of his philosophical ideas about the nature of the phenomenon.

II The Secular Poems

Four of Vaughan's secular poems employ magnetic imagery and all four uses are characterized to some extent by "wit" or learning, qualities not found in the allusions to magnetism which occur in the sacred verse. Of these four poems two, which I shall discuss first, introduce magnetism only for the sake of straightforward analogies while the remaining two exploit, with some ingenuity, what seems to have been a thoroughgoing knowledge, on Vaughan's part, of seventeenth century theories about magnetism.

The final stanzas of the first of the four poems, "To Amoret, of the difference..." (pp. 12–13)[11] read

> Whil'st I by pow'rfull Love, so much refin'd,
> That my absent soule the same is,
> Carelesse to misse,
> A glaunce, or kisse,
> Can with those Elements of lust and sence,
> Freely dispence,
> And court the mind.
>
> Thus to the North the Loadstones move,
> And thus to them th'enamour'd steel aspires:
> Thus, *Amoret*,
> I doe affect;
> And thus by winged beames, and mutuall fire,
> Spirits and Stars conspire,
> And this is LOVE.

Joan Bennett suggests that there is no convincing relationship between the final stanza and the adaptation of Donne's "A Valediction: forbidding mourning" which precedes it.[12] E. L. Marilla, on the other hand, sees "Thus" (1.29) as "an important integral element; through it the statement becomes an explicit assertion of the basic identity in true romantic love and magnetic attraction."[13] I can agree with neither critic. The authority of Mr. Marilla's reading, leading as it does to his finding a statement of the identity of love and magnetism, makes necessary an analysis of the syntax of this undistinguished piece of versifying. "Thus" clearly introduces an analogy, not an assertion of identity, and this analogy in line 29 does tie in (*pace* Mrs. Bennett) with the previous stanza: it likens the North's affecting lodestones *at a distance* with the lover's courting the mind at a distance. Line 30 states a parallel analogy—rather awkwardly in making what was formerly attracted the attractor. Lines 31 and 32 state a new analogy in which the lover's "affection" for, his longing for, Amoret is likened to the "aspiration" of the steel to the lodestones. We now have an almost circular series of analogies: the courting of the mind is like the magnetic phenomena which are like the lover's "affection." An odd construction, this. The fourth and final analogy (ll. 33–34)—which can refer back both to the previous stanza and to lines 31 and 32—likens the mutual influence of spirits and stars to the lover's courting the mind. The series of analogies, then, forms an A-B-A-B pattern in which the A's are the lover's actions, the B's their analogues. Finally comes the assertion "And this is LOVE."

Of this final line Mr. Marilla states: "Here the implication of these last two stanzas emerges into open statement that 'LOVE' is a manifestation of the universal binding force exemplified in magnetic attraction and in the affinity of the 'Spirits and Stars.'"[14] Now, the interlocking A-B-A-B construction in the final stanza seems to preclude selecting as the antecedent of "this," in the final line, the magnetic and the "Spirits and Stars" analogies to the exclusion of the lover's actions; yet we must do so if we are to accept Mr. Marilla's reading. It might be argued that "this" refers back only to the "conspiring" of spirit and stars—though, as I shall show, there are good reasons for not thus limiting it, but "this" cannot also have as antecedents the magnetic analogies without including the interposed "Thus, Amoret,/I do affect." The true antecedent of "this" is, surely, the paradigm of love constituted of the whole string of actions and analogues, or, of course, the Platonic love itself which is discussed in the previous stanzas and which these analogies illuminate. "And this is LOVE" is, then, an assertion that true love is Platonic, distant, able to dispense with "lust and sence." Read thus, the final line concludes the argument of the whole poem, indeed refers us back to its full title: "To Amoret, of the difference 'twixt him, and other Lovers, and what true Love is." We must conclude that in this poem Vaughan does not identify magnetic attraction with love but merely sees magnetism as analogous to love.

In the second secular, magnetic piece, a commendatory poem addressed to Mrs. Katherine Philips (pp. 61–62), Vaughan describes the inspiration her "New miracles of Poetrie" have been on his own writing.

> . . . It was true
> I might at distance worship you
> A *Persian* Votarie, and say
> *It was your light shew'd me the way.*
> So *Lodestones* guide the duller *Steele,*
> And high perfections are the *Wheele*
> Which moves the lesse, for gifts divine
> Are strung upon a *Vital line*
> Which touch'd by you, Excites in all
> Affections *Epidemicall.*

The lodestone analogy in line 31 presents no problem: the final four lines are rather less easy. Mr. Marilla sees in them a continuation of the magnetic analogy. "Basic here," he writes, "is the concept of the 'Universall Magnet' binding the visible and invisible worlds. . . . The fantastic idea is that Mrs. Philips established contact with one of the magnetic lines and imparted inspiration to all others likewise in contact with it."[15] The assumption that needs careful examination is that by "Vital line" Vaughan means "magnetic line."

The basic meaning of "line"—rope or cord or string—clearly accords best with the idea that the gifts are "strung" upon it. Mr. Marilla is, I think, reading modern notions of magnetism back into the seventeenth century. The concept of "lines of force" within a magnetic field originated with Faraday in the nineteenth century; the magnetic philosophers of Vaughan's day spoke of the *orbis virtutis* of the lodestone, using William Gilbert's term.[16]

It is worth noting, in passing, that Edmund Blunden bases much of his claim of a universal magnetism in Vaughan on the assumption that in this passage from one of the pilcrowed elegies, "Line" refers to magnetic influence:

> Sure, there's a tye of Bodyes! and as they
> Dissolve (with it,) to Clay,
> Love languisheth, and memory doth rust
> O'r-cast with that cold dust;

For things thus *Center'd*, without *Beames*, or *Action*
    Nor give, nor take *Contaction*,
And man is such a Marygold, these fled,
    That shuts, and hangs the head.

Absents within the Line Conspire, and *Sense*
    Things distant doth unite,
Herbs sleep unto the *East*, and some fowles thence
    Watch the Returns of light;
But hearts are not so kind....   (p. 429)

"His magnetic theory," Blunden writes, "probably embraces the mysterious interplay and communication between things apparently inanimate.... The 'Line' must be some presumed curve of magnetic influence...."[17] Rejecting, as it seems we must, the connection between "Line" and magnetism, the meaning of the first four lines of the elegy is that the affections tie together the bodies of living friends as *with a cord*.[18] Associating "Line" with "tye"—and with the "Vital line" of the Mrs. Philips poem—we will be tempted to think of it as a cord; but can absent friends be said to be "within" a cord? It seems necessary to divorce "Line" from the imagery of the first stanza and accept Martin's suggestion that the line is that which divides the living from the dead, a boundary line.[19] In "To his Learned Friend..." (p. 623), another poem on the theme of separation which I discuss below, Vaughan points out that it is between living friends that there is an "Effectual informing Influence," not between the living and the dead; and it is the burden of this elegy that the *"Center'd,"* that is interred, body does not communicate.

Turning to the two secular poems which display Vaughan's knowledge of magnetic philosophy, the first of these, *"In Amicum fœneratorem"* (p. 43), contains in its opening lines an intricate and extended magnetic simile:

Thanks mighty *Silver*! I rejoyce to see
How I have spoil'd his thrift, by spending thee.
Now thou art gone, he courts my wants with more,
His *Decoy* gold, and bribes me to restore.
As lesser lode-stones with the *North* consent
Naturally moving to their Element,
As bodyes swarm to th'Center, and that fire
Man stole from heaven, to heav'n doth still aspire,
So this vast crying summe drawes in a lesse,

And hence this bag more Northward layd I guesse,
For 'tis of *Pole-star* force, and in this sphere
Though th'least of many rules the master-bear.[20]

The simile is interesting enough in itself, but it gains in significance when it is realized that the knowledge of magnetic philosophy which it displays is of a kind that predates William Gilbert's—and that was rejected, with much sarcasm, by him—whereas the philosophy behind Vaughan's other extended magnetic conceit, in "To his Learned Friend...," is entirely in accord with the new ideas Gilbert introduced. It seems improbable that Vaughan would have chosen to use the old notions in a learned poem had he known the new, and it is thus probable that between the writing of the two poems Vaughan read *De Magnete* or one of a number of subsequent works that were in part based upon it.

Prior to Gilbert, whose major discovery was that the earth was itself a great lodestone,[21] the common explanations of the lodestone's turning to the North included the idea that a great magnetic body was situated among the polar stars;[22] and we find that the magnetic simile of *"In Amicum fœneratorem"* opens (l. 5) by implying that the North harbors a great lodestone towards which the lesser lodestones turn. The parallel, reinforcing similes of lines 7 and 8 need not concern us here. Line 9 means that the moneylender's offer of gold—the "vast crying sum"—is offered in order to attract back the smaller sum of silver which the speaker owes, a situation analogous to a small lodestone being attracted to the North.

Mr. Marilla explains lines 9 to 12 thus:

> ...since the letter from the moneylender assumes that this offer of a loan may bring in the smaller one, the usurer must have laid this bag [i.e. the gold] more within the magnetic line [again!] than he had placed previous ones.... The visualization of the "Pole-star" and the magnetic attraction to the "North" brings to the author's mind the northern constellations, the "Lesser Bear" and the "Great Bear," and so the bag of gold becomes, in this figure of the lodestone, a "master-bear."[23]

Mr. Marilla's reading is, of course, consonant with the lesser-greater lodestone simile of line 5 but it does nothing to help us with the final, clinching line in which "this bag" is described both as being the "least of many" and as ruling "the master-bear." Clearly the bag, being "the least," must be the smaller sum, the current debt of silver, not the offer of gold as Mr. Marilla would have it; and the "master-bear" must, of course, be the gold. The problem, then, is how within the extended simile the smaller can be said to rule the larger when the basic idea of the simile is that larger beings rule smaller ones.

The solution, I think, lies in there being a witty inversion of the roles of offer and debt at the end of line 9. "Hence" in line 10 does not mean, as Mr. Marilla's reading implies, "it follows from this that" but rather "henceforth."Lines 10 to 12 mean then that, from now on, surprisingly ("I guesse"), the small debt exercises a stronger pull (is "more Northward layd") than the offer of gold. The gold with which the usurer expects to lure back the small current loan is in fact being attracted by the smaller sum into the speaker's pockets. Now this inversion of the simile's original premise that great things attract small is reinforced by the star metaphor. The polestar is, as we have seen, magnetic, attractive; it is "th'least" because it is in the constellation of the Lesser Bear; and yet it "rules the master-bear" because the Great Bear wheels round it— it was, of course, also called Cynosure—in the "sphere" of the fixed stars. This outwitting of the usurer by the speaker accords perfectly with the sense of the rest of the poem, and this modification of Mr. Marilla's reading supports his contention that *"In Amicum fœneratorem"* is "easily one of the 'wittiest' expressions of the time."[24]

The last of the secular poems that contain magnetic imagery, "To his Learned Friend . . . " (p. 623), contains the following argument:

> 'Tis a kind Soul in *Magnets*, that attones
> Such two hard things as *Iron* are and *Stones*,
> And in their dumb *compliance* we learn more
> Of Love, than ever Books could speak before.
> For though *attraction* hath got all the name,
> As if that *power* but from one side came,
> Which both unites; yet, where there is no *sence*,
> There is no *Passion*, nor *Intelligence*:
> And so by consequence we cannot state
> A Commerce, unless both we animate.

The point made in this typically Metaphysical argument-by-analogy is, of course, that friendship is not a one-sided matter but requires that both parties "animate." The magnetic analogy to the necessary give and take of friendship derives from Gilbert who, in a series of definitions prefacing *De Magnete*, offers the following:

> Coitio magnetica: quia in magneticis motus non fit per facultatem attractricem, sed per vtriusque concursum aut concordantiam non vt sit vnius tantum ἑλκτικὴ δύναμις sed vtriusq; συνδρομή, vigoris semper coitio: corporis etiam si moles non obstiterit.[25]

and, in Book II:

> Coitionem dicimus, non attractionem, quòd malè vocabulum attractio irrepsit in magneticam philosophiam, ex veterum ignorantia: vis enim illata videtur vbi attractio est, & imperans violentia dominatur.[26]

The idea of magnetic coition, and with it the rejection of magnetic attraction, occurs among the secular poems only in "To his Learned Friend..." Each of the other secular poems, as we have seen, employs the pre-Gilbertian idea of attraction: "th'enamoured steel aspires" to the lodestones, "*Lodestones* guide the duller *Steele*," and "lesser lodestones with the *North* consent." In each instance the greater attract the lesser and "imperans violentia dominatur." It should be noted, however, that Vaughan did not necessarily adopt the new magnetic philosophy directly from Gilbert. In *Pseudodoxia Epidemica* (1646), Sir Thomas Browne both incorporates a translation of the Gilbert definition of magnetic coition and cites six additional authorities who had published since *De Magnete* (1600) works which incorporate the concept.[27]

In "To his Learned Friend..." which is presumably one of his later secular poems,[28] Vaughan is perhaps moving beyond the merely figurative use of magnetism, which characterizes the three earlier poems I have discussed, towards a view which unifies magnetism and spiritual forces. If in the later poem he is merely drawing another analogy, then lines 11 to 14 refer solely and unambiguously to iron and stones, and this would be difficult to argue. On the other hand, in using an argument based on a single analogue drawn from scientific theory, Vaughan is taking a position far removed from that of his brother on the subject of "universall magnetism." Gilbert can be of further help here.

Book V chapter 12 of *De Magnete* begins:

> Admirabilis in plurimis experimentis magnes, & veluti animatus. Atq; hæc est vna ex illis egregia virtus, quam veteres

in cælo, in globis & stellis, in sole & luna animam existimabant.[29]

and continues, later:

Sed telluris magnetica vis & globorum formata anima siue animata forma, sine sensu absq; errore, sine malorum & morborum tam præsentium iniurijs, actum habet insitum, per totam materialem molem viuidum, certum, constantem, dirigentem, commouentem, imperantem, consentientem; à quo omnium in superficie generationes & interitus propagantur.[30]

Gilbert is here modifying the ancient view of the *anima mundi* by proposing magnetism as the soul of the universe. However, although the language of the argument is Platonic, the cosmos that Gilbert envisages is, as we see in the second excerpt, ultimately mechanistic.

Returning to "To his Learned Friend . . ." we may note that, like Gilbert, the poet ascribes a soul to the magnet and we also, perhaps, get in line 10 a hint that the new, Gilbertian view of magnetism is more apropos than those of the ancients which Vaughan seems to have read "before." I suggest then, that at least at this stage in his career, Vaughan found Gilbert's view of cosmic magnetism, which goes some way to reconciling observed physical fact with the spiritual, more congenial than the scientifically unorthodox views of his brother. It is significant that it is apparently only after the discovery of Gilbert's ideas that Vaughan feels free to use magnetic imagery in any but purely metaphorical ways. This has interesting ramifications in the larger discussion of the general relationship between the ideas of the twin brothers; for whatever the extent of the influence of Thomas's Hermetic ideas on Henry, it seems clear that Henry remained the more orthodox in his religious beliefs as he did, apparently, in the magnetic philosophy expressed in his secular verse.

III Silex Scintillans

Four of the poems in Vaughan's collection of sacred verse contain references to magnetism; in none of them is the subject developed very far. In "The Queer" (p. 539) *"holyness"* is likened to a magnet in a simple metaphor:

> Sure, *holyness* the *Magnet* is,
> And *Love* the *Lure*, that woos thee [joy] down:

That Vaughan's statement is no more than a metaphor is clear from the parallel metaphor in the second of these lines. If we try to read the first line as an assertion that holiness and magnetism are both spiritual forces, then we shall have to propose another spiritual force, the *"Lure."* But Vaughan is using lure in the technical sense of either the falconer's apparatus for calling down his bird or his cry to call it down, and this statement is clearly metaphorical.

The fourth stanza of "Man" (p. 477) begins:

> He [Man] knocks at all doors, strays and roams,
> Nay hath not so much wit as some stones have
> Which in the darkest nights point to their homes,
> By some hid sense their Maker gave;

It may be questioned whether these stones are, in fact, lodestones at all; for elsewhere in *Silex Scintillans* Vaughan notes that even stones, apparently the most inanimate of creatures, keep a "commerce" with God. However, Man in this poem is described as having lost his sense of direction, he "strays and roams," and is contrasted to "some stones" (evidently special ones) which infallibly "point" the way. These are references to direction, not to mutual influence, and Vaughan is talking about the "verticity" of lodestones. That they are capable of thus pointing even "in the darkest nights" has a special significance which I discuss below.

In "The Starre" (p. 489) the speaker, seeking to know what it is "here below" that attracts the light of the star, is sure that the attractor is imbued with "a restless, pure desire / And longing for thy [the star's] bright and vitall fire."

> These [qualities] are the Magnets which so strongly move
> And work all night upon thy light and love.

These lines are *O.E.D.*'s earliest citation of the *figurative* use of the word "magnet," and, indeed, it is possible to read the magnet reference simply as a metaphor. Similarly, *O.E.D.* cites the following passage from "Cock-crowing" (p. 488) as its earliest example of the *figurative* use of "magnetism:"

Father of lights! what Sunnie seed,
What glance of day hast thou confin'd
Into this bird? To all the breed
This busie Ray thou hast assign'd:
  Their magnetisme works all night,
  And dreams of Paradise and light.

It does not seem possible to demonstrate from sense or syntax either
that Vaughan is or is not writing figuratively in these two poems when
he refers to magnetism. The structure of each passage will allow a
metaphorical interpretation—that magnetism is a metaphor for desire—
but at the same time, in these pieces, which are among the richest in
Hermetical reference of all of Vaughan's poems, the poet can hardly
have been unaware, that, given the context, the use of magnetic imagery
must necessarily evoke the idea of a Hermetic universal magnetism. A
close examination of the contexts in which Vaughan refers to magnetism
in *Silex Scintillans* does, however, indicate that the phenomenon had for
him a particular significance which, at the least, makes it a special
manifestation of spiritual force and not identical with other such
manifestations.

Throughout *Silex Scintillans* Vaughan uses sun and light imagery
to indicate communication with the divine and images of clouds and
darkness to indicate an absence of that communication. Light is Vaughan's usual metaphor for (or symbol of, or medium of) the commerce
between inferiors and superiors. It is, then, significant that in three of
the four sacred poems that refer to magnetism, the reference is closely
associated with the night. (The exception, "The Queer," uses magnetism, as we have seen, in a rather offhand metaphor and does not develop
the image.) In his religious verse, then, Vaughan seems to see magnetic
imagery as a suitable substitute for light imagery when he wishes to
express the idea of a commerce between God and His creatures continuing during the darkness of the night.

It is not difficult to see how Vaughan may have arrived at this
specialized use of magnetic imagery. The wonder of the magnetic compass was that it did point the way in mists and darkness when all other
methods of navigation were useless. We need look no further than Edward Wright's commendatory preface to *De Magnete* for an expression
of this wonder couched in language which would have appealed to
Vaughan's penchant for images of mists and storms and darkness:

165

Ferri namque magnete tacti indicio, austri, septentrionis, orientis, occidentisque puncta, cæteræque mundi plage caliginoso cœlo & obscurissimâ nocte nauigantibus innotuerunt. . . . nautus olim (vt ex historijs constat) anxietas incredibilis & ingens periculum sæpiùs imminebat, cum ingruente tempestate, sublatoq; solis, syderumque aspectu, quónam tenderent prorsus ignorarent, nec vlla ratione aut artificio hoc ipsum inuestigare possent.[31]

Within the scheme of Vaughan's recurring theme of Man's estrangement from God, a specialized and restricted use of magnetism as commerce with the divine is all that is possible. The poet's repeated use of cloud and night imagery to indicate the shutting out of that light which is man's commerce with the divine has no parallel in the realm of magnetic phenomena. In fact, Gilbert is at pains to demonstrate that magnetism is by no means readily shut out or cut off,[32] and a poet familiar with Gilbert's ideas, as Vaughan was, and who at the same time felt that Man's communication with God was tenuous and intermittent, could not make extensive use of magnetic imagery to indicate divine commerce. Vaughan's specialized use of magnetism in the divine poems indicates his awareness of this problem, indicates the extent to which he was influenced by the new magnetic philosophy of William Gilbert, and distances him from the Hermetic idea of a universal magnetism.

IV Summary

Two of the four secular poems by Vaughan that employ magnetic imagery do so in conventional, rather trite ways. In contrast the other two, "In amicum fœneratorem" and "To his Learned Friend . . . ," use magnetism as the vehicle of complex, extended conceits. Each of these two poems demonstrates that Vaughan had some detailed knowledge of magnetic philosophy; and the differences between the kind of knowledge displayed in each suggest that between the writing of the two, Vaughan abandoned the ideas of the ancients under the impact of Gilbert's *De Magnete* or of some work derived from it. Among the secular poems it is only in "To his Learned Friend . . ." that Vaughan can be said to move beyond using magnetism as anything more than an analogy for other forces and Gilbert's work, with its idea of a cosmic magnetism, may have brought about the change.

Of Vaughan's four references to magnetism in *Silex Scintillans*, one is demonstrably metaphoric whereas the others, because they occur in contexts containing other Hermetic references, suggest an approach to the idea of the Hermetic "universall magnetism." However Vaughan's uses of magnetic imagery are specialized, occurring as a substitute for his more usual light imagery when he wishes to write of the commerce between inferiors and superiors continuing during the hours of darkness.

Neither in his sacred nor in his secular verse does Vaughan use the terminology of the iron/lodestone phenomenon to describe, unequivocally, the Hermetic concept of magnetism: that by which "all things may be attracted whether physical or metaphysical."[33] Vaughan's magnetic philosophy, when compared with that of his Hermetist brother Thomas, reinforces the impression that he was the more orthodox thinker of the two.

Notes

1. This article is a slightly revised form of a paper originally prepared for a graduate seminar directed by Dr. Alan Rudrum at Kent State University during 1968–69. I am grateful to Dr. Rudrum both for stimulating my interest in Vaughan and for suggesting the specific topic of this paper.

2. Thomas Vaughan, *The Works of Thomas Vaughan*, ed. by A. E. Waite (London, 1919), pp. 192–93.

3. Thomas Vaughan, p. 28.

4. Henry More, "A Particular Interpretation appertaining to the last three books of the Platonic Song of the Soul" in *Democritus Platonissans* (Cambridge, 1646), n.p.

5. Jean Baptiste van Helmont, "The Magnetic Cure of Wounds" in *A Ternary of Paradoxes* "Translated, Illustrated and Ampliated" by Walter Charleton (2nd impression; London, 1650), p. 24.

6. van Helmont, pp. 35–36.

7. See, for example, Edmund Charles Blunden, *On the Poems of Henry Vaughan* (London, 1927) and Elizabeth Holmes, *Henry Vaughan and the Hermetic Philosophy* (Oxford, 1932).

8. Henry Vaughan, *The Works of Henry Vaughan*, ed. by L. C. Martin (2nd edn.; Oxford, 1957), pp. 700–64, *passim*.

9. Henry Vaughan, *Secular Poems*, ed. by E. L. Marilla (Uppsala; Cambridge, Mass.; Copenhagen; 1958), pp. 99–337, *passim*.

10. Examples are: E. C. Pettet, *Of Paradise and Light: a Study of Vaughan's "Silex Scintillans"* (Cambridge, 1960), and R. A. Durr, *On the Mystical Poetry of Henry Vaughan* (Cambridge, Mass, 1962).

11. For Henry Vaughan's works, all page and line numbers refer to the Martin edition.

12. Joan Bennett, *Four Metaphysical Poets* (Cambridge, 1934), pp. 76–77.

CHAPMAN

13. Marilla, pp. 138–39.
14. Marilla, p. 139.
15. Marilla, p. 240.
16. William Gilbert, *De Magnete* (London, 1600), in the prefatory section "Verborum quorundam interpretatio," n.p. For the scientific background of the distinction between "lines of force" and *orbis virtutis*, see Duane H. D. Roller, *The "De Magnete" of William Gilbert* (Amsterdam, 1959), pp. 147–50. Gilbert's work was of the profoundest significance in the establishment of experimental science, remains a great work of scholarship in its recording of historical magnetic philosophy, was widely read, and remained the unchallenged authority on magnetism until the late eighteenth century. I have consulted the English translation by P. Fleury Mottelay (New York, 1893; reprinted New York 1958) but have found the edition unreliable. Roller reports a similar experience with the other English edition, translated by S. P. Thompson (London, 1900). The quotations in this paper are from the first edition of 1600 and all references are made to that edition.
17. Blunden, p. 15. This reading seems at first to gain some support from the notion that memory, which Blunden identifies with magnetism, "doth rust." Gilbert, who as we shall see seems to have influenced Vaughan, writes of the destruction of magnetism by the rusting of the magnet (*De Magnete*, p. 70). However, Vaughan's dangling metallurgical image may possibly be referred to a complicated alchemical conceit. A "tye" is, according to *O.E.D.*, a piece of mining equipment used in the washing of ores. The word is regional, occurring in the West Country and South Wales, Vaughan's native region. "Bodyes" could be a punning reference to "the seven bodies terrestrial," the seven metals of alchemy, a term with which we may assume Vaughan to have been familiar. The bodies, then, washed in the tye, rust, dissolve, return to the elemental earth. One is tempted to go further and find in "o'rcast" a pun on the casting of ores in the "cold dust" of the foundry sand.
18. Vaughan associated "tye" with a fairly explicit cord image in an earlier poem which is also on the theme of separation. "To Amoret gone from him" (p. 8):

> If Creatures then that have no sence
> But the *loose* tye of influence ... [my italics]

"Loose" is easy to associate with a cord, difficult to associate with, for example, magnetic or light "influences."
19. Martin, p. 734.
20. In the analysis of this passage which follows, I have followed Mr. Marilla in taking "master-bear" to be a reference to Ursa Major. I am grateful, however, to Mr. Kevin Magarey for pointing out that "bear" in "master-bear" may well be read in the sense of "bag." As both readings seem to accord perfectly with the sense of the passage, I suggest that Vaughan here intended a pun, one which adds a further dimension to the wit of the poem.
21. Gilbert, p. 39.
22. Gilbert, lib. I cap i, *passim*, ascribes this opinion to, among others, Albertus Magnus, Paracelsus and Ficino.
23. Marilla, pp. 180–1.
24. Marilla, p. 179.
25. Gilbert, n.p. "*Magnetic coition.* [The term is used] because in magnetism motion is not caused by attraction but by a coming together or agreeing together of both parts: the attractive power, as it were, residing not in one only but in both. The coming together, the coition, is always forceful, and even the heavy bulk of an [interposed] body will not hinder it." (This and later translations are my own.)

168

26. Gilbert, p. 60. "We call it coition, not attraction, because the term 'attraction' has erroneously crept into magnetic philosophy from the ignorance of the ancients. Indeed, where there is attraction we see extraneous force, and a controlling power holds sway."

27. Sir Thomas Browne, *Pseudodoxia Epidemica* in *The Works of Sir Thomas Browne* ed. Geoffrey Keynes, v. II (London, 1928), p. 101. Chs. 2 and 3 of Bk. II are, largely, a digest of ideas originating with Gilbert or reported by him. Browne's authorities range from Descartes to van Helmont.

28. The dating of Vaughan's poems has proved difficult. In this paper I assume that the order in which the volumes of secular verse were published related to the order of their composition.

29. Gilbert, p. 208. "The lodestone behaves remarkably in many experiments, behaves, indeed, as if it were filled with life. Moreover, this is one and the same phenomenon which the ancients thought of as the soul in the heavens, in the planets and stars, in the sun and moon."

30. Gilbert, p. 210. "But the magnetic power of the earth—and the created soul, or rather the living form, of the heavenly bodies—is, on the one hand, incapable of perception and, on the other, incapable of error. It is not subject to the injuries of the ills and diseases of the present time. Through the whole material mass it maintains the given motion—purposeful, unchanging, directing, impelling, commanding, harmonizing. From it stems the generation and decay of all things on the surface of the earth."

31. Gilbert, n.p. "Indeed, under murky skies and in the darkest night, the navigators knew by the pointing of the magnetized needle the points of south, north, east and west and all the quarters of the world. . . . mariners (as the histories agree) were once subject to unbelievable anxiety and great peril for, with the approach of a mighty storm, they could not direct their course correctly by sighting the sun and the stars, nor discover it by any reckoning or skill."

32. Gilbert, lib. II cap xvi, *passim.*

33. The same holds true for his prose works. These contain only a single reference to magnetism, the use of "Loadstone" in a simple simile in *The Chymists Key* (p. 606).

GEORGIA B. CHRISTOPHER

In Arcadia, Calvin . . . : A Study
of Nature in Henry Vaughan

Henry Vaughan is the only metaphysical poet ever to be accused of being a poet of nature. The lively sentience and often numinous air of nature in *Silex Scintillans* has led critics in the past to call him a proto-Wordsworthian or a devoté of Hermeticism. In the last two decades criticism has happily dispelled the notion that Vaughan is the Ur-Romantic and has placed him squarely in the Christian tradition.[1] Moreover, Ross Garner has shown that the sentience of nature in *Silex Scintillans* is not the "animism" or pantheism of Hermetic philosophy which endows matter with conscious life.[2] It has yet to be recognized, however, that Vaughan is using a poetic strategy already current in the Renaissance and that his vision of nature's sentience—far from smacking of the occult—is integral to his particular brand of Reformation piety.

Part of the problem is that in Vaughan's poetry, nature appears in such a variety of ways—as metaphor illustrating a doctrinal point,[3] as symbolic description of the state of the heart,[4] and as a source of emblems rich in analogy.[5] In his most characteristic poems, however, he does not depend upon the discursive patterns of Donne and Herbert. He seldom reduces nature to an abstraction—to a world which attends man or to a cupboard of food. Rather Vaughan turns to nature as a presence. He deals in perceptual categories less akin to Herbert and Donne than to the pastoral songs which flooded England between 1590

Reprinted, by permission of The University of North Carolina Press, from *Studies in Philology*, 70:4 (1973), 408–26.

and 1640. Like the often anonymous poets of the miscellanies, Vaughan takes the stance of someone perceiving natural phenomena, even though the details may be entirely conventional.

I

The pattern which Vaughan shares with the pastoral songs is one in which nature becomes a mode of apprehending the divine. Both *Silex Scintillans* and the songs of the miscellanies treat an experience which one might call a contingent paradise—a state of joy and well-being which entirely depends upon the presence of another. In secular pastoral songs there seems to be an assumption that the mistress is a deity controlling man and nature. Whether she be Phillis, Astrea, or Queen Elizabeth, her presence instantly transforms nature into a paradise of sunshine, singing birds, playing fountains, and all the flowers of May. This paradise seems to be eternal. While the goddess is present, time stands still. The paradise, however, is very fragile and vanishes instantly at the lady's departure or disfavor. The paradigm of contingent paradise goes back, of course, to Theocritus and is stated by Menalclas in Idyll VIII:

> Tis ever spring; there meades are ever gaie;
> There strowt the bags; there sheepe are fatly fed,
> When DAPHNE cums; Go she awaie,
> Then both the sheepheard there, and grasse is dead.[6]

The radical transformation of nature in the presence of the beloved often involves not only a change from winter to spring but a change from darkness to sunlight. As Petrarchan conventions cross and mingle with the pastoral stream, sunlight often comes to be the dominant feature of the paradise the mistress brings. Paradise in Renaissance songs often partakes of both eternal spring and eternal morn:

> The Sunne the season in each thing
> Reuiues new pleasures, the sweet Spring
> Hath put to flight the Winter keene:
> To glad our louely Sommer Queene.[7]

This song, attributed to William Hunnis, demonstrates the role of nature generally found in Renaissance pastoral songs. There is no analysis of the perception, however. The song simply continues to elaborate upon the joy and vitality of nature in the presence of Amargana. There is no progression of time or argument. A stanza could be transposed or omitted without detriment to the poem:

> The pathes where *Amargana* treads
> With flowrie tap'stries *Flora* spreads.
> And Nature cloathes the ground in greene:
> To glad our louely Sommer Queene.
>
> The Groaues put on their rich aray,
> With Hawthorne bloomes imbroydered gay,
> And sweet perfum'd with Eglantine:
> To glad our louely Sommer Queene.
>
> The silent Riuer stayes his course,
> Whilst playing on the christall sourse,
> The siluer scaled fish are seene,
> To glad our louely Sommer Queene.
>
> The Woods at her faire sight reioyces,
> The little birds with their lowd voyces,
> In consort on the bryers beene,
> To glad our louely Sommer Queene.
>
> The fleecie Flocks doo scud and skip,
> The wood-Nimphs, Fawnes, and Satires trip,
> And daunce the Mirtle trees betweene:
> To glad our louely Sommer Queene.
>
> (ll. 7–26)

Thus, a typical Renaissance song embodies one epiphanic moment in which nature responds to the presence of the beloved and serves as a transposed description of her glory. At the same time the change in nature reflects the lover's response and serves as a transposed description of his inner state—simple, joyful adoration. Nature stands as a medium which links longing subject and adored object. The glories of spring absorb all individual traits of lover and beloved. The numinous potential of this Theocritan paradigm is not often realized in Renaissance songs, partly because the details have been codified by tradition and have become part of the rhetoric of compliment. The triple identification between lover, nature, and the beloved rarely stands in equilibrium. One finds nature often primarily identified with the lover, in which case nature's response becomes explicitly animistic; that is, nature does not merely respond with springtime vitality but takes on specific human behavior, even becoming articulate. For example, in Sir Charles Sedley's "Song-a-la-Mode," nature itself proposes for the swain:

> Rivers murmur'd from their fountains . . .
> Still admiring,
> And desiring,
> When shall *Phillis* be a Wife?[8]

On the other hand, when nature tends to be identified primarily with the beloved, the details of the paradisal setting tend to become descriptive epithets for the beloved, as in the Countess of Pembroke's "A Dialogue . . . in praise of Astrea."

> *Then.* Soone as *Astrea* shewes her face,
> Strait euery ill auoides the place,
> And euery good aboundeth.
>
> *Then. Astrea* may be iustly sayd,
> A field in flowry Roabe arrayd
> In Season freshly springing.[9]

It is important for our concern with Vaughan to note that the paradigm of contingent paradise had already, in various ways, been applied to Christ. Edmund Bolton's hymn hails the nativity as the advent of pastoral paradise:

> After long night, vp-risen is the morne,
> Renowning *Bethlem* in the Sauiour.
> Sprung is the perfect day,
> By Prophets seene a farre:
> Sprung is the mirthfull May,
> Which Winter cannot marre.
> In *Dauids* Cittie dooth this Sunne appeare:
> Clouded in flesh, yet Sheepheards sit we heere.[10]

Here the identification is primarily between nature and the beloved, so that nature becomes honorific terminology: Christ is very morn and very spring. Conversely, in "Christ's Victorie on Earth," Giles Fletcher the Younger treats the wilderness as a pastoral setting and identifies nature with the poet's response to Christ. As one might expect, nature behaves animistically:

> Wonder doeth call me up to see, O no,
> I cannot see, and therefore sinke in woonder,

The man, that shines as bright as God, not so,
For God he is himselfe, that close lies under
That man, so close, that no time can dissunder
 That band, yet not so close, but from him breake
 Such beames, as mortall eyes are all too weake
Such sight to see, or it, if they should see, to speake.

Upon a grassie hillock he was laid,
With woodie primroses befreckeled,
Over his head the wanton shadowes plaid
Of a wilde olive, that her bowgh's so spread,
As with her leav's she seem'd to crowne his head,
And her greene armes [t'] embrace the Prince of peace,
The Sunne so neere, needs must the winter cease,
The Sunne so neere, another Spring seem'd to increase.[11]

In *Silex Scintillans* one finds a similar range of identifications. Nature sometimes provides honorific rhetoric,[12] sometimes a counterpart of the poet's response,[13] but the paradigm of contingent paradise generally governs the use of nature, even when the object of desire is never mentioned by name.

II

It is easy to see this paradigm at work if one turns first to poems dealing with the life of Christ. In "The Search" Vaughan recounts an imaginative quest from the manger to the sepulcher and chooses to dwell upon Christ's sojourn in the wilderness, which his presence transforms.

He liv'd there safe, 'twas his retreat . . .
With Seraphins there talked he
His fathers flaming ministrie,
He heav'nd their *walks*, and with his eyes
Made those wild shades a Paradise. . . .
   (p. 406, ll. 55, 59–62)

Vaughan expects this imaginary journey to be a pastoral excursion where he will find biblically apt "wells" among the Arcadian properties of secular poetry. "I . . . writ down," he says,

What pleasures should my Journey crown,
What silent paths, what shades, and Cells,
Faire, virgin-flowers, and hallow'd *Wells*
I should rove in. . . .   (ll. 67–71)

In "Ascension-day" the fields of Bethany, in Christ's presence, take on
the look of perpetual spring familiar to secular songs, where there inevitably flow streams of dissolved pearl:

I walk the fields of *Bethani* which shine
All now as fresh as Eden, and as fine.
Such was the bright world, on the first seventh day,
Before man brought forth sin, and sin decay;
When like a Virgin clad in *Flowers* and *green*
The pure earth sat, and the fair woods had seen
No frost, but flourish'd in that youthful vest,
With which their great Creator had them drest:
When Heav'n above them shin'd like molten glass,
While all the Planets did unclouded pass;
And Springs, like dissolv'd Pearls their Streams did pour
Ne'r marr'd with floods, nor anger'd with a showre.
With these fair thoughts I move in this fair place,
And the last steps of my milde Master trace.
                    (p. 482, ll. 37–50)

There is a vast difference between Vaughan's associatively rich use of
this paradigm and the perfunctory use of it by Renaissance poets for
compliment. Nonetheless, Vaughan's meditative attempt to trace the
last steps of his Master with the idyllic scenery makes use of the same
convention that Ben Jonson does in *The Sad Shepheard* when Aeglamour
seeks his missing shepherdess:

Here! she was wont to goe! and here! and here!
   Just where those Daisies, Pincks and Violets grow:
The world may find the Spring by following her.[14]

Vaughan manages to convey a sense of the numinous most pow-
erfully when he applies the paradigm without overt reference to God.
"Regeneration," the first poem in *Silex Scintillans*, is a case in point. The
poem begins with a symbolic description of the heart:

Yet, was it frost within,
   And surly winds

175

Blasted my infant buds, and sinne
Like Clouds ecclips'd my mind.
(p. 397, ll. 5–8)

Thence begins a painful journey through terrain "Rough-cast with
Rocks and snow," from which the speaker is led by a mysterious voice
into a "new spring." Suddenly the scene is rife with the props of pastoral
paradise— clear sunshine, flowers, gentle fountains, and shady grove—
imagery whose conventionality Helen White noted long ago:[15]

Found all was chang'd, and a new spring
Did all my senses greet;

The unthrift Sunne shot vitall gold
A thousand peeces,
And heaven its azure did unfold
Checqur'd with snowie fleeces,
The aire was all in spice
And every bush
A garland wore.... (ll. 39–47)

No explanation is offered for the mysterious voice nor for the radical
change in scenery, but the poet labels the new land *Jacobs Bed* and so
calls up the biblical account of how Jacob in a far country slept at Bethel
and dreamt of God standing at the top of a ladder stretching from heaven
to earth: "And Jacob awaked out of his sleep, and he said, Surely the
Lord is in this place; and I knew it not" (Genesis 28:16). Vaughan, it
seems, is invoking the story of Jacob's discovery as a parallel to his own.
Hence the paradigm of contingent paradise obtains: to discover the
presence of God is to discover spring. After the manner of pastorals,
Vaughan uses a sensuous apprehension of nature to reflect the quality
of consciousness. A sunny spring scene here reflects the emotional quality of the newly regenerate heart in much the same way that sensuous
particulars reflect the swain's love-filled consciousness. Joy, adoration,
awe, and hope find synthesis in the apprehension of nature.

"Regeneration" is a rich poem, whose literary ancestry is far wider
than the pastoral tradition, for it also contains emblems of regeneration
in the flowers and stones,[16] whose sleeping and waking, deadness and
liveliness are parallel to the radical change in nature. The poem has
been seen as representing the early stages of a mystic journey,[17] and the
concluding lines as a prayer for mystic absorption.[18] The poem, however,

may just as easily be read as the *metanoia* of the evangelical tradition—a sudden event in which entry into the Kingdom of God is perceptibly felt as a new state of being. Indeed, Vaughan's emphasis upon the transforming work of the Spirit makes him seem very much like the dissenters whom he contemns. At the end of "Regeneration," the mysterious voice who has led the way speaks from a Rushing Wind and identifies himself as the Holy Spirit by a cryptic whisper, *"Where I please."* Hence it is the Holy Spirit who has called ("Away!"), transformed, and illumined the inner man—with sunlight, emblems, and finally whispered words. These gifts of the Spirit evoke a ratifying response of the will:

> Lord, then said I, *On me one breath,*
> *And let me dye before my death!*

In the context of the poem, these final lines seem to embody Calvin's paradox that regeneration is complete at a stroke and yet is a gradual process of perfection never complete in this life.[19] The fully regenerate man must still pray for the death of the Old Man. Vaughan explores this paradox of the man who is dead to sin, and yet not dead to sin, in "The Timber": he is likened to a felled tree which can still "resent" the storms which felled it and likened to a "murthered man" whose blood can still freeze at the approach of his murderer.

III

The overwhelming experience of "Regeneration" is decisive, but the Spirit blows when it lists and Vaughan begins to evidence the anxieties common to evangelical experience. The new spring is not felt to be eternal, as may be seen by the winter imagery of the poems which follow, and especially of such titles as "The Relapse" and "The Resolve." The mutability of the sense of grace is a frequent theme in Herbert, and Vaughan may have taken his immediate inspiration from the rhetoric of a poem like "The Temper (II)":

> It cannot be. Where is that mightie joy,
> Which just now took up all my heart?
> Lord, if thou must needs use thy dart,
> Save that, and me; or sin for both destroy.

> The grosser world stands to thy word and art;
> But thy diviner world of grace
> Thou suddenly dost raise and race,
> And ev'ry day a new Creatour art.[20]

Vaughan, however, treats the recurrence of the world of grace in perceptible terms. "Mount of Olives [II]" shows the return of grace as the return of a sense of spring:

> [I] wander'd under tempests all the year,
> Went bleak and bare in body as in mind,
> And was blow'n through by ev'ry storm and wind,
> I am so warm'd now by this glance on me,
> That, midst all storms I feel a Ray of thee;
> So have I known some beauteous *Paisage* rise
> In suddain flowres and arbours to my Eies,
> And in the depth and dead of winter bring
> To my Cold thoughts a lively sense of spring.
> (p. 476, ll. 12–20)

One should note that this analogy to sudden, spontaneous memory emphasizes the passive role of man in the experience of grace, just as the initiative of the Rushing Wind does in "Regeneration."

"The Morning-watch" is another poem which connects the presence of the Spirit with a perception of quickening nature, and here we see the paradigm of contingent paradise fulfilling its numinous potential. The poem begins with the state of the heart described in metaphors from nature:

> O Joyes! Infinite sweetnes! With what flowres,
> And shoots of glory, my soul breakes, and buds!
> (p. 424, ll. 1–2)

The moment, Vaughan seems to say, is due to the quiet work of the Holy Spirit during the night which is now come to fruition:

> All the long houres
> Of night, and Rest
> Through the still shrouds
> Of sleep, and Clouds,
> This Dew[21] fell on my Breast;

> O how it *Blouds*,
> And *Spirits* all my Earth!   (ll. 3–9)

From metaphorical description of the heart as earth springing forth at
dawn, Vaughan shifts to perception of the "quick world" outside:

> heark! In what Rings,
> And *Hymning Circulations* the quick world
> Awakes, and sings;
> The rising winds,
> And falling springs,
> Birds, beasts, all things
> Adore him in their kinds.   (ll. 9–15)

With extraordinary deftness Vaughan blurs the line between subject
and object. The morning world springing to life has become the reap-
pearing world of grace.

For periods of estrangement and despair, Vaughan reverses the
Theocritan paradigm, just as did the secular poets. The paradigm in
reverse may be illustrated by Colin Clout's complaint in "Januarye" of
The Shepheardes Calender, when Rosalind's absence and disfavor make the
land a "barrein ground, whome winters wrath hath wasted."[22] Sir Philip
Sidney's famous double sestina offers another:

> She, whose lest word brings from the spheares their musique,
> At whose approach the Sunne rase in the evening,
> Who, where she went, bare in her forhead morning,
> Is gone, is gone from these our spoyled forrests,
> Turning to desarts our best pastur'de mountaines.[23]

A variant just as frequently found in the miscellanies is the one in which
the lover's heart alone partakes of winter while he painfully perceives
that nature all about him is joyful and spring-like. This variant may be
seen in a sonnet by Lodge,

> The earth late choakt with showers
>   Is now araid in greene:
>   Her bosome springs with flowers,
> The aire dissolues her teene,
>   The heauens laugh at her glorie:
>   Yet bide I sad and sorie.
> The woods are deckt with leaues,
> And trees are cloathed gaie . . .

> Where I am clad in blacke,
> The token of my wracke.[24]

and in a song by Thomas Campion,

> Where he such pleasing change doth view
> In eu'ry liuing thing,
> As if the world were borne anew
> To gratifie the Spring.
>
> If all things life present,
> Why die my comforts then?
> Why suffers my content?
> Am I the worst of men?[25]

In Vaughan's poetry it is precisely because he is the worst of men, or at least because he is made of sinful clay, that he often stands estranged from nature. There is, moreover, good doctrinal reason why he does not adopt the stance of Colin Clout, who finds nature a "myrrhour" of his own despair. In Vaughan's Christian scheme, nature depends upon and mirrors God: "Each *tree, herb, flowre* / Are shadows of his *wisedome*, and his Pow'r."[26] Blight and winter touch only the "frail weed" of the heart.[27] Hence whenever Vaughan perceives what is clearly external nature, he finds it Arcadian: birds never prey, streams never flood, and plants never die. Like the swain in Lodge's sonnet, he dramatizes his estrangement from a beloved deity by envying the vitality of the green world about him. In Vaughan's case, nature may not always be shown as specifically springlike, but it never appears wintry, varying only from reliable periodicity to holiday exuberance:

> Thy other Creatures in this Scene
> Thee only aym, and mean.[28]
>
> ...hills and valleys into singing break....[29]
>
> ...heark, how th' *wood* rings,
> *Winds* whisper, and the busie *springs*
> A Consort make.[30]

It is curious that Vaughan mentions the fall of nature on at least two occasions;[31] yet when he presents nature, it is always with the innocent, Arcadian air of Elizabethan songs and madrigals.

IV

Strange as it may seem, this Arcadian vision of nature derives from a piety that owes a great deal to Calvin. Vaughan is usually credited with an Augustinian temper,[32] but has rarely been discussed in the light of the Reformed theologian who drew heavily upon Augustine.[33] It is not my purpose to disentangle minute strands of doctrinal indebtedness, but merely to point out that the Anglican Church whom Vaughan defends against Calvinist dissenters had herself been touched by Calvin's theology. The Thirty-nine Articles had been Calvinist in doctrinal matters, and by Vaughan's time at least two generations at the universities had been exposed to prelections on the *Institutes*. More important, there had been nine editions of Thomas Norton's English translation of the *Institutes* between 1561 and 1634,[34] as well as six editions of English abridgments.[35]

The best evidence that Vaughan's piety derives from Calvin appears in *Silex Scintillans* itself. While it contains several poems on the eucharist, it also contains several poems on the word—"H. Scriptures," "The Book," and "To the Holy Bible." These poems and others like "The Agreement" and "Religion" reveal a habit of reading scripture as a devotional exercise which sometimes yielded numinous moments. Like Calvin, Vaughan stresses that the Spirit and the Word work in tandem. He records walks among biblical groves whose "leaves thy spirit still doth fan."[36] He recalls that the Book "Woulds't convey / A sudden and most searching ray / Into [his] soul" or that it would suddenly disclose the "secret favors of the Dove."[37] There are even moments when Vaughan seems to be taking the Calvinist position that the Word and the Spirit alone are efficacious for salvation. "H. Scriptures," for example, hails the Bible as

> The Doves spotless neast
> Where souls are hatch'd unto Eternitie.
> (p. 441, ll. 3–4)

This is not to insist that Vaughan is narrowly Calvinist, but simply that his poetry reflects the loose synthesis of Catholic and Calvinist patterns found in the Anglican Church prior to 1633.

It is not altogether surprising, then, that Calvin's discussion of the "testimonies of nature" in the *Institutes* should shed light upon Vaughan's curiously Arcadian, curiously sentient nature. Like

181

Vaughan, Calvin notes perfunctorily that creation has fallen,[38] but says very, very little about the ruin of nature. His overriding concern is to recommend nature as a "dazzling theatre" in which God "sets forth to all without exception his presence portrayed by his creatures."[39] Indeed, Calvin's most eloquent passages are those in which he extols the "radiance" and "brightness" present in Creation,[40] even though man's eyes have become "dull" since the fall and cannot perceive it aright. In order to see nature in all its incandescence, man needs faith (or the Spirit working within) and the "spectacles of Scripture":

> Just as old or bleary-eyed men and those with weak vision, if you thrust before them a most beautiful volume, even if they recognize it to be some sort of writing, yet can scarcely construe two words, but with the aid of spectacles will begin to read distinctly; so Scripture, gathering up the otherwise confused knowledge of God in our minds, having dispersed our dullness, clearly shows us the true God [in his works].[41]

It is my contention that Vaughan is visionary in precisely this sense and that he presents nature as specially illumined by faith and the Word. "And do they so? ... " is a poem specifically about reading nature with the spectacles of scripture. The poet begins dramatically by choosing the view of nature in Romans 8:19 over secular wisdom:

Rom. Cap. 8. ver.19

Etenim res Creatae exerto Capite observantes
expectant revelationem Filiorum Dei[42]
And do they so? have they a Sense
    Of ought but Influence?
Can they their heads lift, and expect,
    And grone too? why th'Elect
Can do no more: my volumes sed
    They were all dull, and dead,
They judg'd them senselesse, and their state
    Wholly Inanimate.
Go, go; Seal up they looks,
    And burn thy books.
        (p. 432, ll. 1–10)

Having established a vision committed to the Book rather than to books, he proceeds to make hortatory comparison between nature and man. Nature is steadfast in hope, man is not (ll. 11–30). Here is the application to self which Calvin counsels as reason for contemplating nature, and it is very similar to the application which Calvin himself makes of Romans 8:19:

> Not that [the creatures] are endowed with any perception, but that they naturally long for the undamaged condition whence they have fallen. Accordingly, Paul has *attributed* "groaning" and "birth pangs" (Rom 8:22) to them, that we "who have received the first fruits of the Spirit" (Rom. 8:23), should be ashamed to languish in our corruption, and not at least to *imitate the dead elements....* [43]

The strategy of Vaughan's poem could be summed up paradoxically as: "Imitate the dead elements," for as Ross Garner has shrewdly observed, the point of the last stanzas rests upon knowing that the Creatures do not have any human capabilities.[44] Calvin has happily made explicit Vaughan's assumptions: Paul has painted a verbal vision of nature which is superior to common-sense (or even scientific) vision for the purposes of spiritual exhortation.

"And do they so?..." is typical in showing how Vaughan takes pains to find scriptural warrant for his views and how he finds scripture warranting very much what the *Institutes* claim—at least as regards the natural world. Indeed Calvin's elaboration of the dictum, "The Lord represents both himself and his everlasting Kingdom in the mirror of his works with very great clarity,"[45] serves as a helpful commentary on the meanings of nature in *Silex Scintillans*. First of all, the skill of the great Artificer[46] is revealed in the grandeur, movement, and variety of nature as a total system. Such passages in the *Institutes* as I, xiv, 20 and I, v, 6 offer concise prose counterparts of a celebrated passage from "Rules *and* Lessons":

> Observe God in his works; here *fountains* flow,
> *Birds* sing, *Beasts* feed, *Fish* leap, and th'*Earth* stands fast;
> Above are restles *motions*, running *Lights*,
> Vast Circling *Azure*, giddy *Clouds*, days, nights.

> When *Seasons* change, then lay before thine Eys
> His wondrous *Method*; mark the various *Scenes*
> In heav'n; *Hail, Thunder, Rain-bows, Snow*, and *Ice*,
> *Calmes, Tempests, Light,* and *darknes* by his means;

> Thou canst not misse his Praise; Each *tree, herb, flowre*
> Are shadows of his *wisedome*, and his Pow'r.
>
> (p. 438, ll. 87–96)

However grand nature as God's art may be—and Calvin is often eloquent on the subject—he holds this to be an inferior revelation. The
carnal sense, he says, often stops here; "But faith ought to penetrate
more deeply."[47] Faith's deeper perspective is to see nature in personal
categories. It is to see that every creature "taste[s] God's special care"
and to see that every creature fulfills the end of its creation—to show
forth the glory of its author[48]—to praise. In short, faith sees nature as
a mirror of the kingdom of God, that is, the kingdom of faith. It is
important to remember that Calvin defines faith as a kind of sentience,
as "knowledge of God,"—knowledge not in any speculative sense of
what God is in himself, but knowledge of God "as he is toward us."[49]
It is an experiential knowledge which cannot be separated from man's
response:

> This is the Heart he craves; and who so will
> But give it him, and grudge not; he shall feel
> That God is true, as herbs unseen
> Put on their youth and green.
>
> ("The Starre," p. 490, ll. 29–32)

The sentience of nature in *Silex Scintillans* takes on its proper significance once it is seen in the context of Calvin. Even the celebrated
"mystical" passage in "Rules *and* Lessons," if considered in the whole
of Vaughan's work, appears to treat a knowledge of God somewhat less
spectacular than that of a full, unmediated vision. It seems to treat only
the knowledge of God that is integral to praise—or faith in Calvin's
terms:

> Walk with thy fellow-creatures: note the *hush*
> And *whispers* amongst them. There's not a *Spring*,
> Or *Leafe* but hath his *Morning-Hymn*; Each *Bush*
> And *Oak* doth know *I AM*; canst thou not sing?
>
> (p. 436, ll. 13–16)

The phenomenon of faith is nonetheless mysterious and seems so here,
partly because the content of knowledge is only implied and partly
because the muted whispers of dawn suggest the oaken hymns of praise,
and also perhaps the presence of the Sacred Wind.

"The Bird" is a poem less numinous but more explicit as to what nature knows. It begins with an address to a bird whose nest has been assaulted by rain and wind all night:

> And now as fresh and chearful as the light
> Thy little heart in early hymns doth sing
> Unto that *Providence*, whose unseen arm
> Curb'd them, and cloath'd thee well and warm.
>
> (p. 496, ll. 7–10)

The implication is that the bird sings because she knows God "as he is towards her," and so appears as a model of faith. Then the whole of creation likewise appears sentient and adoring, and so becomes a mirror of the kingdom of faith:[50]

> All things that be, praise him; and had
> Their lesson taught them, when first made.
>
> So hills and valleys into singing break,
> And though poor stones have neither speech nor tongue,
> While active winds and streams both run and speak,
> Yet stones are deep in admiration.
>
> (pp. 496–7, ll. 11–16)

By this point in the poem it has become clear that Vaughan is viewing nature very much through the spectacles of scripture, for this passage is strongly reminiscent of Psalm 65:13 and especially of Psalm 114:4, in which "The mountains skipped like rams, and the little hills like lambs." It is precisely at this point that the strategy of pastoral song and that of psalm coincide. The Psalmist declares that the valleys shout and the hills skip for joy in the presence of the Lord, while William Hunnis declares that the woods ring and the "Fleecie Flocks doo scud and skip" in the presence of Amargana.

Perhaps the clearest indication of the way in Vaughan fuses secular and sacred versions of sentient nature appears in his verse rendition of Psalm 65. The paradigm of contingent paradise obtains, for nature feels God's presence and responds "animistically" with song:

> *Thou visit'st the low earth*, and then
> Water'st it for the sons of men ...
> Thou water'st every ridge of land
> *And settlest with thy secret hand*
> *The furrows of it*; then thy warm

185

And opening showers (restrain'd from harm)
Soften the mould, while all unseen
The blade grows up alive and green...
And hills full of springing pride,
Wear fresh adornments on each side.
The fruitful flocks fill every Dale,
And *purling Corn* doth cloath the Vale;
They shout for joy, and joyntly sing,
Glory to the eternal King!
(p. 532, ll. 27–28; 33–38, 40–48, italics mine)

Here, too, are the ingredients of Calvin's vision of nature, which sees in it the intimate ministrations of Providence and a response of knowing praise. Finally, there is a telltale scrap of diction from pastoral song— "the *purling* Corn"—to indicate how in the hidden channels of Vaughan's mind, secular and biblical treatments of nature have coalesced, so as to yield a compelling vision of nature as an Arcadia of faith.

Notes

1. Ross Garner, *Henry Vaughan: Experience and the Tradition* (Univ. Chicago Press, 1959). E. C. Pettet, *Of Paradise and Light: A Study of Vaughan's* Silex Scintillans (Cambridge Univ. Press, 1960). Louis L. Martz, *The Paradise Within: Studies in Vaughan, Traherne, and Milton* (Yale Univ. Press, 1964).

2. Garner, p. 116.

3. Pettet, pp. 86–87.

4. R. A. Durr finds that the vegetative imagery in *Silex Scintillans* derives primarily from biblical sources, like the parable of the sower, and collectively becomes a symbol for deep religious life. *On the Mystical Poetry of Henry Vaughan* (Harvard University Press, 1962), pp. 60 ff.

5. Frank Kermode, "The Private Imagery of Henry Vaughan," *Review of English Studies, N.S.I.* (1950), 215 and Garner, p. 56.

6. Anonymous translation, 1588, *English Pastoral Poetry*, ed. Frank Kermode (London, 1952), p. 62.

7. W. H., "Wodenfrides *Song in praise of Amargana,*" *England's Helicon,* 1600, 1614, ed. Hyder Edward Rollins (Harvard Univ. Press, 1935), I, 65, ll. 3–6.

8. *The Poetical and Dramatic Works of Sir Charles Sedley*, ed. V. de Sola Pinto (London, 1928), I, 45, ll. 8–14.

9. *A Poetical Rhapsody 1602–1621*, ed. Hyder Edward Rollins (Harvard Univ. Press, 1931), I, 16, ll. 8–10; 20–2.

10. "The Sheepheards Song: a Caroll or Himne for Christmas," *England's Helicon*, I, 132, ll. 24–31.

11. *The Poetical Works of Giles and Phineas Fletcher*, ed. Frederick S. Boas (Cambridge Univ. Press, 1908), I, 41, Stanzas 6–7.

12. "The Relapse," *The Works of Henry Vaughan*, ed. L. C. Martin (Oxford Univ.

Press, 1957), p. 433, ll. 21–28. All further quotations from Vaughan will be from this edition.

13. "The Dawning," p. 452, ll. 22–24; "The Day of Judgment [II]," p. 531. ll. 15–16.

14. *Ben Jonson*, ed. C. H. Herford, Percy and Evelyn Simpson (Clarendon Press, 1925–52), VII (1941), 11.

15. *The Metaphysical Poets: A Study in Religious Experience* (New York, 1936), p. 310.

16. See Garner, pp. 54–55.

17. For readings which relate the structure of "Regeneration" to classical Catholic mysticism, see Durr pp. 82 ff. and Garner pp. 47 ff.

18. Notably Durr, p. 82.

19. *Institutes of the Christian Religion*, ed. John T. McNeill, tr. Ford Lewis Battles (Philadelphia, 1960), III, iii, 3 and 9. All further references to Calvin will be from this edition.

20. *The Works of George Herbert*, ed. F. E. Hutchinson (Clarendon Press, 1941), p. 56, ll. 1–8.

21. Compare with, "sanctifie and supple my heart with the dew of thy divine Spirit, refresh it with the streams of thy grace, that I may bring forth fruit in due season..." (*The Mount of Olives: or Solitary Devotions*, p. 145).

22. *Spenser's Minor Poems*, ed. Ernest de Sélincourt (Clarendon Press, 1960), p. 15, l. 19.

23. *The Poems of Sir Philip Sidney*, ed. William A. Ringler, Jr. (Clarendon Press, 1962), p. 113, ll. 68–72.

24. "Sonnet 7" (appended to *Scillaes Metamorphosis*, 1589), *The Complete Works of Thomas Lodge* (Glasgow, 1883), I, 46, ll. 1–8; 11–12.

25. "The peaceful westerne winde...," *Campion's Works*, ed. Percival Vivian (Clarendon Press, 1909), p. 139, ll. 21–28.

26. "Rules *and* Lessons," p. 438, ll. 95–96.

27. Classic examples are "Disorder *and* frailty," p. 444 and "Unprofitablenes," p. 441.

28. "And do they so?...," p. 432, ll. 23–24.

29. "The Bird," p. 497, l. 13.

30. "Christs Nativity," p. 442, ll. 7–9.

31. "Corruption," p. 440, ll. 13–16 and "Repentance," p. 449, ll. 65–66.

32. Ross Garner traces the pessimistic strain in Vaughan to Augustine, but notes that Vaughan's contempt of the world may be due to Calvinistic interpretations of Augustine, pp. 21–35. Louis L. Martz in *The Paradise Within* finds Vaughan's method of mining memory to be an Augustinian quest, pp. 17–31.

33. For Calvin's indebtedness to Augustine, see Francois Wendel, *Calvin: The Origin and Development of His Religious Thought*, tr. Philip Mairet (New York, 1963), pp. 124 ff.

34. (London, 1561, 1562, 1574, 1578, 1582, 1587, 1599, 1611, 1634), Benjamin B. Warfield, *Calvin and Calvinism* (Oxford University Press, 1931), p. 417.

35. Edward May's version of Edmund Buney's "Compendium" (1580); C. Fetherstone's version of Laune's "Epitome" (1585, 1586, 1587, 1600) and Henry Holland's version of Piscator's "Aphorismes" (1596). *Ibid*.

36. "Religion," p. 404, ll. 1–20. See also "The Agreement," p. 528, ll. 7–12.

37. "To the Holy Bible," p. 541, ll. 19–21, 28.

38. *The Institutes*, II, i, 5.

39. I, vi, 2, I, v, 8, and vi, I.

40. I, vi, I, and vi, I.

41. *Ibid.*

42. It is interesting that Vaughan uses a rare variant (occurring in two of Thomas Vautrollier's printings, London, 1576 and 1582) of a translation by Beza, who was himself a disciple of Calvin, and that the phrase which the variant adds, *capite observantes,* heightens the implication of sentience in Romans 8:19. French Fogle, ed., *The Complete Poetry of Henry Vaughan* (New York, 1965), p. 186 n.

43. III, xxv, 2. Italics mine. See also III, ix, 5.

44. *Henry Vaughan: Experience and the Tradition,* p. 97.

45. I, v, 11.

46. I, v, 2.

47. I, xvi, l.

48. *Ibid.*

49. I, x, 2: See also I, vi, 2. "... all right knowledge of God is born of obedience."

50. Compare with Calvin's comments on nature in his preface to the New Testament in Olivétan's French Bible of 1635: "The little singing birds are singing of God; the beasts cry unto Him; the elements are in awe of Him, the mountains echo his name; the waves and fountains cast their glances at Him; grass and flowers laugh out to Him. Nor indeed need we labor to seek Him afar, since each of us may find Him within himself, inasmuch as we are all upheld and preserved by His power dwelling within us" (tr. and cited by John T. McNeill, *The History and Character of Calvinism* [New York, 1954], p. 232.

ROLAND MATHIAS

In Search of the Silurist

Henry Vaughan is so much associated, in the mind of the informed but
unspecialist reader, with the poems he published in *Silex Scintillans* in
1650, at the age of twenty-nine—and, indeed, with the tone of those
poems and especially such as are anthologised—that his image is that
of a vague figure of Christian devotion, domiciled, it is true, by the
banks of the Usk at Newton, but having little life as man, as doctor, as
husband or father. It is in no sense the intention of this article to touch
up the poet by debunking the man, but it may be possible, by examining
the historical background again and adducing one or two comparisons,
to throw a little fresh light upon the poet's attitudes and reasons. One
point must be sharply urged, however: it is not to be supposed that out
of the facts available there can emerge a personality recognisably akin
to that of a twentieth century poet, understandable in all or most of the
aspects of his life. Not merely were seventeenth century modes of thinking, at least before the Puritan Revolution, very different from our own:
it is also evident that Henry Vaughan, in his affiliations, his loyalties
and most of all in his reading, associated himself with archaic values.
There is a gulf fixed: and though this is bridged, in part, by the Christian
devotional tradition, the images in the poetry, arising as they often do,
from an acquaintance with Hermetic philosophy or with the fancies of
very ancient writers, are completely successful only when they appear
to decorate Christian orthodoxy rather than depart from it. Vaughan
is a man who has to be discovered and understood after much reading.
He is not lightly to be detected using poetry as a pious mask or pre-

Reprinted, by permission of the publisher, from *Poetry Wales*, 11:2 (1975), 6–35.

tending to a love of his native country that he does not feel. The known facts of his life are too few, in any case: there is no simple posture in which the Silurist may be caught and held.

Henry Vaughan and his twin brother Thomas were born in 1621, the sons of Thomas and Denise Vaughan of Trenewydd (Newton), Llansantffraed, in the county of Brecknock.[1] Thomas Vaughan, the father, was the younger son of William Vaughan of Tretower, scion of one of the many Vaughan branches that went back to Roger Vaughan of Bredwardine and his wife Gwladys, daughter of Dafydd Gam. The tree was a vigorous one: other, now separated, branches had produced the Earls of Pembroke and those Herberts of Montgomery Castle to whom, a little before Henry Vaughan's time, the poet George Herbert had been born. Nor did William Vaughan's branch utterly lack distinction: he had married Frances, the illegitimate daughter of Thomas Somerset the recusant, third son of the second Earl of Worcester. The links, moreover, which had been formed in Tudor times between the court and the metropolis and the seemingly distant lands of Breconshire and western Herefordshire were not yet entirely dissolved: Henry Vaughan's maternal grandfather had held his lands in Scethrog from Mistress Blanche Parry, Queen Elizabeth's chief lady of the bedchamber, and from the Queen herself, whose ward his daughter Denise subsequently became. And to whom was this wardship granted but Sir David Williams, that eminently successful judge from Ystradfellte who founded the fortunes of the Gwernyfed line?

At a distance it looks grand enough. But the reality, when seen close to, is undeniably seedy. William Vaughan was heavily in debt: in 1607 Paul Delahay, steward of the Earl of Salisbury's Alltyrynys lands, himself mindful of the credit and the prospects of his own son-in-law (a son of William of Tretower by a former marriage), was complaining of 'the oppressions suffered by mr. William Vaughan', particularly in the detention for two years of his 'soone in lawe younge Walbies [Walbeoffe]'[2]: in 1614 a Bill of Complaint was filed in the Star Chamber by Richard Herbert of Pencelli (but descended from the Montgomery Herberts) alleging unfair prosecution in the Exchequer Court by Charles Vaughan, the poet's uncle and elder son to William, and malicious attacks on his lands by the same Charles, John Walbeoffe of Llanhamlach (the 'younge Walbies' before indicated) and Christopher Johnes. The background to this was that William Vaughan had mortgaged his lands in Pencelli for the sum of £400 to Sir Edward Lewis of Fan,

Caerffili, recently Sheriff of Glamorgan and a notorious land-grabber. Sir Edward was 'quietly to enjoy' these lands against the date of repayment, which was guaranteed by the sum of £2000 in the form of a bond raised by William Vaughan's friends and relatives. Charles Vaughan's answer in the Star Chamber was that Richard Herbert (perhaps acting for the moneylender) had deliberately 'disturbed' Sir Edward's tenure so that the bond should be forfeit.[3] What happened in this particular case is not clear, but the fortunes of the Tretower family and descendants remained depressed. In 1625 Charles Vaughan was said to be 'outlawed for debt' and his second marriage in 1636 to Ursula Coningsby of Hampton Court, Hereford, was a desperate attempt to repair his fortunes with a new wife's dowry.

Thomas Vaughan, the poet's father, seems to have escaped the worst of these actions at law and not to have taken part with his brother in violence. But there can be no doubt that his marriage to Denise Morgan was intended to set him up financially: he was her second husband and it was she, a widow of eighteen, who was possessed of sufficient estate to enable them to live in some comfort. Even so, the marriage did not immediately settle things: Thomas and Denise were involved for some years in litigation whose purpose was to recover moneys from the Newton estate detained by the father of her first husband. It was all somewhat precarious: Thomas brought to the marriage a well-known family name, but little else. All his life he was a busy litigant: a Justice of the Peace but never more than Under-Sheriff for the County, he was arraigned in 1650 for apparent embezzlement of the revenues from the Powell lands at Llangasty and in 1656 of the tithes for Llansantffraed. In the first instance an 'acquittance' was missing and Henry, his son, then twenty-nine and already the author of *Silex Scintillans*, had to depose that he was present when such an acquittance was received by his father. It is at least a little odd that at the end of his own life Henry was in precisely the same trouble over a 'dandy horse' he had bought from William Wynter for £21.10s. Wynter's widow denied that it had been paid for: Henry's insistence that it had was not assisted by the fact that he could not find the receipt. Father and son were very different men, nevertheless: Thomas's honesty was really in question, even if his challengers were political enemies. John Aubrey the diarist, although a relative (by way of Charles Vaughan's first wife), remarked punningly that Thomas was 'a coxcombe and no honester then he should be—he cosened me of 50s once'.

One may wonder a little, therefore, why Henry Vaughan should have interpolated into his translation of *Vita Paulini* a reference to 'a virtuous descent' which, he writes,

> ... is attended with more Divinity, and a sweeter temper, then the indiscrete Issue of the multitude.[4]

Certainly 'the multitude', the populacy, were always for him a source of mistrust and dislike: on the other hand, he condemned both pride of birth and the contemporary passion for heraldry. 'A virtuous descent' may have seemed the only credible alternative, especially since he was probably thinking of his mother, with whom he lived long after his marriage and whom he revered and loved without question.

The arms of the Vaughans—three boys' heads with snake-encircled necks—appear on his tombstone, but there is no certainty that they did so of *his* intent. *Quod in sepulchrum voluit* probably refers only to the six words which follow. In his lifetime he had often been mindful of the follies of aristocratic pride. In his 'Elegie on the death of Mr. R. W.' (who was killed at Rowton Heath in 1645) he affirms that

> ... a private turffe ... can do more
> To keep thy name and memory in store
> Than all those *Lordly fooles* which lock their bones
> In the dumb piles of Chested brasse, and stones.
>   (M.51)

And his general attitude is perhaps best expressed in the happy translation he made from the Jesuit Nieremberg's *De Arte Voluntatis* (1631), where the theme is that common one of the world as a stage:

> The *Actors* care not how the *Scenes* varie: they know, that when the *Play* is ended, the *Conquerour* must put off his Crown in the same *Ward-robe* where the *Fool* puts off his *Cap* ...
> The *stageplayer* is not commended, because he *acts* the *part* of a *Prince*, but because hee *acts* it well, and like a *Prince*. It is more commendable to *act* a foole, a begger, or a mourner to the life; then to *act* a King, or a Philosopher foolishly.
>   (M.275–76)

This is clear enough and Vaughan may have seemed to him no more than Fychan[5] writ foolishly large. But he was 'aristocratic' and conservative by instinct: his youth was spent, as we shall see, in standing for a party that was defeated both politically and militarily: he had no time for the attitudes of the majority, whom he distrusted as at best fickle and for the most part wilfully stupid. The references he makes to his opponents (references which often mar his poems) are intemperate and sometimes ridiculous. In a prefatory poem to *Man in Glory*, for instance, which he translated from the Latin of Anselm (the eleventh century Archbishop of Canterbury), he imagines the Archbishop, driven from the kingdom by 'that little hand/Which clouded him', returning to view 'This fatal wrack . . . these desolations here':

> He would do penance for his old complaint,
> And (weeping) say, That *Rufus* was a Saint.
>   (M.193)

Historically this is ludicrous. And in other outbursts he consistently fails to distinguish any point or points of principle in views which were Parliamentarian, Dissenting or anti-Royalist. What he said (or thought) about local opponents of long standing like Jenkin Jones of Tŷ Mawr does not appear: about persons he was more wisely silent.

My reason for introducing these views thus early will, I trust, be plain: if Henry Vaughan set no great store by the renown of his Vaughan ancestry, and—much more profoundly—distrusted the commonality, what did he mean by describing himself as *Silurist?* The Silures were a Celtic tribe who landed in several parties on the shore of Severn, at Sudbrook Promontory, Caldicot and elsewhere, some time in the second century BC, having arrived there by way of Cornwall and the southwest peninsula. Some of them may also have landed and made camp at Coygen in Carmarthenshire. They distinguished themselves under the leadership of the Marnian prince Caradawg (Caractacus) in their resistance to the Romans and more particularly after his capture when, in 47 AD, leaderless or led by persons unknown, they defeated the Second Legion under Manlius Valens in a pitched battle—an achievement as rare as it was galling to the Romans. Centuries later, these same Silures held up the Norman lords with an obstinacy that only the concentration of castles at the crossings of the Usk, the Monnow and the Wye now testifies to. Their deadly shooting with the longbow Giraldus Cambrensis describes: these were the bowmen who brought the King of England overwhelming victory at Crecy and Poitiers. Theirs was a military tradition which, if flaunted in Elizabethan times by Fluellen-like figures such as Sir Roger Williams, had earlier been based on the stubborn bravery of the individual soldier in the Welsh colours of green and white. For these were the men who had fought in the Hundred Years' War behind the Black Prince: these were the men who, led by Henry of Monmouth, had beaten Glyndwr's forces at Grosmont and elsewhere. The military tradition of south-east Wales had been bent to the King of England's purpose, in a manner quite untypical of the rest of Wales. Dafydd Gam had been both Glyndwr's enemy and the saviour of the King's life at Agincourt. The Silurian tradition had become that of the King's 'Welsh subjects', the object of their loyalty often personalised in the Prince of Wales (however little that may have meant to the unmilitary). Was it this that Henry Vaughan embraced in calling himself 'Silurist'?

Not a word from him speaks of his meaning. And to interpret him, unassisted, is undoubtedly dangerous. Possibly, too, the ethnic spread of the latter-day Silures is in question. If Henry Vaughan was 'Silurist' in the right of his ancestors, he was so because he descended from the Bredwardine family, because his nearer family was 'of Tretower', and much more doubtfully so because of his own birth at Newton, Scethrog. The depth of Silurian penetration of the Usk valley westward is uncertain: they may not, in the true tribal days, have held land west of Bwlch. On the other hand the attitude and influence of Dafydd Gam, who hailed from Penpont, west of Brecon, suggests that in the days of the Hundred Years' War and later the aura of loyalty had spread beyond its original wearers into new country. Henry Vaughan may well have considered Brecon town and its environs fully Silurian and his vision of the military tradition of his ancestors need not have been irredeemably soured and spoiled by the knowledge that Sir Thomas Morgan 'the dwarf' was mining the walls of Raglan Castle and Sir Trevor Williams of Llangybi was commanding the Parliamentarian besiegers—nor, indeed, by the money-wasting ineptitude of his own relatives, the Somersets of that same Raglan, in the King's cause. If the men of Gwent had fallen into division, that was not necessarily the end. There were still the true loyalists of Breconshire, epitomised by Colonel Herbert Price's troop of horse, in which both Henry and his brother Thomas served.

King Charles visited Brecon and stayed at the Priory in June 1645, not long after the disaster at Naseby. He was then intent on raising another army. Shortly afterwards Colonel Price's troop, brought up to strength with a number of new recruits (Henry and Thomas Vaughan among them), moved off northwards. They were at Chester in Septem-

ber and, with other royalist forces, were defeated at Rowton Heath on
the 24th of that month. Survivors from the troop were also part of the
garrison of Beeston Castle, nine miles south-east of Chester, which surrendered in November. It was all futile and too late, but at least King
Charles had been at Chester in person. In that sense Silurian traditions
had been fulfilled.

Henry Vaughan himself says nothing of this directly: his service
can be inferred from the presence of his name amongst those of officers
who made a claim for war-compensation after the Restoration (February
1662/3) and from two poems in particular—'An Elegie on the death of
Mr. R. W. slain in the late unfortunate differences at Routon Heath,
neer Chester, 1645', and 'Upon a Cloke lent him by Mr. J. Ridsley'.
Although not written until over a year later (R. W.'s death not being
certain till then), the first has some of the marks of an eyewitness
account:

> O that day
> When like the *Fathers* in the *Fire* and *Cloud*
> I mist thy face! I might in ev'ry *Crowd*
> See Armes like thine, and men advance, but none
> So neer to lightning mov'd, nor so fell on.
> Have you observ'd how soon the nimble *Eye*
> Brings th' *Object* to *Conceit*, and doth so vie
> Performance with the *Soul*, that you would swear
> The *Act* and *apprehension* both lodg'd there,
> Just so mov'd he: like *shott* his active hand
> Drew bloud, e'r well the foe could understand.
> But here I lost him . . .   (M.50–51)

The second poem is humorously reminiscent: it recalls one night spent
naked ('Pure Adamite') in the cloak, whose '*Wire-embraces*' had by the
morning made such '*Characters* and *Hierogliphicks*' on his body that he
might have been taken for a Pict or 'Some walking *Herball* or *Anatomie*'.
But a few lines establish the poet's presence amongst the garrison of
Beeston Castle:

> Hadst thou been with me on that day, when wee
> Left craggie *Biston*, and the fatall *Dee*,
> When beaten with fresh storms, and late mishap
> It shar'd the office of a *Cloke*, and *Cap*,
> To see how 'bout my clouded head it stood
> Like a thick *Turband*, or some Lawyers *Hood*,

While the stiffe, hollow pletes on ev'ry side
Like *Conduit-pipes* rain'd from the *Bearded hide*,
I know thou wouldst in spite of that day's fate
Let loose thy mirth at my new shape and state...
(M.52)

Despite the humorous intent, the manner of his riding out has the right air of despondency:

Just so Jogg'd I, while my dull horse did trudge
Like a Circuit-beast plagu'd with a goutie Judge.

Vaughan may conceivably have served with Colonel Price before the campaign of late 1645, perhaps at the relief of Nantwich in January 1642/3 and at Hereford in April of that same year, when Price was acting Governor of the city and was compelled to surrender it to Sir William Waller. But whether this is so or not—and the odds are against it—the poet had fought always on the losing side and (except for Price's brave retiring action at Nantwich) there had been little of glory to record, certainly nothing which he could possibly have felt would gild the epic Silurian tradition of stubbornness in battle. He had served as lieutenant (to Captain Bartholomew Price) and his brother Thomas as Captain. No doubt they had done their best, but the poem to Ridsley's cloak was perhaps the easiest way to render a dispiriting experience.

Henry Vaughan's later actions are in doubt. He may have been a prisoner for a short while. Colonel Price was captured again, both at Hereford in December 1645 and at the fall of Raglan Castle in August 1646, but Henry was not with him on either occasion. Nor does he seem to have been involved in the brief stirrings of the Second Civil War in Breconshire. 'Mr. Games and others' made an attempt to raise the gentry of the neighbourhood for the King (personalised for the moment in the rebel ex-Parliamentarians Poyer, Powell and Laugharne) and Colonel Horton hurried to secure the town of Brecon before advancing to the decisive battle of St. Fagans. But of Henry there is not a word. His misery at the King's defeat in 1645/6 may long have been compounded by other factors—by the general distrust felt in Wales of the Catholicism of his grandmother's people, the Somersets, by the pitiable display of the armies that Raglan had raised, and by the hatred felt by Welshmen, even royalist Welshmen, for the King's commander in Wales, the arrogant Colonel Gerard. A splendid loyalty had been confounded by political and religious developments which were irrelevant

locally. In 1610 the Prichard family of Llanover had described themselves on their monumental brass as 'lineally descended from the bodye
of Cradocke Vraichvras, Earle of Hereford & Prince betweene Wye and
Seaverne'[6] and it is not lightly to be supposed that a poet who chose to
call himself 'Silurist' had forgotten the tradition, whether or not he had
a genealogical claim with which to compete. But thirty-five years later
the descendants of the Silures were unnaturally divided. Sir Thomas
Morgan 'the dwarf', the natural military successor to Sir Roger Williams
of Penrhos, to Sir Thomas Morgan 'the Warrior' and his nephew Sir
Charles, of the Pencarn family, had declared unequivocally for the Parliament. Siluria and the King were parted. It was worse than defeat: it
was defeat made possible by folly and turpitude. Withdrawal was the
only answer: when the poet gave 'an Invitation to Brecknock' to 'his
retired friend', he too had *retired* in a sense that may well have been the
same:

> Come then! and while the slow Isicle hangs
> At the stiffe thatch, and Winters frosty pangs
> Benumme the year, blith (as of old) let us
> 'Midst noise and War, of Peace, and mirth discusse.
> This portion thou wert born for: why should wee
> Vex at the times ridiculous miserie?
> An age that thus hath fool'd it selfe, and will
> (Spite of thy teeth and mine) persist so still. (M.47)

Henry Vaughan may well, of course, have intended the term 'Silurist' to carry quite a different emphasis. But before we can examine
other possibilities, it will be necessary to go back in time, to outline his
life before the war.

The twins Henry and Thomas had a younger brother, William,
and a sister who married one William Parry. Their childhood must have
been a happy one: how else could Henry have written, in 'The Retreate',

> Happy those early dayes! when I
> Shin'd in my Angell-infancy.
> (M.419)

or conceived a theme in which every step away from childhood was a
step farther from heaven? But the twins were bright intellectually and
their 'white designs' were not long undisturbed: they were sent, their

MATHIAS

parents' unsteady fortunes notwithstanding, to the tutelage of Matthew
Herbert, rector of Llangattock, who taught the boys Latin and Greek.

> ... Then I went
> To learned Herbert's kind encouragement,
> Herbert, the pride of our Latinity;
> Six years with double gifts he guided me.
> Method and love, and mind and hand conspired,
> Nor ever flagged his mind, nor his hand tired.
> This was my shaping season.

as Edmund Blunden puts it in his translation of Henry's poem 'Ad
Posteros'.[7] The boys were Welsh-speaking from their mother's knee:
their less Welsh father had probably taught them English: and Latin
at least was so firmly grounded in the future poet that much of his
reading in adult life was in that language, from which he also translated
freely.

In 1638, the six years at Llangattock completed, the two young
men, by this time seventeen, went up to Oxford. Thomas, the more
academic of the two at that time, remained there, at Jesus College, for
a number of years. Henry's case is much more puzzling. He himself
said that he was of Jesus College, but his name has never been traced
in the books. Writing to John Aubrey when he was past fifty, however,
he confessed:

> I stayed not att Oxford to take any degree, butt was sent to
> London, beinge then designed by my father for the study of
> the Law, wch the sudden eruption of our late civil warres
> wholie frustrated.   (M.667. Letter dated 15 June 1673).

It is probable that when at Jesus College he began to write verse (there
are certain Latin poems extant signed by an H. Vaughan of Jesus
College, though there was another member of the same name and initial)
and, if he spent only one year there, he would have had near Breconshire
neighbours of his as contemporaries, in the persons of Andrew Watkins
of Llansantffraed and Jenkin Jones of Llanddeti, enrolled as batteler
and servitor respectively. Henry and Thomas would have been gentle-
man commoners and if we read into Jenkin Jones's lower rank the
reflection of an already Puritan persuasion, we must also accept that
there was an aura about the name of Vaughan (whatever Henry may

198

have felt subsequently) which would not permit the twins to be less than 'gentlemen'.

Henry was in London, it is assumed, for two years. Again the silence about him is puzzling. His name is not found in the roll of any of the Inns of Court, though there are others of some fame (notably Oliver Cromwell) of whom this is also true. Whether he studied law very seriously is open to question: certainly he made no very prolonged attempt to engage in it afterwards. But that he was in London can be confirmed from his verse: he interested himself both in literary society and politics and his detestation of 'the populacy' probably dates from the mob scenes at Strafford's execution in 1641. His poem 'A Rhapsodis. Occasionally written upon a meeting with some of his friends at the Globe Taverne' (M.10) is, if obscurely placed in Roman history, undoubtedly intended as a polemic for the contemporary scene: its passionate tone was to be repeated in the secular poems which follow. Violently and immoderately royalist, he shows no signs, in his serious writing, of understanding the political possibilities.

Interested also in the contemporary stage, Henry Vaughan was obviously sociable and no more sober than the majority. His poem 'To my Ingenuous Friend, R. W.' (a companion of his in Oxford and London or in London only and not to be confused with the younger man of the same initials who fell at Rowton Heath) offers an interesting contrast with the tone of the unvaryingly devotional poems of *Silex Scintillans*:

> When we are dead, and now, no more
> Our harmless mirth, our wit, and score
> Distracts the Towne; when all is spent
> That the base niggard world hath lent
> Thy purse, or mine; when the loath'd noise
> Of Drawers, Prentises, and boyes
> Hath left us, and the clam'rous barre
> Items no pints i'th' Moone, or Starre;
> When no calme whisp'rers wait the doores,
> To fright us with forgotten scores;
> And such aged, long bils carry,
> As might start an Antiquary;
> When the sad tumults of the Maze,
> Arrests, suites, and the dreadful face
> Of Seargeants are not seene, and wee
> No Lawyers Ruffes, or Gownes must fee:
> When all these Mulcts are paid, and I

199

From thee, deare wit, must part, and dye;
Wee'le beg the world would be so kinde,
To give's one grave, as wee'de one mind...
(M.3)

Henry had been in London, right enough, and had gone through some form of law studentship. But in 1642, when the Civil War broke out, his father called him home to Breconshire.

For the next three years, according to Aubrey, he acted as clerk or secretary to Judge Sir Marmaduke Lloyd, chief justice of the Brecknockshire, Radnorshire and Glamorgan circuit. Lloyd's committed royalism probably earned the young man's devotion and Henry remained in this post, so far as appears, until his involvement in the abortive Chester campaign which followed the visit of King Charles to Brecon Priory. It is possible, however, as has already been indicated, that he was with Colonel Price's troop some eighteen months earlier.

In 1646 appeared Henry Vaughan's first small volume, entitled simply *Poems*. Apart from a translation from Juvenal and the pieces he had written in Oxford and London, there are in it a number of love-poems addressed to Amoret (a name for the beloved used by Browne, Lovelace and Spenser before him). The tone of these poems, like many of their titles, seems to have been adopted from William Habington's *Castara*, which had been published in the previous decade. Vaughan was an unashamed borrower (as his later debt to George Herbert makes more obvious) and the particular quality of *Castara* which appealed to him was the chasteness of Habington's Muse, the absence of 'wanton heate'. Vaughan's own Preface, in which he claims that 'the fire at its highest is but Platonick' and that 'Danger' is excluded, obviously approves his master's breach with the Petrarchan tradition of celebrating some lady other than the poet's betrothed. The Amoret poems may reasonably be seen as part of the courtship of his first wife.

It was in the Priory Grove, at Brecon, that Henry Vaughan first made love to Catherine Wise of Gilsdon Hall, Coleshill, Warwickshire. He seems to have been living in Brecon at the time and it may have been before his service with Colonel Price at Chester. But his acquaintance with Price was crucial, for it was Price's wife, Goditha, herself from Warwickshire, who had invited the girl there and it was Price's Grove (Henry's 'usual Retyrement', as he tells us) which became the 'Chaste Treasurer' of all his vows. By Catherine Wise Henry Vaughan was to have four children, and when she died, some time between 1651 and 1658, he proceeded to marry her sister Elizabeth, by whom he had another four. This sequence of events, however happy it may have been in some respects, was to involve Henry in sad and bitter quarrels in later years, when the children of the two marriages took their jealousies into litigation which inevitably inculpated their father. For our immediate purpose, however, the important point is that the language of the poet's household *must have been* English and that the dedication of his next volume of poetry, *Olor Iscanus*, to Kildare, Lord Digby (who also had estates in Coleshill), confirms the impression made by his practice of translating Welsh names (as 'the parish of St. Brigits' for Llansantffraed) and by the attitudes implicit in his poetry that he was presenting himself, his people and the countryside he loved to an English audience, which consisted not merely of his acquaintances in Oxford and London but of the Midland conglomeration of his wives' relatives and friends and of those of the mistress of the Priory.

Olor Iscanus (The Swan of Usk), although dated from 'Newton by Usk this 17. of *Decemb*. 1647', was not published (and then probably by his friend Thomas Powell) until April 1651, thirteen months after the appearance of *Silex Scintillans*. The main reason for this was undoubtedly the poet's 'conversion': the author of *Silex Scintillans* was a changed man, one who viewed his secular poems somewhat askance. It is believed that the conversion came about for two reasons: first, the death of his beloved younger brother William in July 1648: then—a state of deep melancholy having overtaken him—the reading of the works of George Herbert. So deep an impression did the latter make on him that he quoted from them as freely as if they were Holy Writ, without need of acknowledgement. 'There is no example in English literature', comments Hutchinson,[8] 'of one poet borrowing so extensively from another'.

What this discipleship did for his poetry cannot concern us here: it must be sufficient to say two things only—first, that his greatest poems escape from all sense of tutelage, and, second, that the change in the man was to last his life long. But perspective was not absolutely destroyed: in the Preface to *Silex Scintillans* he was able to declare:

> ...I have [by God's saving assistance] supprest my *greatest follies*, and those which escaped from me, are (I think) as innoxious, as most of that *vein* use to be; besides, they are interlined with many virtuous, and some pious mixtures.
>
> (M.390)

Some of his secular poems, it is evident, were held back because they were either dangerously royalist or regrettably profane.

The years of the Commonwealth and the Protectorate were years of purgatory for Vaughan. His brother Thomas, who had returned to Llansantffraed as rector, was ejected on a charge (at one time justified) of drunkenness: his friends Thomas Powell and Thomas Lewis were ejected from the incumbencies of Cantref and Llanfeigan respectively: and the poet himself, unable to accept the claim of the Propagators that they were providing a better ministry, believed himself to be in 'a land of darkenesse... where destruction passeth for propagation'. (M.217).[9] It was this conviction that drove him to write his prose work *Solitary Devotions* (the first item printed in *The Mount of Olives*, entered at Stationers' Hall in December 1651). This was a short personal handbook or instructor encouraging his readers to maintain the private exercise of their religion and urging them particularly to prepare themselves for Holy Communion.

We may reflect here on the religious determination of a man who was still no more than thirty, while at the same time aware that the whole man is more complex than this, his complexity largely lost to sight. He was still, for instance, very close to his twin brother Thomas, who had virtually abandoned his priestly ministrations for an involvement in chemical experiment which, at the Resoration, took him into the King's service and, albeit accidentally, brought about his death at Albury in Oxfordshire in February 1665.[10] We catch a glimpse, in 1651, of Thomas, his wife Rebecca, and Henry's wife Catherine making 'a great glass full of eye-water... at the Pinner of Wakefield' in London. There was evidently no separation of Christian practice and Hermetic philosophy, even in Henry's family, but it may be doubted how deeply the poet himself had delved into Hermetic writings. His interest in medical treatises apart, he seems to be indebted to Paracelsus for his idea of the 'sympathy' between terrestrial and celestial things—a 'correspondence' in which every terrestrial creature has its counterpart in the heavens—and there is in his poetry a Hermetic emphasis not to be seen in Herbert's *The Temple* (especially in the use of words like 'white', 'light', 'ray', 'beam'). But Henry Vaughan has harmonised this with the Christian vision, while at the same time enlarging his imaginative bounds. There is nothing in his work to disconcert the orthodox.

At some time uncertain he began to practise as a doctor. It looks as though he cannot have begun his medical training before 1665, though his translation of Nolle's *Hermeticall Physick* in that year shows him already acquainted with Galen and Paracelsus. He was described as M.D.

on his tombstone and he was known as a doctor consistently from 1667 onwards. But the university in which he qualified has not been discovered: neither in English nor Dutch universities is there record of his name. It is assumed that Vaughan treated ordinary people over a wide area (he himself wrote to Aubrey, 'I have practised now for many years with good successe (I thank god!) & a repute big enough for a person of greater parts than my selfe' [M.668. 15 June 1673]) but of the only three patients we can name, two were of high social status and the third a substantial farmer. In June 1673 he was 'att Breckon . . . still attending our Bishops Lady in a tertian feaver' (M.667) and in September 1693, less than two years before he died, he was at Crickhowell attending 'Mr. Serjeant Le Hunts Lady, who is most dangerously sick in a putrid fever with most malignant symptoms'. A deposition of his made in February 1693/4 shows that he attended Thomas Powell of Maesmawr, across the valley from Newton, in his last illness. These are the fragments of information that survive from a busy medical life.

Vaughan's marriage to Elizabeth Wise (probably in 1655) lies under the suspicion that, despite his disparagement of his Puritan opponents, he was not above taking advantage of the fact that they were most unlikely to challenge him about marrying within the prohibited degrees (which the Church in its full Establishment would certainly have done). And the quarrels which ensued, in which the children of the first marriage took the view that their stepmother was favouring her own brood to their disadvantage, embittered Henry Vaughan's last years. Thomas, the eldest son, after several lawsuits and agreements allegedly not kept, took possession of Newton and left his father and stepmother to repair for themselves a ruinous cottage in Scethrog village, which they occupied from 1689 onwards. But it was Catherine, Henry's third daughter by his first wife, who shamed her father in public. One of her hands had been burned in infancy and she later became lame: in April 1693 she petitioned the Justices of the Great Sessions alleging that her father refused to maintain her. Having obtained a judgment for thirty shillings a quarter, she went on to repeat her petition, saying that, the judgment notwithstanding, her father had paid her nothing and that the local magistrates, who evidently sympathised with Henry, had failed to give her any support. This time Henry Vaughan, who admitted that he had attempted to give his daughter half a crown a week instead of thirty shillings a quarter and that she had refused it, answered Mr. Justice Paulett as follows:

... your Lordship will give me leave to tell you that among
heathens noe parents were ever compelld to maintain or relieve
disobedient & rebellious children, that both despise & vilifie
their parents, & publickly give out most scandalous & re-
proachfull lyes concerning them: which this pious petitioner
hath done, & still doth ... I am sure that among Christians
& in all civil governments it is, or should be looked upon as
a practise directly against his precepts & commands, who is
the great Judge of all our actions.

He could obviously be provoked, not merely to rage but to a more
prolonged self-justification. Indeed, the action that brings his reputation
into the greatest doubt is the Bill of Complaint he put forward in Chan-
cery in November 1693, in which he detailed his position (under an
agreement dated 'about December 1688') as trustee for the younger
children of William Wynter of Llanfihangel Talyllyn, whose interests
the father, when alive, had feared might suffer if his Papist widow and
her son by her first marriage had their way. Elinor Wynter in her answer
relied upon a will made by her late husband in September 1690, which
Elizabeth Vaughan had witnessed and of which Henry Vaughan was
one of four Overseers. It is significant that Hugh Powell, rector of
Llansantffraed (and a relative of the Vaughans), and John Prosser had,
by Henry's own account, refused to sign the deed of 1688, and equally
refused to associate themselves with this Bill. The Wynters and the
Vaughans had, before William Wynter's death, been friends, and one
cannot but feel that there was a good deal in Elinor Wynter's assertion
that Henry would never have brought such an action (in which the
partiality of the information is obvious) if he had not been challenged
in the earlier-mentioned matter of the 'dandy-horse'.

Most of this litigation occurred in the last few years of the poet's
life and the old man may have been getting crotchety and unbalanced.
He died on 23 April 1695 and was buried at Llansantffraed, in the
churchyard not within the church: the stone which covers his tomb was
inscribed, at his own wish, *Servus Inutilis: Peccator Maximus/Hic Iaceo*.[11]
His actions in the few years previous remove from those words the
smallest taint of a false modesty that one might have suspected in the
author of *Silex Scintillans*. With the *Gloria Miserere* that follows they read
(and clearly so, after re-cutting, to this day) as a supreme expression
of Christian humility, conviction of sin and faith in the sacrifice made
by Jesus Christ on the cross.

There are, of course, several respects in which the pieces of the picture do not fit: the real everyday face and personality of the poet still elude us. Before we turn briefly to the poems and the few letters extant to elucidate that part of Henry Vaughan which wished to be called 'Silurist', there is one additional area worthy of exploration, however tendentious the results may prove.

A man, be he a poet or not, may be known by his friends and the company he keeps. And here we have a negative, as well as a positive, indicator. Rowland Watkyns was rector of Llanfrynach, the parish between those of Llanfeigan and Cantref, from 1636 to his ejection in 1649, and again from the Restoration to his death in 1663. Three years or so older than Henry Vaughan but a good deal younger than Henry's friend Thomas Powell, he was more than a neighbouring rector: he was a poet, the author of *Flamma Sine Fumo* (1662),[12] and, as his record shows, a royalist. But not one word does he write of Henry Vaughan, and Vaughan not a word of him. And this is the more curious because Watkyns plainly moved in some, at least, of his contemporary's circles: not merely does he dedicate his volume to Colonel Sir Herbert Price, whom he calls 'a walking Library' (Preface, A.2)—he also has two poems for the Lady Goditha and one for Sir Francis Floyd [Lloyd], Sir Marmaduke's son. Thomas Lewis, rector of Llanfeigan (to whom Vaughan wrote that attractive poem which begins: 'Sees not my friend, what a deep snow/*Candies* our Countries wooddy brow?') is named as one of two 'loveing friends' appointed as Overseers in Watkyns's will. There are other poems in *Flamma Sine Fumo* which shoot, like arrows, *around* the mark: one to Lord Herbert, the ineffective commander of the early days of the war (and the representative of Vaughan's relatives, the Somersets), two to members of the Gwernyfed family (linked, if loosely, with the Vaughans since the days of his mother's wardship), one to Sir Randolph Egerton (Vaughan dedicated *Flores Solitudinis* to Sir Charles of the same name, the uncle of both his wives), one to Edward Powell of Maesmawr (whose son Thomas was Vaughan's patient in 1692 or 1693), and one to Edmund Jones of Buckland (for whose son Games Vaughan may have written an obituary).[13] Another poem is dedicated to Roger Vaughan of Moccas, one of the vast Vaughan cousinage. another, with perhaps more impertinence, to Sir John Aubrey of Llantrithid: and yet another—significantly, if coldly—to Dr. Aurelius Williams, Dr. of Physick.

It is as though the outline of Henry Vaughan's effigy is being picked

out with arrow-points. To what may we attribute the silence of these
two poets about each other? Watkyns's attitude to the Commonwealth
and its protagonists cannot have been in question: for him, too, the
common people are 'constant in nothing but inconstancie' ('The Common People', p. 35): for him 'The new illiterate Lay-Teachers' (pp. 43–
44) destroy rather than propagate:

> If this a propagation shall be found,
> These build the house, which pull it to the ground;
> This is meere Hocus-Pocus; a strange sight,
> By putting candles out, to gain more light.

Perhaps the two poets disliked each other: it may have been as
simple as that. Perhaps it was because Watkyns was neither an Oxford
man nor a native of the Usk valley (he came from Longtown, in 'fruitful
Herefordshire', just to the east of the Black Mountains, and said he did
not like Breconshire people). And perhaps—though this seems unlikely
in view of the wide scatter of dedications—Henry Vaughan did not
know that Watkyns wrote verse. I incline to the view that the 'Silurist'
thought too much of Watkyns's output to be 'begging verse' (his poems
were written mainly during the period when he was ousted from his
living) and that Watkyns objected both to Vaughan's Hermetic interests
(and particularly those of his brother Thomas) and his personal manner—which he regarded as high-flown. Something of this sort may be
inferred from Watkyns's commendation of his work in *Flamma Sine Fumo*
'To the Reader':

> I am not Eagle ey'd to face the Sun,
> My mind is low, and so my Verse doth run.
> I do not write of Stars to make men wonder
> Or planets how remote they move asunder.
> My shallow River thou may'st foord with ease,
> Ways, which are fair, and plain can nere displease.

The volume's sub-title is 'Poems without Fictions'.

As for Henry Vaughan, the friendships of which we are aware show
a strongly conservative tendency—though whether it is fair to infer this
from poem-dedications and the few letters to Aubrey and Wood that
are extant is open to question. The friends of his youth appear in *Poems*
and in *Olor Iscanus*: there are the two R. W.s, the R. Hall slain at Pon-

tefract, J. Ridsley of the cloak, a friend James (whom some have suggested as James Howell, despite his sixteen years' seniority), a 'retired friend' whom he invites to Brecknock, Thomas Lewis and Thomas Powell, clerics (the latter a powerful literary influence), and Mrs. K. Philipps ('The Matchless Orinda'), with whom he had, presumably, a literary correspondence. To *Olor Iscanus* T. Powell, I. Rowlandson and Eugenius Philalethes (Thomas Vaughan), all calling themselves *Oxoniensis*, contribute poems of commendation, in which they emphasise the poet's 'wit': Powell wonders under what 'wittie star' the Vaughan twins were born and expects a new *Gemini* in the skies: Rowlandson writes of the 'pow'rfull shine' of his friend's verse: and his brother Thomas, attempting the improbable, suspects,

> The *Puritans* will turn thy Proselytes,
> And that thy *flame* when once abroad it shines.
> Will bring thee as many *friends*, as thou hast lines.
>
> (M.38)

Thalia Rediviva, though not published until 1678, contains a number of early poems not previously approved and a few, like the elegy for his cousin Charles Walbeoffe, who died in 1653, which post-date *Silex Scintillans*. Thomas Powell of Cantref, though long dead, has two pieces dedicated to him: John Morgan of the Wenallt ('of White-Hall Esq.', as the title puts it), a neighbour of Vaughan's and related both to the Powells of Maesmawr and to Jenkin Jones, earns a poem '*upon his sudden Journey and succeeding Marriage*' which cannot be dated: and there is another to Judge Arthur Trevor of the Brecknock Circuit upon his '*much lamented death*' in 1666. 'Daphnis' is an elegy for Eugenius Philalethes, the poet's brother. The poem in *Thalia* of latest date is that '*To the Editor of the matchless Orinda*', which belongs to 1667, but Orinda's poem in commendation of Henry Vaughan, like that of Thomas Powell, was written many years before. There remain commendatory poems from N. W. and J. W., the latter of whom also contributes the book's dedication to the Marquis of Worcester. Hutchinson identifies these with Nathaniel and John Williams, both of Jesus College but much younger than Henry Vaughan. John, the elder, was in his thirtieth year in 1678 and a prebendary of St. David's. In 1680 he became Archdeacon of Cardigan.

Outside the books we may add Edmund Jones of Buckland and his son Games (if we accept the view of William Force Stead), a known friendship with the Wynter family (before the days of the lawsuits) and the circle comprised of Colonel Sir Herbert Price, his wife, and the Midland acquaintances made through Henry's marriages. It is necessarily a very incomplete picture and its dominant constituents—Oxford friends, relatives, churchmen and lawyers—may very well be misleading, as any social portrait based on *occasional poems* is likely to be. But for what it is worth Henry Vaughan appears to move very little outside the circle of those who in politics, churchmanship, literary and professional interest, were naturally closest to him. It is one of the misfortunes we suffer under that his period as an active physician, when he may have encountered neighbours of lower social status and different attitudes of mind, produced no poems at all.

It remains to attempt to show what, if not military glory or populist sympathy, the poet may have meant by his choice of the term 'Silurist'. One possibility is that he intended it as an oblique word for 'Welshman'. Hutchinson has argued at length[14] the evidence that Vaughan was not merely acquainted with Welsh poetry but so well acquainted with it that his own practice in writing poetry in English was markedly affected by it. There is no space here to set out Hutchinson's arguments in detail: it must be enough to note his headings—the use of personal pronouns for *things* (not merely *his* and *her*, still common in 1650, but *he* and *she*): the frequent ascriptions of Welsh genders to nouns in English, even against English practice: the rhyming of *s* and *z*, both probably pronounced by Vaughan as *ss*: the rhyming of stressed and unstressed syllables (not common in English verse), the unstressed rhyme probably getting clearer enunciation according to the Welsh practice: a love of alliteration, and particularly of sibilants, alien to the practices of contemporary verse in English: a fondness for assonance, amounting often to laxity in rhyming: a deficiency in organising the whole poem because of the emphasis on polishing individual lines (a frequent weakness in Welsh poetry): the importance to Vaughan of the word *white*, which appears to echo the meanings of the Welsh *gwyn*, not merely *white*, but *fair, happy, holy, blessed*; the prevalence of *dyfalu*, a piling up of comparisons, often practised in Welsh poetry: and the use of antitheses, again in a manner which seems peculiarly Welsh. Hutchinson suggests, because of the identity of *s* and *z* in his poetry, that Henry Vaughan stressed his sibilants heavily and probably spoke English with a pronounced accent.

All this has to be inferred. What the poet wrote about Welsh poetry—or rather what has survived of what he wrote about it—is very little. John Aubrey and Anthony à Wood had been pressing him for information about Dr. John David Rhys, an Anglesey man who lived the latter part of his life in Breconshire and died about 1609 (he 'had the unhappiness to sojourn heer in an age that understood him not', writes Vaughan in 1689) (M.674) and in the last year of his life the poet made answer in the only letter that assists us at all (dated 9 October 1694, M.675–76). After saying that he had enquired in vain of the few people he thought might have known about the 'ancient Bards' and excusing himself on the ground that those same Bards, like the Druids, passed on their knowledge by word of mouth only,[15] he continues as follows:

As to the later Bards, who were no such men, butt had a societie & some rules & orders among themselves: & severall sorts of measures & a kind of Lyric poetrie: wch are all sett down exactly In the learned John David Rhees, or Resus his welch, or British grammer: you shall have there (in the later end of his book) a most curious Account of them. This vein of poetrie they called Awen, which in their language signifies as much as Raptus, or a poetic furor; & (in truth) as many of them as I have conversed with are (as I may say) gifted or inspired with it. I was told by a very sober & knowing person (now dead) that in his time, there was a young lad father & motherless, & soe very poor that he was forced to beg; butt att last was taken up by a rich man, that kept a great stock of sheep upon the mountains not far from the place where I now dwell. who cloathed him & sent him into the mountains to keep his sheep. There in Summer time following the sheep & looking to their lambs, he fell into a deep sleep; In wch he dreamt, that he saw a beautifull young man with a garland of green leafs upon his head, & a hawk upon his fist: with a quiver of Arrows att his back, coming towards him (whistling several measures or tunes all the way) & att last lett the hawk fly att him, wch (he dreamt) gott into his mouth & inward parts, & suddenly awaked in a great fear & consternation: but possessed with such a vein, or gift of poetrie, that he left the sheep & went about the Countrey, making songs upon all occasions, and came to be the most famous Bard in all the Countrey in his time.

This was just such a tale as Aubrey loved, of course, but the letter which gives such prominence to it and says so little else has an air either tired or genuinely ignorant. Vaughan may have felt too old and forgetful to be bothered with such queries: he admits to having talked to Welsh bards (presumably in Welsh) but gives the impression that his knowledge of their 'poetic furor' comes from the declamation of their verse to him at meeting: there is not a word of *his* having *read* Welsh poetry, much less written it. And for the rest he refers Aubrey to Rhys's 'grammer'. He admitted (letter to Wood of 25 March 1689, M.674) that he failed to answer a much earlier letter from Aubrey about Rhys, pleading 'a tedious and severe sickness with a very slow recovery' as excuse, and earlier still (in 1673, M.670) he could not tell Aubrey of the books of any Jesus College men except his brother and himself and his friend Thomas Powell.[16] Either he responded to these enquiries with some reluctance or he really was not a man well informed about books in Welsh or by Welshmen. His reaction to a suggestion from Aubrey that he should collaborate (as far as his native county was concerned) with Dr. Robert Plott, Keeper of the Ashmolean Museum at Oxford, who intended a natural history of England and Wales, shows markedly more enthusiasm: he returns 'humble & hearty thanks' for being told of it, and continues,

> I shall take Care to assist him with a short account of natures Dispensatorie heer, & in order to it, I beg you would acquaint me with the method of his writinge.
>
> (9 December 1675. M.672)

But it was six years later before Aubrey, after much asking, obtained the 'halfe a dozen printed Queres' from Plott to send to Vaughan, and nothing seems ever to have come of the poet's intended collaboration. He was still interested in 1680 (M.672) but perhaps his frequent absences from home (in the interests of patients) and the advance of old age disinclined him to write at length on anything. It is a great pity that the only letters we have belong to years when this was increasingly true.

If we transfer our investigation to the books of devotion and medicine which he read in earlier periods of his life, the 'Silurist' is harder still to find. His translations from the Latin are taken from Juvenal, Ovid, Ausonius, Boëthius, Mathias Casimir (a contemporary work of 1632), Plutarch, Maximus Tyrius, 'a Platonick Philosopher', Archbishop Anselm, Nieremberg the Jesuit, Eucherius, Bishop of Lyons (a fifth century example of *contemptus mundi*) and Paulinus, Bishop of Nola (whom Ausonius taught and Eucherius, and as a near-contemporary, venerated). It would be worthy of remark indeed if it could be proved that Vaughan's interest in Eucherius, Paulinus and perhaps Ausonius (who wrote a poem on the Moselle) arose because they were Gaulish Celts: but the truth is more probably that Eucherius justified his feelings of withdrawal from a distasteful world, whose end 'truely draws near, if it be not *at the door*', and that Paulinus was an example to him of the way in which a man, once converted, may become a true poet by employing his talents in sacred poetry. Vaughan also translated the work of Henry Nollius, already mentioned, and in the case of Antonio de Guevara, Bishop of Carthagena, appears to have translated him direct from the Spanish.

Many of these books were more contemporary than the dates of their original composition would suggest. Indeed, it is the date of a new edition *in Latin* that should be our guide to Henry Vaughan's reading. All the pieces 'Collected in his Sicknesse and Retirement' (M.211) for *Flores Solitudinis*, for example, had been newly latinised by Jesuit editors. But many of these works must have been difficult to obtain. How had the poet got his hands on such books? And even more, why, as a Welshman—as 'Silurist'—does he never consider translating from, or into, the Welsh? It may be argued that there was no work in Welsh worthy of translation that had not itself been translated from the English, and that this was particularly true in the two fields of Vaughan's interest. One cannot but suspect, however, that Rhys Prichard's popularisations of doctrine and practice (not, it is true, *published* until 1659/60) had been circulating widely from Llandovery long before. If they were known and ignored, as seems possible, the reasons would lie in Prichard's Puritanical leanings and Vaughan's aristocratic distaste for the popular. Again, it is worthy of note that Vaughan betrays no knowledge of Lewis Bayly's *Practice of Piety*, an extremely well-known work first published in 1611 and akin in spirit to Vaughan's *Solitary Devotions*. Rowland Vaughan of Caergai translated it into Welsh in 1630 and that translation went into five editions in the next hundred years. Should we perhaps suppose that Bayly's world (he was Bishop of Bangor) was largely cut off from Vaughan's Breconshire? In a letter of 15 June 1673 (M.668) Vaughan told Aubrey that the 'other persons mentioned in yor lre were Northwales gent & unknowne to any in these parts'. He advised him to enquire of Dr. Thomas Ellis of Dolgellau, sometime of Jesus College. But even if we grant such insulation, the point remains that Vaughan apparently intended *Solitary Devotions* only for those of his friends and neighbours who could read English. Or it was meant for the consumption of royalist churchmen in general. Arguments from silence are always suspect, but once again it must be noted that Henry Vaughan shows no sign of being a Welshman living in what was then Welsh-speaking Wales.

It must be obvious that the kind of education the Vaughan twins received from Matthew Herbert and which they afterwards compounded at Oxford is central to these considerations. It was an education in the classical languages and their literatures, intended ultimately to adorn and cultivate the speaker and writer of English. If Wales and the Welsh language played any part in the thinking of Welshmen so educated, they provided, for one generation only, some access to the affections of the commonalty and, in the longer term, permitted minor sentimental attachments such as the pride due to pedigree and descent. But in other, major respects, there were serious disadvantages to be overcome. I conclude that Henry Vaughan, despite his long residence in his native spot, was able to vary the direction in which his education pressed him only in declaring an origin (in a fashion which his English readers might well fail to understand) and in presenting often, in the Latin which was the mark of the sufficiently educated, the native scene he loved as eminently fit (despite the peculiarities of language) for the attention of a discriminating English public.

This is a theme which I have left myself too little space to illustrate at any length. But it is worth making two assertions, if only for provocation's sake. Henry Vaughan does not, in my view, *describe* the Usk and the scenes on its banks in a way that modern readers would recognise. Those who would seek to identify aspects of the landscape from his poems, whether secular or religious, very soon find themselves scrambling for a line or two. Topographical emphasis in English verse was appearing, only slowly, in Vaughan's day: its earliest examples are probably Sir John Denham's 'Cooper's Hill',[17] written between 1642 and 1655, and Edmund Waller's 'On St. James's Park' (1661).[18] John Dyer's 'Grongar Hill' (1726), the earliest such poem from Wales, belongs still to the first phase of topographical writing in verse. But Vaughan's purpose was unmistakably to *celebrate* his landscape and that he did so in the manner of his favourite Vergil (with *groves, fountains, arbours, nymphs, shepherds* and *pipes*) was largely a matter not merely of personal habit and predilection but of a thus far unbroken tradition. But that may not have been the only reason. It seems to me possible that the Vergilian tradition was needed, or felt by the poet to be needed, to support the disadvantaged culture and habitat which he wished to celebrate. It was essential that he, the poet, should appear to have credentials that were unassailable. The second point is more detailed. The greatest daring shown in the presentation of his native countryside is to be seen in 'To the River Isca' (M.39). After an introduction in which Eurotas and Hebrus, Tyber and Thames, Mosella and Severn, are seen to be celebrated by poets already renowned, the poem continues:

> Poets (like Angels) where they once appear
> Hallow the place, and each succeeding year
> Adds rev'rence to't, such as at length doth give
> This aged faith, That there their Genii live.

The poet's status is undoubtedly a lofty one, but there is no recognition of Welsh bards gone before, of a countryside already hallowed in another language. The poet himself, the 'Silurist', is the man who will make Isca celebrated, as these later lines show:

> But Isca, whenso'er those shades I see,
> And thy lov'd Arbours must no more know me,
> When I am layd to rest hard by thy streams,
> And my Sun sets, where first it sprang in beams,
> I'le leave behind me such a large, kind light,
> As shall redeem thee from oblivious night,
> And in these vowes which (living yet) I pay
> Shed such a Previous and Enduring Ray,
> As shall from age to age thy fair name lead
> 'Till Rivers leave to run, and men to read.

I am not so unkind as to think that these lines are intended as mere self-aggrandisement: the 'Silurist's' is an 'Enduring Ray' but it is also a 'Previous' one—other poets will be born after him: the Usk is the glory behind the poetry and both will last. But it is plain as can be that Henry Vaughan sees himself not as any kind of successor in a Welsh tradition but as a pioneer in English verse, a writer for an English audience who is bringing a previously uncelebrated and distant region to their civilised notice. The Welshness is in the place and not intentionally, if at all, in the poetry. We have here a poet whose purpose it is to bring his loved world into the orbit of the classical heritage of the English. It is an early version of the purpose of most Welsh writers in English before the middle of the present century.

213

Notes

1. All facts in this article, unless otherwise stated, are derived from F. E. Hutchinson, *Henry Vaughan: A Life and Interpretation* (Oxford, 1947).

2. *Calendar of the Manuscripts of the Marquis of Salisbury*, Part XIX, pp. 127–28. 11 May 1607.

3. Star Chamber Proceedings, James 1:8/169/17.

4. L. C. Martin, *The Works of Henry Vaughan* (in two volumes), Oxford 1914, p. 363. The pages in these two volumes are numbered consecutively and future quotations from them will be designated simply by the letter M, and the page number.

5. Fychan was the original Welsh form of Vaughan. It meant 'little' or 'the lesser' and was used as an appendage to the name of the younger of two brothers who, though born of the same parents and therefore *full* brothers, had yet been given the same Christian name.

6. J. M. Lewis, *Welsh Monumental Brasses*, p. 66. Cradocke Vraichvras (though not identified by Lewis) is identical with Caradawg, the leader of the first century AD.

7. M.32. Blunden's translation, from *On the Poems of Henry Vaughan* (1927), p. 9, is quoted by Hutchinson, *op. cit.*, p. 27.

8. pp. 102–03.

9. Preface to *Flores Solitudinis*, dated from 'Newton by Usk in South-wales. April, 17, 1652'.

10. Antony à Wood records: 'Eugenius Philalethes died as twere suddenly wn he was operating strong mercurie, some of wch by chance getting up his nose marched him off. So Harris of Jesus Coll.'

11. 'A useless servant (slave): the greatest of sinners/here I lie.'

12. Edited with an Introduction and Notes by Paul C. Davies, 1968. All the information about Watkyns of which this article makes use is to be found in Davies, unless otherwise stated.

13. William Force Stead, in The Times Literary Supplement of 8 February 1952, advanced the view that a tablet in the church at Llansantffraed which is inscribed with 22 lines of verse in memory of 'Games Jones late of Grays-Inn Esq. & Recorder of Brecknock, who dyed in ye 31th year of His Age May the 18th 1681' may in fact carry the last of all Henry Vaughan's poems. Curiously, Rowland Watkyns refers to the dead man, much earlier in his life, as James Jones.

14. *Op. cit.*, pp. 156–64.

15. It is not clear why he could not have consulted the work of his long-dead friend Thomas Powell, who wrote *A short account of the lives, manners & religion of the British Druids and the Bards &c*. Unpublished, this had been left in Vaughan's custody. M.670.

16. This reply makes it extremely unlikely that he was acquainted with James Howell, who had left Jesus College as long before as 1613.

17. Curiously, Sir Herbert Price's eldest son, Sir Thomas Price, married Elizabeth, the daughter of Sir John Denham. (Theophilus Jones, *History of Brecknockshire*, Glanusk Edition, II. 139) Rowland Watkyns's description of Sir Herbert as 'a walking library', coupled with the evidence that amongst Sir John Price's descendants there was one in each generation who was described as 'learned', should prompt attention to the family at the Priory as a possible focus of literary interest. It may even be that Henry Vaughan was writing for *them*.

18. John Wilson Foster, 'The Topographical Tradition in Anglo-Irish Poetry' (*The Irish University Review*, Autumn 1974).

CLAUDE J. SUMMERS and TED-LARRY PEBWORTH

Vaughan's Temple in Nature
and the Context of "Regeneration"

Although Henry Vaughan's "Regeneration" has received much attention from modern readers,[1] it has not yet been placed in the religio-
political context which can illuminate its apparent obscurity. A difficult
poem, placed first in *Silex Scintillans*, "Regeneration" traces the poet's
own pilgrim's progress. The quest for personal regeneration is a private
one, but Vaughan recounts it in terms which reverberate with public
implications. Taking its impetus from Herbert's "The Pilgrimage,"
Vaughan's poem is finally much different. In the late 1640's and early
1650's, Vaughan was writing under conditions far removed from those
experienced by Herbert two decades earlier. In addition to many personal differences between the two poets, the external conditions under
which they lived are crucial, for they provide the Silurist's painful quest
a context quite opposed to the ecclesiastical tradition in which Herbert
wrote. An understanding of this context helps reveal a hitherto unap-
preciated dimension of "Regeneration" and of Vaughan's reliance on
nature, and explains concretely an important difference between
Vaughan and his mentor.

Louis Martz observes that Herbert's eucharistic imagery is his
dominant field of reference, whereas in "Regeneration" there is no such
allusion, adding: "Nothing could speak more eloquently of the vast
difference between these two poets."[2] Martz further notes that Vaugh-

Reprinted, by permission of The University of Illinois Press, from *Journal of English
and Germanic Philology*, 74 (1975), 351–60.

an's poems characteristically develop in terms of the Bible, nature, and the self, remarking pointedly: "it is as though the earthly church had vanished, and man were left to work alone with God."[3] For Anglicans such as Vaughan, the triumph of those who would suppress the Church of England as it had existed in the first four decades of the seventeenth century did in fact signal the banishment of the earthly church. In 1646, after the defeat of the Royalist forces in the first Civil War, the Puritan regime firmly established itself in south Wales. From the vantage point of the twentieth century, we are aware that the Parliamentarian suppression of Anglicanism was, to a large degree, incomplete and ineffective. But Henry Vaughan's apprehension of the politicoreligious situation of his day was far more restricted than our view of it. In 1646, Vaughan saw his schoolmaster, Matthew Herbert, rector of Llangattock, and his neighbors Thomas Powell, rector of Cantref, and Thomas Lewes, rector of Llanfigan, displaced by Puritan ministers. And in 1650, Henry's twin brother Thomas, the incumbent of the poet's own parish, was evicted from his living and the position left vacant.[4] When he was writing the poems of *Silex Scintillans*, Vaughan had no way of knowing that there would be a Restoration of the Church in 1660, nor did he have much opportunity to know that in various parts of England and Wales Anglicanism successfully defied its Parliamentarian enemies. He only knew that the Puritan desecration of the Established Church, including the abolition of the Book of Common Prayer,[5] had robbed him of the public sources of inspiration and imagery so vital to Herbert.

Vaughan regarded the Parliamentarian displacement of Anglicanism with horror. In *The Mount of Olives*: or, *Solitary Devotions* (written, 1651), he addresses God as "O thou, that art every where" and laments that the churches ("These reverend and sacred buildings") are "now vilified and shut up."[6] In the same work, he offers "A Prayer in time of persecution and Heresie," indignantly and sorrowfully rehearsing the disfigurement of the Church by the Puritans: "Consider, O Lord, the teares of thy Spouse which are daily upon her cheeks, whose adversaries are grown mighty, and her enemies prosper. The wayes of *Zion* do mourne, our beautiful gates are shut up, and the Comforter that should relieve our souls is gone from us. Thy Service and thy Sabbaths, thy own sacred Institutions and the pledges of thy love are denied unto us; Thy Ministers are trodden down, and the basest of the people are set up in thy holy place" (p. 166). And in "Man in Darkness, or A Discourse of Death," appended to *Solitary Devotions*, Vaughan again comments on the adversity visited upon the Church as a result of the Parliamentarian victory: "We have seen such vicissitudes and examples of humane frailty, as the former world (had they happened in those ages) would have judged prodigies. We have seen Princes brought to their graves by a new way, and the highest order of humane honours trampled upon by the lowest. We have seene Judgement beginning at Gods Church, and (what hath beene never heard of, since it was redeem'd and established by his blessed Son,) . . . his Ministers cast out of the Sanctuary, & barbarous persons without *light* or *perfection*, usurping holy offices" (pp. 170–71). This context of the Puritan destruction of Anglicanism helps to explain Vaughan's neglect of the liturgical tradition so important to Herbert.

The religiopolitical context also helps explicate "Regeneration" and provides important implications for a complete evaluation of Vaughan's reliance on nature. In "Regeneration," Vaughan finds in nature not simply "that universall and publik Manuscript"[7] of the Book of the Creatures which supplements the Scriptures and the conscience as guides to salvation; he also discovers Beth-el, the House of God. Not only does he come to the realization that God is indeed everywhere; but he also finds in the enclosed garden the Spouse of Christ, His Church, a temple more rewarding and more intimate than that edifice now so "destituted" and rent by the Puritans. Indeed, it may be precisely because the Anglican fabric has been destroyed that Vaughan is led to a new apprehension of a temple in nature, one expressed in terms of the architecture of Anglicanism.

"Regeneration" develops as a traditional spiritual quest. The speaker, though fascinated by the "smoake, and pleasures" (l. 23) of worldly pursuits, is nevertheless unfulfilled by them. The "Ward" of line one suggests both his youth, his spiritual immaturity, and his condition of bondage. He is, as George Williamson observes, a ward of the world and of sin;[8] for "whosoever committeth sin is the servant of sin" (John 8:34b). So much is he a slave, under the control of earthly pleasure, that he must take pains to elude his master's eye: "I stole abroad" (l. 2). He embarks on a pilgrimage which eventually culminates in his plea to be received "into the congregation of Christ's flock"[9] and his prayer to die to the world so that he may be born in Christ.

The pilgrim's initial encounter with nature confirms his disquiet. Vaughan emphasizes the moral ambiguity of nature unaccompanied by

Christian revelation. The external renewal of vegetation does not automatically generate a renewal of the pilgrim's soul. The primrose (l. 4) may be the earliest flower to bloom in the spring, but it is also a traditional symbol of sadness and early death.[10] It may be "high-spring" without (l. 3), but it is "frost within" (l. 5). The speaker finds this initial spring to be only the "Meere stage, and show" of renewal (l. 10) while sin "Like Clouds ecclips'd my mind" (l. 8).

He ascends the "monstrous, mountain'd thing" (l. 11), finally achieving the pinnacle. He learns by this pursuit that pain is a *sine qua non* of a meaningful quest. But he is yet able to interpret its lesson fully. The "late paines" (l. 22) are outweighed by the insubstantial worldly things he holds dear, reminding the reader of the warning to Belshazzar: "Thou art weighed in the balances, and art found wanting" (Daniel 5:27). Vaughan's metaphor of the scales works on another level as well: the "smoake, and pleasures" are heavy and bear one downward in much the same way that later the "ill-shap'd, and dull" stones (l. 56) in the cistern stand "Nail'd to the Center" (l. 60), while the pains are light and elevate one toward heaven like the bright stones "quick as light" (l.57) which dance in the water. The pilgrim does, however, recognize the emptiness of his soul, and that recognition prepares him to heed the instruction of God:

> With that, some cryed, *Away*; straight I
> Obey'd, and led
> Full East, a faire, fresh field could spy
> Some call'd it, *Jacobs Bed.*
> (ll. 25–28)

Through God's injunction, he is led to the revealed temple of nature.

The first overt Biblical allusion in the poem (*Jacobs Bed*) informs us that God has directed the pilgrim to His House, Beth-el. For George Herbert, though himself not wholly satisfied with the church of his day, Beth-el was the Anglican fabric in both its spiritual and physical manifestations. But Parliament closed the physical doors of that church to Vaughan, and even desanctified its buildings;[11] thus it is only in the landscape of a poem that he can discover that holy place, "A Virgin-soile, which no / Rude feet ere trod" (ll. 29–30). There is no building here, not even the stone which Jacob set up: "And this stone, which I have set for a pillar, shall be God's house" (Genesis 28:22a). There can be no physical House of God so long as the Puritans rule. But God told

Jacob, "behold, I am with thee, and will keep thee in all places whither thou goest" (Genesis 28:15a). The spiritual House of God can be anywhere, and the poet-pilgrim discovers in a grove (actually a garden encircled by trees) the architecture of Anglicanism. In this natural temple, he experiences a true springtime of the soul.

Jacob's field is the church porch. The nave is the grove "Of stately height, whose branches met / And mixt on every side" (ll. 35–36). Since the pilgrim has been traveling toward the east, he obviously, and appropriately, enters the grove through its west "door." He is at first struck by the sensuous sights and fragrances of the interior, those objects "purified" out of Anglicanism by the dissenters.[12] There is the richness of stained glass: the "unthrift Sunne" (l. 41) shoots "A thousand peeces" of gold (l. 42), and the sky is "Checqur'd with snowie fleeces" (l. 44). The air has been censed and the whole interior decked in garlands (presumably, since it is spring, for Eastertide):

> The aire was all in spice
> And every bush
> A garland wore. . . .   (ll. 45–47)

Near the entrance is the baptismal font, "a little Fountain" (l. 49). This is the first element of the interior to provide the pilgrim with more than mere sense impressions. Drawing near, he is shown a lesson in the stones which fill the cistern, a lesson of the mystery of Grace. The "bright, and round" stones (l. 55) are those souls Elect by God; the stones "Nail'd to the Center" are the reprobates. In addition to the mystery of Grace, however, the stones impart a message of comfort. Those souls which have experienced the Grace of God through the Church and have remained true to her have undergone a shaping and polishing by God's chastisement (Heb. 12:5–11, esp. 6) and by external adversity (II Cor. 4:8–18). They will be everlastingly alive ("quick," l. 57). By contrast, the "ill-shap'd, and dull" (l. 56), those who have not suffered the pains of adversity, are—despite a physical act of baptism—borne downward to damnation ("more heavy then the night / Nail'd to the Center," ll. 59–60). This lesson of faith is embedded in the earlier metaphor of the scales. The "quick" stones also echo the "lively stones" of I Peter 2:4–5, the "chosen of God" who are built into "a spiritual house." They have "purified" their "souls in obeying the truth" and have been "born again, not of corruptible seed, but of incorruptible"

219

(I Peter 1:22, 23). At this point, however, the pilgrim cannot yet interpret the lessons:

> I wonder'd much, but tyr'd
> At last with thought,
> My restless Eye that still desir'd
> As strange an object brought.
>
> (ll. 61–64)

The speaker's inability to comprehend these lessons emphasizes the mysteriousness of Election and faith and their imperviousness to rational explanation.

The "banke of flowers" (l. 65), that object which he next examines, suggests a raised altar.[13] The contrast between awake and sleeping flowers implies a message similar to that expressed by the stones in the fountain: the saved are open to and thus warmed by Grace, while the unsaved are asleep to God and to eternal life, not having been offered God's gift of salvation. The image of some flowers "fast asleepe, others broad-eyed" (l. 67) also recalls the parable of the watchful servants (Mark 13:34–37; Luke 12:35–40) and is thereby linked not only with the Second Coming, but also, in Luke's account, with the metaphor of Christ and His Church as bridegroom and bride: "[Be] ye yourselves like unto men that wait for their lord, when he will return from the wedding; that when he cometh and knocketh, they may open unto him immediately. Blessed are those servants, whom the lord when he cometh shall find watching. . . . And this know, that if the goodman of the house had known what hour the thief would come, he would have watched, and not have suffered his house to be broken through." Vaughan in his epigraph from The Song of Songs will later emphasize the bridegroom-bride metaphor. The obvious lesson of the watchful servants here is a lesson of vigilance in an hour of adversity. In the moment of the Parliamentarian triumph, the pilgrim must be alert to the presence of God in unexpected places. He must be prepared to discover a temple in nature when the "thief" has broken through the traditional House of God. And in the temple, he must be "broad-eyed" and receptive to the presence of God.

In the natural temple, the pilgrim is regenerated through a metaphorical death to worldly concerns and a consequent rebirth to the spiritual. "Musing long" (l. 69) in the enclosed garden, he hears

> A rushing wind
> Which still increas'd but whence it stirr'd
> No where I could not find.[14]
> (11. 70–72)

The Biblical allusion informing lines 69–80 is John 3:8: "The wind bloweth where it listeth, and thou hearest the sound thereof, but canst not tell whence it cometh, and whither it goeth." This allusion operates on two levels in "Regeneration." It is God's declaration that He cannot be restricted by anything, not even by the closing of His church. When denied Him in an edifice of stone and mortar, the pilgrim has been able to find God in the architecture of a grove. On another level, the wind is the offer of salvation to the individual soul, an invitation to be "born of water and of the Spirit" (John 3:5). It is for this invitation that the speaker pleads in the poem's conclusion: "Lord, then said I, *On me one breath, / And let me dye before my death!*" (ll. 81–82). By dying to the world and being reborn in the spirit, the pilgrim can be "regenerate and grafted into the body of Christs congregation."[15]

Louis Martz has called attention to the context of the epigraph from The Song of Songs and has applied it on a sensual level to the metaphors with which Vaughan describes the scene within the grove.[16] But Martz has neglected to make a more significant application of the passage to the poem. The Song is frankly erotic, and both Jewish and Christian theologians have insisted, from the beginning, that it be allegorized in some fashion or other to make it spiritually acceptable. The most common Christian interpretation is that the bridegroom and the bride represent Christ and His Church.[17] And in the passage from which Vaughan took his epigraph, the bride is described as an enclosed garden, where are to be found a cistern and many kinds of spicy plants.

One of the most influential Anglican interpretations of The Song in the seventeenth century is Bishop Joseph Hall's *An Open and Plaine Paraphrase, upon The Song of Songs* (1609).[18] Hall's interpretation of the verses most pertinent to "Regeneration" helps illuminate Vaughan's position. Hall assigns to Christ the verses immediately preceding the one Vaughan uses as an epigraph: "A garden inclosed is my sister, my spouse; a spring shut up, a fountain sealed. Thy plants are an orchard of pomegranates, with pleasant fruits; camphire, with spikenard. Spikenard and saffron; calamus and cinnamon, with all trees of frankincense; myrrh and aloes, with all the chief spices: A fountain of gardens, a well of living waters, and streams from Lebanon."[19] Hall explains that

221

the garden is enclosed so that it will not be "carelessly open, either to the loue of strangers, or to the rage of enemies, which like the wilde Bore out of the wood, might root vp and destroy her choise plants: but safely hedged and walled . . . a Spring & Well of wholsome waters, from whom flow forth the pure streames of my Word; but, both inclosed and sealed vp: partly, that shee may the better (by this closenesse) preserue her owne naturall taste and vigour, from the corruptions of the world; and partly, that shee may not be defiled and mudded by the prophane feet of the wicked" (pp. 245–46). Vaughan's temple in nature, the "garden inclosed," is, then, unlike the organized church, safe from the "rage of enemies" and is:

> A Virgin-soile, which no
> Rude feet ere trod,
> Where (since he stept there,) only go
> Prophets, and friends of God.
> (ll.29–32)

Significantly, Hall interprets the plants of the garden as faithful children who grow up in the Church, and the fragrances as symbols of their holy obedience. In Vaughan's description of the grove, he emphasizes those sensuous aspects of the Anglican worship to which the Puritans particularly objected, the stained glass and the incense. In light of Hall's interpretation, Vaughan's description ironically redounds against the defilers of the Anglican ritual who were—in Vaughan's view—anything but obedient.

The half-verse that Vaughan quotes as the epigraph ("Arise O North, and come thou South-wind, and blow upon my garden, that the spices thereof may flow out")[20] Hall assigns to the Church, interpreting it as her plea for Christ to come "and breathe vpon this garden of my soule; that the sweet odours of these my plants may both bee increased, and may also bee dispersed afarre, and carried into the nostrils of my Well-beloued" (p. 246). Significantly, the pilgrim in "Regeneration" hears God's breath, the "rushing wind" (l. 70) in the grove, the temple he comes to recognize as the House of God. God's presence in the garden is the answer to both the Church's plea and the pilgrim's search for personal regeneration.

Vaughan's "Regeneration," then, is an account of the poet's own personal pilgrimage from a false spring of worldly pursuits to a genuine springtime of the soul. Brilliantly developed by means of rich and pregnant allusions, the poem charts a quest for spiritual rebirth. Central to this journey is the pilgrim's discovery of the House of God in nature, where he learns lessons of the mysterious working of Grace and of faith in times of adversity. It is in the enclosed garden that he hears the rushing wind whisper *"Where I please"* (l. 80). Vaughan describes this temple of nature in terms that remind the reader of Anglican architecture and ritual, the earthly church denied to Vaughan by the Parliamentary triumph. As a result of that triumph, Vaughan apprehends in nature the enduring Church, the Spouse of God, which is safe from the vicissitudes of the religiopolitical strife of his immediate experience. In this sense, "Regeneration" is a public poem as well as a personal one.

Vaughan's discovery of a temple in nature has implications for the continuing evaluation of him as a nature poet. In the best of the many studies emphasizing Vaughan's relationship to nature, James D. Simmonds speculates that among the motives that prompted the poet's interest in nature imagery "may have been partly a reaction against dualistic and Manichean elements in Puritan polemics.... Their attitude tended to minimize the possibility that matter was sanctified by pious uses and ultimately to weaken belief in God's love for the Creation. ... The violent contemporary attacks on the traditional liturgy may have contributed to the intensity of [Vaughan's] interest in the traditional view of the relation of Nature to God on which the liturgy was based."[21] One can go beyond this to the view that Vaughan, driven from his church, found the immanence of God in nature, as Herbert found it in the liturgy of Anglicanism and Jacob in the vision at Beth-el.[22]

Notes

1. See, e.g., Edmund Blunden, *On the Poems of Henry Vaughan* (London, 1927), pp. 20–21; Itrait-Husain, *The Mystical Element in the Metaphysical Poets of the Seventeenth Century* (Edinburgh, 1948), p. 214; Ross Garner, *Henry Vaughan: Experience and the Tradition* (Chicago, 1959), pp. 47–62; E. C. Pettet, *Of Paradise and Light: A Study of Vaughan's* Silex Scintillans (Cambridge, Eng., 1960), pp. 104–107; R. A. Durr, *On the Mystical Poetry of Henry Vaughan* (Cambridge, Mass., 1962), pp. 82–89; Louis Martz, *The Paradise Within: Studies in Vaughan, Traherne and Milton* (New Haven, 1964), pp. 8–12; George Williamson, "Structure in Vaughan's Poetry" in *Milton and Others* (London, 1965), pp. 176–79; Stanley Stewart, *The Enclosed Garden: The Tradition and the Image in Seventeenth-Century Poetry* (Madison, 1966), pp. 105–11; and William H. Halewood, *The Poetry of Grace* (New Haven, 1970), pp. 125–33.
2. Martz, *The Paradise Within*, p. 12. Other considerations of the differences between Herbert and Vaughan include George Williamson, *The Donne Tradition* (Cam-

SUMMERS and PEBWORTH

bridge, Mass., 1930), pp. 123–33; Helen C. White, *The Metaphysical Poets* (New York, 1936), pp. 240–88; Pettet, pp. 51–70; Durr, pp. 9–13; Joan Bennett, *Five Metaphysical Poets*, 3rd ed. (Cambridge, Eng., 1964), pp. 71–89; and Joseph H. Summers, *The Heirs of Donne and Jonson* (New York, 1970), pp. 121–29.

3. Martz, p. 13.

4. F. E. Hutchinson, *Henry Vaughan: A Life and Interpretation* (Oxford, 1947), pp. 109–12. Between 1646 and 1650, the Brecon County Sequestration Committee ordered the displacement of many Anglican ministers. An even more vigorous purge of royalist clergy was initiated on 22 February 1649/50 with the passage of "An Act for the better Propagation and Preaching of the Gospel in Wales . . . ," *Acts and Ordinances of the Interregnum, 1642–1660*, ed. C. H. Firth and R. S. Rait, 3 vols. (London, 1911), II, 342–48. Although we are aware that there were reformers of various persuasions in control of Parliament at different times between 1642 and 1660 and that inevitably the term "Puritan" is imprecise, we use the term "Puritan" and "Parliamentarian" interchangeably as convenient inclusive references.

5. On 4 January 1644/5, Parliament ordered that the "Book of Common Prayer, shall not remain, or be from henceforth used in any Church, Chapel, or place of publique Worship, within the Kingdome of England, or Dominion of Wales," replacing it with a Puritan "Directory for the Publique Worship of God" ("An Ordinance for taking away the Book of Common Prayer, and for establishing and putting in execution of the Directory for the publique worship of God," *Acts and Ordinances*, I, 582).

6. *The Works of Henry Vaughan*, ed. L. C. Martin, 2nd ed. (Oxford, 1957), p. 147. All subsequent quotations from Vaughan are from this edition and are cited parenthetically in the text.

7. Sir Thomas Browne, *Religio Medici*, Part I, Section 16, in *The Prose of Sir Thomas Browne*, ed. Norman Endicott (Garden City, N.Y., 1967), p. 21.

8. Williamson, *Milton and Others*, p. 177.

9. From the service of "Publique Baptisme" in *The Booke of Common Prayer . . .* (London: Imprinted . . . by Robert Barker . . . And by the Assignes of Iohn Bill, 1636), sig. D3 verso.

10. Cf. Spenser's *Daphnaïda*, ll. 232–39; Shakespeare's *Cymbeline*, IV.2.218–21; and Milton's *Lycidas*, l. 142. On the metaphorical significance of the primrose, see, e.g., Hilderic Friend, *Flowers and Flower Lore*, 2 vols. (London, 1884), II, 461–62.

11. "The Directory for the Publique Worship of God," promulgated in England and Wales on 4 January 1644/5 as the replacement for the Book of Common Prayer, excuses the Puritans' use of Church of England edifices by declaring that "no place is capable of any holiness under pretence of whatsoever Dedication or Consecration" (*Acts and Ordinances*, I, 607).

12. "An Ordinance for the utter demolishing, removing and taking away of all Monuments of Superstition or Idolatry" (26 August 1643) orders the destruction by 1 November 1643 of "all Images and Pictures of any one or more Persons of the Trinity, or of the Virgin Mary, and all other Images and Pictures of Saints," including those in stained glass, in all and every the Churches and Chappels . . . within this Realm of England and Dominion of Wales," excepting only "any Image, Picture, or Coat of Arms . . . of any King, Prince, or Nobleman, or other dead Person which hath not been commonly reputed or taken for a Saint." "An Ordinance for the further demolishing of Monuments of Idolatry and Superstition" (9 May 1644) reiterates the order for such destruction (*Acts and Ordinances* I, 265–66, 425–26). Censing the altar, one of the "Romish" practices repopularized by Archbishop Laud, was repugnant to Puritans of all persuasions.

13. In addition to ordering the destruction of church altars in England and

Wales, Parliament decreed on 26 August 1643 that the floors of all chancels "raised for any Altar or Communion Table to stand upon, shall before [1 November 1643] be laid down, and levelled." The order was repeated on 9 May 1644 (*Acts and Ordinances*, I, 265, 425).

14. Edgar F. Daniels ("Vaughan's 'Regeneration': An Emendation, " *AN&Q*, 9 [1970], 19–20) suggests that "No" in line 72 be emended to "Nor."

15. "Publique Baptisme," sig. D3 verso.

16. Martz, pp. 9–11.

17. For an account of this tradition, particularly as it is manifested in the sixteenth and seventeenth centuries, see Stewart, pp. 3–30.

18. We quote from the 1620 folio (London: Imprinted ... for Henry Fetherstone) bound and paged into *A Recollection of Such Treatises as have been heretofore seuerallie published ... By Jos. Hall....* (London: Printed for Hen. Fetherstone ..., 1621) pp. 233–55.

19. The Authorized Version, which we quote, numbers these verses as 12–15 of Chapter 4; Hall's text numbers them 12–14, designating "Thy plants.... the chief spices" as one verse. The translation that Hall reproduces differs little from the Authorized Version.

20. The first half of 4:16 in the Authorized Version; in Hall's text, the first half of verse 15. The first edition of *Silex Scintillans* erroneously identifies it as 5:17; in his notes, Martin corrects the chapter number, but lets the verse number stand (p. 728). Hutchinson points out Vaughan's eclectic use of various translations of the Bible (p. 122, n. 4).

21. James D. Simmonds, *Masques of God: Form and Theme in the Poetry of Henry Vaughan* (Pittsburgh, 1972), pp. 146–47.

JAMES CARSCALLEN

Editing Vaughan

Professor Rudrum's edition of Vaughan's complete poetry should prove
very useful both to the non-scholarly reader for whom the Penguin series
is designed and to students of Vaughan. Like other volumes in the series
it uses modern spelling, although Rudrum has rightly kept Vaughan's
italicizations, which, as he says, normally make allusions or indicate
special senses of words. There are occasional losses with Rudrum's
modernizations. The metre suffers when an ordinary seventeenth-century form like 'flowr' becomes 'flower,' and at the same time modern
spelling lulls us out of whatever alertness we might bring to forms like
'lovest,' which become monosyllabic when the metre requires it as it
does in the first line of *Dressing*. Modernization also forfeits a certain
amount of wordplay (which might have been more extensively noted),
as when 'Adamant' in *Man's Fall, and Recovery* loses its capital A and
no longer hints at Adam. What is gained is, of course, readability for
the non-specialist; and Rudrum's edition is scholarly at the same time.

Rudrum has carefully examined Vaughan's text as such, and while
it does not present many cruxes he has been able to introduce some
new emendations, all of them quite convincing. I might suggest a couple
that he has not introduced. In *Jacob's Pillow, and Pillar* the line 'But a
strong wind must break thy lofty rocks' is puzzling, since 'thy' does not
seem to refer to Jacob, the only person Vaughan has been addressing;
I suspect that he meant 'the,' although Vaughan does use possessive
pronouns in special ways, as with 'my Earth' in *The Morning-watch*. In

Reprinted, by permission of the publisher, from *University of Toronto Quarterly*, 47
(1971), 267–73.

the elegy for R. Hall there seems to be the opposite mistake: all editions have 'The fair and open valour was thy shield,' but the line would be more idiomatic if it began 'Thy.' This would be a very minor change; one a bit more substantial would be the substitution of 'who' for 'whom' in the line 'By his breath whom my dead heart heaves' in *The Agreement*. Rudrum notes an old sense of 'heave,' 'to move, to rouse the feelings of,' and interprets the clause as meaning that 'the deadness of the poet's heart is distressing to Christ.' This is possible, but in a passage dealing with God's life-giving power it seems more likely to be God who heaves the poet's dead heart (which would come to life like a plant rising out of the ground); and 'whom my' would be a very easy mistake for 'who my.' Another possible substitution would be 'earth' for 'ear' in the line 'But all the ear lay hush' in *Regeneration*. This was proposed by Grosart, and I wish that Rudrum had at least recorded Grosart's proposal: 'ear' would be an easy slip for a typesetter after 'eye' in the previous line, and 'earth' gives a more natural reading. If 'earth' is right, Vaughan is probably thinking of Habbakuk 2:20: 'The Lord is in his holy temple: let all the earth keep silence before him'; and this seems appropriate in a passage where Vaughan is entering a kind of temple in order to observe worship. (At this point I should add one printer's error I have noticed in Rudrum's edition: 'you' for 'your' in line 7 of the poem on Powell's translation of Malvezzi.)

Rudrum's editing is at its most helpful in his construing of individual words for the modern reader. To a great extent his success derives from unremitting attention to the OED. Vaughan's diction is sometimes awkward, but it can also be surprisingly precise and suggestive if one knows the old senses of the words he is using, and these are not always apparent from the context. The lover in *The World* who 'his eyes did pour / Upon a flower' is evidently weeping as well as looking, but Vaughan's expression becomes less strained and more witty when we know that as late as Fielding one could 'pore one's eyes out,' thereby becoming blind. Here we distinctly have a pun, and puns are somewhat commoner in Vaughan than one may at first perceive. I wish that Rudrum had noted the allusion to royal sons and successions at the end of *Resurrection and Immortality*—'One everlasting *Sabbath* there shall run / Without *succession*, and without a *sun*'; he might also have explained the delightful touch in *The Importunate Fortune* when Vaughan says of the spheres 'I hold them all *in capite*,' meaning both that he holds them directly from the crown and that he holds them in his head. Elsewhere

Vaughan's way of assimilating conceptual and physical senses of words makes it harder to be sure about puns: Rudrum feels that we have a pun when Vaughan's breath 'aspires' in *Joy*, but for Vaughan there may have been no pun at all. At any rate there are two distinct meanings of 'aspire' for a modern reader, and an editor is right to indicate the breadth of Vaughan's meaning. Similarly, Rudrum is right to note the special legal and financial applications of 'deed' and 'earnest' at the end of *To his Retired Friend* (to which, for that matter, he could have added 'use' and 'lease').

In his commentary Rudrum takes issue, implicitly and explicitly, with much that can only be called silliness in Marilla's edition of the secular poetry, and is able to correct even Martin's usually sound standard edition about some things. He is right, I think, about the 'they' in line 54 of *To my Ingenuous Friend* who are going to forget 'us' when they arrive in Elysium. 'They' are almost certainly the souls of 'us': interestingly, the Vaughan of the 1646 poems is already prepared to imagine a higher self that moves away from all knowledge of a lower one. In his references to hermetic writings Rudrum goes beyond Martin, and he is particularly good on Vaughan's brother Thomas—not many readers would have caught an echo of Thomas (as well as of Herbert's *Church Militant*) in the 'poor, despised Truth' of *The World*. What is even more important is that Rudrum has supplied copious biblical references. Martin refrained from doing this as a matter of policy, which was hardly justifiable in 1914 and would be disastrous today. My only objection is that Rudrum has not always gone far enough. No editor could include all Vaughan's echoes of the Bible or even of Herbert, but echoes should be noted wherever they function to call up the whole of their original context or to illuminate a poem's general structure and significance. Rudrum does not tell us that *Faith* is largely a paraphrase of Hebrews 9 and 10, or that the first *Day of Judgment* is a paraphrase of the *Dies irae*. Glossing the passage in *The Night* where Vaughan rejects a 'mercy-seat of gold,' he makes a connection with George Fox and comments that the Vaughan brothers 'shared their mystical doctrines with the sectaries rather than with their political and ecclesiastical allies.' In the first place, the English translators of Boehme, from whom Rudrum has just quoted, were Anglicans who probably worked under the patronage of Charles I. Moreover, Vaughan does not mean any disrespect for church buildings, as the prose *Mount of Olives* makes clear. What he does mean is a contrast between the old temple as carnal, merely 'dead and dusty,' and the 'living works' associated with Christ: the most pertinent biblical text is the same passage from Hebrews as in *Faith*, a passage which Rudrum has in fact used very helpfully to explain the 'sacred veil' at the beginning of the poem. Then there is the notorious line in *Looking Back* which found its way into *The Stuffed Owl*: 'How brave a prospect is a bright *back-side*!' Allowing that it is biblical, Rudrum notes that the 'backside' was already used in its modern sense in the seventeenth century, and feels that Vaughan's use of it was incautious. Perhaps it was: Milton seems to be using the word humorously in *PL* III. 494, where the rags of superstition 'Fly o'er the backside of the world'; but Vaughan does not hesitate to use the same word in the delicate epitaph for Princess Elizabeth, and if it is biblical we might have been told where in the Bible it occurs. Moses led his flock 'to the back-side of the desert, and came to the mountain of God,' where he saw the burning bush; he later saw the back-parts of God, and not only lived to tell the tale but managed to escape the pages of *The Stuffed Owl*.

A poem that will send a larger number of readers in search of help is *Regeneration*. Rudrum has a note on 'A ward, and still in bonds,' but he does not connect it with Paul's analogy between the Law and childhood: Vaughan may be thinking especially of the comparison of the Law to a schoolmaster in Galatians. Rudrum does not identify the mountain in *Regeneration* as Sinai, or the scales on its top as those of justice and hence of the Law. When Vaughan proceeds 'full east,' Rudrum connects 'east' with 'Easter,' which does no harm, but he does not mention Jacob, who after his dream found his bride Rachel in the 'land of the people of the east' (Genesis 29:1). Yet the reader needs to know a bit about Jacob as Vaughan interpreted him, if not about other biblical figures who find refuge in the east. As *Jacob's Pillow, and Pillar* explains, his stone and his solitude were 'Law and command'; they also prefigured the true temple, and in *Regeneration*, the 'fair, fresh field' at which Vaughan arrives is similarly '*Jacob's bed*.' It is beyond the job of an editor to interpret Vaughan's characteristic double perspective here, but he can point the reader to the most essential materials. The animate stones which Vaughan sees in the fountain may well be related to a passage in Thomas Vaughan which Rudrum quotes; both passages are certainly related to the living stones of 1 Peter. In this last case there is an important principle involved: it is misleading to give a secondary reference while omitting a primary one. Vaughan himself would surely have felt that a biblical allusion precedes others not only in degree but in kind, and that a long (and illuminating) gloss on the relation between *Resurrection and Immortality* and the Hermetica should have found room somewhere for the spirit that passes through all things in the Wisdom of Solomon. For the same reason the questions about the maker of the world that Vaughan cannot answer in *Vanity of Spirit* should have been linked with similar questions in Job and Proverbs if they were also to be linked with the Hermetica. If we step outside the Bible, St. Augustine is as primary a source as any for *Vanity of Spirit*: for this reason a reference to Louis Martz should have included the opening chapter of *The Paradise Within*.

A different reservation that I feel about Rudrum's edition is perhaps less important. I wish that he had gone further not only to indicate but to settle questions of dating and order. Where an issue cannot be settled it is no doubt best to state that fact plainly: we cannot know, for instance, whether the R. W. of the 1646 poems is the same person as the R. W. of *Olor Iscanus*, and Rudrum is right not to press the matter. On the other hand, he might have reviewed the case for identifying the 'Amoret' of the 1646 poems with the 'Etesia' of *Thalia Rediviva*. Hutchinson's reasons for making the identification, to which Rudrum refers, are admittedly not conclusive, but there may be a further clue in the name 'Etesia' itself. Rudrum mentions the cooling effect of the Etesian winds: their literary association seems to have been more generally with mildness (as when Thomas Nabbes in his *Microcosmus* of 1637 speaks of 'mildest ayre / Breath'd by Etesian winds'), and in antiquity they were thought of as favourable to sailing. Since Etesia goes 'beyond sea,' Vaughan may have chosen her name to wish her well in her voyage. His first wife Catherine Wise had connections with both the Digbys in Ireland (to whom Vaughan later expressed indebtedness) and to Colonel Price, the owner of the Priory Grove in Brecon where he first met Amoret. Was Catherine Wise staying with the Prices when he met her, either on her way to Ireland or on a previous visit? It seems not unlikely; and we can see why by 1646 the name 'Amoret,' traditionally associated with a bride, was more appropriate for her. The Etesia poems, then, would be early—earlier than the Amoret poems.

Again, there seem to be good reasons for dating *To his Retired Friend, an Invitation to Brecknock* in or shortly after the winter of 1645/6: Marilla was right, if for questionable reasons; and Hutchinson wrong in dating the poem in 1649, since its first part refers most plausibly to the arrival of the parliamentary army with Laugharne in November of 1645. If this is correct, then the poems of *Olor Iscanus* seem to have been printed in their order of composition, which is worth knowing. This seems not to be true of the poems in the first part of *Thalia Rediviva*, and with a poem like *The Importunate Fortune* conjectures about dating must rest on style and thought. Marilla thought it must be contemporaneous with *The Proffer* in Part II of *Silex Scintillans*, but such a jaunty claim to a scholar's freedom of the universe looks earlier to me, allowing the possibility that Vaughan might have returned to an earlier manner for a genre he had practised in earlier years. These questions of dating are not as academic as they may look, since our understanding of Vaughan's development towards the *Silex* poems would be given much solider ground by more certain dating of poems like *The Importunate Fortune* and *On Sir Thomas Bodley's Library*: even the love-poems, which seem to have so little in common with *Silex*, use metaphors and philosophical notions in a way that throws light on *Silex* and one would welcome any facts or arguments that would help in dating them.

In the explication of particular passages Rudrum has done an important service: one's only general complaint can be that readers may need even more help than he has given them. In *To Amoret, The Sigh*, to give only a single example, a reader may not see that the 'holy spring' of the third stanza is the same thing as Amoret's bosom in the second, and anything an editor might do to clarify this confusing little poem would be welcome. Rudrum's interpretations can themselves be questioned in a few places. When Vaughan prays in *To the River Isca* that the *'green banks* and *streams'* of the Usk may become the *Hill* and *Helicon'* of poets, it is unlikely that the hill in question is Zion: 'Helicon' probably refers to the sacred well, and 'Hill' to the mountain itself, the two being identified with the water and the banks of the Usk respectively. In the elegy *In Amicum Foeneratorem* Rudrum accepts Chapman's explanation of the opening, that the silver of Vaughan's earlier loan has magnetically drawn the gold of his later one into his pocket. Perhaps, though I do not feel very sure about it, Vaughan means rather that the gold is intended to draw in the silver, and when he says of the gold that 'in this sphere/ though the least of many [it] rules the master bear,' he means that even if it were the lesser sum, which it is not, it would be the 'master bear' because of its polar position ('though' is used in the same way in the following poem, *To his Friend*, and in any case is common in this sense).

I feel similarly tentative in offering a suggestion about the *'mouths*

and *elbows*' produced by the cloak which Vaughan borrowed from J.
Ridsley (*Upon a Cloak*, line 76): perhaps Vaughan means that the cloak
hardened as it dried after a wet day, thus either developing mouths and
elbows of its own or moulded them in the wearer (in which case the
'mouth' would be the surly expression into which the experience would
make him set his mouth). I am ready to be more aggressive about certain
other passages. If Malvezzi's *Christian Politician* is 'languaged like our
infancy,' it is not because Powell has used children's language in his
translation: Vaughan is simply writing for convenience' sake as if English
were his native language, although it probably was not, and thus included himself in the typical 'we' of this kind of seventeenth-century
poem. The fountain in line 8 of *Religion* can hardly be that where the
angel found Hagar, since the other members of Vaughan's catalogue
here are all patriarchs and prophets, and what the Bible has made him
see in each of its 'shades' is 'an angel talking with a man.' As a parallel
passage in the prose *Mount of Olives* indicates (p 146 in Martin's edition),
Vaughan is thinking of Abraham's servant Eliezer, named in Genesis
15: Eliezer was traditionally identified (in the Glossa Ordinaria, for
instance), with the servant in Genesis 24 who was led by an angel to a
well outside Nahor, and who prayed in order to choose a wife for Isaac.
In the second *Begging* Vaughan tells us that birds 'sing best, and prettiest
show, / When their nest is fall'n and broken.' Rudrum comments that
'there are many references to birds in *Silex Scintillans*, and several which
manifest careful observation.' If any of these references manifest careful
observation, which is doubtful, this is hardly one of them: it looks more
like a proverb or other commonplace, though Tilley's *Proverbs* and Erasmus are of no help.

The two poems in *Thalia Rediviva* entitled *Fida: Or the Country Beauty:
to Lysimachus* present a special problem. They indicate a situation in
which a humble country-girl is seduced and abandoned by a man of
higher rank, who has been directed to the girl by a friend. Rudrum sees
this as fiction, but thinks that Fida is 'Lysimachus' beloved,' in spite of
the fact that Lysimachus appears in another poem as a real person, a
friend of Vaughan. This Lysimachus is not a nobleman or a gallant,
but a poor scholar. My guess is that he is the dedicatee of the Fida
poems rather than a character in them, and that Vaughan expected him
to sympathize with Fida's indignation. (Since there was an ancient
grammarian called Lysimachus, and since the person so named seems
to be on terms of some familiarity with Vaughan, he may be Vaughan's

old schoolmaster Matthew Herbert.) Fida herself is a conventional 'nymph complaining,' and a likely influence on both the matter and form of the work is Randolph's *Pastoral Courtship*. I would question Rudrum's interpretation of the first stanza of *Fida Forsaken*, which I shall have to quote in full.

> Fool that I was! to believe blood
> While swoll'n with greatness, then most good;
> And the false thing, forgetful man:
> To trust more than our true God, *Pan*,
> Such swellings to a dropsy tend,
> And meanest things such great ones bend.

According to Rudrum Fida is saying that it is foolish to trust Pan, the god of nature and sexuality, more than the true God. This reading is supported by the punctuation of the original edition, but the stanza as we have it reads very awkwardly, and it would be unusual for a shepherdess to think of Pan as other than 'our true God.' If we replace the colon after 'man' by a comma and put a full stop after 'Pan' the stanza gives much better sense: it was foolish of Fida to trust man more than God, called 'Pan' in a pastoral poem. The last two lines now function easily as a separate statement about the men whose blood is swollen with greatness. 'Meanest' in the last line does not refer to 'mean or sordid' things, as Rudrum has it, but to humble things—that is, to Fida herself.

This review has consisted mainly of notes and queries, which are of greater potential use to an editor than general value-judgments; and inevitably I have recorded cavils far more than agreements. There are any number of helpful references and perceptive readings in this edition that I shall have to lump together in making a final statement of admiration. Rudrum has done an excellent piece of work, and one that should be welcomed by readers of whatever kind who are looking for a good edition of Vaughan.

JONATHAN F. S. POST

Spitting out the Phlegm: The Conflict of Voices in Vaughan's *Silex Scintillans*

> *There must be some "sons," and some "servants," to prophesy to, to whom these Prophets may be sent, to whom this prophecy may come. "All flesh" may not be cut out into tongues; some left for ears, some auditors needs. Else a Cyclopian Church will grow upon us, where all were speakers, nobody heard another.*
>
> Lancelot Andrewes,
> "Sermon Preached on May 24, 1618"

For most readers Henry Vaughan is primarily a poet of the visual imagination, a writer who displays nearly an endless fascination with the stunning ocular effects one can achieve in verse either through the use of sudden shards of light or through more subtly woven contrasts between shadow and color. Lines such as the famous opening to "The World" ("I saw Eternity the other night / Like a great *Ring* of pure and endless light")[1] cut so deeply into the memory that visionary and vintage seem almost synonymous in *Silex Scintillans*, with the result that many critics, like the pilgrim in "Regeneration," have "fed" hungrily on the vital gold of the poet's imagery.[2] But one of the things the pilgrim discovers in his travels is that however glorious the "unthrift Sunne" (41) might be, the mediation between God and man turns on fundamentally an aural experience. The poem concludes with Vaughan attributing unmistakably the knowledge of God's presence to the act of

Reprinted, by permission of the publisher, from *Philological Quarterly*, 59:2 (1980), 165–86.

speech: "But while I listning sought / My mind to ease / By knowing, where 'twas, or where not, / It whisper'd; *Where I please*" (77–80, Martin, p. 399).

In finding "Some use for Eares" (50) in this poem, Vaughan keeps within an established line of Christian thought, intensified by the Protestant Reformation, that regarded the ear and not the eye as the superior sensory organ.[3] The basic authority for elevating one over the other was, of course, the familiar cry of the Apostle Paul that "faith cometh by hearing" (Romans 10.17), a claim repeated by Christians as distant in time as Augustine and Bunyan and asserted with increasing frequency during Vaughan's day when the visible church was forced underground. The poet's own translation from the fifth-century Bishop Eucherius' *The World Contemned* dilates on the central reason for valuing sound over sight:

> Why with so much dotage do we fixe our Eyes upon the deceitfull lookes of temporal things? Why do we rest our selves upon those thornes onely, which wee see beneath us? Is it the Eye alone that wee live by? Is there nothing usefull about us but that wanderer? We live also by the eare, and at that Inlet wee receive the glad tydings of Salvation, which fill us with earnest grones for our glorious liberty and the consumation of the promises.
>
> (Martin, p. 326)

Not every image leads to a vision of eternity. The Odyssean eye could easily be tricked in its wanderings while the humbler ear offered some of the securer comforts of home: always open to the "glad tydings of Salvation," it seemed a surer passage way for Christian truth to enter. Moreover, a person need only hear the sounds of his own "ernest grones" to realize that a "*Hymning Circulation*" (10, Martin, p. 424) had once more been restored between the chime of heaven and the tongue of man.

It is not my intention to devalue the visionary experience in Vaughan, but it does seem to me that the importance of the aural imagination in his religious verse has not received the full attention it deserves. As Herbert's heir attempting to extend the Anglican tradition during a time of intense religious confusion, it was only natural that the younger poet should prize the role of a good listener. Vaughan was, in effect, one of the sons to whom a "seer" was sent, and part of his purpose as poet and apostle was to help spread the gospel of his master's "in-

comparable prophetick Poems" (Martin, p. 186). In the face of a growing "Cyclopian Church... where all were speakers," the thicket of
echoes in *Silex* from Herbert both signals the continued survival of the
Anglican Church and serves as a hedge that separates the collection
from the *"frequent* Extasies, *and raptures to the third heaven"* (Martin, p. 140)
which Vaughan witnessed with disdain in the world about him. But the
thicket did not offer complete protection. Vaughan was a poet, and as
a poet, he chose to range abroad and speak in his own voice, shaped
and modulated by circumstances very different from those in Herbert's
day. Although a devotional lyricist wishing to retain the inner melody
of Christ's "still, soft call," the younger author—as James Simmonds
has shown[4]—did not refrain from the savagery of political attack occasioned by the historical moment. Largely missing from Herbert, such
a polemical response could also threaten to override the "Christian
intent" of any poem.

One consequence of this difference between *The Temple* and *Silex
Scintillans* is that the later collection is fundamentally more divided in
its attitude toward the sound of language or, rather, the language of
sounds. Herbert worried mainly about the "sincerity" of an utterance—
the dangers of "Decking the sense, as if it were to sell";[5] Vaughan, on
the other hand, attended more deeply to both the moral attitudes reflected in a person's tone of voice and the corruptibility of language
itself. Like his famous contemporary, Milton, he was keenly aware that
the fall of man brought about also a fallen language in which words
surrendered the pristine clarity of their original signifying powers to the
corrupt habits of the flesh. In his well known poem "The Retreate," for
instance, the author looks back to the past through a haze created partly
by language, and he indicts the tongue for its Satanic powers to wound
the conscience and soil the other senses: Adamic innocence exists

> Before I taught my tongue to wound
> My Conscience with a sinfull sound,
> Or had the black art to dispence
> A sev'rall sinne to ev'ry sence,
> But felt through all this fleshly dresse
> Bright *shootes* of everlastingnesse.
> (15–20, Martin, p. 419)

Vaughan seems almost to platonize language here when he divides it
into two realms in which the "black art" of the fallen tongue stands in

direct contrast with the flesh that feels "Bright *shootes* of everlasting-nesse." The distinction is an absolutely traditional one, of course, with clear verbal ramifications. Dante and Milton assign the greatest linguistic confusion to the characters in Hell and the purest modes of communion to those in heaven, and Vaughan follows suit. His one view into "that dark, dreadful pit" in *Silex* ("The Relapse," 3, Martin, p. 433) concentrates almost solely on the cries of the damned while his many visions of heavenly splendor are often inaugurated by song.[6] "Howling is the noyse of hell," Donne reminds us, "singing the voyce of heaven."[7]

Given these polar views of language, it is hardly surprising to discover the presence of two voices in *Silex*. There are perhaps others, but these two seem particularly conspicuous in the way Vaughan plays one off against the other, with each receiving clearer definition in the light of its opposite and both serving as a synecdoche of sorts for a broad spectrum of human behavior with precise moral equivalents. The first is the voice of fallen Adam, whose language, when unrestrained, could easily move toward chaos. Inevitably associated with the Tower of Babel, the confusion of tongues that radiates from the entire species also identifies the particular individual:

> For whereas our mindes are distracted with varietie of opinions, and our hearts carried headlong to divers inordinate lusts; so the tongue should likewise bee confounded with many base and barbarous languages, some of them very harsh in pronunciation, that a man must wrong his own visiage, and disfigure himself to speake them.[8]

Vaughan only occasionally draws such caricatures through language, but the many changes he rings on "loud" in *Silex*—and their association with the fallen—show him equally sensitive to the disruptive and barbarous potential of human speech. Whether describing the impulsive murmurings of the heart or the more conspicuous clamorings of God's foes, the young poet knew the tones of disobedience.

The other voice of course is Christ's, whose sounds Vaughan identifies with all true followers of God. "How comes He?" asks Lancelot Andrewes. " 'He shal come down like the dew in a fleece of wool,' and that is scarce to be heard. 'He, He shall not roar nor cry, nor His voice be heard out into the street.' "[9] In *Silex*, Christ, while potentially present to all who are obedient, is also "scarce to be heard": the ear needs to be finely tuned to catch the whisperings at the end of "Regeneration" or the "still, soft call" at the center of "The Night." Nowhere in the devotional verse does He "roar or cry." As the antitype to fallen man's "babble," moreover, Christ's voice speaks usually with clarity and precision, and his language has a palpable "softness" that contrasts with either the crudeness of man's sometimes clumsy cadences or the shrill tightening of accents that occurs with intemperance. During the mid-century strife, Vaughan thought of God's Word as his sole guide— "Were not thy word (dear Lord!) my light, / How would I run to endless night" ("The Men of War," 9–10, Martin, p. 517)—and as a model for imitation, it had only one tone and one message: "Let *Mildness*, and *Religion* guide thee out, / If truth be thine, what needs a brutish force?" ("Rules *and* Lessons," 38–39, Martin, p. 437).

To appreciate how Vaughan plays off these different voices in his verse is to see that his poetry is not always so haphazardly composed as is sometimes thought. The spiritual fullness of the edenic past and the resurrected future, for instance, is repeatedly defined by the way language verges on silence and highlights a present riddled with the strains of verbal abuse and confusion. "Religion" (Martin, pp. 404–05) and "*Isaacs* Marriage" (Martin, pp. 408–10), Vaughan's most complete portrayals of an earthly paradise in the devotional verse, evoke many of the familiar, Christian-pastoral views of an harmonious ideal where man communes with both angel and animal; they also underscore the necessity of civilized discourse made possible only by "soft" voices. Both poems take considerable care to describe an ideal tone of speech; both counterpoint these descriptions with a disturbing cacophony of sounds. Whether it is the "mild, chast language" of Rebecca (41) or the soothing, natural tones of God's "*soft voice*" as He speaks in "*fire*, / *Whirle-winds*, and *Clouds*" (17–18), each of these ritual acts of communion has been destroyed by the intruding noise pollution: the "False Ecchoes, and Confused sounds" of religious disputes ("Religion," 38) and the "*Antick* crowd / Of young, gay swearers, with their needlesse, lowd / Retinue" ("*Issacs* Marriage," 21–23). The possibility of a quiet "Conf'rence in these daies" ("Religion," 20) is a dream as far removed as the golden age itself. In each poem, also, Vaughan gives his verbal thematics a summary twist. He sharpens to a point his resentment in "Religion" by acidly concluding, "Nor must we for the Kernell crave / Because most voices like the *shell*"—the kernel at the heart of Puritanism is as hollow as the "*False Ecchoes*" it generates—while in the second poem he underscores the current perversion of language by drawing a picture of a modern Adam in the "odde dull sutor" who spends his time coining "twenty/New sev'ral oathes, and Complements" (15–16): the act of naming has degenerated into the art of defaming.

Vaughan also extended his ideal of "soft" voices in the past into the future where he could further refine it into an image of quietude. The favorite anthology poem, "Peace," describes a remote outpost of the elect more picturesque than sublime. Ordered, aesthetic, and still, it envisions a new "model army" neatly detached from any real acts of military destruction:

> My Soul, there is a Countrie
> Far beyond the stars,
> Where stands a winged Centrie
> All skillful in the wars,
> There above noise, and danger
> Sweet peace sits crown'd with smiles,
> And one born in a Manger
> Commands the Beauteous files.
> (1–8, Martin, p. 430)

The "noise, and danger" of the world have been mediated and transcended, not conquered, by Christ, whose "commands" create "Beauteous files" of order. Furthermore, as one who does not actually speak in the poem, Christ's smile seems to be a beckoning gesture of the silent rewards that await the obedient but which the speaker's sleeping soul has yet to enjoy (10). The waking that Vaughan prays for is to the tranquility of Christ: the soul that sleeps in this poem can only hear the noise of life below.

Living in a world, though, "where all [things] mix and tyre" (44, Martin, p. 523), Vaughan rarely sculpted such statuesque visions of peace. More often, he would frame momentary communions against a larger backdrop of chaos and noise and heighten the tension of a poem by fusing antithetical attitudes toward sound with larger image patterns of contrasting light and darkness. "The Night" (Martin, pp. 522–23), for instance, develops the paradox of speaking with the "Sun" (Christ) at midnight—a time naturally suited to hearing His voice—and in the central stanzas, five and six, darkness of night becomes the tent in which the poem listens to the private and selective voice of Christ's "still, soft call":

Dear night! this worlds defeat;
The stop to busie fools; cares check and curb;
The day of Spirits; my souls calm retreat
    Which none disturb!
Christs progress, and his prayer time;
The hours to which high Heaven doth chime.

Gods silent, searching flight:
When my Lords head is fill'd with dew, and all
His locks are wet with the clear drops of night;
    His still, soft call;
His knocking time; The souls dumb watch,
When Spirits their fair kinred catch.

                                                    (25-36)

God's "silent, searching flight"[10] is a version of what Vaughan describes in "The Constellation" as "motion without noise"; it is a delicate spiritual hovering easily shattered for both poet and reader by the intruding noise of the larger world:

Were all my loud, evil days
Calm and unhaunted as is thy dark Tent,
Whose peace but by some *Angels* wing or voice
    Is seldom rent;
Then I in Heaven all the long year
Would keep, and never wander here.

                                                    (37-42)

The real "hauntings" here belong not to the whispering sounds of the night but to the loud utterances of the day. Temptation lurks "where the Sun / Doth all things wake" (43-44); without the ritualized communion with the "Sun" that should be occurring during the day in the form of traditional, Anglican services, the wanderings of man cannot be checked. It is not up to Christ to increase the volume of his voice to offer salvation to man: "He shall not roar, nor cry, nor his voice be heard out into the street."[11]

Wider in geographic scope but even more precise in the verbal distinctions it makes, "The Constellation" (Martin, pp. 469-70), like "The Night," combines both auditory and visual senses to discriminate between proper and improper modes of religious behavior. The poem pairs off the "Fair, order'd lights whose motions without noise / Resemble those true Joys" of heaven (1-2) against the sounds created this time not just by the world at large but by the "zeale" (40) of Puritan enthusiasm. Identified throughout with "Silence and light" (13), the stars serve as distant patterns of obedience for all to observe; they also serve as a means for the reader to measure and imagine degrees of human depravity during these war-torn years. The speaker, of course, comes across as an individual most attentive to the constellation, and his meditative address and quiet ruminations at least imitate, if not equal, the serene motion of the stars. Man in general, though, gropes in an intermediary range of darkness associated with "Musick and mirth (if there be music here)." In this case, music is no symbol for heavenly harmony in the traditional Pythagorean scheme; Vaughan's crystalline spheres are silent, and the sounds heard characterize only the sensual pleasures on which man slavishly depends:

> Musick and mirth (if there be musick here)
> Take up, and tune his year,
> These things are Kin to him, and must be had,
> Who kneels, or sighs a life is mad.   (21–24)

This description of a general indifference to God and partially apprehended noise prepares us in turn for a further descent into the demonic particulars of Puritan behavior. More than half way through the poem, Vaughan takes us deep into the center of an *Inferno*:

> But here Commission'd by a black self-wil
> The sons the father kil,
> The Children Chase the mother, and would heal
> The wounds they give, by crying, zeale.

> Then Cast her bloud, and tears upon thy book
> Where they for fashion look,
> And like that Lamb which had the Dragons voice
> Seem mild, but are known by their noise.
> (37–44)

"Silence and light" have been extinguished by the cries of the damned. Here, the inversion of all moral codes, symbolized in Dante by Satan's inverted posture (as viewed from God's perspective), finds its equivalent in the deadly primitive rites of offspring killing their parents. Like the devil, the children repudiate their source of life, and again, like him, they dissemble and feign; but their failure to keep silent gives them away: they are "known by their noise" (44). The dragon in their voice links them with the Beast of the Apocalypse (Rev. 13:11) who, for a

241

POST

while, is allowed to overpower God's saints before being driven to perdition. After such a journey, Vaughan returns to contemplate the heavens with increased urgency, but he does not forget the role of sound in the poem. The concluding line of "The Constellation" locates the restoration of social order at a time only when men can "say," not cry, "*Where God is, all agree*" (60); the manner is as important as the matter. Speech cannot be separated from action. Without a return to simple, familiar (and Vaughan would say humane) discourse, it is both foolish and hypocritical to preach of Christ and religious toleration.

Vaughan's sharpest division of voices belongs to his finest "war poem"—"Abels blood" (Martin, pp. 523–24). Indeed, one of the best of the many poems about mid-century strife, Vaughan's attempts to balance the cries of vengeance against a plea for patience, and the result testifies to the poet's ability to imagine, even to identify with, both impulses. Like Milton's sonnet, "On the Late Massacre in Piemont," "Abels blood" taxes God to protect the righteous and punish the wicked. Abel, of course, was the archetype of all martyrs who, despite being murdered, was not silenced: his "blood crie[d] unto [God] from the ground" (Gen. 4:10) and placed a curse on Cain. Vaughan begins by establishing the lines of continuity between past and present symbolized in the sound of Abel's cry that still rings loudly around the land:

> Sad, purple well! whose bubling eye
> Did first against a Murth'rer cry;
> Whose streams still vocal, still complain
>   Of bloody *Cain*,
> And now at evening are as red
> As in the morning when first shed.
>   (1–6)

But after drawing the initial parallel, etched precisely in the scarlet image of the setting sun, Vaughan lets his auditory imagination work on the basic difference between the first murder and the present slaughter. Abel's voice is but a whisper when compared to the sounding complaints of the accumulated dead:

> If single thou
> (Though single voices are but low,)
> Could'st such a shrill and long cry rear
> As speaks still in thy makers ear,
> What thunders shall those men arraign

242

Who cannot count those they have slain,
Who bath not in a shallow flood,
But in a deep, wide sea of blood?
A sea, whose lowd waves cannot sleep,
But *Deep* still calleth upon *deep*:
Whose urgent *sound* like unto that
Of many waters, beateth at
The everlasting doors above,
Where souls behinde the altar move,
And with one strong, incessant cry
Inquire *How long?* of the most high.

(7–22)

There is much to admire here poetically, particularly the sustained imagery of spreading blood: the streams of the third line are more than "a shallow flood" by the thirteenth, where they expand quickly into a "deep, wide sea" (14) before they broaden into "many waters" (18) that collectively beat on heaven's doors above. But the poet's voice also demands attention. One "long cry" (the sentence covers sixteen lines), Vaughan's initially low pitched description quickly increases in volume and power through a series of verbal repetitions and appositional phrases that sweep forward and backward on their way to gathering energy for the "one, strong, incessant cry" of "*How long?*" (21–22). One phrase fades impatiently into another—the "*Deep* still calleth upon the *deep*" (16)—as the murmur of confusion builds steadily into a challenge of God's authority.

Within the mention of "most high," though, the poem snaps back on itself. Exactly halfway through (line 23 of the 44 line poem), the speaker turns to face the "Almighty Judge" (24), and he adopts a new tone, a new voice, and a new message. Vaughan remembers that the blood of Abel is cancelled by the blood of Christ (Heb. 12:14), a cancellation that penetrates into the fabric of the verse and results in a new address identical in length to the first one. The revisions begin theologically with the poet's assertion that at God's "just laws no just men grudge" (25); they continue in the images of blood that now should remain "Speechless and calm" (35); and they are summed up in the restrained posture of prayer the poet adopts throughout. The only cry to reach heaven should "*speak better things*" (40), and Vaughan's does:

Almighty Judge!
At whose just laws no just men grudge;

Whose blessed, sweet commands do pour
Comforts and joys, and hopes each hour
On those that keep them; O accept
Of his vow'd heart, whom thou hast kept
From bloody men! and grant, I may
That sworn memorial duly pay
To thy bright arm, which was my light
And leader through thick death and night!
   I [Aye], may that flood,
That proudly spilt and despis'd blood,
Speechless and calm, as Infants sleep!
Or if it watch, forgive and weep
For those that spilt it! May no cries
From the low earth to high Heaven rise,
But what (like his, whose blood peace brings)
Shall (when they rise) *speak better things.*
Then *Abels* doth! may *Abel* be
Still single heard, while these agree
With his milde blood in voice and will,
Who pray'd for those that did him kill!(24–44)

Moreover, the second half of the poem seems literally to transform or
"reform" in the light of Christ's "mild blood" the turbulent wake of
voices in the first half of the poem. Clearly marked, each thought begins
with an apostrophe (23, 27, 33, 37, and 41); each proceeds in a similar
tone of penitence, with the poet concluding that Abel should still be
"single heard" (42)—to remind us of the sufferings of the slain—but
that it is Christ whom we should follow, "not for revenge, but for
'remission of sins.' "

    "Abels blood" is exemplary for showing the devotional Vaughan
trespassing into the sounds of the world and making a successful return
to the ways of Christ. But the gap in language represented here so
clearly has broader implications for the writer of "heavenly poesy." As
a descendant of Adam, Vaughan, like Sidney, understood that the corruption of language could be momentarily refined by Christ but not
altogether restored to its original Adamic purity: the poet makes us, "*as
it were*, see God comming in his majestie" (italics mine); the need for
similitude is still necessary since "our erected wit maketh us know what
perfection is, and yet our infected will keepth us from reaching unto
it."[12] For Vaughan, the gap is felt most deeply in the verbal alternatives
before him. Not enough of a precursor of Romanticism to wish away

altogether the need for language, he was sufficiently a child of the Reformation to realize that the "wilde / Murmurings of his youth" (35–36, Martin, p. 395, "Dedication") did not simply stop with his "conversion" to religious verse. Along with those whom he criticized, Vaughan knew that he also possessed the "black art" of the tongue; he, too, inherited the potential to "babble," to speak without Christ, where the noise from his own throat might reveal him as a disciple of the devil rather than an apostle of Christ.

He signals this concern in a place no less conspicuous than the epigram to the finished *Silex Scintillans* (1655). While a number of Herbert's other followers explicitly identified themselves with David—the traditional type of the devotional poet—Vaughan thought of himself as a latter day Job, in some respects the prototype of David, whose eloquent plea for knowledge of God's favor he fixed on the title page to his collection: *"Where is God my Maker, who giveth Songs in the night? / Who teacheth us more then the beasts of the earth, and maketh us wiser then the fowls of heaven?"* (Job 35:10–11).[13] The inscription fuses the political with the personal. An obvious choice for a poet conscious of writing *"out of a land of darkenesse"* (Martin, p. 217), the quotation from Job asks whether he has been the recipient of divine inspiration for his "Sacred Poems and Private Ejaculations" or whether, like Job, he "opens his mouth in vain [and] multiplieth words without knowledge" (Job 35:16). Sensitive to the sounds of others, Vaughan was equally sensitive to the sounds generated by his own voice. It, too, was a measure of grace.

It is not surprising, therefore, to find that a number of Vaughan's most "afflicted" moments take the form of a verbal struggle between the language of the world and the language of Christ. "The Check" and "Distraction," for instance, are designed to represent the difficulties that beset a poet who is unable to transform the voices of temptation into the sounds of Christ: in both poems language has surrendered its control to the corrupt flesh and, consequently, both poems are in the process of disintegrating. "The Check" (Martin, pp. 443–44) is written precisely at the moment when things are falling apart, when the center is not holding because the poet can barely hear Christ's voice. As a result, the poem is on its way to becoming the "speechlesse heap" (3) which is its threatened end. But first it must suffer the fate of all fictions which are created without God at the center and lose its symmetry and order before crumbling to dust. Vaughan begins by attempting literally to hush the sound of his own flesh:

Peace, peace! I blush to hear thee; when thou art
    A dusty story
A speechlesse heap, and in the midst my heart
    In the same livery drest
    Lyes tame all the rest;
When six years thence digg'd up, some youthfull Eie
    Seeks there for Symmetry
But finding none, shal leave thee to the wind,
    Or the next foot to Crush,
        Scatt'ring thy kind
And humble dust, tell then dear flesh
    Where is thy glory?   (1–12)

E. L. Marilla has insisted that we read this poem in connection with "The Charnel-house"[14]—another dramatization of human vanity—but such a connection needs to be mediated by Herbert. As the allusion to "dear flesh" (11) indicates, Vaughan has his master's "Church-momuments" in mind when he wrote the opening stanza. The speaker, with teacherly condescension, chides his body, but the task is not so cooly performed here as it is in Herbert. There is obvious embarrassment on the speaker's part for even having heard the call of the flesh, the effects of which Vaughan represents in the fragmented structure of the verse itself. The verbally mimetic pattern of dissolution which occurs phonetically, rhythmically, and syntactically in Herbert's poem[15] reappears here in the way flesh and fiction become curiously fused to share in a parallel rite of disintegration. "The Check," like the body, possesses a certain skeletal symmetry in the fairly elaborate rhyme scheme and the parallel adverbial clauses, but the joints of the poem keep being jolted by the abruptly halting speech rhythms and the variously drawn out and suddenly truncated lines. Even down to the details of a crushed poetic foot, the formal disorderliness of the verse anticipates the "dusty story" of the flesh which some youth will later find. Moreover, the visual structure does not and, in fact, cannot impose "a diagram which otherwise has no existence,"[16] a situation which Wimsatt points to as frequently happening in the shaped poems of the classical tradition. On the contrary, Vaughan's refusal to allow the speaker's response to achieve a firm symmetrical pattern is exactly the point: so long as he attends to the flesh, we will always witness a partially corrupted form of address. The "dusty story" (2) cannot be the neatly carved devotional poem.

The reflexive process continues into the center of the poem. "All things," the speaker tells the flesh in the second stanza, "teach us to die" (20). "View thy fore-runners," he goes on to say: "All that have growth, or breath / Have one large language, *Death*" (28–29); and it is impossible to escape the suggestion that the poem is just one more such emblem. Death seems writ large in the speaker's own breath and in the shape his words assume on the page itself. The only way to reverse the decaying process, Vaughan hints, is through Christ, whose word can make "true glory dwell / In dust, and stones" (35–36). His voice, if heard, cannot only save "dear flesh," but the way in which it can transform a "dusty story" into a dwelling of "true glory" bears significantly on the speaker's own mode of address. The final stanza brings to a point the conflict between Christ's voice "Of Love, and sorrow" (38), and the speaker's own intensifying warnings to the unregenerate self:

> Heark how he doth Invite thee! with what voice
> Of Love, and sorrow
> He begs, and calls; *O that in these thy days*
> *Thou knew'st but thy own good!*
> Shall not the Crys of bloud,
> Of Gods own bloud awake thee? He bids beware
> Of drunknes, surfeits, Care,
> But thou sleep'st on; wher's now thy protestation,
> Thy Lines, thy Love? Away,
> Redeem the day,
> The day that gives no observation,
> Perhaps to morrow.   (37–48)

Shuttling between Christ's invitation and the obstinate flesh, the speaker only partially grasps the voice "Of Love and sorrow" (38) in the italicized lament, before he turns abruptly to castigating his body. At this point his own intemperance takes over—"Thou knew'st but thy own good!" (40)—and his own reinterpretation of Christ's invitation as "Crys of bloud" (41) makes the flesh shrink further away, with the speaker chasing choppily after him: "Wher's now thy protestation, / Thy Lines, thy Love?" (44–45). The remark seems one last reflexive gesture by Vaughan that indicts the tongue of the speaker as well as the unregenerate flesh: neither possesses lines of love. The speaker's stumbling conclusion, "Away / Redeem the day, / The day that gives

POST

no observation, / Perhaps to morrow" (45–48), seems almost to fall in
on itself in a "speechlesse heap" (3).

"Distraction" (Martin, p. 413) is the spiritual sequel to "The
Check." The most visually chaotic lyric in all of Vaughan, the poem is
a picture of human babble: "a man must wrong his own visiage, and
disfigure himself to speak [it]." Not only does it record a "world... full
of voices" (11–12), but the verse reflects in its own verbal disjointedness,
how one "man is call'd, and hurld / By each [voice]" (12–13). The
opening few lines initiate an experience of sudden stops and starts that
continue throughout the poem and indicate the spasms of living without
God:

> O knit me, that am crumbled dust! the heape
> Is all dispers'd, and cheape;
> Give for a handfull, but a thought
> And it is bought;
> Hadst thou
> Made me a starre, a pearle, or a rain-bow,
> The beams I then had shot
> My light had lessend not,
> But now
> I find my selfe the lesse, the more I grow.
> (1–10)

Few lines measure the meter adequately. A phrase either fails to span
the full line or it bends loosely around the end where the rhyme keeps
catching the voice by surprise to add another jolt to the poem. It is little
wonder that the speaker complains that "I find my self the lesse, the
more I grow" (10): the flips and starts weary.

Like "The Check," "Distraction" also records its debts to Herbert—this time to some of his master's wilder poems such as "Deniall"
and "The Collar." The resemblances to the latter are especially instructive since, like "The Collar," Vaughan's lyric is one long, disorganized
poem that looks as if it should be divided into stanzas but offers no
convenient place to do so. Moreover, the two poems are also nearly
identical in length, with Vaughan's falling just two lines short of Herbert's; but the shortcoming is a crucial one, for it is here that Herbert's
rebellious speaker hears the sound of God's voice—"Me thoughts I
heard one calling, *Child!*" (35)—and the poem closes on a note of communion that orders all that has gone before: "And I reply'd, *My Lord*"

$(36).^{17}$ In "Distraction," there is no intervening voice, no "glad tydings of Salvation," that might assure the speaker that his groans have been in "ernest." Instead, the poem concludes with the speaker's confession that still "Amidst the noise, and throng" (32) he is "full of voices" (12) but none of them Christ's.

> Come, and releive
> And tame, and keepe downe with thy light
> Dust that would rise, and dimme my sight,
> Lest left alone too long
> Amidst the noise, and throng,
> Oppressed I
> Striving to save the whole, by parcells dye.
>
> (28–34)

The final lines do give a clue, however, to Vaughan's "formal" purposes in the poem. Like the speaker who, in striving for all, has begun to disintegrate, so the poem is in the process of crumbling from the standard pentameter couplet that lies beneath the lines: both "by parcells dye"; each needs to be "reformed," but neither is given the chance. Unlike "The Collar," "Distraction" measures only the fall, for which there is no single pattern, either human or verbal.

The noise without was within, and in both locations it was equally difficult for Vaughan to ignore. "When the sounds will not unite," writes Walter Ong in pointing to the victimizing powers of the aural sense, "when they are cacophonous, hearing is in agony, for it cannot eliminate selectively—there is no equivalent of averting one's face or eyes."[18] To escape from the weight of his own tongue, Vaughan was led at times into a practice of verbal self-effacement that paralleled his own ascetic instincts. The quotations from Scripture—"God in the *Voice*" (8, Martin, p. 441, "H. Scriptures")—placed at the end of his poems, for instance, serve to absorb the poet's own language into that of another order. "Regeneration," "Religion," "The Brittish Church," "The World," and "The Mutinie" all conclude with sizeable inscriptions from the Bible that sometimes verify and at other times correct the speaker's attitude; but in either case they deliver an intervening voice that seals off the poem on a gnomic note of authority. Among seventeenth-century poets, Vaughan was unusual in this respect, and among his own verse, the most interesting example is perhaps "The Mutinie" (Martin, p. 468–69).

"The Mutinie" presents the paradox inherent in a rebellious deliverance, for what the speaker learns, reluctantly, is that no deliverance which is truly one can be rebellious. Vaughan begins by presenting the self's captivity in typological terms that have both personal and political significance. As Martin notes (p. 743), the images of clay and straw are from Exodus; the speaker, like Israel, is in bondage, and the God to whom he initially prays is more theirs than his, more Old Testament than New:

> Weary of this same Clay, and straw, I laid
> Me down to breath, and casting in my heart
> The after-burthens, and griefs yet to come,
> > The heavy sum
> So shook my brest, that (sick and sore dismai'd)
> My thoughts, like water which some stone doth start
> Did quit their troubled Channel, and retire
> Unto the banks, where, storming at those bounds,
> They murmur'd sore: But I, who felt them boyl
> > And knew their Coyl,
> Turning to him, who made poor sand to tire
> And tame proud waves, If yet these barren grounds
> > And thirstie brick must be (said I)
> > My taske, and Destinie,
>
> > 2.
>
> Let me so strive and struggle with thy foes
> (Not thine alone, but mine too,) that when all
> Their Arts and force are built unto the height
> > That Babel-weight
> May prove thy glory, and their shame.   (1–19)

Vaughan asks that his murmurings be channeled into action, not quieted. His wish is to join God in the punishment of the wicked and, incidently, to share in the glory of His victory. But the speaker also keeps bargaining with God for favors. The unregenerate thoughts "storming at those bounds" (8) continue in the speaker's wish to be part of a victory in which he remains protected by God from all the "frothie noise which up and down doth flie" (25). He wants it both ways. Even as he begins the third stanza—"Not but I know thou hast a shorter Cut / To bring me home" (29)—he still partially resists complete identification with the milder ways of Christ and the New Testament. Only gradually does he assent to a will greater than his own that is not an extension of his earlier anger: concession ("O be pleas'd / To fix my steps" [35–36]) becomes desire ("O give it ful obedience" [39]) that finally relaxes into an attitude of patient acceptance ("soft and mild / Both live and die thy Child" [41–42]). But the finishing touches are left to Christ, "the finisher / And Author of my faith" (22–23). His voice closes off the poem through an inscription from Revelation that plays on the two ways of "overcoming" and presents the only bargain of any importance to remember:

> *To him that overcometh wil I give to eate of the hidden* Manna, *and I wil give him a white stone, and in the stone a new name written, which no man knoweth, saving he that receiveth it.*
>
> [Rev. 2.17]

The "frothie noise" (25) of the speaker, gradually refined from the poem, is altogether excluded from the quotation. Permanently fixed on the page, set in place with italic solidity, the inscription, like Christ's promise, buttresses the verbal order and assures us of the difference between a momentary mutiny and complete distraction.

"Joy" (Martin, p. 491) extends the ascetic into the hermetic and goes so far as to equate all unholy mirth with "False, jugling sounds" (3) and "forc'd accents" (7). The poem pushes the genre of melancholy complaints mediated by song into a realm of pseudo-suffering whose "course measures" (1) offend the poet's ears. Associated most often with the literary pastoral, these "grone[s] well drest" (3) contrast with nature's music—"a lesson plaid . . . by a winde or wave" (8)—and threaten to lure the listener away from the harmonies of God's creation. To spoil our sense of their melodies, Vaughan twists these lesser creations into a series of "jugling" oxymora, highly conventional in their description but harshly presented by the poet:

> Be dumb course measures, jar no more; to me
> There is no discord, but your harmony.
> False, jugling sounds; a grone well drest, where care
> Moves in disguise, and sighs afflict the air:
> Sorrows in white; griefs tun'd; a sugerd Dosis
> Of Wormwood, and a Deaths-head crown'd with Roses.
>
> (1–6)

The speaker, responsive to "the lesson plaid . . . by a wind or a wave," delivers a different sound altogether, signalled by a change in the poem's meter that eventually tightens into the whispering dimeters describing the sounds around "Hermit-wells" before they expand into an epigram written, once more, in a pentameter couplet:

> Therefore while the various showers
> Kill and cure the tender flowers,
> While the winds refresh the year
> Now with clouds, now making clear,
> Be sure under pains of death
> To ply both thine eyes and breath.
> As leafs in Bowers
> Whisper their hours,
> And Hermit-wells
> Drop in their Cells:
> So in sighs and unseen tears
> Pass thy solitary years,
> And going hence, leave written on some Tree,
> *Sighs make joy sure, and shaking fastens thee.*
>
> (17–30)

Like "The Mutinie," "Joy" seems to undergo its own rite of verbal purification. The closing couplet, precisely chiselled, points to its own well-carved art in the inscription the hermit should leave on the tree, one whose message neatly reverses the one usually left by lovers who roam the pastoral woods. Yet lest it seem that the hermit is presumptuous—too satisfied with his note of wisdom—we should remember that what he writes has already been written. All he is doing is what Vaughan, the poet, has been doing: imitating the imitator of Christ, George Herbert, whose "Affliction [V]" describes man as "We are the trees, whom shaking fastens more" (20).

Finally, "The Proffer" (Martin, pp. 486–88) extends the ascetic into the transcendent by way of the world as the poem represents perhaps the quintessential example in *Silex* of a battle of voices both within and without Vaughan. The poem is a *tour de force*, a remarkable display of verbal power. Viewing it either biographically, allegorically, or a fusion of the two,[19] its critics all agree that the good fight has been fought and fought well. Simmonds sums up this position when he sums up the poem in a gloss from the prose. The lyric expresses "Vaughan's acceptance of the advice which he gave the reader of *The Mount of Olives*: "running thy race with patience, look to JESUS the Author and finisher of thy faith, who when he was reviled, reviled not again. Presse thou towards the mark, *and let the people and their Seducers rage*; be faithful unto the death, and he will give thee a Crowne of life' (Martin, p. 141)."[20] The poem might be a demonstration of personal fortitude on Vaughan's part, but to read it retrospectively is ultimately to drain away from it the dramatic process of language and fail to appreciate the moral risks inherent in a devotional poet's very choice of words.

For while the poem does end with Vaughan looking to Jesus, the first seven stanzas hardly reveal a poet running his race patiently, or refusing to revile his enemies, or even distinguishing carefully between his calm self and the raging world of seducers. Indeed, just the opposite is true. Vaughan simmers with indignation as he reviles his enemies with some of the most bone cracking rhetoric he ever wrote. "Some *Syllables* are *Swords*," the poet writes in "Rules *and* Lessons": "Unbitted tongues are in their penance double, / They shame their *owners*, and the *hearers* trouble" (70–72). During most of "The Proffer," Vaughan forgets about the possibility of shame and concentrates on giving his "*hearers* trouble."

The poem does not unfold in a linear pattern marking a pilgrim's progress. Instead, Vaughan keeps using language to create, extend, and widen a gulf between his tempters and himself, one in which the poet's violent denunciations stand in sharp contrast with the "Sorcery / And smooth seducements of the Commonwealth." He begins by pummelling his opponents immediately. The alliteration stings throughout the first stanza but especially in the final line, which turns nature's symbiotic process into a parasitic raid that borders on the obscene:

> Be still black Parasites,
> Flutter no more;
> Were it still winter, as it was before,
> You'd make no flights;
> But now the dew and Sun have warm'd my bowres,
> You flie and flock to such the flowers.   (1–6)

In stanza after stanza, Vaughan attempts to "still" the sounds of the "poys'nous, subtile fowls" through the force of his verbal barrage; he slides between irony and invective but never softens in his attitude toward them:

> O poys'nous, subtile fowls!
> The flyes of hell
> That buz in every ear, and blow on souls
> Until they smell

And rot, descend not here, nor think to stay,
I've read, who 'twas, drove you away.
                                    (13–18)

But the language used to create a distance between the two on one front also serves to connect them on another. So long as the speaker directs his diatribe against these fiends, he is to some extent bound to their claims; and inasmuch as he continues in his cankered assault, he reveals, in fact, that he is in danger of being infected by their rotten breath. Righteous indignation has its problems as well as its rewards. The example, for instance, of Christ casting the money changers from the Temple—sometimes seen as an authority here for Vaughan's fuming[21]—was a tricky model at best to imitate. "Every Christian is not Christ," preached Donne:

> And therefore as he that would fast forty days, as Christ did, might starve; and he that would whip Merchants out of the Temple, as Christ did, might be knockt down in the Temple; so he [that] knowing his owne inclinations, or but the general ill inclination of all mankind, as he is infected with Originall sin, should converse so much with publicans and sinners, might participate of their sins. The rule is, we must avoid inordinatenesse of affections; but when we come to examples of that rule, our selves well understood by our selves, must be our owne examples.[22]

The conclusion Donne reaches forms the conclusion of Vaughan's poem: "our selves well understood by our selves, must be our owne examples." In the final stanza Vaughan takes stock of his associations with the enemy and "spit[s] out their phlegm":

> Then keep the antient way!
>   Spit out their phlegm
> And fill thy breast with home, think on thy dream:
>   A calm, bright day!
> A land of flowers and spices! the word given,
>   If these be fair, O what is Heaven!   (43–48)

The first three lines continue in the imperative, but then one of those remarkable shifts occurs in Vaughan where the force of language suddenly alters its course, leaving a ripple in the seam of the poem that declares at once the gap which distinguishes the life of human fury and restricted movement from the world of transcendent calm, the restless activity of the verb from the motionless and atemporal noun in apposition. The former is the fallen world—a world of poets as well as publicans—whose limitations are best signalled in the tight closure on which each of the first seven stanzas end. The latter is, as Vaughan says, "the word given," a sign of grace bestowed from above and available for all to imitate; its endless potentiality for creation and freedom is signalled through the openness of apostrophe.

Moreover, when Vaughan exhorts himself to "Spit out their phlegm," he repeats almost exactly Herbert's command for England to "Spit out thy flegme" in "The Church-Porch"; but through the simple substitution of "their" for "thy" and of himself as the implied subject for England, the poet admits to his recognition that in the act of writing, he has already been in contact too long with the slothful commonwealth. He has, in fact, begun to decay spiritually. Without necessarily knowing, or believing in, contemporary arguments that "satyr" and satire were etymologically linked to the devil,[23] Vaughan nonetheless seems to have understood the risky position of the satirist in general, summed up by Alvin Kernan in the old adage: "He who sups with the devil needs a long spoon."[24] By spitting out their phlegm, Vaughan clears his throat of whatever sickness may have lodged in his lungs during his attack. He also clears the way for a new verbal order: for "where the Holy Ghost is received," remarks Lancelot Andrewes, "there is ever a change in the dialect, a change from cursed, unclean, 'corrupt communication,' unto 'such as becometh Saints.' "[25] The good fight in "The Proffer" is finally as much within the poet as it is with others, and it centers on Vaughan's own all too human impulse to indulge too fervently in the language of overkill, so that while winning this battle, he should lose the larger war for his soul. The victory assures us, and is meant to assure us, that on this occasion at least the poet of *Silex* has heard "the glad tydings of Salvation" and at last "giveth Songs in the night."

Notes

1 *The Works of Henry Vaughan*, ed. L. C. Martin, 2nd ed. (Oxford: Clarendon Press, 1957), p. 466. All further references to and quotations from Vaughan's writings will be to this edition and hereafter included in the text of this essay.

2. Discussion of Vaughan's visionary power dates back to the nineteenth century when the poet was thought a precursor of Wordsworth and continues into the present to cover the full range of Vaughan criticism, regardless of whether the

POST

poet is viewed as a nature worshipper, religious mystic, Renaissance hermeticist, or simply as an author of some fine lines. For representative examples of each, see *The Works in Prose and Verse of Henry Vaughan*, ed. Alexander B. Grosart, 4 vols. (Lancashire: The Fuller Worthies Library, 1871), II, 13–14 and 68–88 in the Introd.; Itrat-Husain, *The Mystical Element in the Metaphysical Poets of the Seventeenth Century* (London: Oliver and Boyd, 1948), pp. 210–36; Patrick Grant, *The Transformation of Sin: Studies in Donne, Herbert, Vaughan, and Traherne* (U. of Massachusetts Press, 1974), pp. 155–60, and E. C. Pettet, *Of Paradise and Light: A Study of Vaughan's "Silex Scintillans"* (Cambridge U. Press, 1960), pp. 3–11 *passim*.

3. William G. Madsen, *From Shadowy Types to Truth: Studies in Milton's Symbolism* (Yale U. Press, 1968), pp. 155–62, gives a brief but excellent account of Classical and Christian attitudes towards the rival senses and cities the lines I quote below from Eucherius to place Vaughan in that tradition. Objecting to Madsen's placement of Vaughan with Humanists rather than with Neoplatonists Florence Sandler, "The Ascents of the Spirit: Henry Vaughan on the Atonement," *JEGP*, 73(1974), 209–26, has argued that "no reader of Vaughan will be reassured by [this quotation], for it is doubtful that he took to heart Eucherius' maxim, let alone attached to it the significance that the Protestant Reformers had placed upon the ministry of the Word" (pp. 209–210). Barbara K. Lewalski, *Protestant Poetics and the Seventeenth-Century Religious Lyric* (Princeton U. Press, 1979), pp. 317–51, esp. pp. 332 and 493, demonstrates Vaughan's pervasive debt to Protestant Reformers; but even if there is still room for disputing theological influences on this most eclectic of authors, I hope to show in this essay how Vaughan, as a poet, was certainly responsive in his verse to the auditory imagination, a sensitivity with inevitable theological overtones that places him in a line with Protestant Reformers, like Luther and Calvin, who valued the "inner voice" over visual ceremony.

4. *Masques of God: Form and Theme in the Poetry of Henry Vaughan* (U. of Pittsburgh Press, 1972), pp. 85–137, esp. pp. 110–13.

5. *The Works of George Herbert*, ed. F. E. Hutchinson, 2nd ed. (Oxford: Clarendon Press, 1945), p. 102 ("Jordan [II]"). All further references to Herbert's poetry will be to this edition.

6. See, for instance, "The Search" (Martin, p. 407), "Me thought I heard one singing thus" (74), which transforms the "call" at the end of Herbert's "The Collar" to emphasize the shift to song (75–94), one that prepares the reader for "another world" (95). "Ascension-day" (9–14) also depends on the sudden intrusion of "song" into the pentameter norm to signal the spirit's ascent.

7. *The Sermons of John Donne*, ed. Evelyn M. Simpson and George R. Potter, 10 vols. (U. of California Press, 1953–62), VII (1954), 70.

8. Godfrey Goodman, *The Fall of Man* (London, 1616), p. 293. For a survey of Renaissance commentaries describing the effects of the fall on the human tongue, see Beverly Sherry's helpful essay "Speech in *Paradise Lost*," *Milton Studies*, VIII, ed. James D. Simmonds (U. of Pittsburgh Press, 1975), pp. 247–66.

9. *Ninety-Six Sermons by...Lancelot Andrewes*, ed. J. P. Parkinson, 5 vols. (Oxford: John Henry Parker, 1843–60), III (1850), 267.

10. I have analyzed in more detail the verbal structure of these middle stanzas and their relationship to the poem at large in "Vaughan's 'The Night' and his 'late and dusky' Age," *SEL*, 19, (1979), 127–41.

11. *Ninety-Six Sermons by...Lancelot Andrewes*, III (1850), 321. The passage from which this quotation is taken describes at some length the different "keys" in which Abel and Christ speak. See also *The Sermons of John Donne*, VII (1954), 69–70, and the discussion of Abel in Vaughan's 1654 translation of Nieremberg's *Of Temperance and Patience* (Martin, pp. 236–37).

256

12. *The Prose Works of Sir Philip Sidney*, ed. Albert Feuillerat, 4 vols (Cambridge U. Press, 1962), III, 7, 9. respectively (spelling slightly modernized).

13. Lewalski, *Protestant Poetics and the Seventeenth-Century Religious Lyric*, pp. 31–53 *passim*, gives the most recent discussion of the pervasive influence of the Psalms of David on sixteenth and seventeenth-century poets. She is undoubtedly right in down-playing the generic influence of the Book of Psalms on Vaughan (p. 332) given the importance he attached to *The Temple* as a literary model; but David was also thought of as "the most glorious pattern, not only of the sacred music of the day, but of Songs also in the Night", *The Works of Joseph Hall*, 12 vols. (Oxford: D. A. Talboys, 1837), pp. 7, 524. The quotation comes from Hall's pamphlet, *Songs in the Night* (1660) and forms a valuable, albeit histrionic, gloss on these lines from Job, particularly in connection with the issue of election discussed below: "And if we, out of strength of our moral powers, shall be setting Songs to ourselves in the Night of our utmost disconsolation [as opposed to the songs which God puts in our mouths], woe is me, how miserably out of tune they are! how mis-accented, how discordous even to the sense of our own souls" (p. 522).

14. "The Secular and Religious Poetry of Henry Vaughan," *MLQ*, 9 (1948), 408.

15. Joseph H. Summers, *George Herbert: His Religion and Art* (Harvard U. Press, 1954), p. 134, followed by Stanley E. Fish, *Self-Consuming Artifacts: The Experience of Seventeenth-Century Literature* (U. of California Press, 1972), pp. 164–69, have commented extensively on these aspects of "Church-monuments."

16. "In Search of Verbal Mimesis" in William K. Wimsatt, *Day of the Leopards* (Yale U. Press, 1976), p. 72.

17. For an excellent discussion of the formal aspects of "The Collar" that describes how the final lines "order" the poem both theologically and structurally, see Summers, *George Herbert*, p. 92.

18. *The Presence of the Word: Some Prolegomena for Cultural and Religious History* (Yale U. Press, 1967), p. 130.

19. See, respectively, F. E. Hutchinson, *Henry Vaughan: A Life and Interpretation* (Oxford: Clarendon Press, 1947), p. 125; R. A. Durr, *On the Mystical Poetry of Henry Vaughan* (Harvard U. Press, 1962), pp. 101–11, and James Simmonds, *Masques of God*, pp. 105–07.

20. *Masques of God*, p. 107.

21. Durr, *On the Mystical Poetry*, p. 109.

22. *The Sermons of John Donne*, IV (1959), 329.

23. "This word *satyr*, many verbal Grammatists labour to derive from the Greek ... but we must derive it from the first *maternall* tongue, the *Hebrew* word *Shagnar*, *Lev.* 17.1: *Ye Shall not offer your children* Leshegnirim, *to the hairie ones*. That is to the Devils, who appeared in the liknes of hairy Goats & therefore were called *Satyres* by some small interchange." *The Works of Mr. John Weesme*, 3 vols. (London, 1636), I, 16.

24. Alvin B. Kernan, *The Cankered Muse: Satire of the English Renaissance* (Yale U. Press, 1959), p. 24. For variations on this proverb in the Renaissance see *The Home Book of Proverbs, Maxims, and Familiar Phrases*, selected and arranged by Burton Stevenson (New York: Macmillan, 1948), p. 559.

25. *Ninety-Six Sermons*, III (1850), 193. The punishment Dante assigns the wrathful in hell throws a macabre light on Vaughan's own actions in the final stanza: in the fifth circle, the incontinent are immersed in black mire where, unable ever to clear their throats, they nonetheless keep attempting to sing but only gurgle inarticulate hymns to God. See, *The Divine Comedy of Dante Alighieri: Inferno*, trans. John D. Sinclair (1938; rpt. New York: Oxford U. Press, 1961), pp. 104–05.

THOMAS WILLARD

The Publisher of *Olor Iscanus*

On the title page of Henry Vaughan's *Olor Iscanus* (London, 1651) is
the note "Published by a Friend." Throughout the nineteenth century
and into the twentieth, readers thought the friend was Vaughan's twin
brother, Thomas Vaughan.[1] Then in the 1940s scholars argued that the
friend must have been Vaughan's neighbor Thomas Powell[2] or his book-
seller Humphrey Moseley.[3] Since then Vaughan's editors have named
Powell or Moseley as the friend,[4] and no one has suggested, as I will,
that Thomas Vaughan published the book. But the evidence marshalled
in support of Powell and Moseley raises a question: what was the role
of a "publisher" in the mid-seventeenth century?

A prefatory note from "The Publisher to the Reader" says that
Olor Iscanus was released without "*the Author's* Approbation" (sig. A6ᵛ).
The word "publisher" is used here to mean one who makes a book
public or, in Samuel Johnson's phrase, "one who puts out a book into
the world."[5] This meaning became common in the mid-seventeenth
century—the first instance in the *OED* is from 1654—and is now rare,
supplanted by the modern commercial meaning. Two early examples
seem instructive. When Thomas Vaughan inserted a note from "The
Publisher to the Reader" in *The Fame and Confession of the Fraternity of R:
C:* (1652), he was not to be mistaken for the printer who produced the
copies or the stationer who sold them (respectively identified on the title
page as J. M. and Giles Calvert). He simply made public a translation
that had been "*communicated*" to him, adding a publisher's note and a

Reprinted, by permission of the publisher, from *Papers of the Bibliographical Society of
America*, 75 (1981), 174–79.

long preface (sig. A3ᵛ). And after he wrote a message "To the Reader" of Henry Vaughan's translation *The Chymists Key* (1657), using the pseudonym Eugenius Philalethes, Thomas Vaughan added a phrase on the title page: "*Published by* Eugenius Philalethes." The chief task of a publisher like Thomas Vaughan was to get a book into print, doing what he could to see that an accurate, attractive text reached a reliable stationer.

Olor Iscanus was printed by T[homas] W[arren], who printed Thomas Vaughan's *Lumen de Lumine* at about the same time. But Moseley registered Henry's book on 28 April 1651, five days after Humphrey Blunden registered Thomas's. Since Moseley also registered Powell's *Stoa Triumphans* on the twenty-eighth,[6] W. R. Parker concludes that Powell published Henry's book. But Powell's book was printed by J. G[rismond], who also printed his *Elementa Opticae* that year, and it may not have gone through the press until June or later: Powell's dedication is dated 3 June, the year being presumably 1651, and his book did not reach the stationer George Thomason until 7 September.[7] Powell may have taken *Olor Iscanus* to Moseley, but Thomas Vaughan most likely saw it through the press. Perhaps he did the same for Powell's books. For like *Olor Iscanus* and *Lumen de Lumine*, *Elementa Opticae* has an engraving by Robert Vaughan, who made the famous engravings for Elias Ashmole's *Theatrum Chemicum Britannicum*.[8] Thomas Vaughan may have obtained the plates for all three books, and he wrote a prefatory poem for *Elementa Opticae*. Living in London, he was in the best position to deal with printers and stationers.

The word "stationer" referred to a clearly defined position in a closely regulated guild. It carried more weight than the fledgling "publisher," and a stationer would normally call himself one. Moseley titled his note to Milton's poems of 1645 "The Stationer to the Reader," even though he had solicited the poems and could therefore have called himself the publisher, had he been familiar with the usage. Yet after saying, "*I have not the Author's* Approbation *to the* Fact," the friend continues, "*but I have* Law *on my* Side...." F. E. Hutchinson ingeniously suggests that Henry Vaughan agreed to let Moseley sell *Olor Iscanus* and received an advance on the book; Vaughan changed his mind, possibly after a religious conversion, and Moseley stepped forward to claim what was his by law. But perhaps Hutchinson is quoting out of context. The sentence concludes, "*I have* Law *on my* Side, *though never a* Sword: *I hold it no man's* Prærogative *to* fire *his* own House." The law here governs arson rather than breach of contract, and the sentence harkens back to an opening reference to Virgil, *"that referr'd his* Legacies *to the* Fire" (sig. A6ʳ). It seems unlikely that Moseley was the friend who published *Olor Iscanus* and very unlikely that he published it against Vaughan's wishes. Otherwise Vaughan would hardly have sent two other books to Moseley.[9]

It does seem likely, however, that Thomas Vaughan would have preferred Moseley as a vendor for *Olor Iscanus*. Blunden was a good choice for the first part of Henry's *Silex Scintillans* (1650), a volume of religious poems with many hermetic echoes. But he was not one to attract the urbane, royalist audience for which Henry had written his "secular poems." For Blunden was a leading occultist—a publisher of the astrologer William Lilly, an authority on Jacob Boehme, and "an extraordinary Chymist."[10] Moreover, Thomas Vaughan, whom Blunden praised as a young Hermes and employed in alchemical research,[11] may have fallen out with Blunden. *Lumen de Lumine* was the last book he had Blunden issue, and his next book, *Aula Lucis*, referred to his break with an occult circle of some sort. Moseley, on the other hand, was perhaps the leading publisher of fine literature, the perfect choice for *Olor Iscanus*.[12]

We must now consider two pieces of internal evidence, first Thomas Vaughan's lines "Vpon the following *Poems*," which come after the commendatory verses by Powell and Rowland in *Olor Iscanus*. The poem begins:

> I Write not here, as if thy *last* in store
> Of learned *friends*, 'tis known that thou hast *more*;
> Who, were they told of this, would find a way
> To rise a guard of *Poets* without *pay*,
> And bring as many *hands* to thy *Edition*,
> As th' *City* should unto their *May'rs* Petition,
> But thou wouldst none of this . . .   (sig. A8ʳ)

Since Thomas refers to notes "licens'd *By the King*" (sig. A8ᵛ), he must have written the poem before 1648. Parker thinks he would have revised it, had he readied the volume for publication. For Henry had become a religious poet who would later say of his secular poems, "I do here most humbly and earnestly beg that none would read them."[13] Were he the friend, Thomas would have removed any suggestion that Henry had been consulted about the publication of what the title page said he had "Formerly written." But such revision is impossible, since Thomas's poem turns on the image of Henry as a feudal lord of poetry, with many loyal friends. It is also unnecessary, since "wouldst" is the conditional tense of "will" and can reflect an attitude as well as a decision. Further, the plea just quoted is dated 30 September 1654 and has a tone of posturing about it. Since Henry included *Olor Iscanus* in the list of his works that he later sent to John Aubrey, we may wonder whether he ever meant to suppress it.[14]

Equally important as internal evidence is "The Publisher to the Reader." If by Powell, it has more levity than his other prefaces, far more than the preface to *Stoa Triumphans*.[15] If by Moseley, it comes closest in tone to his preface to Cartwright's works and his remark there on an act of plagiarism *"which would have forc'd us to an* Act of Trover *for recovery of* stollen *Wit."*[16] But it bears most of all the impress of Thomas Vaughan's wit, and it has the rhythms of his prose. Here are the final sentences:

> *Thou seest how* Saucie *I am* grown, *and if thou doest expect I should* Commend *what is* published, *I* must tell thee, I crie no Sivill [i.e., Seville] Oranges. *I will not say,* Here *is* Fine *or* Cheap: *that were an* Injurie *to the* Verse *it selfe, and to the* Effects *it can* produce. *Read on, and thou wilt find thy* Spirit ingag'd: *not by the* Deserts *of what wee call* Tolerable, *but by the* Commands *of a* Pen, *that is* Above *it.*　　　　　　(sig. A6ᵛ)

If one will compare this passage with the opening jibe at astrologers in *Anima Magica Abscondita* or the preface to *Magia Adamica*, one will likely conclude with Louise Guiney: "the preface is in Eugenius Philalethes' own gallant style."[17]

When Parker argued that Thomas Vaughan did not publish *Olor Iscanus* he went on to show that this was the exception to the rule: from 1650 to 1657 Thomas probably helped issue all of Henry's other books.[18] But *Olor Iscanus* may not be such an exception after all. The evidence remains inconclusive: Henry had many "learned friends." But I suspect the nineteenth-century readers just happened to be right when they named Thomas as the friend and the twentieth-century scholars just happened to be wrong when they suggested Powell or Moseley instead. When the friend remarked, *"Here is a* Flame *hath been sometimes* extinguished: *Thoughts that have been* lost *and* forgot, *but now they* break out *again like the* Platonic Reminiscencie," he may have recalled Henry Vaughan's statement to the reader of his 1646 poems, *"You have here a* Flame, *bright only in its* owne Innocence."[19] But if the publisher was Thomas Vaughan, as I think, he doubtless recalled his recent exchanges with Henry More about that Platonic doctrine and the final lines of his commendatory poem:

> Yet I suspect (thy fancy so delights)
> The *Puritans* will turn thy *Proselytes,*
> And that thy *flame* when once abroad it *shines,*
> Will bring thee as many *friends,* as thou hast *lines.*
>
> (sig. A8ᵛ)

Notes

1. H. F. Lyte, ed., *The Sacred Poems and Private Ejaculations of Henry Vaughan* (Boston: Little, Brown, 1854), pp. xxvi f.; H. C. Beeching, Introduction, *Poems of Henry Vaughan, Silurist,* ed. E. K. Chambers, I (London: Routledge, 1890), xxv.

2. William R. Parker, "Henry Vaughan and his Publishers," *The Library,* 4th ser., 20 (1940), 401–11; Harold R. Walley, "The Strange Case of *Olor Iscanus,*" *RES,* 18 (1942), 27–37.

3. F. E. Hutchinson, "The Strange Case of *Olor Iscanus,*" *RES,* 18 (1942), 302–21, and *Henry Vaughan: A Life and Interpretation* (Oxford: Clarendon, 1947), p. 76.

4. L. C. Martin, ed., *The Works of Henry Vaughan,* 2nd ed. (Oxford: Clarendon, 1957), p. 704; French Fogle, ed., *The Complete Poetry of Henry Vaughan* (Garden City, N.Y.: Anchor, 1964), p. 50; E. L. Marilla, ed., *The Secular Poems of Henry Vaughan* (Uppsala: Lundequistska, 1958), p. 158; Alan Rudrum, ed., *Henry Vaughan: The Complete Poems* (Harmondsworth: Penguin, 1976), p. 467.

5. Quoted in *Oxford English Dictionary,* s.v. "publisher" (2a).

6. The astrologer William Lilly, whose books Blunden sold, wrote of "Mr. *Warren* the Printer, an assured Cavalier," in sec. 16 of *Mr William Lilly's History of his Life and Times,* rpt. as *The Last of the Astrologers* (London: Folklore Society, 1974). Warren is the only London printer with the initials T. W. listed in H. R. Plomer, *A Dictionary of the Booksellers and Printers Who Were at Work in England, Scotland and Ireland from 1641 to 1667* (1907; rpt. Oxford: Bibliographical Society, 1968).

7. G. B. Briscoe Eyre, ed., *A Transcript of the Registers of the Worshipful Company of Stationers, From 1640–1708 A.D.,* I (London: privately printed, 1913), 364, 365.

8. G. K. Fortesque, ed., *Catalogue of the Pamphlets, Books, Newspapers, and Manuscripts . . . Collected by George Thomason, 1640–1661* (London: British Museum, 1908), I, 846.

9. Registered by Nath. Brooke on 15 April 1651, printed by Grismond in 1652. Both Ashmole and Thomas knew Thomas Henshaw, of whom the first wrote in *The Way to Bliss* (1658) and the second wrote in *Magia Adamica* (1650).

10. *Flores Solitudinis* (1654) and *Hermetical Physick* (1655).

11. Durant Hotham, *The Life of Jacob Behmen* (London, 1654), sig. B2ʳ; Richard Baxter, *Reliquiae Baxterianae* (London, 1696), I, 11.

12. "To his ever honour'd friend, the Learned Author" in Thomas Vaughan,

Anima Magica Abscondita (London, 1650), sig. E4^r; Henry More, *The Second Lash of Alazonomastix* (1651; rpt. London, 1656), p. 208.

13. Both Vaughans contributed commendatory poems to William Cartwright, *Tragedies, Tragi-Comedies, with Other Poems*, issued by Moseley in 1651.

14. *Works*, ed. Martin, p. 390.

15. *Ibid*, p. 688.

16. For an attribution to Powell with a close reading see E. L. Marilla, " 'The Publisher to the Reader' of *Olor Iscanus*," *RES*, 24 (1948), 36–41.

17. Cartwright, sig. A2^r.

18. *A Little English Gallery* (New York: Harper, 1894), p. 76.

19. Parker's case that Thomas saw Henry's other books through the press may be strengthened on two counts. Though William Leake registered Thomas's *Aula Lucis* on 12 Sept. 1651, four months before he registered Henry's *Mount of Olives* on 16 Dec., the two books may have been printed at about the same time: both are dated 1652 on their title pages and reached Thomason early that year. And though Mosely registered Thomas's *Euphrates* on 16 Aug. 1655, Thomason received a copy of it on 30 June 1655, only 5 days after getting a copy of Henry's *Hermetical Physick*, registered by Moseley on 16 Jan. 1655. See Eyre, I, 378, 386, 463; II, 7; and Fortesque, I, 858, 861; II, 119.

20. *Works*, ed. Martin, p. 2. See Observation 1 in Thomas Vaughan, *The Second Wash*, printed in 1651 and registered by Blunden at the same time as *Lumen de Lumine*.

RACHEL TRICKETT

Henry Vaughan
and the Poetry of Vision

Critics frequently disagree over the landscape of Vaughan's poetry; whether it is recognizable as that of the Usk valley where he spent most of his life, or is rather a landscape of the mind, emblematic and bearing little relation to natural description. F. E. Hutchinson in his *Life*, and E. C. Pettet in *Of Paradise and Light*, both take it as an instance of Vaughan's uniqueness in his age that he possesses a topographical quality. John Dixon Hunt in *The Figure in the Landscape*, on the other hand, takes precisely the opposite point of view, and Barbara Lewalski in her chapter on Vaughan in *Protestant Poetics and the Seventeenth-Century Religious Lyric*, is so determined to pursue Vaughan's use of the image of pilgrimage to its scriptural and theological sources, that you would think any simple association of the natural objects encountered on the way with those among which Vaughan actually lived, almost too naively superficial.

For all this, there can be little doubt that Hutchinson and Pettet are right. Vaughan thought of himself as the poet of a particular place. 'To the River Isca' is only the best and the best-known of several allusions to his native place in *Olor Iscanus*:

> CAMBRIA *me genuit,* patulis *ubi* vallibus *errans*
> *Subjacet* aeriis montibus ISCA pater...
>> ('*Ad Posteros*'),[1]

and the volume itself is prefaced by this adaptation of Virgil:

Reprinted, by permission of the English Association, from *Essays and Studies*, 34 (1981), 88–104.

O quis me gelidis in vallibus ISCAE
Sistat, et ingenti ramorum protegat umbra!

In his final publication, *Thalia Rediviva*, the elegiac eclogue 'Daphnis',
commemorating the death of Thomas Vaughan his twin brother, refers
again to the beloved river:

> So where swift *Isca* from our lofty hills
> With loud farewells descends, and foaming fills
> A wider channel, like some great port-vein,
> With large rich streams to feed the humble plain.
>
> (43–6)

At the same time, conventional though the topics and images of Vaughan's poems are, the showers, storms, springs, waterfalls, stars, groves
and seasons of his meditations, they are all observed with peculiarly
intense physical, as well as imaginative, vision.

Take, as an example, Vaughan's water imagery. It is remarkably
detailed and returns to the observed river again and again; the falls,
the eddying water tinged with foam, the rapid flow, the spreading out
into a wider channel which Vaughan described in 'Daphnis' as the Usk's
especial features, are recurrent figures in his work:

> But as this restless, vocal *spring*
> All day, and night doth run, and sing,
> And though here born, yet is acquainted
> Elsewhere, and flowing keeps untainted...
> ('The Dawning', 33–6)

> As waters here, headlong and loose
> The lower ground still chase, and choose,
> Where spreading all the way they seek
> And search out every hole, and creek.
> ('Misery', 9–12)

> My thoughts, like water which some stone doth start
> Did quit their troubled channel, and retire
> Unto the banks, where, storming at those bounds,
> They murmured sore...   ('The Mutiny', 6–9)

The immensely detailed poem 'The Water-fall' is only the most elaborate
of a series of such river images. One aspect of still or stagnant water
also obviously fascinated him: the way in which mist is exhaled from
its surface. Hutchinson has plausibly supposed that 'that drowsy lake'

of 'The Shower (I)' may be Llangorse Pool, near to Vaughan's birth-place, since 'a hot mist would rise from a lowland lake in cultivated country, whereas most of the Welsh lakes are clear mountain tarns'.[2] Vaughan had evidently seen this phenomenon and been struck by it. He uses it outside 'The Shower' several times—in 'Isaac's Marriage' (53–62), in 'Disorder and Frailty' (31–45), and in 'The Tempest' (26). In each case it is seen as a type of the soul's imperfect aspiration to God and its dissolution into the rain or dew of tears. And in each case it is clear from the detail that Vaughan had closely observed the vapour he applies so effectively to his devotional theme.

Climate and weather play an important part in his work, sudden storms especially. He would have found the topic of a storm in Herbert's *The Temple*, but the only time the elder poet gives us the feeling of climate is when he writes, "I once more smell the dew and rain'. By contrast Vaughan's poems are full of weather:

> Many fair *evenings*, many *flowers*
> Sweetened with rich and gentle showers
> Have I enjoyed, and down have run
> Many a fine and shining *sun*,
> But never till this happy hour
> Was blest with such an *evening-shower*!
> ('The Shower (I)', 5–10)

Abraham, 'the first believer' in 'Retirement (II)', has pitched his tent

> Where he might view the boundless *sky*,
> With all those glorious *lights* on high,
> With flying *meteors*, *mists* and *showers*,
> Subjected *hills, trees, meads* and flowers.
> (7–10)

Joy is

> Another mirth, a mirth though overcast
> With clouds and rain, yet full as calm and fine
> As those *clear heights* which above tempests shine...
> ('Joy', 14–16)

a phenomenon only to be observed in hilly country. In 'The Tempest' Vaughan refers to a recent drought when saying how everything in nature can show to man 'himself, or something he should see':

This late, long heat may his instruction be.

(3)

And the Welsh climate must have given him occasion often to experience what he writes in *Son-days*: 'A gleam of glory, after six-days-showers'. Important as it is to see a poet in the context of his age's thought and conventions, something of the peculiarity of his imagination may be neglected if we tie him too closely to his historical setting. Thus, to see Vaughan against his native landscape as much as against his times, may draw attention to some aspects of his work which are as important to their imaginative effect on readers as his indebtedness to Herbert, his use of Protestant poetics, or his addiction to emblem. The old comparison between Vaughan and Wordsworth still has some value, even though we have acquired a more sophisticated knowledge of the poetic conventions and the theology of the seventeenth century than those who first made it. For it continues to draw attention to certain aspects of their imagination which may properly be compared. Both of them write a poetry of vision in which sight, the physical seeing of a local landscape, can be realized as the necessary prelude to insight or revelation, though the insight of each is inevitably distinct. Neither Vaughan nor Wordsworth is a visionary poet of the same sort as Traherne or Blake. But the landscapes of their poems, like the mountainous rainy regions in which they lived, are illuminated very deliberately by each poet with various kinds of light, from the simplest—'all the sweetness of a common dawn' or 'those faint beams in which this hill is dressed, after the sun's remove', to the most intense and supernatural, 'the light that never was on sea or land', the dying of the light of sense 'in flashes that reveal the invisible world', the 'great ring of pure and endless light', or 'bright shoots of everlastingess'. For each poet the consciousness of light has a peculiar importance.

Vaughan's vocabulary of light needs only to be compared to his contemporaries' for us to realize what a very different poet he is from them. Even in his early love poetry to Amoret there is none of that tired gem imagery Cavalier lyrists inherited from the Renaissance which at its worst produces a flashy glitter and no feeling of genuine radiance.[3] The object illuminated in good metaphysical poetry—Donne's 'bracelet of bright hair' for instance, or Marvell's 'hatching throstle's shining eye' is brilliant and defined, but never suggestive of the play or movement of light. This is conspicuously lacking in Herbert, whose poems are full of the light items of devotional poetry, stars, sparks, flames, and all of them almost entirely static and emblematic.

The metaphysicals took a profound interest in the symbolic and philosophical implications of light and darkness, day and night, as Sir Thomas Browne indicates:

Light that makes things seen, makes some things invisible; were it not for darkness and the shadow of the earth the noblest part of Creation had remained unseen and the Stars in heaven as invisible as on the fourth day when they were created above the Horizon with the sun or there was not an eye to behold them. The greatest mystery of Religion is expressed by ad-umbration and in the noblest part of Jewish types we find the Cherubims shadowing the Mercy-seat. Life itself is but the shadow of death, and souls departed but the shadows of the living. All things fall under this name. The Sun itself is but a dark Simulacrum, and light but the shadow of God.

(*The Garden of Cyrus*, Chapter IV)[4]

Vaughan's poem 'The Night' might be set side by side with this passage, for they could be read as commentaries on each other as far as ideas go, yet what a different imaginative world we are in with Browne! Though furnished with so many paradoxes and phrased in such splen-didly elaborate cadences that it seems richly-textured at once, it is an almost entirely unvisual world, a world in which the eye has nothing to do.

Similarly, the popularity of the shadow as a subject from Donne to Henry King is in complete contrast to the way Vaughan uses it; in them the shadow's relation to light and body are essential elements in an intellectual exercise, but it is not *seen* as a visible phenomenon. Indeed poems or prose passages on light, or objects of light, or lack of light, in this period are for the most part meditations on the aboriginal concepts of light and darkness in their actual and extended metaphorical mean-ings. No other seventeenth-century poet appears to create for us, as Vaughan does, a real world of sights and objects, illuminated with sunshafts and clouded with shadows, and all, like the play of light itself in the hilly landscape of the Usk valley, various, broken and full of movement.

Vaughan's poems use as repeated images the natural shows as-sociated with light—clouds, dews, rainbows, shadows, stars, moonlight, sunlight, and they are, of course, used emblematically and scripturally

as his epigraphs often indicate. But they create over the whole spread
of his work a strong sense of place and climate. This is something we
never find in Traherne, for example. Traherne writes:

> Tis not the Object, but the Light
> That maketh Heaven; Tis a pure sight.
> Felicity
> Appears to none but them that truly see.[5]

What is missing in Traherne is precisely the object; he is too absolutely
fixed in heaven, in the purity of vision. The rich and varied landscape
of Herefordshire in which he was reared and where he lived at various
times in his life is equally absent from his poems and his meditations.

Revelation in Vaughan comes from its true source, the God both
immanent and transcendent, who is present in his creation and yet exists
beyond it. His illumination shines through and suffuses the natural
world so that it seems to glow from the objects themselves even if they
are only 'masques and shadows'. Often these objects, though part of a
conscious system of emblems, are curiously changed by this illumination
into familiar particulars of the local scene. A good example is from 'They
are all gone into the World of Light!', where the memory of the dead

> glows and glitters in my cloudy breast
> Like stars upon some gloomy grove,
> Or those faint beams with which this hill is dressed,
> After the sun's remove.   (5–8)

The movement here is from a state of mind to an immediate scene—
precisely the opposite direction from that which became so popular with
topographical poetry in the next age. (In *Grongar Hill*, for instance, a
poem again celebrating the landscape of South Wales, Dyer depicts the
scene first and draws from it appropriate moral reflections.) Later in
his poem, Vaughan, meditating on death—'What mysteries do lie beyond thy dust;/Could man outlook that mark!'—makes another delicate
transition to metaphor:

> He that hath found some fledged bird's nest, may know
> At first sight, if the bird be flown;
> But what fair dell, or grove he sings in now,
> That is to him unknown.   (21–4)

And here again the metaphor *solidifies* into a recollection of the local,
natural world. The final stanza of the poem seems to epitomize its whole

intricate pattern of the interchangeable relations between theme and image, between fact and figure:

> Either disperse these mists, which blot and fill
> My perspective (still) as they pass,
> Or else remove me hence unto that hill,
> Where I shall need no glass.   (37–40)

In this imagery from Corinthians, of seeing through a glass darkly, Vaughan conveys not only the traditional aspiration to the fullness of knowledge in union with God, but also a longing for the barriers between the inner and the outer world to disappear, between the world of insight and the world of physical sight which shift and turn so subtly in their relationship to each other in his poetry. The insistent repetition of words of seeing and looking makes Vaughan's 'world of light' a dual one, a spiritual and a material world, so that however distinct they are, he can move easily in his imagination from one to the other, and the transitions from the longed-for imagined world to the real natural world, from statement to metaphor, are an essential part of the discourse of the poem.

The repertoire of natural objects and effects in Wordsworth's poetry is strikingly similar to Vaughan's: clouds, reflecting dews, rainbows, raindrops, moonlight, sunlight, starlight, movement and the noise of water. Some of his best-known passages illustrate this:

> The rainbow comes and goes,
> And lovely is the rose,
> The moon does with delight
> Look round her when the heavens are bare,
> Waters on a starry night
> Are beautiful and fair . . .
> ('Ode on the Intimations of Immortality', 10–15)

> All things that love the sun are out of doors,
> The sky rejoices in the morning's birth,
> The grass is bright with raindrops;—on the moors
> The hare is running races in her mirth;
> And with her feet she from the plashy earth

Raises a mist, that, glittering in the sun,
Runs with her all the way wherever she doth run.
('Resolution and Independence', 8–14)

But for Wordsworth the process of revelation is a very different one from Vaughan's. Insight or perception is reached by an accumulation of sense impressions, and it is as if the surface forms disintegrate and undergo a kind of metamorphosis: the lovely morning of 'Resolution and Independence' turns suddenly grey, from the pressure of a deeper apprehension. Wordsworth tells us how as a child he had to hold on to material objects to assure himself of their existence. As a poet, it was equally necessary to him to enumerate with laborious authenticity each particular of scene or circumstance as a prelude to the moment of illumination he attempts so often (and often in such strangely negative terms), to define. The 'obscure sense of possible sublimity', the mind 'working with a dim and undetermined sense/Of unknown modes of being', the moment when Imagination 'that awful power,/Rose from the mind's abyss', and which, in the difficult conclusion to Book V of *The Prelude* he attempts to follow through, all are parts of the mysterious, transforming process of poetic creation:

Visionary Power
Attends the motion of the viewless winds
Embodied in the mystery of words:
There darkness makes abode, and all the host
Of shadowy things work endless changes: there
As in a mansion like their former home
Even forms and substances are circumfused
By that transparent veil with light divine
And, through the turnings intricate of verse,
Present themselves as objects recognised,
In flashes, and with glory not their own.
(*The Prelude*, Bk. V, 595–605)

Here Wordsworth is trying to analyse what is perhaps not susceptible to analysis in the last resort—the imaginative process of seeing, transforming and transcribing, or verbalizing. The forms and substances are the essences of the 'substantial things' with which Wordsworth's poetry deals, and which remain, however changed, *idem et alter*, through the

271

power of the creative process. And they are the phenomena of the natural world; the loved landscape.

Vaughan, of course, has no such concern with examining the creative process. He is only eager to examine states of soul; the 'deep but dazzling darkness' of 'The Night' is the excess of God's brightness; he appeals to God, not to any self-generating poetic power, to 'brush me with thy light'. Vaughan's task is, perhaps, a simpler one, but within the changing spiritual climate of his poems we are continually returned to the various world of creatures, so lovingly itemized together with their use in 'Rules and Lessons':

> To heighten thy *devotions*, and keep low
> All mutinous thoughts, what business e'er thou hast
> Observe God in his works, here *fountains* flow,
> *Birds* sings, *beasts* feed, *fish* leap, and the *earth* stands fast;
> Above are restless *motions*, running *lights*,
> Vast circling *azure*, giddy *clouds*, days, nights.
>
> When *seasons* change, then lay before thine eyes
> His wondrous *method*; mark the various *scenes*
> In heaven; *hail, thunder, rain-bows, snow*, and *ice*,
> *Calms, tempest, light* and *darkness* by his means;
> Thou canst not miss his praise; each *tree, herb, flower*
> Are shadows of his *wisdom*, and his power. (85–96)

He works within a rhetorical structure where the metamorphosizing process that so fascinated Wordsworth has been regulated into a system of analogies and formal figures. Yet the idea of light and its function in the natural world, of sight as a co-relative of insight, is imaginatively of profound importance to both. In 'To the River Isca', an early celebratory topographical poem, Vaughan had written:

> But *Isca*, whensoe'r these *shades* I see,
> And thy *loved arbours* must no more *know* me,
> When I am laid to *rest* hard by thy *streams*,
> And my *sun sets* where first it *sprang* in beams,
> I'll leave behind me such a *large, kind light*,
> As shall *redeem* thee from *oblivious night*.
> (25–30)

Images of light and darkness are commonplace in complimentary poems, but Vaughan uses them here with a peculiar, almost obsessive intensity. It is impossible not to feel in reading him that he is a poet who has actually observed the play of light over landscape, and has become as

imaginatively haunted by this property as by the movement and flow
of the water of his native river. Both carry wide imaginative implications
beyond the simple symbolic equivalents—grace, human life, transience,
that they superficially represent. Their function in Vaughan's poems
could be said to act, in Wordsworth's phrase, 'As objects recognized,/
In flashes, and with glory not their own.'

'The Water-fall' is perhaps the best example of this intricate quality
of implication. The cascade itself is both an emblem of human life and
a real waterfall throughout. It is almost impossible to disentangle the
two strands in the opening paragraph where the movement of the fall
is so deliberately and delicately imitated in the metre and vocabulary:

> With what deep murmurs through time's silent stealth
> Does thy transparent, cool and watery wealth
>> Here flowing fall,
>> And chide, and call,
> As if his liquid, loose retinue stayed
> Ling'ring, and were of this steep place afraid,
>> The common pass
>> Where, clear as glass,
>> All must descend
>> Not to an end;
> But quickened by this deep and rocky grave,
> Rise to a course more bright and brave.   (1–12)

The tone changes to a simpler exclamation and an almost Wordsworthian directness in the recollection of the second paragraph:

> Dear stream! dear bank; where often I
> Have sat, and pleased my pensive eye,
> Why, since each drop of thy quick store
> Runs thither, whence it flowed before,
> Should poor souls fear a shade or night,
> Who came (sure) from a sea of light?
>> (12–18)

Vaughan's fascination with the movement of the water leads to a sense
of perpetual return to the source which can at once receive a religious
application. And this application is extended in the last section of the
poem to the more obvious associations of the element—baptismal renewal and redemption. The conclusion disentangles the various strands

of metaphor and actual seeing, till something *beyond* sight supersedes
the physical imagery of the poem, as death releases the soul:

> As this loud brook's incessant fall
> In streaming rings restagnates all,
> Which reach by course the bank, and then
> Are no more seen, just so pass men.
> O my invisible estate,
> My glorious liberty, still late!
> Thou art the channel my soul seeks,
> Not this with cataracts and creeks. (33–40)

Vaughan had alluded before to the noise of the Usk ('this loud brook'
is like the 'shrill spring' of 'Vanity and Spirit' and the 'restless, vocal
spring' of 'The Dawning'), and its other qualities of rapid movement,
eddying flow (restagnating all), its widening course, its creeks and inlets.
But here even the familiar river is at last relinquished, as Vaughan's
poetry of vision reaches out, ultimately, to an *invisible* estate. For him
light itself, as Browne wrote, is but the shadow of God.

The vocabulary of 'The Water-fall' is especially characteristic of
Vaughan. Neither he nor Wordsworth cares much for colour epithets
(except for Vaughan's often noted use of green, the symbolic colour,
and white the non-colour, which those who know Welsh tell us means
happy and blessed also in that language). Both may be contrasted in
this with Keats, or with Tennyson whose luxurious topography has
nothing of their peculiar kind of vision. Vaughan limits his descriptive
words to such as suggest the lively, lucent quality of the element—
transparent, cool, liquid, clear, quick, streaming. By this economy he
achieves an extraordinarily intense and effective descriptive effect which
is to some extent illusory (since little has been described), just as the
natural world itself is illusory in contrast to the world of paradise. A
similar economy of language has often been remarked in Wordsworth's
style. In each case this kind of poetry of vision, though so intimately
associated with a familiar and local landscape, does not try to characterize such detail by the use of epithets; there is no 'loading every rift
with ore' in them. Vaughan and Wordsworth *clarify* the world they depict
almost as if they were imitating in language the function of light.

A clumsy congratulatory poem by N. W. of Jesus College (Nathaniel Williams), printed in *Thalia Rediviva*, suggests that Vaughan's
contemporaries recognized his peculiarity in making so much of his own
landscape.

Where reverend bards of old have sate
And sung the pleasant interludes of Fate,
Thou takest the *hereditary shade*
Which Nature's homely Art has made
And then thou giv'st thy Muse her swing, and she
Advances to the galaxy.   (1–6; italics mine)

The 'hereditary shade' of Nature's 'homely art', the local landscape in
which Vaughan's family had lived for so long, is the means the poet
uses to reach his vision. He appears remarkably early as a poet who
can at one and the same time *see* his own landscape in sensitive visual
terms, and use it as a paradigm of his true theme—eternity. The idea
of 'the prayer of creatures' is Vaughan's justification of his love of the
natural world; God has 'hid in these low things snares to gain his heart',
and to turn man to his eternal destiny. Of course Vaughan was not
alone in his time in his love of the creaturely world. Marvell shows as
great a fascination with it, but 'Nature's mystic book' is a much less
localized volume to him than to Vaughan. No one would claim to
recognize the landscape of mid-Yorkshire from *Upon Appleton House*, exact
though many of its naturalistic details are. Marvell is quite a different
kind of poet from Vaughan, and neither landscape nor light plays a
very important part in his work. Though he shares many conventions
of thought and belief with Vaughan, 'vision', seeing and seeing *beyond*,
is not what interests Marvell.

I am suggesting in this essay a way of looking at poetry which is
not historical or scholarly. Both these approaches are necessary; but in
the last resort we read poetry which survives outside the classroom in
a way that ignores chronological strait-jackets. It is a peculiarity of
English poetry that some of it, major or minor, in any century, may
seem to reflect a personal response to the landscape and climate of an
island where the sense of boundary, limitation and locality is excep-
tionally strong, and where the effect of climate is various and unpre-
dictable. Vaughan, though I am not suggesting that it is his main claim
to survival, is a good example of this. And though he is in no sense so
great a poet as Wordsworth, he can properly be compared with him for
this reason as much as for his interest in the state of childhood, innocence
and preexistence, among the topics they share. My argument is strengthened rather than weakened by the fact that there seems to be no evidence
that Wordsworth ever read Vaughan.

It is just as likely that the effect of climate and weather on a particular kind of landscape should affect the imagination of some poets as it obviously does of some painters. No one doubts the influence on Turner and Constable of the countryside and the climates they depict. They were fortunate in living at a time when what stimulated their imagination was already aesthetically and theoretically respectable. Wordsworth has been compared to both of them, and Ruskin in *Modern Painters*, that great defence of Turner which developed into a whole new system of aesthetics, prefaces the finished work with a passage from *The Excursion*. The poet Edmund Blunden has compared the effect of Vaughan's poetry with a Claude painting,[6] but this seems altogether too calm, expansive, generalized and idealized for the particular movement and variety of Vaughan's scene. Molly Mahood makes a more convincing comparison with Samuel Palmer,[7] though Palmer's rich and heavy, thickly-wooded and static landscapes represent a different vision and a different countryside from the Welsh poet's. But both Blunden and Mahood are right, surely, in recognizing the strong visual as well as visionary quality in Vaughan.

Some lines from a recent sonnet, 'Conscious Light', by the glass engraver Laurence Whistler, attempt to convey the act and art of seeing:

> One field beneath the flying sun grows bright,
> Seems held for recognition and let lapse.
> You'd say that field was being thought by light.
> Perhaps earth is what light reflects on, thinking
> This field—that clump—those cottages. Perhaps
> The dark areas live in the same mind,
> Only not thought, put by, patiently shrinking,
> Back into darkness, reconciled though blind.[8]

The last two and a half lines of the same poem seem to me to epitomize very vividly the odd relationship in this art between the natural world, the fact, and the vision, one which I have tried to examine in Vaughan and more briefly in Wordsworth:

> O glory explaining
> How heaven, for a flash, is fact more than we know;
> Now it translates us, now we are the meaning.

Notes

1. Unless otherwise noted, all quotations from Vaughan refer to the edition by Alan Rudrum in the Penguin English Poets Series (Harmondsworth, 1976).

2. F. E. Hutchinson, *Henry Vaughan*, a Life and Interpretation (Oxford, 1947), p. 23.

3. A typical example might be these stanzas from Edward Benlowes' 'The Sweetness of Retirement' (Benlowes, being a pastoral and devotional poet, may well be compared with Vaughan):

> When early Phosphor lights from eastern bed
> The grey-eyed morn, with blushes red;
> When opal colours prank the orient tulip's head.
>
> Then walk we forth, where twinkling spangles shew,
> Entinselling like stars the dew,
> Where buds, like pearls, and where we leaves like em'ralds view.

See Saintsbury (ed.), *The Caroline Poets*, Oxford, 1905, Vol. I, P. 449.

4. Sir Thomas Browne, 'The Garden of Cyrus', ch. IV, in *Religio Medici and other Works*, ed. L. C. Martin (Oxford, 1964), p. 167.

5. 'The Praeparation'. Wade ed. *The Poetical Works of Thomas Traherne* (1932), p. 13.

6. Edmund Blunden, *On the Poetry of Henry Vaughan* (1927), p. 41.

7. M. M. Mahood, *Poetry and Humanism* (1950), p. 255.

8. Laurence Whistler, *To Celebrate Her Living* (1967), p. 107.

MICHAEL BIRD

Nowhere but in the Dark:
On the Poetry of Henry Vaughan

'Vaughan is usually considered as the poet of occasional fine lines, and
of no perfect poem', and he meets often enough, and at greater length,
with this sort of assessment. The same thing is loosely true of other
poets—Wyatt, for instance, or Coleridge—but the fact asserts itself that
any thought about Vaughan's work tends to be haunted less by the
inadequacy of this remark than by its blighting justness. The poet of
patchy and unsustained éclat makes his appearance, or rather conspicuously fails to, almost everywhere in the surrounding critical literature
and more seems to be needed than a relaxed acceptance that it is, really,
a rare lyric that runs at even pitch of creative energy and vigilance.

The quoted statement happens here to be T. S. Eliot reviewing
Blunden's Vaughan book[1] in *The Dial*. The whole piece might be seen
as nothing more than a minor demonstration of Eliot's knack for gauging
critical state-of-play, although, as a casual summary, it has held its
ground better than anything more affirmative in Blunden's commentary.
If, now, Vaughan is much thought about at all (for, while he has always
had readers, he's never had a 'public') it is in these terms. Amid much
that is inscrutably introspective—a private dialogue to which we have
finally no access—the 'fine lines' lift up chance clarities and at once
leap beyond whatever niche we had been mentally preparing for their
17th century devotional intimacies. In this sense every reader's Vaughan
is the same poet. No-one thinking of 'They are all gone into the world

Reprinted, by permission of Oxford University Press for the English Association,
from *English*, 33:145 (1984), 1–20.

of light' ever remarks that there's a more important or at least more interesting side to him (as some Keats readers look to *Hyperion* rather than *The Eve of St. Agnes*); and among the less anthologised pieces it would be difficult to mistake the successes:

> 'Tis now clear day: I see a Rose
> Bud in the bright East, and disclose
> The Pilgrim-Sun.

Hard to imagine a less assertive exclamation; yet the fragment could only be Vaughan. The quiet and radiant dynamic enforces a chariness, sending the critic to look elsewhere for something to say. Blake's lyrics come to mind here, in the way their visuality, thrust to the very surface of the poems, deflects argument endlessly towards other aspects of the work; towards turbid privacy and away from the radiantly evident.

Why *say* anything at all? Except that the tenacious approximateness of Eliot's remark (and his 'no' is critical tradition's too) dogs the poetry like a dismissal. In place of it there is both everything and nothing to be said, but it is uniquely the case with Vaughan that he appears to incite the nothing to an extent that his work is often written about as though it engendered possibility of discussion largely, even wholly, in terms of its borrowings and failures.

Of course the borrowings and influences his verse displays provide more mental handhold than anything else we find there,[2] and it is to this fact, with Blunden's criticism rather than the poems in view, that Eliot's review applies itself. He turfs out with brusque accuracy a series of false, because deflected, approaches:

> Some readers have professed to discover in Vaughan the traces of an hermetic philosophy of profound depths. It may be there; if so it belongs not to literature but to cryptography. The mystical element in Vaughan which belongs to his poetry is there for anyone to see; it is 'mysticism' only by a not uncommon extension of the term.

We say 'mystical' partly out of our awareness that Vaughan is often addressing himself from and to something which awakens in us no response to its truth but which is, nevertheless, not felt to be mere failure to communicate. George Herbert provides the defining contrast. His truth stands unqualified; he addresses himself to God and we need no proviso of Christian faith to accept the relation and respond to its exigencies. Herbert's work stays readable because the cloudless sanity of temper the verse reveals remains what it always was, while Vaughan's capacity to live as a poet has very little to do with the personal or doctrinal psychology of his lyrics.

To remark that Vaughan is in no sense intellectually in Herbert's shadow still leaves us free to notice that the work is peppered with all kinds of fragments and echoes from Herbert's verse, unhidden and traceable as a trail of flour from a punctured bag. These traces are the pieties of Vaughan's discipleship, writing and living in consciousness of cherished creative affinity with the older poet (who died in Vaughan's twelfth year). They don't point to the sources of his art, though they are a striking, wearisome and revealing phenomenon, and it is likely that he never outgrew the imitative need that binds Herbert's poetry (and before that Randolph's, Donne's and others') so closely with his own.[3]

The following lines, for example, come from *The Mutiny*:

> Let me so strive and struggle with thy foes
> (Not thine alone, but mine too,) that when all
> Their arts and force are built unto the height
>   That Babel-weight
> May prove thy glory, and their shame.

Apparently a fluent remoulding of Herbetian inflexion and clarity, (the poem follows, in various aspects, his *Collar*), the effect of this is in fact not to concentrate but to disperse attention. 'Strive and struggle' is so intent on its own gesturing that, isolated by the shrill ardour of the parenthesis, it fails to lay imaginative hold on the 'Babel-weight', which is itself suspended in floating inertia by the building metaphor's upward–tending weightlessness. The stanza's final, cancelling two-way pull between glory and shame impresses further the sense that Vaughan's meditative logic suffers in projection (like Claudius's: 'an auspicious and a dropping eye') a thwarting conceptual astigmatism. And this couldn't even be called an obscure passage; nor careless, nor inept. The mutinous restlessness it speaks of has nothing to do with the way attention is unseated; jolted and thrown without being able to fix on any particular illogicality. There is none. So, if we can be bothered, we're already mentally decoding the piece: 'Vaughan is saying that...' Which is where discussion of themes[4] begins, and attempts to refer this to 'what belongs to the poetry' gratefully capitulate.

Vaughan's debt to Herbert almost entirely takes the form of this kind of fractured ventriloquism, which makes it all the stranger that he should be thought of as having a very uneasy relation to, even transcendent disclocation from, both the Metaphysicals of the previous generation and his own contemporaries. Linguistically I relate this to a sea-change process of transposition in which the Metaphysical syntactic and verbal gestures become severed and denatured when deployed by Vaughan. Only compare Herbert's *The Collar*, from first to last a syntactic *coup*, with the way so many of Vaughan's lyrics seem, amid analogous rhythmic flourishes, to fall to pieces of their own accord,[5] leaving single lines and images endowed with a disconnectedly self-signalling quality.

It is a quality that irretrievably distances poet from reader. With the exception of Shakespeare there is no other English poet of any stature who has been found so open to colonisation by later periods than his own. Those who want to admire Vaughan as a 17th century spirit are oddly on the defensive, as though 'the romantic conspiracy to redeem the poet from a period cursed with obsolete learning'[6] had somehow succeeded in capturing him outright.

Nor is it difficult to understand the alacrity with which post-Romantic readers have warmed to the theme of childhood recovered. The evoked and longed-for child-state of *The Retreat* has been taken as a proleptic Wordsworthian visioning in which innocence and nearness to nature are held in fuzzy, dazzled synthesis, while the more obvious inference, that Wordsworth learnt substantially from Vaughan, has never gained much ground. And Frank Kermode's remark that the poem takes its place in the mid-century by representing 'an advanced contemporary interpretation of the Fall as a psychological as well as an historical phenomenon' could, with slightly adjusted emphasis, be applied to Blake's *Garden of Love*.

> Happy those early days! when I
> Shined in my Angel-infancy.

This is prelapsarian dawn and innocent child and soul before birth. There is nothing surprising about this triad in its period context except— and importantly—that it is himself Vaughan is searching back to re cover. The disarming directness of the rhyme-clinched pronoun surprises too. Perhaps we'd expected some particularisation; 'my heart' or mind or soul? Then at once simple wholeness of self vanishes in the angel-brilliance of its visualisation. Are the 'early days' a generalised paradisal dream after all? But 'I' returns, though not at all as a self played upon by the external corrupting world and so reenacting the primal loss of innocence. 'I' is an original and strangely unqualitied self that teaches its own soul both to imagine and utter evil and 'dispenses' (actively giving and passively permitting) sins to each of the senses. *Unqualitied* not vacuous, because, however perplexing its behaviour, this self is a presence; shining, understanding, walking, teaching, longing, leaving and comparable with other men (the forward-motion-lovers of 1.29). Yet, distinct as it is, Vaughan's self has nothing of the human and complete first-person address of the Metaphysicals ('Sweetest love, I do not go'), and its vigorous prompting and affective participation in the poem's unfolding seems to draw on an unlocatable and supra-mental reserve that is at once as potent and vacant as the white thought.

What's the nature of the 'white, celestial thought'; suffused, radiant and held in the Vaughan-spell that can't ever be mistaken? This question evokes an instance of what I mean by the poet who incites the nothing sayable; whiteness *is* everything and nothing, and its secondary symbolisms here drop back into an area of more or less inconsequential afterthought. This first conception, without object or subject, is quickly replaced in the soul by images of emblematic clarity as 'on some *gilded cloud*, or *flower*/ My gazing soul would dwell an hour,/ And in those weaker glories spy/ Some shadows of eternity'. The metaphor is sight, both actual and inward, but instead of bringing cloud and flower into the single scope of its own processes the gazing soul is fragmented, distributed between the things it contemplates. It 'dwells on' them in the commonplace figurative sense, but also literally, so that the hour is simultaneously a long time to sustain this tranced intensity and a brief, capricious instant (*eternity* in the next line but one 'shadows' both).

The soul disperses itself by gazing, and the remaining four senses provide no surer anchor in an external world of flowers or clouds. In the happy early days Vaughan says he 'felt through all this fleshly dress/ Bright shoots of everlastingness'. Attention is urged towards these 'bright shoots' as the effective focus of the string of before and after clauses. They are *felt*, however, more in their metaphoric brightness than in any Marvellian 'vegetable' quality, and they are not, in this visuality, an image of enhanced and concentrated sense-awareness but an annihilation of the point at which sensual apprehension can dilate into the truth of a lived relation. *Bright* is an exploded focus and shares with *The Retreat*'s other sight-words an effect at once insistently visual and blindingly unseeable.

The Retreat's infancy entirely fails to make contact either with a reflected-on idea of childhood or the human fact. Vaughan's poem doesn't gaze into the lost purity of infancy but into the lost infancy of self, and this distinguishes it as sharply from anything contemporary as its theme of primal dissociation does from the primal connection that is the essence of the Romantic idea. Compare Herbert's assertion that 'Childhood is Health'. And compare Marvell's young girl in *The Picture of Little T. C. in a Prospect of Flowers*:

> See with what simplicity
> This nymph begins her golden days!
> In the green grass she loves to lie,
> And there with her fair aspect tames
> The wilder flowers, and gives them names.

Relation to Vaughan is suggested first by the 'golden days' and only then by the child. And the nearness is more than, and different from, that kind of contemporaneity which links, for instance, Herbert and Donne. Jacob's children, in *The Search*,

> In those calm, golden evenings lay
> Watering their flocks, and having spent
> Those white days, drove home...

And the sixth stanza of *The Garden* could stand alone as commentary on the hypostatised thought in *The Retreat*:

> Meanwhile the mind, from pleasures less,
> Withdraws into its happiness:
> The mind, that ocean where each kind
> Does straight its own resemblance find,
> Yet it creates, transcending these,
> Far other worlds, and other seas,
> Annihilating all that's made
> To a green thought in a green shade.

Mind annihilates and creates in one impulse. The Romantics would have recognised this; it's the phoenix-fire of Keats's *Lear* sonnet. But the static, irreducible translucence of the last line yields a pungent absentness, a marriage of mind and world in which both are annihilated, that

283

couldn't be more different from the characteristic kind of restless, heuristic pattern Romantic lyrics follow.

Marvell, however, by insisting on the far-otherness of the imagination's worlds, insists on the actuality of the world outside and independent of the operation of mind: an *out there* that Vaughan never gives the impression of touching. In *The Picture of Little T. C.* Marvell's invitation to 'see' puts the living child before us and makes her the focal image in the mind's 'prospect'. The flush of adept, modish wit in the idea that she can tame with her pretty face 'the wilder flowers' diffuses magically with the realisation that at the source of the tender conceit lies the word *simplicity*. We respond to a magnanimity that like a charm centres the poem on the mortal child.

Nothing of this in *The Retreat*. Nor does Vaughan's poem offer a reflection on innocence, infancy, sin, or anything else. He has nothing interesting to say about the soul's progress, except that it derives from a place *before*. Before teaching and before understanding; a supramental, pre-sensual state that haunts his poetry in images of light and night, sleep and death, scattering and returning. *The Retreat* of the title is threefold; a return, a haven and a withdrawal. The journey ends where it begins. The dark, protecting and confining urn exists not in opposition to but in identity with the original celestial shining.

It is every reader's experience that Vaughan's images of night and light—the quiet and radiant dynamic that marks those 'fine lines'—remain distinctly and disconnectedly in memory. Whatever their context, once the poem is no longer in front of us they become dissociated from everything but themselves, moments of fortuitous psychic arrest. In *The Mutiny* I noted how Vaughan's shadowing of Herbertian rhythm and syntax doesn't bind and impel the poem, but instead induces an effect of self-cancelling dispersal. The Metaphysical gestures fly loose from his hands in minor anarchy within the stanza form and the images, like lights on water, touch and coalesce without linkage. Yet Vaughan's visuality—the gazing soul of *The Retreat* calls up a host of visioned instants from other poems—is a thread of gold that his critics have always tried to anchor in a world of sense or, at spiritual remove, in cogent mysticism. So we inherit the Nature Poet and the Mystic, and once these two make their appearance it is difficult to keep either the Hermetic Books or the Romantics at arm's length and Vaughan himself disappears under a historical or a proleptic tyranny.

William Empson commented on lines from '*Joy of my Life*':

> God's saints are shining lights: who stays
> Here long must pass
> O'er dark hills, swift streams, and steep ways
> As smooth as glass.

'One does not separate them in one's mind; it is the Romantic Movement's technique; dark hair, tidal water, landscape at dusk are dissolved into your mind, as often in dreams, into an apparently direct sensory image which cannot be connected to any of the senses.'[7]

The last phrase is felicitously accurate. But 'dark hair'? Empson wants to anchor the words in a world, in this case the world of dreams, and he already has Shelley more in mind than he has Vaughan. Why doesn't this convince; why aren't the lines sensory or Shelleyan? We glance back and note the lights, the travelling, the succession of images that impart a gliding velocity. The 'sensory immediacy', however, founders on the emphatic stasis of 'who stays/ Here long' which itself drags against the imagined swift release of the next lines. This is another two-way pull. It makes a toneless vacancy of that vigorous Metaphysical *must*. Think of Herbert's 'He builds a house which quickly down must go' or Donne's 'Must to thy motions lovers seasons run?'; brisk, taut, impulsive. Vaughan's conceit offers to fuse the saint's guiding example with the necessity of lights for avoiding obstacles on our way home and to bed; but the lights of the poem are held to nothing but their own shining. Stars, candles, pillar-fires; they scatter attention in untethered disunity.

> They are that City's shining spires
> We travel to;
> A swordlike gleam
> Kept man for sin
> First *out*; this beam
> Will guide him *in*.

Bright saints and sword-gleam, apparently identified with each other in their gleaming, are functionally opposite and disconnected, so that the intended clasp of the final out/in paradox falls in two like a split log.

These untethered image-impressions proffer a logic of sustained conceit, achieved through syntactic sleight of hand, while their imagi-

native effect is at once heightened and wholly disintegrative. It is as
though thought could bypass the brooding and associative operation of
mind:

> The mind that ocean, where each kind
> Does straight its own resemblance find.

In relation to the Metaphysical Conceit, these lines reveal a looking-
glass world within whose terms the question 'how does this relate . . . ?'
cannot be asked. Green shade *is* green thought; identity or nothing.[8]

However, where Marvell's mind-ocean proves to be of infinite com-
prehensive unity, boundlessly integral, Vaughan repeatedly suggests
and develops an entirely opposite frame of imaginative consciousness.
Here is an example from *Church Service*:

> O how in this thy choir of souls I stand
>   (Propped by thy hand)
>   A heap of sand!
> Which busy thoughts (like winds) would scatter quite
>   And put to flight,
>   But for thy might;
>   Thy hand alone doth tame
> Those blasts, and knit my frame.

Busy thoughts defeat and disperse the self. The notion of minor anarchy,
of coalescence without linkage, finds its image in the propped-up heap
of grains of sand, supported but ready to collapse and scatter. And this
suggests why Vaughan transmits no settled sense of personality or per-
sona in his verse, almost no identity. His is a self that can conceive its
own existence nowhere but in the annulment of reflective consciousness,
the extinction of thought.

If that heap of sand seems on its own a fortuitous and quirky image,
it must be stressed that Vaughan returns often to the motif of scattered
consciousness, assuaged and gathered and contained by God. The poem
that follows in *Silex I, Burial*, begins:

> O thou! the first fruits of the dead
>   And their dark bed,
> When I am cast into that deep
>   And senseless sleep
>   The wages of my sin,

NOWHERE BUT IN THE DARK

O then,
Thou great Preserver of all men!
Watch o'er that loose
And empty house,
Which I sometimes lived in.

It's not finally clear whether this represents the body or the mind or just an empty house. In effect, it is all three equally. Then, in the third and fourth stanzas, the self that survives death appears as storm-swept dust contained;

The world's thy box: how then (there tossed,)
Can I be lost?

Vaughan appends *Romans viii* 23:

And not only they, but our selves also, which have the first fruits of the spirit, even we our selves groan within our selves, waiting for the adoption, *to wit*, the redemption of our body.

I have used the word *self* to house both body and spirit, and the distinction isn't conclusively made in *Burial*. Moreover, the ruined dwelling is felt to have housed life in a way analogous to Christ's boxing-in of the scattered self after death. The ruined life-house evokes so poignant a sense of inhabitable, forsaken locality that the 'dark bed' of Death-in-Christ seems as though it's been mysteriously and physically transferred from the place where 'scarce a room but wind, and rain/ Beat through, and stain/ The seats and cells within.' The soaked boards, the weather's chill and damp airiness within disinhabited walls, are more present to the mind than any of Donne's little rooms, so that we want to ask what it is that, in a poet of inward seeing, throws out this instant of unemphatic actuality.

In the 'dark bed', belonging to but transferred from the life-lorn dwelling, Vaughan's scatterings and homings meet, and the burial of the title draws towards itself the curtains, beds and sleep of other poems. It is as though his one hold on the rhythms of physical life were in a domestic gentleness of imagined death:

But I would be
With him I weep

287

> A bed, and sleep
> To wake in thee.
> (*Come, come, what do I here*)

The self of *The Retreat* comes from a place 'before' and just as sleep unites life with death, the pre-sensual security and enfolding darkness of the womb are not only like but, in this case, the same thing as death:

> Perhaps some think a tomb
> No house of store,
> But a dark, and sealed up womb,
> Which ne'er breeds more.

The strangeness of these lines is that a *sealed* womb isn't a *dead* womb, yet what is the function of a womb that 'ne'er breeds more'? Breeding is a sending-out, the connection between life and world, and the womb is sealed not to prevent it breeding but as though in order that it may breed to itself in darkness. And if this intimation of passive and withheld fertility seems peculiarly self-cancelling (or rather, peculiarly *not* self-cancelling), it is so in the same transfigured, evident 'simplicity' that unites sleep with death and in which Vaughan's darknesses are rendered in terms of pellucid luminosity. The womb-tomb in its enfolded darkness, the Angel-infancy in its unseeable brilliance end and begin *The Retreat*, a double homing:

> Some men a forward motion love,
> But I by backward steps would move,
> And when this dust falls to the urn
> In that state I came return.

'Came return'. Nothing separates the words. They merge in the housing urn where death gathers life's dust and absolves it from distinctness and, thereby, from consciousness.

> Dear, beauteous death! the jewel of the just,
> Shining nowhere, but in the dark.
> (*They are all gone into a world of light*)

Everywhere in Vaughan's work are the invitations to look, to see. 'I saw eternity the other night'; 'Sees not my friend?'; 'I saw thy truth'; 'I see the use'. And these would be unremarkable if this poet were the Wordsworthianised minor-Herbert of critical tradition, revealing and celebrating God's immanence in created nature—feathers, shells, pearls, the rainbow, a nest, groves, clouds and lakes:

> But his own living works did my Lord hold
> And lodge alone.

Restore these lines to their place in *The Night*, however, and their apparently signal statement hazes. Vaughan refers the night of the title to *John iii 2*, where Nicodemus asks Jesus, among other things, 'can a man enter a second time into his mother's womb, and be born?' This inquiry is so suggestive of the motif of backward cyclical progression— the strong spiritual undertow exerted by the notion of pre-rational infancy in *The Retreat* and in the poem that precedes *The Night*, *Childhood*—that Vaughan's failure to seize that very question is itself strange. Instead, the poem centres on the fact that Nicodemus came after dark 'And what can never more be done/ Did at mid-night speak with the sun'. The imagined sun-communing night is 'my soul's calm *retreat*', the Lord's 'dark Tent', 'the soul's dumb watch' and the image of womb-darkness, raised arrestingly in the scripture dialogue and apparently ignored by Vaughan, is clearly cognate.

The Night rides on light-in-darkness and releases with that centrifugal, corruscating action I have called untethered disunity one of the most striking image-sequences in any single poem of Vaughan's.

> God's silent, searching flight:
> When my Lord's head is filled with dew, and all
> His locks are wet with the clear drops of night.

'Mystical' this obviously is, both vaguely and precisely (the night sky *is* Christ's body, the 'Virgin shrine'[9]), but the refulgent dewiness owes nothing to symbolic tradition and is there, in fact, despite it. For we are aware how easily that dew-filled head might slip into pietistic grotesque, outcast, like much Mystical Verse, unrescuably from the language (a 'bad translation' effect that blights the genre up to and beyond T. S. Eliot's 'indigestible portions/Which the leopards reject'). Again, seeing's special quality is pushed to the fore. Sight is not merely the primary but almost the single exclusive sense-faculty of Vaughan's poetry. Other senses tend to announce themselves gauchely: 'only a little fountain lent/ Some use for ears'. All the same, it's difficult to put aside Empson's Shelley-shaded insight about the 'apparently direct sensory image that cannot be attached to any of the senses'.

The purely visual always everywhere has an abstract tilt, but why do Vaughan's images in particular shake so unattachably free from the senses? In an oddly straightforward way, in part shared by other naïf or visionary writers (Christopher Smart, or Blake), he lacks instinctive purchase on the world of contingent reality where things happen and lives are affected. He echoes, but does not reproduce, poetry of forged Metaphysical connection. He owes almost every dramatic or asseverating inflexion in his verse, directly or indirectly, to some other poet. Often these are simple magpie thefts:

> Just so base, sublunary lovers' hearts
> Fed on loose profane desires,
> May for an eye,
> Or face comply.

Particularly, there is always a disconcerting, braking jolt when Vaughan announces the kind of major-key *attacca* sequences both Donne and Herbert were and are admired (and overvalued) for: 'I struck the board', 'Batter my heart', 'Look not for mind in women'. His opening exclamations have, by comparison, a puzzled, airy equanimity: 'Sad, purple well!', 'Fair, solitary path!', 'How shrill are silent tears!'[10] Nothing *matters* for Vaughan in any coercive or impinging way, and his deep instinct is to anaesthetise rather than, in Hopkins' phrase, 'make capital' of crisis. This reflexive withdrawal from and blurring of the point of emotional or intellectual address pervades both the prose works and the verse. In *Man in Darkness* the crisis is the instant when 'the pangs of death come thick' upon the soul, but it is absorbed painlessly into death-as-sleep. The meditation lights on the image of a creature in hibernation, 'that dark state of dormition', which, he avows, 'is so strong a symbol of the resurrection, that I think it needless to make any application'. The sleep that precedes renewal here doesn't, of course, *change* the sleeping animal and to take Vaughan's word for the clarity of this symbol is to draw the Resurrection into the instinctual and somnambulistic rhythm of life's death-comprehending cycle:

> I say then, do we not see that these *birds* and inferior creatures which in the *spring* and *summer* continue here very merry and *musical*, do on a sudden leave us, and all *winter*-long suffer a kind of *death*, and with the *Sun's* warmth in the *youth* of the year *awake* again, and *refresh* the world with *revived notes*? For the singing of birds is *naturalis musica mundi*, to which all *arted strains* are but *discord* and *hardness*; How much more shall *Jesus Christ* the *Sun of righteousness rising with healing under his wings,*

awake those that sleep in him, and bring them again with
joyful resurrection?[11]

The 'natural' world carries both literal and symbolic import, not because
its life is evident but because it is unconscious and unwilled. Out of
those two slumberous negations, however, the winged Christ, like a
phoenix-bird, leads the resurgent seasonal cycle of resurrection.

Hibernation is a secure, concealed, life-nurturing retreat and this
is precisely the sense death bears for Vaughan, as though it compre-
hended renewal so implicitly that it would be 'needless to make any
application'. Thus the cognate motifs of secure sleep and night and light
make no symbolic announcement, but signal wherever they occur a
withdrawal from cogitated sensation into rapt awareness, an unbrooding
inward-folding of the mind.

> Were all my loud, evil days
> Calm and unhaunted as is thy dark Tent,
> Whose peace but by some Angel's wing or voice
> Is seldom rent;
> Then I in heaven all the long year
> Would keep, and never wander here.

Vaughan incites the nothing sayable. It may be that I reach for
negation too often as a means of soliciting his poetry, although it is clear
that the quality even, and especially, of his best work rides on its own
abstention and withdrawal. Notice here, for instance, how the 'calm
and unhaunted' darkness is so much 'louder' than the evil days. It is
the nature of his gift that this absence of purchase on the world, this
inability to dramatise a lived relation or to brood on pain, both produces
and liberates a poetry of effortless naturalism. Though we are unable
to call it humane or magnanimous, its achievement is in a real sense
psychic-state transfigured. As with Marvell's small girl, conceit falls
from an image like a tender joke, restoring to it a precious simplicity,
its nature as original and modest truth.

The 'truth' of *The Shower* is sudden rainfall and a sinner's remorse.
This much-anthologised piece bears superficial relation to Herbert's *The
Flower*, though no single line suggests anyone but Vaughan. It is actually
unclear whether the longed-for repentant relief has or is still to come,
but the last stanza bestows a translucent bright ambience, a released,
cleansed clarity:

> Yet, if as thou dost melt, and with thy train
> Of drops make soft the earth, my eyes could weep
> O'er my hard heart that's bound up, and asleep,
>   Perhaps at last
>   (Some such showers past,)
> My God would give a sun-shine after rain.

Another two-way pull here disperses the heart's hardness. Is 'bound up' toughly constricted or gently swathed—the idea of being wrapped in sleep? It is, in effect, not metaphorically physicalised remorse that this stanza impresses, but a showery amplitude of living day. Set beside it, those few of Herbert's poems that glance outside the window offer something redemptively intellectual, a fully self-recognised psychic weather:

> After so many deaths I live and write;
> I once more smell the dew and rain,
>   And relish versing.

Here writing 'some such shower past' he wakes to the same sweet redolence of drenched earth and wide air and peace at heart. Connection is briskly established, however, by the way *relish* reflects from the versing (as in a man wholly possessed of his poet's faculty) directly back to the smell of dew and rainsoaked earth and air. It is impossible *not* to grasp that this is largely the same sort of thing Vaughan anticipates, the 'sunshine after rain'; and yet Vaughan's remains sunshine; no more, no less. 'Simplicity' reveals itself under cover of metaphor, and—recalling the green thought in the green shade—symbol and thing symbolised are the same.

Again, it is almost the case that the receive the effect of Vaughan's verse is to evade its import. This is finally what is felt to make it so unsatisfactorily comparable with Herbert's. In *The Flower* the regenerate soul is disclosed with every honesty of metaphor; 'I bud again'. Nothing could be, to our habits of healthy complex thought, simpler. But those three words in a Vaughan poem would set growing an uneasily edgeless image of the soul actually having leaves, or being plant-shaped or in reality a plant. The fusions that we recognise as Vaughan's pseudo-conceits are looking-glass metaphors; to understand them is to effect a disjunction between abstract and concrete, or between what is being 'talked about' and what invades the imagination.

Vaughan conjures the bright ambience, but is unable to make it

participate any further in metaphor, to make it at all eloquent about
sin or prayer or mercy:

> 'Twas so, I saw thy birth: that drowsy lake
> From her faint bosom breathed thee, the disease
> Of her sick waters, and infectious ease,
> > But, now at even
> > Too gross for heaven,
> Thou fall'st in tears, and weep'st for thy mistake.

What *is* the mistake? And what is the unheard discussion to which the
poem addresses itself? 'Twas so' is planted and gestural, as Donne would
plant a 'by my troth' to compel the reader into a sense of situation and
relation. But the verbal gesture is impotent here. Where this kind of
phrase often signals the Metaphysical lyric's public, talkative, urbane
facet, in Vaughan's poem it turns inwards. *The Shower* begins by ab-
sorbing all possible thought about what's been seen into the fact of
seeing.

Lack of purchase is part of Vaughan's gift. There could be no 'fine
lines' without minor anarchy and disjunction. It is also, like the reso-
nance of *The Night*'s 'unhaunted' darkness, paradoxical and mysterious,
but it permeates his language in quite observable ways. Note how often
words that offer relation and contact are frozen, abstracted from their
function:

> and sin
> Like clouds eclipsed my mind.
> *(Regeneration)*

It may be that this appears perfectly commonplace. Fleshly sin can
easily be figured as eclipsing clouds, but Vaughan's simile puts such an
airy space between body and mind that the idea of sinful contamination
loses all concentration. And how can mind simultaneously sin *and* be
the bright object sin obliterates? Already 'like' is dispersing the poem's
import among shades and contradictions. It is powerless to suggest how
sin corresponds to the eclipsing clouds. If sin is 'like' clouds, blown in
from somewhere else, windborne and transient, in what sense is it sin?
The Retreat's notion of a self that dispenses 'a several sin to every sense'
is echoed in this disjunction of sin from mind, only in this case the clear,
dominating image of eclipsing clouds makes that oddness seem periph-
eral. Like the clouds of *Regeneration* the rains of *The Shower* carry neither

menace nor pain and, like an eclipse, must pass as surely as they come.
And this transience anaesthetises crisis; sin and remorse will only tell
their story if the critic wakes them up himself.

The 'hard heart' which is the object of *The Shower* is 'bound up
and asleep'; as distant and unconscious as a fairytale giant beneath a
hill. If Vaughan communicates nothing about the psychological state
of hardheartedness, his words still have a fairytale uncontradictability.
It is a tone we meet often:

> Thy heavens (some say,)
> Are a firy-liquid light . . .

> And though poor stones have neither speech nor tongue,
> While active winds and stream both run and speak,
> Yet stones are deep in admiration . . .

There is no disproving the stones' admiration. But neither is there any
access to it. Like the bound-up heart, and unlike Marvell's glowworms
or Blake's Clod and Pebble, they announce nothing for themselves.[12]
What *can* stones announce—or unhaunted darkness, or pure and endless
light? Vaughan's entities all aspire to the condition of 'white thought',
which contains everything and nothing, which possesses identity without
having 'significance' and is both beginning and end of the process of
cogitation. White thought has no part to play in the expository or the
heuristic lyric modes, which explains why Vaughan has, as I put it,
nothing to say. All the same, talk of fairytale uncontradictability denotes
more than a rephrasing of 'naïf'. It is, for instance, this quality more
than anything else that makes Vaughan Marvell's contemporary, with
the difference that inside the miracle of Marvell's mind-ocean device,
the generative action of art which creates its own relevance, works to
achieve a symmetry of parts:

> But when the vigilant patrol
> Of stars walks round about the Pole,
> Their leaves, that to the stalks are curled,
> Seem to their staves the ensigns furled.
> Then in some flower's beloved hut
> Each bee as sentinel is shut,
> And sleeps so too: but, if once stirred,
> She runs you through, nor asks the word.

These metaphors bears the same relation to 'the stars shine in their
watches' that Mercutio's Mab speech bears to Marcellus's 'It faded on

the crowing of the cock'. Vaughan's world of nature is the world where, during the hallowed time (some say) 'the bird of dawning singeth all night long'.

Looking at this essay, I think Vaughan might easily have had it his own way again and absconded from between the lines. But there can be no defining the liberating qualities of his verse while this absentness is treated as a nuisance. Rather, it is the whole story. Resurrection is the other side of absentness and resurrection, if anything, is Vaughan's abiding theme. Remember the hibernating animal 'in that dark state of dormition', and the winged sun of righteousness' spring awakening. Unconscious nature shares the darkness of death-as-sleep with the redemptive, resurrected light. The Angel-infancy and the housing urn cancel each other out and, if not the same place, are the same thing. Thus Vaughan's isolation is not illusory. His apartness often becomes apparent in the very terms in which conformity is suggested. 'In mystical or related types of writing, says Rosemond Tuve,[13] 'the images themselves are likely to be perspicuous...Crashaw need not pause to explain the twofold applicability of each phrase when he says ... "Where he meant *frost*, he scatter'd *flowrs*" ... Vaughan says " 'Twas but just now *my bleak leaves* hopeless hung", and Herbert, "And now in age *I bud again*"; we...accept without pausing the transferred epithet *bleak* as a psychological description.'

Vaughan's line comes from *Unprofitableness*, a poem that has clearly been modelled on Herbert's *The Flower* and which is very much less successful. 'My bleak leaves' is nothing on its own, but even within the poem Vaughan creates no very illuminating juncture of psyche and tree. The man is a tree, but the tree is not a man. The devotional anecdote stumbles through a series of touch/smell images in which Herbert's dew and rain become 'all perfumes and spice'. Vaughan is directly indebted here, yet the anaesthetising, withdrawing impulse that effectively annuls contact between the two poems is manifest. The point at which Herbert's makes its cleanest psycho-physical connection, asserting truth to experience, is exactly where Vaughan's withdraws most blindly into emblematic confection. 'I smell a dew like *myrrh*' he claims; but when he continues, 'and all the day/ Wear in my bosom a full Sun', the heraldic crudity begins to give way to the brighter, vaguer truth; it can be assimilated to the thought that 'glows and glitters in my cloudy breast/ Like stars upon some gloomy grove'.

There remains, too, a wisdom in our recognition of the difficulty

of defining the proper context for Vaughan's verse. For what he does
finely shares itself effortlessly widely. And this is where talk of Wordsworth, or of Shelley or the Shakespeare of *A Midsummer Night's Dream*
and the *Tempest* masque, falls as naturally as it does imprecisely:

> The active air, the gentlest showers,
> Shall from his wings rain on thy flowers;
> And the Moon from her dewy locks
> Shall deck thee with her brightest drops.

The *Poetical Sketches* don't seem far from this, nor the spirit songs from
Prometheus. Yet 'Romantic' is never the word. When we hear Shelley's
'Some say that gleams of a remoter world/ Visit the soul in sleep' we
are aware that this poet's invocation of the unconscious solicits something quite other than Vaughan's imagined pre-sensual haven. We are
returned to the elusively evident visuality that simultaneously centres
and scatters the poems: the self, also, centred and scattered on the cycle
of light:

> There is in God (some say)
> A deep, but dazzling darkness; as men here
> Say it is late and dusky, because they
>   See not all clear;
> O for that night! where I in him
> Might live invisible and dim.

Notes

1. *On the Poems of Henry Vaughan* (1927). Blunden, as Eliot acerbically points
out, makes a Nature Poet of Vaughan: 'The Vaughan landscape is inimitable. Its
clouds are so fleecy... its sunbeams so vital, its pasturing life so unalarmed and
unalterable, that it needs no signature.'
2. In E. C. Pettet's *Of Paradise and Light* (1960) the influences dictate the form
of the study: The Bible, Herbert and Hermetic Philosophy watch over it as section
headings.
3. T. S. Eliot writes of the adolescent experiences of poetry: 'At this period,
the poem, or the poetry of a single poet, invades the youthful consciousness and
assumes complete possession for a time... The frequent result is an outburst of
scribbling which we may call imitation, so long as we are aware of the meaning of
the word 'imitation' which we employ. It is not deliberate choice of a poet to mimic,
but writing under a kind of daemonic possession by one poet.' *The Use of Poetry and
the Use of Criticism* (1933).
4. For example, Joan Bennett asserts that Vaughan's work is 'passionately

concerned . . . with the relation between God and the individual soul' and that 'Nature for Vaughan is the revelation and fulfilment of God's will.' Her *Five Metaphysical Poets* (1934) offers something like the consensus view Eliot had in mind. Vaughan is now more commonly seen as rapt occultist than visionary rambler.

5. Anne Righter (Barton) cites *I saw Eternity the other night* as a characteristic instance: 'After a staggering opening, Vaughan's poem collapses into triviality.' (British Academy Chatterton Lecture 1967) The effect is related, through Rochester's verse, to 'a double crisis' facing English poetry generally in the late C. 17th. The poets had run out of things to say and ways of saying them.

6. Frank Kermode, 'The Private Imagery of Henry Vaughan', *R.E.S.* July 1950. Perhaps the most 'private account' of Vaughan. In the service of ratiocinative clarity, it misses simply by attributing cogently metaphorical 'ideas' to Vaughan. Is 'the idea of the dead as stars' a mental entity in any quality similar to, for instance, Donne's idea of the world as a little room?

7. William Empson, *Seven Types of Ambiguity* (3rd [revised] ed. 1953), p. 175.

8. Similarly, the drop of dew shines 'Like its own tear' and in *Eyes and Tears*, 'These weeping eyes, those seeing tears' are, despite the apparent dichotomy, 'these . . . those', the same thing.

9. 'Virgin-shrine': the irradiated shrine may be contrasted with the image of the 'dark' womb, or aligned with that of the tomb-confined star. Vaughan seems, in fact, to be applying the epithet separately to the night and to the divine body. See Alan Rudrum's 'Vaughan's *The Night*: Some Hermetic Notes,' *MLR*, LXIV (1969), pp. 11–19.

10. Herbert has 'What is so shrill as silent tears?' Vaughan's preference for exclamation over question is another aspect of withdrawal from consecutive thought into rapt awareness. The interrogative form interposes itself between mind and object it contemplates. Vaughan's questions, like Blake's, are all disguised exclamations.

11. From *The Mount of Olives*, (1652). I quote from L. C. Martin, *The Works of Henry Vaughan*, (2nd ed. 1957). Elsewhere, quotation from Vaughan's poetry is from Alan Rudrum's edition (Penguin, London, 1976). For Marvell, I use Elizabeth Story Donno's edition (Penguin, London, 1972).

12. *Fairytale uncontradictability* could never apply to Herbert, and may not seem to relate aptly to the C. 17th at all. But what end does, for example, *The Indifferent's* unboastful catalogue serve, beyond Donne's pleasure in telling the tale itself? 'I can love both fair and browne . . .'

13. Rosemond Tuve, Elizabethan and Metaphysical Imagery, (1947), p. 218.

A. J. SMITH

Appraising the World

In canto xxvii of the *Paradiso* Dante and Beatrice ascend to the Crystalline Sphere of heaven, marking as they go our world of lust and pride—'this threshing-floor'—which now turns far away below them. At this outer limit of natural being Beatrice appropriately defines for the pilgrim the relation of eternity to time, of absolute love and providence to contingent events, 'smiling so happily that God appeared to joy in her face':

> La natura del mondo, che quieta
> il mezzo e tutto l'altro intorno move,
> quinci comincia come da sua meta;
> e questo cielo non ha altro dove
> che la mente divina, in che s'accende
> l'amor che il volge e la virtù ch'ei piove.
> Luce ed amor d'un cerchio lui comprende,
> sì come questo li altri; e quel precinto
> colui che 'l cinge solamente intende.
> Non è suo moto per altro distinto;
> ma li altri son misurati da questo,
> sì come diece da mezzo e da quinto.
> E come il tempo tegna in cotal testo
> le sue radici e ne li altri le fronde,
> omai a te può esser manifesto.

The nature of the universe which holds its centre still and moves all else about it begins here as from its hub; and this

Reprinted, by permission of Cambridge University Press, from *The Metaphysics of Love*, Cambridge (1985), 290–302.

heaven has no other seat but the divine mind, in which is
kindled both the love that turns it and the virtue which it
rains down.

Light and love comprehend it in one circle, as it com-
prehends the other spheres; and that girdle is moved solely
by him who makes it.

Its motion is not set apart from all else; rather, the others
take their measure from it, just as ten is made up of a half
and a fifth.

And how time may have its roots in that pot and its
leaves in the other [spheres] may now be plain to you.

Paradiso xxvii, 106–20

Time has its roots in eternity, temporal being is sustained by the
virtue of eternal light and love; whatever has identity in the world is a
mode of that eternal light and love. Beatrice's words offer us the image
of a universal reciprocity of love in which natural creatures, no less than
the seraphim and cherubim, receive that lifegiving power to the extent
that they will to return it. When Beatrice at once bursts out to condemn
cupidity—

> Oh cupidigia che i mortali affonde
> sì sotto te, che nessuno ha podere
> di trarre li occhi fuor delle tue onde!

—we understand that 'cupidigia' is so damnable precisely because it
completely overwhelms mortal beings who, once they have succumbed
to it, lose the power to 'lift their eyes above your waves'. Such a love
of self, or greed for self, works directly counter to the universal disposition
of a loving providence and denies the very principle of God's creation.

Dante's conceit of a creation vitalised by love given and returned
is illuminatingly akin to Vaughan's. So it is scarcely a surprise when a
commentator on the *Paradiso* discovers 'a notable parallel with these
lines' in Vaughan's 'The World', a poem which he thinks 'was written,
probably, with no reference to Dante, but drawing from the same tradition'. He points the parallel from the first stanza and the last two
lines of 'The World'.

'The World' is one of the few poems in which Vaughan confronts
the ordinary activities of secular men. It is a revealing piece, not least
in its intermittent imaginative power:

299

'The World'
I saw Eternity the other night
Like a great *Ring* of pure and endless light,
    All calm, as it was bright,
And round beneath it, Time in hours, days, years
        Driv'n by the spheres
Like a vast shadow mov'd, In which the world
    And all her train were hurl'd;
The doting Lover in his queintest strain
        Did their Complain,
Neer him, his Lute, his fancy, and his flights,
        Wits sour delights,
With gloves, and knots the silly snares of pleasure
        Yet his dear Treasure
All scatter'd lay, while he his eys did pour
        Upon a flowr.

2

The darksome States-man hung with weights and woe
Like a thick midnight-fog mov'd there so slow
    He did nor stay, nor go;
Condemning thoughts (like sad Ecclipses) scowl
        Upon his soul,
And Clouds of crying witnesses without
        Pursued him with one shout.
Yet dig'd the Mole, and lest his ways be found
        Workt under ground,
Where he did Clutch his prey, but one did see
        That policie,
Churches and altars fed him, Perjuries
        Were gnats and flies,
It rain'd about him bloud and tears, but he
        Drank them as free.

3

The fearfull miser on a heap of rust
Sate pining all his life there, did scarce trust
    His own hands with the dust,
Yet would not place one peece above, but lives
        In feare of theeves.
Thousands there were as frantick as himself

And hug'd each one his pelf,
The down-right Epicure plac'd heav'n in sense
And scornd pretence
While others slipt into a wide Excesse
Said little less;
The weaker sort slight, triviall wares Inslave
Who think them brave,
And poor, despised truth sate Counting by
Their victory.

4

Yet some, who all this while did weep and sing,
And sing, and weep, soar'd up into the *Ring*,
But most would use no wing.
O fools (said I,) thus to prefer dark night
Before true light,
To live in grots, and caves, and hate the day
Because it shews the way,
The way which from this dead and dark abode
Leads up to God,
A way where you might tread the Sun, and be
More bright than he.
But as I did their madnes so discusse
One whisper'd thus,
This Ring the Bride-groome did for none provide
But for his bride.

All that is in the world, the lust of the flesh, the lust of the Eys, and
the pride of life, is not of the father, but is of the world.
And the world passeth away, and the lusts thereof, but he that
doth the will of God abideth for ever.

If Vaughan does not always seem to know the vision from the banal
moralising it may be because his grasp of moral life is less sure than
Donne's or Herbert's or Marvell's. Certainly he attributes less than they
do to the power of man's will, and lacks their keen sense of moral peril.
You do not find him posing that immediate choice which gives Herbert's
poems their terrible directness:

My throat, my soul is hoarse;
My heart is wither'd like a ground
Which thou dost curse.

> My thoughts turn round,
> And make me giddie; Lord, I fall,
> Yet call.   'Longing'

For Vaughan moral life is not so much a conflict as a wooing, a matter
of a man's response to the force that holds the whole creation in the
magnetic power of its love. He sees himself more as inadequate lover
than as agonist:

> I long, and grone, and grieve for thee,
> For thee my words, my tears do gush,
> *O that I were but where I see!*
> Is all the note within my Bush.
> 'The Pilgrimage'

Hardly less noticeable throughout *Silex Scintillans* is the poet's inclination
to cope with mundane designs by dissevering himself from them. Vaughan's contempt of the world becomes a party alignment. For him 'the
world' is simply that part of human activity (and human kind as well)
which stands outside the pale of regenerate life, and hence beyond the
scope of Christ's saving love. This indeed is the stark presumption which
'The World' sets out to try. The subject of this slight lyric poem is
nothing less than the relation of time and the world to eternity, the real
value of worldly activities and motives. That a man should turn so
naturally to lyric poetry when he has these imperative metaphysical
questions to pose to himself is remarkable enough, and it is just the
kind of sudden raid upon the eternal which distinguishes English poetry
in the brief era between Donne and Rochester. To find anything like it
you would have to go back to Cavalcanti and Dante; and the difference
between that Florentine poetry and the English metaphysical lyrics
marks a drastic shift in European consciousness over some three
centuries.

'The World' is a vivid poem, full of life and sudden surprises, but
it does not engage us in the dynamic process of a tough argument, as
though the mind must there and then fight its way to a new truth. On
the contrary, it puts the resolved state of things in a few vivid images
and simply spells out their purport, by way of bringing home to the
poet and us the true condition of human existence in our lapsed creation.
So the poem presents an encounter of opposites, but a clear and simple
one which arises out of our instantaneous perception of the contrast
between the image of eternity and the image of time. The attributes of

302

eternal being—calm stability, refulgent beauty, permanence and the like—stand point-by-point against the condition of the dark, distracted, insubstantial time-hurled world. Vaughan has something of Milton's cosmic grandeur of imagination. But the breathtaking casualness of his opening announcement here, and the irresistible onward sweep of the vision, all but distract us from the point of the juxtaposition which is the absolute opposition between the two parts of the conceit.

Vaughan amplifies the second part first, with his emblems of such representative activities of the world as love, statecraft, money-grubbing, sensual pleasure-seeking, riotous living, lightminded triviality. This part of the poem gives substance to an argument which by stanza four he is ready to develop; and he takes it further in that simple but powerful return to the opening contrast. The two images, as we now vividly see, do not wholly exclude each other after all for some few souls escape the world and make the perilous transference from time to eternity, impelled by motives to which Vaughan's images give spatial amplitude. Plainly it is the difference we feel between that elevating virtue and the supineness of the rest which allows him to sweep in so superbly, and moralise the division between the few and the many:

> O fools (said I,) thus to prefer dark night
> Before true light

This time there will be no dismal lapse into platitude at the climax of his argument. Logical necessity and lyric fervour coincide to elevate the mood of the assault on the benighted worldlings, which brings out what their worldliness really entails. Carried up so into lofty denunciation the voice is ready to spring that last dramatic surprise, the sudden shift into an exalted whisper which resolves at a stroke both the play of images in the poem and the implicit opposition they set up between the worldly and the eternal conditions. The pure circle of eternity becomes the ring of marriage; and all further argument is stopped short, for only the bride of Christ can make the transference in any case, and gain this ring:

> *This Ring the Bride-groome did for none provide*
> *But for his bride*

The *sotto voce* simplicity of that conclusion is convincing, and might even strike us with a sense of relief if we are accustomed to Vaughan's mode of virtuoso tightrope walking. More than any other great seventeenth-century poet (and he may be most characteristically Welsh in this) he lives by his momentary excitements, and by the fortunate coming together in his imagination of elements not obviously at one, vivid visual apprehensions, adroit effects of wit, lyric passion. It does not always happen that his first imaginative impulse can extend itself into a tightly sustained argument, or even maintain its lyric impetus. Donne, Herbert, Marvell are of stabler poetic temper than Vaughan. Without fervour he is nowhere.

The closure of 'The World' has its difficulties if Vaughan meant it to answer the questions he has raised. What can it really mean to say that the bridegroom provided the ring for none but his bride? Vaughan is undoubtedly thinking of a choice rather than a predestination, and the voice announces that the ring is reserved for those few who are willing to make themselves the brides of Christ by detaching themselves altogether from the love of worldly objects. The poem categorically (and curiously) distinguishes between their activities and the worldly concerns of all the rest. For them there will be no sexual love, policy, money, sensual delights, or anything but weeping and singing. Penitence and praise oddly become the means to salvation, while all else is damning distraction.

This is uncompromising enough, but we must assume that Vaughan means it. He is not the man to be seduced by a poetic flourish into a sense he would not stand by elsewhere; and in any case this is a critical moment in *Silex Scintillans*. We seem no longer to be countenancing a society in which Christian activity has place and grace. In Vaughan's poem the world claims its own as they choose it, and simply holds them down; the ring is not for them. All that matters, or can matter, is that we detach ourselves from this world so that we make the crossing spontaneously. We must live our eternity here and now.

This is not the kind of detachment from the world which follows out a resolve to live the life of spirit, rather than the life of sense. It is the proof of a moral exclusiveness which separates a few regenerate beings from most of human kind. Vaughan is not so much attacking a character he shares with all other men in virtue of our common humanity, as condemning those men who cut themselves off from the truth he sees. The poem mounts no general assault on our moral nature, or drama of the moral will. Vaughan does not involve himself in the human activities he condemns, or admit himself a citizen of that world at all.

Elsewhere in *Silex Scintillans* Vaughan's denunciations of 'the world' may prompt us to ask what it is in common life that merits such cat-

egorical dismissal. No doubt he needed to confirm his will in a renunciation which was not wholly easy to him, as Donne turns his keenest
raillery on the life of affairs he had involuntarily lost. But Donne knew
just what he was mocking, and partly mocked his own attachment to
that teeming life. The evidence of 'The World' is that in contrast with
Donne's enforced rustication Vaughan's was a self-chosen retirement,
which sustained itself by moral isolation and wholesale contempt. On
the one hand stands the regenerate poet, with a very few such solitary
strivers towards original innocence; on the other hand there is the world
of ordinary men, unregenerate and perhaps unredeemable. It is not
unlike the view of the depraved Old Testament world which Adam sees
from the high mount:

> Grey-headed men and grave, with Warriours mixt,
> Assemble, and Harangues are heard, but soon
> In factious opposition, till at last
> Of middle Age one rising, eminent
> In wise deport, spake much of Right and Wrong,
> Of Justice, of Religion, Truth and Peace,
> And Judgement from above: him old and young
> Exploded, and had seis'd with violent hands,
> Had not a Cloud descending snatcht him thence
> Unseen amid the throng: so Violence
> Proceeded, and Oppression, and Sword-Law
> Through all the Plain, and refuge none was found.
>
> *Paradise Lost* xi, 661–73

Vaughan regularly assumes such a view of his own situation but
rarely exposes the sense of the world in which it is founded, or shows
what his grasp of human motives really amounts to. Our interest in the
matter cannot be just that it is we who are being condemned. There is
no doubt that it was the attempt to define his own predicament in the
critical years around 1650 which fired his imagination; and the sources
of his power, as the reasons for his lapses, must concern us. 'The World'
has no such awful flats as some of the poems submit us to but the part
of the poem which rehearses the activities of us worldlings, though lively
enough, scarcely operates at the level of the rest. So often in Vaughan
the imaginative vitality comes and goes quite abruptly, and here we
may see where mere adroitness takes over.

After the casual splendour of his opening vision Vaughan's representative worldlings seem a farcical lot whom the poet himself cannot

take in earnest. His lover is a comic stereotype, silly rather than sinful and lacking even the dignity of lust; Vaughan characterises him as a foppish fool who scarcely knows what he is after, and asks no more than to dote on his mistress's beauty. Even Spenser's lustful monsters have more force than this, for at least they answer to something brutish in sensual nature. The miser is no better, a stock figure who hardly bears upon the monetary realities of Vaughan's or anybody else's day, and has little force even as a picture of covetousness. The dangerous world needs a better representative than this terrified accumulator of dust, whose self-destructive obsession with material things scarcely mirrors a human reality. Vaughan is not thinking concretely of the life around him at this point, as we see when we come to the epicures and light-minded people, about whose corrupting activities he cannot find anything specific to say at all.

The statesman is a different matter when his comportment is rendered with such Shelleyan savagery, which at least evinces some grasp of a real moral character, and of the baneful effects of politic schemings. Here Vaughan does show concern for civic action, and an awareness that life in the world may merit moral appraisal:

> but one did see
> That policie

To impute to the divine judge even that much concern for the unregenerate world is something. Vaughan more often writes as though God has simply withdrawn himself from that part of mankind which has turned its back upon him—'Ah! he is fled!' ('The British Church'). But he seems here to be writing of events which he knows too well to reduce or dismiss, and which merit their condemnation—'And Clouds of crying witnesses without/ Pursued him ... Churches and altars fed him ... It rain'd about him bloud and tears ... ' The writing at least shows up the flimsiness of the emblematic caricature he goes in for elsewhere, which simply evades the need to take civic life seriously.

The luminous beauty of the vision recommends the contrasting account of regenerate life:

> Yet some, who all this while did weep and sing,
> And sing, and weep, soar'd up into the *Ring*,
> But most would use no wing.

That 'soar'd up' lights the whole conceit, with its miming of a sudden marvellous release into universal grace from the drudgery of those earthbound pieties:

weep and sing,/ and sing, and weep, *soar'd* . . .

Away they go quite suddenly, as though launched by a power they had stored up in that laborious alternation of lament and hymning, by which they showed their preference for true light while the rest of us lived in grots and caves, and hated the day. That heavy ritual of devotion is recompensed by the bold flight which it makes possible:

> Because it shews the way,
> The way which from this dead and dark abode
> Leads up to God

Yet it seems strange that so many people should hate the day, and knowingly refuse the way to God. In Vaughan's terms their continuance in worldly enterprises is madness, for he simply does not allow that what they do may be useful and offer as much moral scope as single-minded devotion. As he represents it, sexual love no less than politics merits only stark condemnation and dismissal, since it is manifestly halfwitted to prefer such foolery to eternal life. He leaves us to ask why only lives devoted to penitence and praise should earn an eternal world.

To question the poem so is to resist that splendid sweep of the unfolding impulse with a cavil which does not trouble Vaughan. His whole concern is to display the gap between mere worldly bustle and vital life; and expressions of sheer vitality of spirit excited his imagination, whereas moral behaviour challenged his wit. He renders the activity of the creation with a vividness which persuades us of its spiritual life:

> stars nod and sleepe,
> And through the dark aire spin a firie thread
> Such as doth gild the lazie glow-worms bed.
> 'The Lampe'

How far do intelligence and imagination come together in the resolution of 'The World'? That sudden drop of the voice at the end is expressive, and the echo of Herbert lends authority to the last simple words. This cannot be God or Christ who speaks however, and it is evidently not one of the fools in his madness. We must take it for the voice of truth sounding through space, which settles rather than resolves the conflict of values the poem has opened. The poet's vision, thus dramatically completed, carries its own assurance that it is pointless for him to dispute with the fools, or seek to relieve their frenzy, since none of them can

307

make the vital leap anyway. Only those who love Christ rather than the world will be gathered into the pure and endless light of divine love. Vaughan's conceit puts an unbridgeable distance between the bride and the lovers of the world. Yet he seems to mean nothing more severe than that there is no easy way of finding the path which leads to God, or of learning to tread the sun:

> and be
> More bright than he.

A man must divorce himself from the world before he may betroth himself to Christ, for a life in the world can only distract him from the true end of love. The point of the whole movement, which the figure of the ring now completes with an emblematic quibble, seems to be that the way is there all right but worldly men cannot take it even if they would. Here there can be no doubting Vaughan's drift. He means that we fix ourselves in our eternal attitude here and now in our present existence, either as distracted dust or as singleminded lovers. When we put our worldly concerns behind us and betroth ourselves to Christ we leave the world while still physically existing in it, and move spontaneously and inevitably towards the ring. 'The World' turns out to be a celebration of love from its opening image to its final words, marking the distance between those who fit themselves to love, and those who fail to love aright.

The poem intimates that the greater part of mankind will not be saved, but that the few who attain the ring, and the many who cannot reach it, alike will their condition; we save ourselves by our resolute choice of Christ rather than the world. If his antithesis between Christ and 'the world' is valid then eternal being and our human activities in the world simply exclude each other, and the election of one or other is enough in itself to settle all merely moral issues. Once we make our choice then the frailties of human nature remain with the worldlings, and the elect must simply seek to avoid the occasions of frailty; as though the battle with the self is then over and people can do no more than confirm themselves in their chosen course, hastening their own dissolution in a myriad of worldly pursuits, or heightening the fervour of their aspiration towards that country beyond the stars. Such conflict as remains must thereafter be fought out not within the self but between two camps; though what Vaughan anticipates is not a conflict but an implacable mutual disdain.

Like Dante, Vaughan offers us an image of the spheres for an emblem of love. Yet Vaughan's device quite disjoins time from eternity, directly opposing the activities of the fallen world to the ardours that gain us Christ's love and the ring of espousal. Dante's shaping conceit of the continuity, or interpenetration, of the orders of being is crucially modified in this poem by Vaughan's conviction that men must recover their innocence before they may rise from earth to light. 'The World' offers us at best a heroic leap across the gulf, and tells us that for most men there will be no crossing at all. We need not look for a Beatrice to mediate the espousals of *Silex Scintillans*.

Vaughan's self-isolation from the public life of his day after the debacle of 1648–9 made a bogy of every distraction from regenerative love. The arch-adversaries of the poet of *Silex Scintillans* are not the forces of hell, or even the sins that make him unreceptive to grace, but the world itself, and death. It is what he makes of our encounters with these corruptions that proves him. No other seventeenth-century poet who concerns us, not even Traherne, believes anything like this. Vaughan's radical attack on worldly life gives him more in common with Bunyan than with Herbert; indeed his supposed discipleship to Herbert must be called in question when the two men took such different views of their spiritual situation, and of themselves. To see *Silex Scintillans* as a visionary version of *The Temple* is to harm Vaughan with a false expectation, for the two works use devotional poetry to quite different ends. Yet Vaughan is no spiritual sport; on the contrary, he gives imaginative authenticity to some of the most powerful ideas which were running in the seventeenth century, and part of the excitement of his writing comes from his perception of a wholeness in those ideas which he took for final truth.

Vaughan is unlike other seventeenth-century devotional poets in that he does not undertake to speak for all men. A man may have no thought of publication when he writes out of his own solitary circumstances, and yet suppose himself to stand in the same predicament as all other human beings; so that his own spiritual wrestlings have a common substance. Donne's *Holy Sonnets*, written for himself and a few friends, express the general dilemma of fallen men who must seek God's grace before they can move to save themselves. Yet Vaughan's concern extends no further than the 'some' of the present poem; and we might ask how far his devotional attitudes as such could have drawn in anyone beyond that small circle even in his own day, when their tendency is so exclusive. But then even his 'some' expresses a notional allegiance, for one of the idiosyncrasies of *Silex Scintillans* is that it conveys no effective sense of community with living men at all, or of a communion with that regenerate few. Vaughan's relationship with his God, as with the countryside in which he lived, is regulated by the sheer force of his own apprehensions and ardours. The common sympathy he feels and most movingly expresses is with the dead, and with those living processes of nature which intimated to him a spiritual renewal beyond the grave, or a possible rebirth into our lost innocence. In his poems he stands alone amidst the natural creation, seeking his own rehabilitation in the order of love:

> I will not fear what man,
> With all his plots and power can;
> Bags that wax old may plundered be,
> But none can sequester or let
> A state that with the Sun doth set
> And comes next morning fresh as he
> 'Providence'

After the civil wars many men, and not only Royalists, must have felt themselves to be lone survivors in a dangerous world. But Vaughan has far more than historical testimony to offer us. He is one of those artists who strive to live out their vision; and for all our cavils, it was no mean prospect of love that he fashioned for himself out of the great legacy of Christian metaphysics. *Silex Scintillans* is the attempt of a man reborn from corruption to see the universe anew, and aright, by the sheer force of his purged imagination. Small wonder if his glimpses of glory isolated him from the ruinous world he saw around him, and were not readily reducible to lessons for life.

Notes

1. J. D. Sinclair, *The Divine Comedy of Dante Alighieri*, 1971, III, p. 400.

ROGER D. SELL

The Unstable Discourse
of Henry Vaughan:
A Literary-Pragmatic Account

The vast majority of Vaughan's poems, secular and religious, are competent and readable enough, and should offer few problems to the critical commentator. We find familiar diction and themes—of love, of satire, of retirement, of devotion—which we can classify by reference to other poets Cavalier and Metaphysical. In the devotional poems the forepresence of Herbert is especially strong, and we find echoes of the Bible and hermetic writers as well. Perhaps we sometimes feel that he's actually derivative.[1] And certainly, although *Silex Scintillans* is sometimes explicated as a sustained devotional achievement in the manner of *The Temple*, the comparison is mainly to Herbert's advantage. But for all that, and despite some clumsinesses and quaintnesses, nobody would wish to deny that the general level of Vaughan's workmanship is respectable.[2]

The problem comes with Vaughan at his best. Here he does at least, by common consent, transmute his borrowings to his own uses. Nor can there be much disagreement about where the best is actually to be found: in a number of poems in *Silex Scintillans*. What very much is at issue are two main points. First, the question of this best's precise extent. In the past thirty or forty years, whole poems by Vaughan have sometimes been praised as organic unities of a high imaginative inten-

Published here for the first time by permission of Roger D. Sell.

sity. On the other hand, there have always been those who experience Vaughan's best as a more Longinian sublimity, spasmodic as flashes of lightning. Secondly, Vaughan's best seems insistently to raise the question of his own involvement in his writing. Some modern critics have made an Eliotian separation between the man who suffers and the mind which creates, so that *Silex Scintillans* becomes an exclusively literary monument. In the older tradition of criticism, the collection is seen as a record of Vaughan's own spiritual life, which in turn gives rise to further debate on that life's precise quality. Was he a sudden convert?[3] Did illness play a part?[4] Was he a mystic?[5]

It is not part of my intention to label individual critics as either modern or traditional. For one thing, some of them have divided loyalties. Frank Kermode, for instance, takes up the traditional topic of the precise quality of Vaughan's religious life—"he is in no sense a mystic"—yet in the same sentence reiterates his modern claim that *Silex Scintillans* is a purely literary monument—"he makes a poet's use of the mystic's language." Kermode muddies the water by supporting his traditional biographical argument by reference to the poems, which on his more modern view are only literary.[6] For another thing, too tidy a classification of Vaughan critics might conceal another instructive truth: that some traditional critics are not as fully traditional as the terms of such a classification would suggest, and some modern ones not as modern. Not every modern critic has detected both organic unity and purely literary scope.[7] Not every traditional critic has found Vaughan's best poetry both intermittent in its magnificence, and autobiographical.[8]

In Anglo-American criticism a lack of completeness and system can never be surprising, and actually offers some dividends. If you have a system and it happens to be wrong, then much of what you say will be wrong as well. If you have no system but you happen to be a good reader, you may hit on the truth pretty often. A fully thought-out account does have its usefulness, however, if only by making its own weaknesses more apparent. And in the case of Vaughan, the two halves of both the traditional and the modern tendencies have a close relation to each other which we should not allow their piecemeal expression by some flesh-and-blood critics to obscure. If, with the traditionalists, you believe that Vaughan's poetry is true to autobiographical origins, then erratic splendours will make it seem the more authentic, the wind of the spirit blowing as it lists through the Aeolian lyre of his sensibility. Conversely, if you believe that none of the poetry is in a real sense autobiographical and account for the best of it in terms of artistry, then the more artistry you can find the better. Every lapse from the perfect form of the aesthetic heterocosm is presumably a lapse into something else, which might just be life.

Especially with its two theses thus explicitly connected, the formalism of the modern tendency now looks decidedly old-fashioned. It stems from a period when, not only many literary critics, but also some philosophers and linguists were deeply suspicious of ordinary speech and tried to isolate something "better"—the "special language" of literature, Russell's logic, *langue* as opposed to *parole*. Three major branches of the humanities were actually in danger of forgetting something major about human beings: the ways in which language is actually used and experienced.

This lack of reality has sadly persisted in some literary theorizing,[9] but in Philosophy and Linguistics there have long been other developments: the later Wittgenstein's explorations of language in use, followed by the speech-act theory developed by Searle from Austin and Grice; and Anthropological Linguistics, Sociolinguistics, Psycholinguistics, Discourse Analysis and Pragmatics. Broadening the philosophical focus from abstract truth values, and the linguistic focus from syntax and semantics, such developments have emphasized that both meaning and linguistic form are always inextricably bound up with ongoing sociocultural and interpersonal contexts. Without such contexts, no particular meanings or forms would become applicable in the first place.

Since this insight relates to written no less than to spoken texts, it is no longer possible to speak of a formalist hermetic seal between "literary" discourse and "ordinary" discourse. The "world of literature" and the "real world" interpenetrate, and although in the texts we call literary there are certainly features of patterning, structure and beauty, no such features are peculiar to those texts. Certain texts, rather, are called literary under certain conditions, and all texts perform actions of one sort or another in the real world. The questions for textual research are: What kind of action? When? And how? When I speak of Literary Pragmatics I have in mind a body of textual research, now at last growing in volume and strength, which is devoted, not to quintessentializing a special literary immanence, but to studying the enabling relations between those text-acts we designate as literary and their context. Not the least concern is with how the designation actually comes to be made. Other general problems include the various kinds of socio-

313

cultural and interpersonal acts that a literary text can perform, the definition of contexts, and the textual encoding of context in lexis and syntax. This last problem is tied up with a phenomenon known as deixis, which will be of central importance to the present paper. More specialized problems have to do with different levels and strategies of politeness and, for narrative texts, with different kinds of "tellability." These problems I have touched on elsewhere.[10]

Now from the standpoint of Literary Pragmatics, the traditional account of Vaughan seems decidedly up-to-date. It is at least based, after all, on a firm conception of how *Silex Scintillans* acts or acted in the world: through Vaughan's self-expression and personal example, the flagging faith of Christian readers might be encouraged. The modern account, on the other hand, not only lacks a theory of text action but is also much more difficult to prove. With Literary Pragmatics to back us up, we can even claim that the modern account is to no small degree counter-intuitive.

In its opposition to autobiographical considerations it is counter-intuitive partly because Vaughan himself, in the preliminary matter for both the first (1650) and the expanded (1655) editions of *Silex Scintillans*, clearly states what one might call the poems' autobiographical corollary, and because the collection subtitle states that some of the contents are in fact "private ejaculations." On what grounds can we ignore these statements? Certainly not by claiming that they offer merely extrinsic information. The whole force of Literary Pragmatics is to remind us what they really are: part of the introductory guidance Vaughan offers the reader, given special prominence by their position in the book and the different format—the title-page and an emblem with a Latin poem in italics in 1650, a discursive prose preface directly addressing the reader in 1655. They sensitize the reader to the autobiographical undercurrent, and imply Vaughan's hope that the reader will find the poems a stimulus to spiritual activity of his own. Up until the present century most readers obviously took them at face value and, on reading the poems, perhaps found Vaughan's hope being realized. Many readers still do so today, and even non-religious readers often take the poems as a moving expression of Vaughan's sincere hopes, despondencies and exhortations, something which could never happen if the writing were not felt to come from the heart. For some passages, it's true, the 1655 preface admits that 'the *history* or *reason* may seem something remote'. But it continues:

> Were they <this history and reason> brought *nearer*, and
> plainly exposed to your view, (though that (perhaps) might
> quiet your *curiosity*) yet would it not conduce to your greater
> *advantage*. And therefore I must desire you to accept them in
> that *latitude*, which is already allowed them.
>
> (P. 143.)

Vaughan is understandably reluctant to reveal very personal details,
yet still wishes the personal vibration to register. None of which necessarily means that he records a sudden conversion or all five steps of
the *via mystica*, or that, in order to be an act of expressive devotion and
exhortation, the poems have to be 'action' poems as well: as much as
anything, they are probably remembered, or re-created experience. No,
the point is only that, if we are to read the poems as anything other
than autobiographical, we shall have to include as part of our account
of standard reading competence a rule to the effect that when an author
prefaces a text with a statement of sincerity, and actually seems in the
text to be sincere, we do not take him literally. Such a rule may seem
to work for Swift, but in Swift there are actually irony signals, and for
Vaughan it is patently no good at all. We must always be allowed, when
due occasion arises, to take poetry straight, and to take it as personal,
just like much other discourse.

The prefatory materials also challenge the modern critics' organ-
icist claims for Vaughan. The 1650 emblematic conceit of the flashing
heart-flint suggests an intensity that is intermittent (*"En lacerum! coelosque
tuos ardentia tandem/ Fragmenta"*), and the 1655 preface even states that
the poems' artistry is much less important than the true perfection and
holiness of spirit in which Vaughan has tried to conceive them. Men-
tioning Herbert as the first 'that with any effectual success attempted
a diversion of . . . /the/ foul and overflowing *stream*' of vicious and sensual
verse, Vaughan says that Herbert's record in winning over "pious con-
verts" has not been matched by those aiming

> more at *verse*, than perfection; . . . for not flowing from a true,
> practic piety, it was impossible they should effect those things
> abroad, which they never had acquaintance with at home.
>
> (P. 142.)

There is more than a hint, indeed, that artistic excellence and sincerity
of spirit don't always go hand in hand. This, the attitude of countless
statements of pious intention from Southwell, Sir John Beaumont and

Herbert up to hymnbooks published in our own time, again anticipates what I am calling the traditional account of Vaughan. And once again, the perspective is essentially pragmatic. Given the discoursal circumstances, most of Vaughan's poems have precisely the degree of formal excellence one might expect. Texts intended as vehicles of devotion to be used by a large community—and Vaughan, I shall soon suggest, did have a large community in mind—must obviously stick to essentials. Too many refinements of style or structure would almost amount to bad taste. In this light, then, that merely respectable level of workmanship and readability in Vaughan of which I spoke at the outset begins to look much more like a considerable merit. Which is not to deny that some of his devotional poems have an intensity far more impressive than others. But clearly, if some critics wish to claim that his best work is always a matter, not only of sublime flashes, but of sustained wholes, then the onus of proof is decidedly on them.

The kind of unity for which modern critics have argued is really a unity of thought, a thematic unity in the arrangement of ideas and subject matter. George Williamson says that many poems depend on the witty exploration of contrasts, religious ideas and paradoxes in particular.[11] Others seek to show that poems are structured along the lines of well established practices of devotional meditation. Louis L. Martz, for instance, claims that "I walked the other day," the poem on which the present paper will eventually focus in detail and which is printed here as an appendix, falls into three groups of three stanzas: I-III, the evocation of the image for analysis; IV-VI, the process of understanding; and VII-IX, the colloquy with God. This corresponds to a traditional contemplative structure.[12]

Yet while Vaughan's best work may have such structures, they are not what makes it sometimes verge on greatness. Similar structures will be found in many of his run-of-the-mill pieces of 'practic piety', and to talk as if part of the impression made by his best writing is of a strict tidiness gives the wrong idea. For there is, in Vaughan's best, something peculiarly unaccountable and disconcerting, a quality, quite inimitable, that does not need an extensive structure to make its presence felt. Sometimes it is something in the way he uses a short line after a long. Often we feel it in just a line, a clause, a phrase. Here are three examples, each preceded by two alternatives designed to make Vaughan's oddity more obvious:

1 a. And peep into the box
  b. And into glory soar
  c. And into glory peep
    ('They are all gone into a world of light', pp. 246–47)
2 a. You two villains, get you packing
  b. Death and darkness be not proud
  c. Death, and darkness get you packing
    ("Easter-Hymn," p. 216)
3 a. I saw your grandmother the other night
  b. And with eternity my sight was dazzled
  c. I saw Eternity the other night
    (The World," pp. 227–28)

In each case, the colloquial-mundane (a) and the eschatological-sublime (b) are juxtaposed in Vaughan's colloquial-sublime (c). I say juxtaposed, and not fused, deliberately. The reader does not necessarily experience such items as a reconciliation of opposites made possible in an aesthetic heterocosm. In our own minds, the two types of perception may actually remain in friction, so that Vaughan emerges as somebody who, envisaging or recording something astonishing, is himself astonishing by apparently not being astonished. Astonishing, and a source of potential strength to others, his words setting our nerves slightly on edge as a still living example of metaphysics domesticated. Where the wit and style of Donne's "Death be not proud" nobly fights to lord it over death for fourteen magnificent lines, the single line of example 2 above, by breaking style, has won without a thought.

Large structures such as those sometimes correctly described by Williamson and Martz are the Procrustean beds on which Vaughan's elusive best refuses to be bound. Martz's discussion of "I walked the other day" itself has some sense of this, for Martz is clearly a little disconcerted by stanza V. This stanza seems to contain a sudden shift from the doctrine so appropriate to the middle, "understanding" phase of meditation into a passionate personal outburst. Martz calls the shift natural, and is able to point out that stanza VI concludes the "understanding" stage with greater objectivity. But he does seem to feel that passionate personal outbursts shouldn't really come before phase three, the colloquy with God. I shall soon be arguing that the poem is distinctively Vaughan's precisely by thwarting such expectations, both here and elsewhere.[13] Also, it so happens that stanza V's shift is at once a shift and not a shift. As so often, and in so many different ways, Vaughan is irreducibly polyvocal.

Another most distinctive poem that has been sadly reduced is "The World," from which, of course, example 3 above was taken.

> I saw Eternity the other night
> Like a great *Ring* of pure and endless light,
> All calm, as it was bright.... (P. 227.)

What the modern critic effectually says at this point is: "Wait! Don't let the lines reverberate too much. They don't mean what they say. Vaughan is not Dante. He's not a mystic either, and even if he were his poems are purely literary. The ring is a conceit which he uses in several other contexts as well. Here, he cleverly resumes it at the end of the poem, as the ring which Christ the bridegroom places on the finger of his church-bride. In the main body of the poem Vaughan satirizes the worldly by way of a telling and carefully structured contrast."[14] Once again, the traditionalist-cum-pragmaticist will be perfectly ready to acquiesce in the broad outline of the structure described. It is impossible to read the poem without registering the witty turn of the close. Yet the turn is just that: at the close. And although the pragmaticist will disagree with Stanley Fish about how we receive individual sentences—since we can hold our perception of meaning in suspense until we reach a pause and punctuation—Fish's "affective stylistics" can certainly be applied to entire poems. In "The World," eternity is first perceived as a great ring of pure and endless light, and nothing can stop us immediately responding accordingly: the witty turn fifty-eight lines later cannot erase the experience. What could, ever? The poem has us, rather, responding in two different ways at two different points. Or, to be more accurate, three different ways, since the central, Juvenalian section has a most stirring severity of tone. Mystical serenity, then, followed by *saeva indignatio*, followed by devout wit. "Decorum" or "artistic unity" are the last labels we should apply to such a poem, for they would obscure what is surely our strongest impression: the interpersonal challenge generated by a most uncannily erratic individual.

So do the best poems have coherence thanks to Vaughan's very individuality? In part, yes. The pragmaticist, who does not believe in "the death of the author," and who does not believe that authors never mean what they say, will regard the reader's developing sense of Vaughan's personality as part of the ongoing context in which each new poem is read. It is part of what gives his words significance, an exemplary significance which will, I have suggested, be apparent to readers, prophane or religious, in any age.

Yet that significance is still significance in the abstract. And although it just might seem to cover the domestication of metaphysics in a phrase like "into glory peep," or a bi-vocality of mystic serenity and devout wit, the actual polyvocality of "The World" is less tractable. What rime or reason can there be to such an individual? Is the poem just whirling words or a parade of poses? Well no, it isn't. But the only way of now restoring coherence to it is, not by forcing an alien aesthetic unity upon it or by making its wit do service for such a unity, but through the use of our historical knowledge and imagination. Beauty of a kind the poem—the poem as a whole—does have. But beauty, I submit, is sometimes of history, and in this case has something to do with the unique fit of Vaughan, himself a part of the context, with the larger situation in which he wrote. Knowledge of this situation pragmatically sensitizes a reader to a larger dimension of exemplariness in poems bi-vocal and polyvocal alike, an exemplariness which as a response to the situation is nothing if not magnificently beautiful. The situation is, of course, the period of rule by the Puritans, whose statesmen and bourgeoisie "The World" is satirizing, and under whom well-descended Cavalier Anglicans like Vaughan and the large community of readers he envisaged were suffering such severe restraints.[15] "The World" rages, and shows how to rage, yet is still able to offer alternatives to rage in serenity and wit, setting an example probably more effective than Vaughan's several prose translations and treatises on such subjects as retirement, devotion, and how to benefit by our enemies. And clearly, this fuller significance, once one has begun to grasp it, so far from explaining the strangenesses of the poem away, only makes it the more surprising. It represents a moral achievement that is disconcertingly resistant to artistic decorum.

Every text, however, whether written or spoken, not only needs a context to clinch the significance. It also has to pay a kind of linguistic deference to the context's pragmatic importance. More precisely, it must encode a certain minimal amount of context within itself, so that its recipients can begin to work pragmatically from context to significance. Students of pragmatics refer to this self-contextualization by texts as deixis. I shall close by examining some of the deixis of "I walked the other day," in an attempt to show that here is yet another source, also best discussed in terms of pragmatics, of Vaughan's queerly disconcerting power.

Deixis is usually subdivided into person deixis, time deixis, place deixis, social deixis and discourse deixis.[16] Person deixis helps to situate the discourse in relation to the addresser (the first person role), the addressee (the second person role) and the thing or person discussed (the third person role). It is achieved largely by the choice of pronouns and nominals and concordant verb forms. Time deixis assigns a point of time to both the thing discussed (content-time, in my own terminology) and the addressee's reception of the discourse (receiving time), both points being defined in relation to the time at which the addresser makes the utterance (coding time). It is achieved largely through tense and adverbials of time. Place deixis locates both the thing discussed and the addressee in spatial relation to the addresser, mainly using different types of definite expression (e.g. this one/that one) and place adverbials. Social deixis is a matter of the addressee's indicating his assessment of his own social status relative to the addressee and the thing or persons discussed. In some languages it is partly achieved by special honorific forms. Discourse deixis is rather different from all the other types, since it is reflexive or metadiscoursal. It relates one section of discourse to another section of the same discourse, largely by means of signpost expressions such as "therefore," "in the previous paragraph" and so on.

A more detailed account of deixis would strongly suggest that languages originally developed for communication in face-to-face interaction.[17] The canonical situation involves one-one or one-many signalling in the phonic medium along the vocal-auditory channel, with all the participants able to see one another and perceive the paralinguistic concomitants of speech, and with different participants assuming the roles of speaker and receiver in turn. Furthermore, the deixis of most utterances tends to anchor them to their context, not randomly, but in such a way that the anchorage points constitute a so-called deictic centre. The central person is the speaker. The central time is his coding time. The central place is his location at coding time. The social centre is the speaker's own rank. And the discourse centre is the point in the discourse at which the speaker has currently arrived.

Needless to say, however, changes are constantly rung on the canonical situation of language use, and there are many ways in which the deictic centre can be shifted or projected. Livia Polanyi has shown, for instance, that the deixis of oral narratives is a factor in setting up the intradiegetic world of the story over against an extradiegetic world of the narrator, with its own "I-now-here." She analyses the subtle ways in which an oral narrator can exploit this circumstance.[18]

But what of written texts? Livia Polanyi's article is actually one of a collection devoted to exploring the differences between written and oral discourse. The conclusion she comes to is that written narratives actually offer fewer openings for sophistication, because they don't have, in addition to the intradiegetic world, the real-life "I-now-here" of the teller facing his audience eye to eye. But perhaps this matter needs re-thinking. Whereas for oral texts coding time and receiving time are identical, thus providing only one alternative to an intradiegetic content-time, for written texts coding time and receiving time are never the same, thus providing two alternatives and far more openings for deictic projection.

Few writers seize on them with the opportunistic brio of Laurence Sterne, but Vaughan sometimes comes fairly close. One sentence in the 1655 preface to *Silex Scintillans* could almost be straight from *Tristram Shandy*—

> By the last *poems* in the book (were not that mistake here prevented) you would judge all to be *fatherless*, and the *edition* posthume; for (indeed) *I was nigh unto death*, and am still at no great distance from it; which was the necessary reason for that solemn and accomplished *dress*, you will now find this *impression* in. (P. 143.)

—and it sensitizes the reader to further deictic projections in the poems themselves. "The Search" opens in the present tense, "Tis now clear day: I see a Rose/Bud in the bright East, and disclose/The Pilgrim-Sun." Coding time and content-time, then, are purportedly the same. Lines 3–65, however, separate them from each other, describing in past tenses how he has reached this, the poem's apparent time centre, by roving all night in search of his Saviour. By lines 65–66 he has brought the account up to date, as it seems, and again we have present tense and a purported concurrence of coding time and content-time: "... see, it is day,/The sun's broke through to guide my way." But then, in a move reminiscent of Herbert's "The Collar," but with a shift of deictic

321

centre which in Herbert was ruled out by the use of past tense *throughout* a characteristically much more stable discourse, Vaughan starts a new verse paragraph:

> ...see, it is day,
> The sun's broke through to guide my way.
> But as I urged thus and writ down
> What pleasures should my journey crown....

Coding time is again separated from content-time, on this occasion through the setting up of a new coding time subsequent to the previous one. Person deixis, on the other hand, remains the same as in lines 3–65: both the first person role and the third person role are filled by "I," while the reader fills the second person role. Then, however, comes another shift:

> But as I urged thus and writ down
> What pleasures should my journey crown, ...
> Me thought I heard one singing thus;
> l
> Leave, leave, thy gadding thoughts;
> > Who pores
> > and spies
> Still out of doors
> > descries
> Within them nought.   (Pp. 157–59)

Here person deixis is involved, the first person role being taken over by that of the singer of the monitory song (God? An angel? The Christian church? Wisdom?), and the "I" taking the second person role, or part of the second person role, rather, since the reader has already been established in this role and is not explicitly released from it. The reader, in other words, has to attend to the warning as well. Or to express it another way, the deixis shift makes the poem's "I" a representative for all mankind. This happens in several other poems by Vaughan, the most strikingly obvious case perhaps being "Man's Fall, and Recovery": with the help of several time shifts, the "I" becomes at once Vaughan, Adam, and everyone in between. In some poems the "you" or implied "you" actually merges with "I" to give "we," while the second person role is taken over by God. Thus, in shorthand form, a frequent devotional pattern is: "I have sinned. O god, forgive us!" or "I rejoice in my Saviour. O god, accept our thanks." Deictic place centre often shifts just as conspicuously, with coding-time "here" coinciding with receiving-time "there." And so on.

Some such marked shifting occurs in much writing, and in many texts it is as conspicuous as in these examples from Vaughan. The "I ... O God ... we" movement, for instance, could have been learnt from Sir John Beaumont (from whom, incidentally, I think Vaughan could have learnt other things as well).[19] More distinctive of Vaughan at his slightly disconcerting best are less self-advertizing shifts, so rapid as to be hardly noticeable. By this means the field of interpersonal activity between writer and reader is electrified, the reader for ever drawn into the communicative act, partly through sheer perceptual curiosity as to its deixis and never quite sure where he will be led, often unable to remember, when he arrives somewhere, quite how he got there. "I walked the other day" is in this respect one of Vaughan's most miraculous oddities, and I now invite my reader to examine its person, time and place deixis in some detail.[20]

The title and first line of the poem make us expect that Vaughan himself is going to play both first and third person roles, and we ourselves the second person role: he will tell us about something he himself did in a content-time$_1$ prior to coding time. The pilcrow, which we have already seen at the head of the collection's most personal poems, serves to strengthen this expectation, and line 2 sets up the story-place naturally enough: a field, which is neither the coding place nor our receiving place. But then line 3's pluperfect helps to thrust us immediately further back to a content-time$_2$ before content-time$_1$. In line 5, 'winter now had ruffled' seems to bring things back to content-time$_1$, yet the *erlebte Rede* of the 'now' also narrows the gap between content-time$_1$ and coding time, an effect which is heightened by the remarkable jumble of PROXIMATENESS and NON-PROXIMATENESS semes in line 7's 'I knew there heretofore'. This line may even begin to narrow the gap between coding time and receiving time.

Certainly, the reader's involvement in the story is intensified by the shift to direct speech in lines 10–14, with the forms "this here" and "sees," both marked for PROXIMATENESS. There is even a concomitant hint of the first and second person roles coalescing: "sees *us* but once a year" (my italics). This hint is developing in line 21, and by then content-time has already been separated off (by "Then," "could," "digged," "That place," "saw," all marked for NON-PROXIMATE-NESS), so that the author-in-first-person-role and the reader stand in a shared time and place, contemplating the author-in-third-person-role in content-time₁.

The author in content-time₁, in his turn, contemplates a new third person emerging: the bulb. This, very unexpectedly for twentieth-century users of English, but a little less unexpectedly for seventeenth-century users, which is more characteristic of the *slight* unease Vaughan creates, is referred to (ll. 17, 21, 24, 26) by the humanizing, masculine pronoun. It even teeters on the brink of a first-person role: the "that" of l.24 introduces an indirect speech construction which holds it to content-time, but it nevertheless becomes the subject of the verbs in lines 25–28, temporarily replacing the author.

"There" in line 23 and line 25 again suggests content-time, but "this air" in line 26, disconcertingly, is at once content-air, coding air and receiving air, just as "ere long come forth" in line 27 relates to a future soon after content-, coding and receiving time. The "This passed" of line 29 seems firmly to separate content-time off again, yet from line 33 to line 42 the direct speech, with its present tenses and PROXI-MATENESS semes in "now" and "here" (ll. 34, 38), brings about both a temporal and a spatial coalescence. Again there is continuing oddity in the lexicalization of the bulb and its immediate surroundings. One could even be forgiven for wondering whether the content-place has shifted from the field to a deathbed. In the diction of line 42 there seems to be an equal and opposite *de*humanization of real people to earth, with eternal-present time reference. The story seems to be happening in more than one place, in more than one simple time, between agents of oddly shifting quality.

Lines 33–35, which Martz describes simply as a passionately personal deviation from objective doctrine, are actually, as the italics indicate, at the same time objective doctrine as well. Cf. Revelation XIV 13: 'And I heard a voice from heaven saying unto me, Write, Blessed are the dead which die in the Lord from henceforth: Yea, saith the Spirit, that they may rest from their labours . . .'²¹ Who, then, actually speaks these lines? In one sense, certainly, the poet in content-time ("I" in l. 29). But don't we also hear other voices?—the voice from heaven, or the spirit, in Revelation the writer of Revelation; the poet at coding time; all Christians always. Such allusiveness is clearly a much more subtle event than irony. Pragmaticists have defined irony as the mention of an utterance that is not an actual use of it.²² If, in pouring rain, somebody says, "Nice day!" this is the mention of an utterance that would be more accurate in other circumstances, and it is interpreted by the hearer as ironically not meaning what it seems to say in the abstract. But Vaughan both mentions the biblical idea and uses it. The wish he addresses to the Bible in "Holy Scriptures" has been fulfilled: "O that I had deep cut in my hard heart/ Each line in thee!" He can now speak "in lines of my Lord's penning." All of which means that the words we read are of more than one time as well. The poem's deixis is increasingly multivalent.

At line 43 there is some sharp deictic switching, as the second person role is transferred to God and we are referred back to an earliest time of all. "This frame" (1. 46) seems to refer to the created universe in which both coding place and receiving place have hitherto been located, but the "I" in lines 48–63 still keeps the speaker separate from the "other" recipient (that reader or "overhearer" who is not God Himself) and at coding time only. Nevertheless, the invocation of God is so sustained, God actually becoming the subject of many verbs from line 43 to line 61, that the real reader is almost forced, as at the end of "The Search," to align with the "I," associating himself in the pious ejaculation. The sustained PROXIMATENESS semes assist this ("here below," "in these masks," "this care"), especially since their only contrast is with NON-PROXIMATENESS semes used of heaven ("those hid ascents," "that day," "above," "there"). Similarly, the point of future time in which the "I" hopes the spiritual uplifting will take place is unspecific: it could be between coding time and receiving time, but it could just as well be after receiving time, so that the reader could share it simultaneously. In that future time, access will be achieved to a realm in which God's glory can only be expressed in the eternal present ("breaks," "art," "move"), thus occasioning the poem its most striking deictic shift so far.

This is one of the reasons why the last three lines are so irreducibly unsettling. The focus suddenly shifts right back, to before receiving time, to coding time. Furthermore, though, there is a slight shock as the earlier odd references to the bulb are suddenly recycled as—what we had perhaps begun to suspect—metaphor for a dead loved-one. Thirdly, the speaker is suddenly highlighted in very sharp isolation from everything and everybody he has previously spoken of or to: God, the bulb, the loved-one, and, most oddly of all, us, the reader. The colloquy with God, with emotional upsurge which Martz rightly detected as part of the larger structure, and in which the reader was deictically encouraged to participate, unaccountably tails off. We feel left up in the air, awkward and embarrassed for Vaughan's sake. We half look up towards God. We half look down at Vaughan, so inveterately fixed in his eternal present of grief: an hour in the field the other day has been only the briefest intermission. In the poem's last two lines its deictic centre finally comes to rest: a grieving "I" in first person role, a grieving "I" in third, with no very definite second person to hear him (God? us?), in the eternity of grief, at the particular place of grief. The text's one piece of discourse deixis, the "Thus" of the last line, sets the seal on this stabilization. And by the same token the poem comes to an end. No further search for happiness, no further deictic projection from the heavy reality, can for the moment be sustained.

The poem's conclusion, then, gives us Vaughan at his lowest spiritual ebb. Clearly, the exemplary function of *Silex Scintillans* resides not so much in the individual poems as in the movement between the poles of eternal grief and eternal hope throughout the sequence as a whole— the movement between "I walked the other day" and "The World." But my discussion of the deixis of the one instance and the strangely polyvocal coherence of the other also hints that in Vaughan's best poems both poles can be represented on the smaller scale. In "I walked the other day," the nervous instability of the deictic projections through which Vaughan tries to move from the one pole to the other is in no small degree the source of the poem's odd power to disconcert.

So by way of conclusion I can now perhaps state my general argument in its sharpest form. The power to disconcert, in all Vaughan's best work, ultimately has very little to do with what we should normally understand by artistry and structure. Artistry and structure are certainly to be found in abundance in his poems, both the run-of-the-mill ones and the best ones. Without artistry and structure they might not hold together at all, and from this point of view his modern critics have performed a valuable service. The traditional view of him is more profoundly true, however, since what lifts him to a more remarkable kind of writing is frankly a matter of psychic input. This varies, giving his best texts, whether poems of hope or poems of grief, a live, unplanned— despite the obvious planning—flavour, which is actually reminiscent of informal oral communication.[23] As written discourse, and even more as literary discourse, they have a fascinating instability in style, coherence and deixis, whose workings in their full context we can now begin to study in the spirit of Literary Pragmatics.

Appendix

'*I walked the other day*'

1

I walked the other day (to spend my hour)
    Into a field
Where I sometimes had seen the soil to yield
    A gallant flower,
But winter now had ruffled all the bower
    And curious store
    I knew there heretofore.

2

Yet I whose search loved not to peep and peer
    I'the face of things
10   Thought with my self, there might be other springs
    Besides this here
Which, like cold friends, sees us but once a year,
    And so the flower
    Might have some other bower.

3

Then taking up what I could nearest spy
    I digged about
That place where I had seen him to grow out,
    And by and by
I saw the warm recluse alone to lie
20   Where fresh and green
    He lived of us unseen.

4

Many a question intricate and rare
    Did I there strow,
But all I could extort was, that he now
    Did there repair
Such losses as befell him in this air

(Reprinted from: *Henry Vaughan: The Complete Poems*, edited by Alan Rudrum, Penguin Books (1976) 1983, pp. 240–42)

And would ere long
Come forth most fair and young.

5

This passed, I threw the clothes quite o'er his head,
30   And stung with fear
Of my own frailty dropped down many a tear
     Upon his bed,
Then sighing whispered, *Happy are the dead!*
     What peace doth now
     Rock him asleep below?

6

And yet, how few believe such doctrine springs
     From a poor root
Which all the winter sleeps here under foot
     And hath no wings
40 To raise it to the truth and light of things,
     But is still trod
     By every wandering clod.

7

O thou! whose spirit did at first inflame
     And warm the dead,
And by a sacred incubation fed
     With life this frame
Which once had neither being, form, nor name,
     Grant I may so
     Thy steps track here below,

8

50 That in these masques and shadows I may see
     Thy sacred way,
And by those hid ascents climb to that day
     Which breaks from thee
Who art in all things, though invisibly;
     Show me thy peace,
     Thy mercy, love, and ease,

9

And from this care, where dreams and sorrows reign
     Lead me above

UNSTABLE DISCOURSE OF VAUGHAN

60
Where light, joy, leisure, and true comforts move
Without all pain,
There, hid in thee, show me his life again
At whose dumb urn
Thus all the year I mourn.

Notes

1. A feeling that receives a somewhat surprising formulation in T. S. Eliot, who says that Vaughan is good insofar as he resembles other seventeenth century poets, to whom his immaturity and sporadicalness make him inferior ("The Silurist," *The Dial* 83 (1927) 259–63).

2. Useful descriptive bibliographies of much recent Vaughan scholarship are to be found in: Robert E. Bourdette, 'Recent Studies in Henry Vaughan', *English Literary Renaissance* 4 (1974), 299–310; and Kenneth Friedenreich, *Henry Vaughan*, Twayne Publishers, Boston 1978.

3. As will soon emerge, the pragmaticist accepts the general autobiographical slant of the traditional approach. On this particular point, much turns on the two sets of introductory matter to *Silex Scintillans*, which the pragmaticist, as I soon explain, is inclined to take at their word. The emblem and the Latin poem of the 1650 edition say that Vaughan has long been so insensitive to God's approaches that God has suddenly decided upon stronger measures: "*Accedis proprior, molemque et saxea rumpis/ Pectora, fitque caro, quod fuit ante lapis.*" (All quotations from: *Henry Vaughan: The Complete Poems*, ed. Alan Rudrum, Penguin Books (1976) 1983.) It is natural to take this as an allusion to his feelings at the loss of his brother William, especially in the light of some of the opening poems such as "Thou that know'st for whom I mourn," where the grief is seen as essentially chastening, and "Joy of my life! while left me here," where the dead loved-one is said to be a "pillar-fire" which leads to the heavenly city. In the preface of 1655 Vaughan regrets his earlier non-devotional verse and speaks of himself as one who has been converted by the religious poetry of Herbert. He has tried to suppress his "greatest follies" and is glad that "those which escaped from me" are "innoxious" and "interlined with many virtuous, and some pious mixtures." One of the reasons for the new preface to the second edition may have been a desire to account in this way for the publication of *Olor Iscanus* in 1651. Vaughan wrote the dedication of *Olor Iscanus* in December 1647. In July 1648 William died. And in the publisher's note to *Olor Iscanus* it is clearly stated that Vaughan had tried to withdraw the poems and they were being published against his will. This statement is corroborated by William R. Parker's examination of the circumstances of publication ("Henry Vaughan and his Publishers," *The Library*, 4th ser., 20 (1940) 401–11): neither Vaughan himself nor, unusually, his brother Thomas apparently had anything to do with it. Nothing, to my own mind, could be more likely than that the impacts of Herbert's example and William's death fell within roughly the same period, contributing to a fairly sudden shift in Vaughan's spiritual life and poetic aims, a likelihood that suits with other poems as well. For a more cautious and less traditional view of the "conversion," see Jonathan F. S. Post, *Henry Vaughan: The Unfolding Vision*, Princeton University Press, 1982. E. L. Marilla ("The Religious Conversion of Henry Vaughan," *Review of English Studies* 21 (1945) 15–22) and James D. Simmonds (*Masques*

329

of God: Form and Theme in the Poetry of Henry Vaughan, University of Pittsburgh Press, 1972) argue for a much more gradual development of religious interest. For the argument of the present article, it suffices that Vaughan's serious religious concerns had at least begun to take shape by the time he wrote the earliest poems in *Silex Scintillans*.

4. Again, the 1655 preface speaks of illness and the pragmaticist, finding this concordant with some poems, will be inclined to believe it. Marilla is probably correct, however, in assigning its onset to 1653–54.

5. The book-length discussions of this question include: Elizabeth Holmes, *Henry Vaughan and the Hermetic Philosophy*, Oxford, 1932; Ross Garner, *Henry Vaughan: Experience and the Tradition*, University of Chicago Press, Chicago 1959; E. C. Pettet, *Of Paradise and Light: A Study of Vaughan's* Silex Scintillans, (Cambridge University Press, Cambridge 1960; and R. A. Durr, *On the Mystical Poetry of Henry Vaughan*, Harvard University Press, Cambridge, Mass. 1962. All of these implicitly or explicitly take issue with the anti-autobiographical trend in modern criticism, Garner and Pettet with particularly sharp words on Frank Kermode (cf. fn. 6). Holmes credits Vaughan with mystic glimpses. Garner says that the poems embody, not so much mystic experience itself, as a longing for mystic experience. Pettet finds a development towards a greater peace in the 1655 edition. And Durr finds the first three stages of the traditional *via mystica*, but not the last two: awakening, purgation and illumination, but not the dark night and final union.

6. Frank Kermode, "The Private Imagery of Henry Vaughan," *Review of English Studies*, new ser., 1 (1950) 206–25.

7. Kermode would probably be the critic who comes closest to this.

8. Elizabeth Holmes is a fairly clear case.

9. Cf. Roger D. Sell, "The Drama of Fictionalized Author and Reader: A Formalistic Obstacle to Literary Pragmatics," forthcoming.

10. Roger D. Sell, "Tellability and Politeness in 'The Miller's Tale': First Steps in Literary Pragmatics," forthcoming in *English Studies*; and "Politeness in Chaucer: Suggestions towards a Methodology for Pragmatic Stylistics," forthcoming in *Studia Neophilologica*.

11. George Williamson, *Milton and Others*, Faber and Faber, London 1965, pp. 165–79.

12. Louis L. Martz, *The Poetry of Meditation: A Study in English Religious Literature of the Seventeenth Century*, Yale University Press, New Haven (1954), 1962, pp. 64–67.

13. Many critics have had the impression that Vaughan's poetry is poetry of experience whereas Herbert's is more wilful and cerebral. Sharon Cadmon Seelig contrasts in these terms "I walked the other day" with Herbert's "Peace," from which the idea of digging up a bulb is drawn (*The Shadow of Eternity: Belief and Structure in Herbert Vaughan and Traherne*, University Press of Kentucky, 1981, pp. 63–65). Such comments are, I think, a response to the quality I am here trying to pin down. Cf. my final paragraph.

14. Cf. Kermode, pp. 210–12.

15. Friedenreich and Simmonds are among the recent scholars who see Vaughan's satirical and devotional poems, treatises and translations as a concerted effort to fill the gap during the repression of true religion, as Vaughan saw it. Friedenreich argues, for instance, that Vaughan cultivated the theme of pastoral retirement, not as an epicurean escape, but with a sense of spiritual husbandry and self-discipline, through which he hoped to prepare himself for commitment in the contemporary situation. Simmonds argues that Vaughan wished to preserve traditional disciplines of regulated worship and devotion: he was suspicious of extemporary prayer and the inner light and ecstasy of some of the Puritans. I largely agree here, though I should

still emphasize that his best work is so *in spite of* discipline rather than because of it. Louis Martz argues that much in the themes, imagery and style of his poems can be seen as a consequence of his own church's regulated worship not actually being accessible: whereas earlier religious poetry reflects the liturgy, the eucharist, the life of communal worship, Vaughan's best poetry centres on the bible, Nature, the inner self ("Henry Vaughan: the Man Within," *PMLA* 78 (1963) 40–49).

16. My account of deixis is mainly based on Stephen Levinson (*Pragmatics*, Cambridge University Press, Cambridge 1983, pp. 54–96), who gives further references.

17. Cf. J. Lyons, *Semantics*, Vols. I & II (consecutively paginated), Cambridge University Press, Cambridge 1977, pp. 637–38.

18. Livia Polanyi, "Literary Complexity in Everyday Storytelling," in Deborah Tannen (ed.), *Spoken and Written Language: Exploring Orality and Literacy* (Advances in Discourse Processes vol. IX), Ablex Publishing Corporation, Norwood, N.J. 1982, pp. 155–70.

19. As a recusant at the time of the Gunpowder Plot scare, Beaumont also had to enter on a life of rural retirement. He found that poems by Juvenal, Horace, Ausonius and Claudian spoke to his situation, and translated some of them, often into iambic pentameter couplets. Vaughan likewise. Beaumont also, in what I have elsewhere called his "autobiographical" and "sacerdotal" poems, wrote poetry intended to bolster the faith of his persecuted fellow-religionists (Roger D. Sell (ed.), *The Shorter Poems of Sir John Beaumont: A Critical Edition with an Introduction and Commentary*, Acta Academiae Aboensis, ser. A. Humaniora, vol. 49, Abo 1974, pp. 40–44). I sometimes wonder if Vaughan could have learnt of Beaumont senior's example from the eldest son, Sir John Beaumont junior, who published his father's poems after his death, was himself a minor poet, and died a Royalist colonel at Gloucester in 1644.

20. One of the few more explicit responses to the poem's shifting deixis is in a comment by Thomas A. Calhoun (*Henry Vaughan: The Achievement of* Silex Scintillans, University of Delaware Press, Newark 1981, p. 64): "...the earth [in stanza v] becomes "Clothes," a hole dug in the ground becomes a bed, and the reburied 'Recluse' is fully personified. The logic of these shifting terms is made apparent at the end of the poem. The poet has been, all along, meditating and mourning before the burial urn of a dead companion. But in the movement of the verse there is no clear transition from past to present, from field and flower to funeral urn. Two places, times, and objects merge. The poet elides whatever verbal directions are necessary from a sense of metaphor. The narrative action cannot be designated as an explanatory fiction or parable, since it is inseparable from the present, reflective experience." The deixis, I hope to show, is a good deal more unsettled than even this. In Vaughan criticism generally, the problem of deixis is in fact largely overlooked. Fredson Bower's article, "Henry Vaughan's Multiple Time Scheme" (*MLQ*, 33 (1963) 291–326), has a very promising title, but is actually about the way Vaughan uses time as an idea and part of his Christian allegory. It is not about time as a dimension of his discourse. For pragmatic and psycholinguistic accounts of contextualization by narrative texts, see for instance: Wallace L. Chafe, "The Deployment of Consciousness in the Production of Narrative," in Chafe (ed.), *The Pear Stories: Cognitive, Cultural and Linguistic Aspects of Narrative Production* (Advances in Discourse Processes vol. III), Ablex Publishing Corporation, Norwood, N.J. 1980, pp. 9–50; Charles J. Fillmore," Pragmatics and the Description of Discourse," in Peter Cole (ed.), *Radical Pragmatics*, Academic Press, New York 1981, pp. 143–81; Margaret Rader, "Context in Written Language: The Case of Imaginative Fiction," in Deborah Tannen (ed.), *Spoken and Written Language*, pp. 185–98.

SELL

21. I owe this reference to Alan Rudrum, *Henry Vaughan*, University of Wales Press, 1981, p. 48.

22. Dan Sperber and Deidre Wilson, "Irony and the Use-Mention Distinction," in Peter Cole (ed.), *Radical Pragmatics*, pp. 295–318.

23. This, I think, is partly what those critics mean who describe Vaughan's work as "poetry of experience." Cf. fn. 13.